Narcotics and Narcotic Addiction

Publication Number 668

AMERICAN LECTURE SERIES®

A Monograph in

The BANNERSTONE DIVISION of
AMERICAN LECTURES IN PUBLIC PROTECTION

Edited by

Le MOYNE SNYDER, M.D.
Medicolegal Consultant
Paradise, California

RALPH F. TURNER
Associate Professor of Police Administration
Michigan State College
East Lansing, Michigan

CHARLES M. WILSON
Superintendent, Wisconsin State Crime Laboratory
Madison, Wisconsin

O. W. WILSON
Superintendent of Police
Chicago Police Department
Chicago, Illinois

RUSSELL S. FISHER
Office of Chief Medical Examiner
State of Maryland
Baltimore, Maryland

Narcotics and Narcotic Addiction

(Third Edition, Fifth Printing)

———————— By ————————

DAVID W. MAURER, PH.D.
Professor of English and the Humanities
University of Louisville
Formerly Lecturer on Narcotic Addiction and Criminal Argots
Southern Police Institute
Louisville, Kentucky

and

VICTOR H. VOGEL, M.P.H., M.D.
Chairman, California Narcotic Addict Evaluation Authority
Formerly Medical Officer in Charge
U.S. Public Health Service Hospital
Lexington, Kentucky

Andrew S. Thomas Memorial Library
MORRIS HARVEY COLLEGE, CHARLESTON, W. VA.

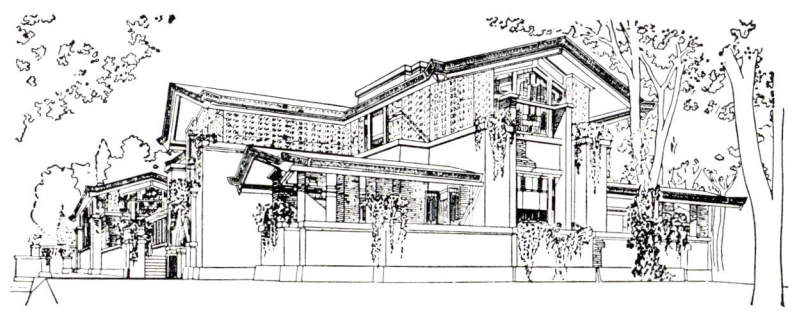

CHARLES C THOMAS · PUBLISHER
Springfield · Illinois · U.S.A.

84825

Published and Distributed Throughout the World by
CHARLES C THOMAS • PUBLISHER
BANNERSTONE HOUSE
301-327 East Lawrence Avenue, Springfield, Illinois, U.S.A.
NATCHEZ PLANTATION HOUSE
735 North Atlantic Boulevard, Fort Lauderdale, Florida, U.S.A.

This book is protected by copyright. No part of it may be reproduced in any manner without written permission from the publisher.

© 1954, 1962, and 1967, *by* DAVID W. MAURER *and* VICTOR H. VOGEL
Library of Congress Catalog Card Number: 66-23014

First Edition, 1954, 4000 copies
Second Edition, 1962, 3000 copies
Third Edition, 1967, 3000 copies
Third Edition, Second Printing, 1968, 2000 copies
Third Edition, Third Printing, 1969, 2000 copies
Third Edition, Fourth Printing, 1970, 2000 copies
Third Edition, Fifth Printing, 1971, 4000 copies

With THOMAS BOOKS *careful attention is given to all details of manufacturing and design. It is the Publisher's desire to present books that are satisfactory as to their physical qualities and artistic possibilities and appropriate for their particular use.* THOMAS BOOKS *will be true to those laws of quality that assure a good name and good will.*

Printed in the United States of America

To Virginia and Barbara

INTRODUCTION

NARCOTIC drugs, as well as most other drugs of addiction, are among the most useful devices of modern medicine; at the same time they threaten us because they are, or may be, addicting. In the last analysis, these drugs are important only because of their effects on human beings and, in the larger sense, on human society. Both of the authors have had occasion to observe the phenomenon of drug addiction over a period of years. At the same time, they have been able to check their personal observations against the work of a number of specialists in pharmacology, psychology and psychiatry, human and animal physiology, criminology and the social sciences. This book, then, is an attempt to describe the various drugs of addiction and to report on the effects which these drugs have on the physiology and psychology of those who are addicted; some attention is also given the methods of administration used by addicts, since these techniques differ markedly from standard medical procedures.

The authors have, in addition, ventured to make some generalizations regarding the social implications of addiction, especially in the United States. In fact, as a background for this book, the authors have conducted a rather intensive study, both anthropological and linguistic, of the sub-culture of the addict. While this book is not intended for the layman, the material has been so presented that any educated person should be able to read it with both interest and understanding. It is intended primarily for government officials and law enforcement officers, including the police, narcotic and customs agents, physicians, judges, probation officers, social and welfare workers, prison and reformatory officials, attorneys, criminologists, the clergy, teachers and writers. The book is not sufficiently technical to be a text for psychiatrists or toxicologists but should be of interest to anyone who desires a general knowledge of narcotics and narcotic addiction.

In the course of this work the authors have had the help of many others, both as individuals and as sources from which data could be drawn. Those technical and medical writers whose works have been referred to are credited both in the text and in the full notes at the end of each chapter. Because of the number of titles used, it would be awkward to acknowledge individual indebtedness here. Inevitably, the views of some writers both here and abroad have not been included, either because they escaped the authors' attention or because they could not be brought within the scope of the present work. Some idea of the number of writers (often expressing divergent views) who have treated opiates alone within the first quarter of the present century can be had from such a classic as *The Opium Problem* by Terry and Pellens, published in 1928. Since then a host of modern investigators have contributed a heavy volume of material, and within the past few years the Department of Social Affairs of the United Nations has not only published a large body of valuable text dealing with all phases of narcotics, but currently issues a most useful bibliography in several languages.

This book could not have been written without the clinical and research work accomplished at the Lexington hospital under the direction of the three Medical Officers in Charge who preceded one of the authors in that position: Dr. Lawrence Kolb, who himself made significant contributions to the literature of addiction; Dr. Walter Treadway; and Dr. J. D. Reichard. Important works of Dr. Clifton K. Himmelsbach and Dr. Edwin G. Williams, previous directors of research at the Lexington hospital, are referred to repeatedly in the bibliography.

Dr. Harris Isbell, Director of Research at the Lexington hospital at the time this book was prepared, must be thanked particularly, not only because of his publications to which frequent reference is made, but for his personal assistance in the preparation of various parts of the manuscript. From long association with Dr. Abraham Wikler, also of the research staff, concepts of drug addiction are frequently used for which he should be given more specific credit. And the authors wish to thank their secretaries, Hester Anderson, Margaret Grant, Varena Stalker, Mary Rapaport, Joan Paul, Elenore Miller, Ida Massey, Myrna Rodriguez,

Dolores Carter, and Leona Fort, for their invaluable patience and labor through several editions of this book. Thanks is also expressed to Martha Ellison, Curriculum Director for the State of Kentucky, for expert technical assistance.

Dr. William Furnish and Dr. William McIntosh of the University of Louisville both deserve warm thanks for reading and criticizing the manuscript. Mrs. Lowry Danser of Wilmington, Delaware, generously and skillfully assisted with the proof, and Virginia Vogel handled the detail connecting with indexing. Mr. Frank Null of the Lexington hospital is thanked for his assistance in preparing some of the illustrations; others are credited to the *Bulletin on Narcotics* of the United Nations. Mr. H. J. Anslinger, former Commissioner of the Federal Bureau of Narcotics, and his successor, Mr. Harry Giordano, made statistics and graphic material available.

Detective Fred Henley of Norfolk, Virginia, a most knowledgeable officer in narcotics, was very helpful in facilitating some phases of the field work, both sociological and linguistic. Thanks is also expressed to Neal Collins for linguistic assistance in the field work for the Third Edition.

In addition, appreciation is expressed to various members of the progressive California Youth and Adult Corrections Agency whose cooperation to a large extent made this edition possible.

Finally, assistance must be acknowledged from those numerous and anonymous narcotic addicts ranging through criminal types to well-educated professional people, both in and out of Federal institutions, who supplied information without which this book would not be authentic.

DAVID W. MAURER
VICTOR H. VOGEL

CONTENTS

	Page
Introduction	vii

Chapter

1. THE NATURE OF DRUG ADDICTION 3
   - The History of Drug Addiction 3
   - The Social Distribution of Addiction 10
   - The Nature of Addiction 28
   - Methods of Taking Drugs 42
   - References 58
2. OPIATES AND THEIR SYNTHETIC EQUIVALENTS 60
   - Opium 61
   - Derivatives of Opium 67
   - Derivatives of Codeine 73
   - Synthetic Equivalents of Opiate Drugs 76
   - Physiological and Psychological Effects of Opiate Drugs . 81
   - Withdrawal Illness 94
   - References 98
3. ADDICTING NON-OPIATE SEDATIVES 102
   - Barbiturates 102
   - Chloral Hydrate 111
   - Paraldehyde 112
   - Bromides 113
   - Marihuana 116
   - Physiological and Psychological Aspects of Addiction to Non-opiate Drugs 122
   - Tranquilizers 128
   - References 129
4. STIMULANT DRUGS 131
   - Cocaine 131
   - Amphetamines: Benzedrine, Dexedrine, Methedrine . 135

Chapter	Page
Hallucinogenic, Psychedelic or Psychotomimetic Drugs: Peyote and Mescaline, Psilacybin, LSD, Morning Glory Seeds, DMT	142
References	157
5. IDENTIFICATION OF DRUGS AND PROOF OF ADDICTION	159
The Need for Proof of Addiction	159
The Identification of Drugs	174
Laboratory Tests for Opium, Its Derivatives and Synthetic Equivalents	175
Tests for Powders and Simple Solutions	176
Specific Test for Opium and Its Derivatives	176
Identification of Synthetic Equivalents of Opiates	179
Tests for Opiates in Body Fluids and Complex Solutions	180
Certification of Laboratory Procedures for Court Purposes	180
Laboratory Tests for Barbiturates	182
Qualitative Test for Barbiturates in Powder Form and Simple Solutions	182
Tests for Barbiturates in Urine and in Complex Solutions	182
Chloral Hydrate Qualitative Test	184
Paraldehyde	184
Bromides	184
Marihuana	186
Cocaine	187
Benzedrine	188
Peyote and Mescaline	188
References	189
6. TREATMENT OF NARCOTIC ADDICTION	192
Drug Addiction as a Social Disease	192
Prevention of Addiction	194
Treatment of the Opiate Addict	196
The Question of Government Clinics	198
The California Civil Addict Rehabilitation Program	220
Prognosis or Results of Treatment of Addicts	225
The Treatment of Acute Drug Poisoning	228
References	236
7. LEGAL CONTROLS FOR DRUGS OF ADDICTION	239
International Controls	239

Contents

Chapter	Page
National Controls	242
References	261
8. Narcotic Addiction and Crime	262
References	300
9. Drug Addiction and Youth	302
References	316
10. The Argot of Narcotic Addicts	318
The Social Aspects of Argot Formation	318
Argots and the Narcotic Addict	325
References	335
A Glossary of Terms Commonly Used by Underworld Addicts	339
Index	399

Narcotics and Narcotic Addiction

Chapter 1

THE NATURE OF DRUG ADDICTION

THE HISTORY OF DRUG ADDICTION

SINCE prehistoric times, human beings have sought methods to make life more pleasurable, and, at the same time, to mitigate or diminish the discomforts which inevitably accompany human existence. The ingenuity which they have shown is extensive, and the perseverance with which they have experimented upon the human physiology is truly remarkable. In a broad sense, all improvements in human living, physical, esthetic, mechanical and scientific, have resulted from this tendency; the motives behind this activity are, on the whole, sound—if we accept human civilization as a healthy state—and the results have, in the cumulative sense, been desirable. While, on the one hand, this experimentation has given us such advantages as insulin and surgical anesthesia, it has, on the other, introduced into human society certain drugs which have the capacity to enslave people beyond any other power known. These are the drugs of addiction.

Basically, they are not recent developments, although some of their more dangerous forms—as well as certain methods of administration—are very recent products of medical and pharmacological research. However, three of the most dangerous drugs known to man go back so far into historic times that we are justified in suspecting that they were known to Stone Age peoples. These are opium, hashish and cocaine. They are all vegetable products, the active ingredients of which occur naturally in plants. However, great skill is necessary to cultivate the plants and recover the concentrated ingredients of both hashish and opium; the active ingredient in cocaine is—and has been for centuries untold—extracted by simply chewing the leaves of the coca plant. The concentrated form of cocaine used in medicine was extracted only as late as 1844. Alcohol, which also has many of the properties of an addicting drug, goes back to early historic or possibly into prehistoric times.

These basic drugs—along with a host of others, ranging from deadly poisons to some highly beneficial pharmaceuticals which comprised the pharmacopoeia of primitive man—were discovered by trial and error over countless centuries of experiment. The total amount of activity concentrated on this primitive and unscientific type of research must have been almost incredible, and the human casualties innumerable, whether they resulted from design or accident. But it did produce interesting and valuable results, many of which—like the *curare* of South American Indians—are just beginning to be appreciated for their medical value. It is not too late to investigate many more of the still obscure drugs used by primitives, although, undoubtedly, many of them have been lost with the rapid and ruthless encroachments of civilization.

Because of the nature of primitive religions (most of which are based on one of the principles of sympathetic magic or animism) primitive peoples tended to use drugs mainly for religious purposes. That is, they employed them to induce states of intoxication ranging from complete catalepsy to the rather mild nicotine intoxication of the American Indians. These states were thought to facilitate communication with the spirit world or with superhuman forces and were used not only by the priestly groups, including medicine men, witch doctors, sachems, etc., but also, on occasion, by larger groups of lay people to produce mass intoxication. Some drugs, such as hashish, were used to prepare warriors for battle; others were used in the puberty rites and in combating, preventing or neutralizing the thousands of taboos with which primitives had to deal. In many instances, the use of drugs was undoubtedly deleterious, especially when whole communities habitually used them to the extent of debauchery. On the other hand, the natives of the Andes and adjacent territory believe that the chewing of coca leaves enables them to perform the extraordinary feats of strength and endurance of which they are capable in altitudes where most non-natives become weak and faint; the effects of mass consumption of the coca leaf are now under consideration by the United Nations (Department of Social Affairs) in an attempt to determine to what extent it is deleterious and how it may be controlled. In spite of the control act of 1962, Bolivia alone produces from 12,000 to 18,000 tons of leaves a year,

50 per cent of which is used locally for chewing, the rest for legitimate production of cocaine.

The knowledge of opium must go back many thousands of years, for a description of its cultivation and preparation is included in the clay tablets left by the Sumerians and debated some 7,000 years B.C.[1] In Dr. R. Campbell Thompson's translations of the medical tablets referred to by Neglian, opium is mentioned forty-two times, along with a list of 115 commonly known drugs of botanical origin. Because of the fact that the cultivation and collection processes described there are substantially the same as those used today, the production of opium must have been, even at that time, a very well-known art. The Egyptians, Persians and Greeks (all very advanced, for their day, in pharmacology) also knew opium very early and used it medicinally. The Arabs are thought to have taken opium into China by the ninth century, although the extensive modern use of opium in China stemmed from India and did not become widespread until the nineteenth century. The Opium War induced China to accept the British-sponsored opium trade from India, thus reenforcing a habit which was already socially acceptable with a new source for a cheap and extensive supply. While opium was used and known in Europe as a medicament at least since the time of Christ, the widespread use of it as a drug of addiction did not develop until the East India Company imported it on a large scale. It was enthusiastically used as a remedy in the American colonies from the eighteenth century on, and, judging from the medical literature of the nineteenth century, must have been very widely abused as a drug of addiction. However, in the past, the opium was taken orally either in infusions or in combination with other substances, and the concentrated derivatives of opium such as morphine and heroin, together with the hypodermic syringe, were, perhaps fortunately, not known until very modern times. The smoking of opium was not known in this country until the Chinese brought it to California and did not become relatively popular until the last quarter of the nineteenth century. Even today, most of the opium taken by addicts in India is eaten.

It was not until 1805 that morphine was isolated in Germany, but by 1832 the French had produced codeine and numerous other alkaloids of opium. All these preparations were thought to have virtue in curing the opium habit, for controlled research was unknown and cross-tolerance had not been discovered. By 1898, the Germans produced diacetyl-morphine (heroin), which was hailed by the medical profession as a miracle drug with all of the virtues of an opiate without any of the dangers thereof. It was not realized that the most addicting of all drugs had been discovered, and heroin was used freely, both alone and in innumerable popular and pharmaceutical preparations, not only in Europe but in the Americas. Addicts were made literally by the millions.

The hypodermic needle did not come into use until the middle of the nineteenth century, although Macht[2] points out that Sir Christopher Wren in 1656 succeeded in injecting drugs intravenously with a quill to which a small bladder was attached. The modern hypodermic, however, dates from the work of Rynd (1845), Taylor (1839) and Wood (1853). The first needle addict was probably Mrs. Alexander Wood, whose husband, Dr. Wood, was prominent in the development of the modern needle some 200 years after Sir Christopher Wren's initial experiment. Considering the importance of the serpent in early human religion, as well as the concentration of technology in the priestly classes, it is remarkable that primitive physicians did not observe and reproduce the hollow fang as an instrument of injection many millenia ago.

The Civil War in America provided the first opportunity for the widespread use of morphine administered hypodermically, and the Pension Bureau had difficulties well into the twentieth century as a result of the large numbers of Civil War veterans who became addicts to morphine or other opiates, euphemistically referred to as suffering from the "army disease." While it soon became obvious that the hypodermic needle, especially when given to patients for self-administration of morphine, was not an unmitigated blessing, the free use of the needle was continued, and, with the advent of heroin, became a most dangerous instrument of addiction. This was especially true since heroin was for some time accepted as a cure for the morphine or opium habit. However, it only substituted another opiate drug for the one taken. At the present time, of course, heroin is outlawed as a medical drug in the United States, but large quantities are being illegally imported through contraband channels. Present-day heroin addicts purchase their drug entirely through the bootleg market. As this is being written, several large seizures of contraband drugs are reported, but the price of bootleg heroin remains steady, and the national market does not seem to be seriously affected. However, there is no doubt that constant raiding and confiscation are all that keep the traffic within bounds.

By the beginning of the twentieth century, the number of opiate addicts in the United States was legion. Estimates ranged from 100,000 to a million. There were no reputable places of treatment, physicians regularly treated withdrawal as an office procedure, and opiate drugs were sold very cheaply over the counter of every drugstore and in some rural grocery stores.

Patent medicines were loaded with narcotics, and soft drinks were charged with them in an effort to guarantee that the customer would return. As a result of public indignation, the Harrison Narcotic Act was passed in 1914. The intentions behind the law were good, and its long-term effect salutary, but the immediate effect was to drive tens of thousands of addicts to underworld connections for the drugs necessary to support their habits. No hospitals were provided for their treatment until years later; the federal Lexington hospital was opened in 1935.

There were, of course, many questionable institutions set up by unscrupulous medical men and others for the cure of opiate addiction. Many of the earliest of these sanitaria were put out of business by the Harrison Act, which regulated their use of narcotics. This was an improvement, except for the fact that it still left the problem unsolved. Some forty clinics were established in the various states for the treatment of opiate addiction and these represented, in the words of Terry and Pellens,[3] "a pioneer movement directed at the solution of certain phases of this complex problem. As in all pioneer movements, they underwent a period of experimentation in which mistakes were made which, eventually, according to their proponents, might have led to valuable findings and encouraging results. Here again, however, the interpretations and enforcement procedures originating in certain regulations of the Department of Internal Revenue in its administration of the

Harrison Narcotic Act resulted in their closing before their development could bear fruit through practical administrative and medical procedures. They were declared illegal, and closed."

However, that was written in 1928. In the interim, strict enforcement has proved to be one effective way to reduce addiction, and most authorities today have abandoned the idea of clinics or dispensaries because they are impractical tools with which to control addiction. Registration of addicts and legal administration of drugs to them does not abolish the contraband drug traffic. Old addicts seek increasing doses, and new addicts denied registration go to the criminal peddler. Furthermore, clinics are based on the false premise that addicts are better off with drugs and that rehabilitative efforts are futile. (See Chapter 6 for a discussion of clinics and the so-called "British System.")

This sudden and drastic change in the attitude of the government toward narcotics as of 1914 immediately affected the medical profession as well as the pharmacist. Ethical physicians hesitated to prescribe and pharmacists refused to fill prescriptions until they learned how the new law was to be enforced. Some less ethical doctors and pharmacists used the law to increase their profits from illegal or questionable dispensing of drugs to addicts. Had more emphasis been placed on education regarding the dangers of narcotics, in the opinion of the authors, the transition from legal addiction to rehabilitation and law compliance might have been smoother. An earlier educational effort might also have prevented some spread of addiction among people who had not yet been exposed to opiates. However, according to the estimates of the Bureau of Narcotics, police action had reduced the number of addicts to an estimated 50,000 by 1948, but at the same time the illicit narcotic traffic was forced into the underworld, and a new and vicious racket was born.

Beginning in 1949, there was a marked increase in addiction, with the highest incidence of increase apparently in the teen-age and young adult groups. Although statistics regarding the exact number of addicts as of the present date are at variance, there is no doubt that addiction is on the increase. The press has claimed that there are from 25,000 to 100,000 addicts in New York City alone, most of them being young people. Proportionate figures have been suggested for Chicago and Detroit, and in those cities, numbers of young addicts are being handled as police problems rather than as medical cases.

By 1951, the District Attorney for New York City estimated, as reported in the *New York Times* for June 18 of that year, that in New York alone the street sales of narcotics amounted to $100,000,000 yearly, and investigations in other large cities indicated similar conditions. The number of patients admitted for treatment in the Federal hospitals, on the other hand, suggested that the amount of juvenile addiction, although significantly larger than in previous years, was not as large as was popularly believed. (For statistics on these admissions, see Chapter 9, *Drug Addiction and Youth*.)

The latest estimate of the Bureau of Narcotics as of December 31, 1965, lists 57,199 active narcotic addicts. This figure is presented for what it may be worth, and probably includes only those known to be using opiates or synthetic substitutes. In the opinion of the authors, if the users of marihuana, the barbiturates and the amphetamines are included, the number would be very much larger. Also, there must be many opiate users unknown to the authorities. It is difficult to understand how some 50,000 addicts can support a contraband market of the proportions generally assumed to exist.

The estimate of the Bureau of Narcotics seems to be very conservative, considering the figures from the various states, but we believe the Federal figures, being arrived at in a consistent manner, do indicate a valid trend over the years since the Harrison Act became law (see Fig. 1). We believe it is safe to state that there are fewer than 100,000 opiate addicts in the United States today. Because of the increasing high price and adulteration of contraband narcotics, fewer addicts have heavy habits compared to the thirties. Very few severe withdrawal illnesses are seen compared with those treated when the Lexington hospital was opened in 1935. More users are *chippying* with irregular *joy pops* than in previous years. Few addicts now are able to get four or five shots of heroin a day for months or weeks or even days continuously.

The Attorney General of California reported for 1965 a total

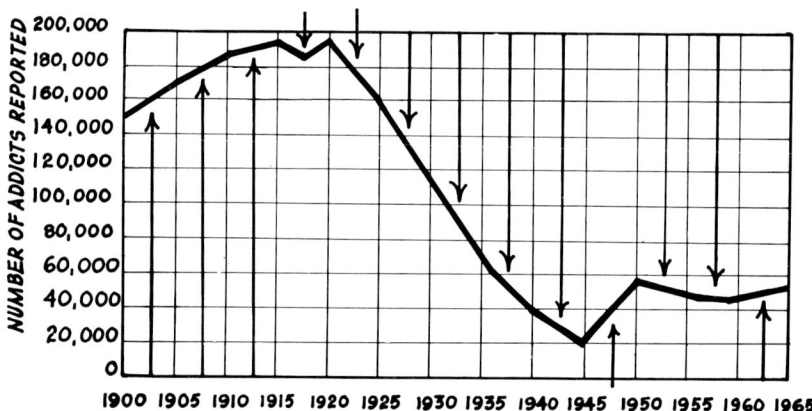

FIGURE 1. Ups and downs of drug addiction.

of 21,434 arrests of adults for drug violations of all kinds. This was 11.4 per cent more than the arrests in 1964; however, arrests for heroin and other hard narcotics decreased by 22 per cent while marihuana offenses increased by 33 per cent and other "dangerous drugs" (principally amphetamine stimulants and barbiturate sedatives) increased by 40.4 per cent.

A broader approach to addiction has come through the United States Public Health Service, which has sponsored two large hospitals, authorized by Congress for the treatment of narcotic addiction, as well as for research into the problem. As part of the Federal program, a certain amount of information concerning addiction has been given circulation by the U. S. Public Health Service. Several states, notably California, New Jersey and New York are aggressively attacking the problem from the standpoint of rehabilitation. It is certain that the narcotics racket is a profitable one which cannot be broken without vigorous law enforcement as well as intelligent therapy and, in the authors' opinion, by long-range education programs sponsored by the public schools, the medical profession and public health agencies.

THE SOCIAL DISTRIBUTION OF ADDICTION

From the earliest times, narcotics have been used by all classes of people ranging from the very wealthy, who indulged in opium as a vice, to the poverty-stricken, who needed a palliative for life itself. In some cultures, narcotics are inexpensive and easy to obtain; in others, they are rare and expensive. Some societies (such as the Oriental opium-producing countries) show a much higher rate of addiction than do others as, for instance the Scandinavian countries, where the rate of addiction is quite low. In some groups, certain narcotics are tolerated or even well accepted, while others are prohibited. Moslems, for instance, generally reject alcohol but accept the consumption of hashish, although both are officially banned by the Moslem religion. In the United States the per capita consumption of alcohol is quite high, but the use of hashish is not only frowned upon; it is a crime punishable by imprisonment.

This social acceptability has a great deal to do with determining the kinds and amounts of drugs which are used in any society. Religion, economics, class-consciousness, ethics, group mores, availability of the drug and a dozen other factors influence the acceptance or rejection of certain drugs. Usually, the more individuals who take a drug, the more respectable its use becomes; also, if many people take it in one form and a few in another, the most popular form attains an edge of respectability over the other. This phenomenon underlies the current shift from cigarettes to pipes and cigars and thus follows well-known behavior patterns which are widespread if not universal in human society. If we consider the taking of tobacco in our own society, we have an example which can be looked at objectively, since its use is so widespread that it takes in all classes of people. Also, like the opiates, it at one time was regarded as having very superior medicinal qualities, having been first introduced into Europe from America in the sixteenth century by the Spanish physician Francisco de Monardes as a cure for syphilis, and later used in a multitude of ways; also, it was the object of much criticism, especially on the part of Puritan groups both here and abroad. The controversy concerning its use still goes on, along both medical and moral lines, heightened by the recent association of cigarettes with cancer, pulmonary and cardiovascular diseases.

While an analysis of the history of the use of tobacco would be very enlightening to anyone interested in the social forces operating to make a drug acceptable, space does not permit so extensive a treatment here. However, if we look at the use of tobacco within the twentieth century, we can observe many of the factors involved in social acceptability. In 1900, tobacco was generally available to the entire population of the United States at a very nominal cost. Most of the adult male population used it. Cigars were a mark of economic status and were not generally consumed by the working classes, where tobacco was taken by pipe or was chewed. Both cigars and pipes were considered less deleterious than cigarettes, which were rated as morally and physiologically dangerous—almost as dangerous as marihuana is regarded by the public today—and their use was generally deplored by most respectable people, especially the medical profession, the teaching profession and the clergy. Chewing was generally recognized as less offensive than smoking in the presence of ladies, who were believed to be unable to tolerate tobacco fumes; hence the cuspidor was standard equipment in all public buildings and in most homes. Snuff was sold in large quantities, but was generally taken by mouth rather than by sniffing. Both men and women used it.

There were certain qualifications to these generalities. Cigars were more popular in the East than in the West, probably due in part to the difficulty of transporting and preserving them fresh for sale. Cigarettes were acceptable in the far West largely because of the Mexican influence, but a sharp distinction was made between those rolled by the smoker and those which were "tailor made" and therefore, for some obscure reason, more deleterious; there was in 1900 a widespread belief that the paper used to manufacture cigarettes was impregnated with some form of slow poison. The paper has only recently (1950) been exonerated as a deleterious factor in tobacco smoking. The chewing of tobacco, while generally deplored by the genteel class of ladies, was accepted as a natural shortcoming of the male and was almost universal among the lower and middle classes; visiting Europeans were constantly astounded not only at the great numbers of tobacco-chewers, but at their range and accuracy as well. Snuff, the survival of a once genteel vice in Europe, was taken largely by older people of rural origin. The only women who smoked (pipes) were old crones, who were excused because of their age and bad teeth, and prostitutes (cigarettes), who were, of course, not excused for any reason. A few socialite women (emancipated from social pressures because of their wealth) smoked cigarettes as an affectation, usually in private.

If we observe what has happened in the past fifty years, we see how certain forces have changed the social acceptability of tobacco. First, the morality or immorality of smoking has ceased to be a very potent factor in the controversy. Smoking has become so universal that persons who do not smoke, especially young persons, may feel considerable social pressure to smoke whether they like it or not. While the cigar is still associated with economic prosperity, its use is much more widespread among all classes and is constantly reenforced by advertising. The pipe has risen (perhaps largely due to its affectation by several generations of college boys and stimulated by British influence) from the mark of the laborer to the mark of the scholar and even the connoisseur of fine tobacco. The cigarette, partly because of its relative cheapness and convenience, has come to be used almost universally by both men and women; this phenomenon of establishing within a few years social acceptability for a form of tobacco formerly universally rejected is a good example of what a strong catalytic agent modern advertising may be when it comes to precipitating social change. Even in the face of strong evidence that cigarettes are a carcinogenic agent, the government agencies responsible for the proper labeling of dangerous foods and drugs sidestep the issue when so popular a habit as cigarette smoking is involved, although a mild "May Be Hazardous to Health" label was required in 1966. Chewing is today so unpopular that one seldom sees it except in rural areas and among older men. The use of snuff is sufficiently rare to be a curiosity, except in certain rural areas where old women occasionally still smoke clay or corncob pipes also. On the other hand, small groups of younger women in the larger cities have taken to smoking pipes, and while this social group is small and exclusive, it is large enough that some pipe manufacturers design pipes especially for ladies; there is a vast difference between these women and those in rural areas who smoke clay or corncob pipes.

It is obvious that we have changed radically in our view toward tobacco because of the desire to imitate others, the desire to belong to another, usually higher, class, the need for recognition by others, the impulse toward conspicious expenditure, the compulsion to break taboos and the seeking for esthetic gratification. These same social forces operate even more potently in shaping our attitudes toward drinking. But a strict Mohammedan, looking at our society, would not be aware of these finer distinctions in the way alcohol is consumed. He might regard the heavy consumption of alcohol, especially by women, as evidence that the entire Western world is corrupt and depraved.

To return to the social acceptance of drugs, we have the same problems that were so obvious in the use of tobacco, except that, related to the use of drugs, these problems are somewhat more obscure, and the groups who are involved in the consumption of drugs are more thinly dispersed throughout the population than those who use tobacco. Therefore, we must try to be more understanding than the Mohammedan who condemns Western civilization; we must understand the propriety of the Chinese custom of moderate opium smoking—for a given Chinese in a specific social group; we must understand that hashish smoking (or eating) may not appeal to us, but that in India and Africa it is as common, and as acceptable, as the consumption of alcoholic beverages in the United States. We cannot condemn the ancient peoples of the Andes as depraved cocaine addicts because they chew coca leaves —at least until we can show them how to duplicate their physical feats on the diet which is available to them. The whole point is that, in a careful consideration of the use of narcotics, we cannot deal in absolutes of right and wrong; we cannot assume that our own customs are necessarily right, while those of the rest of the world are wrong; and we must admit that some individuals in some cultures may, while behaving in a way which seems unjustified to us, be in fact meeting the social demands of their group punctiliously and with complete decorum.

Wikler[4] has expressed interesting views on the choice of addicting drugs in various societies. In the Orient, where human life is less highly regarded than in the West, and where the ideal of the calm, aloof, reserved fatalistic man is held, opiates may be used with little social stigma and perhaps with some social approval, especially since opiates make the vicissitudes of life easier for people who have at best a short and difficult life. Opium itself, especially when smoked, not only produces a feeling of great mental calm and clarity, but brings out, in the personality as well as in the conversation of the user, the qualities of detachment, reserve and dignity. Therefore, large portions of Oriental society accept the use of opium partly because it brings out in people those characteristics which have been traditionally admired. In the United States, however, most social groups would not recognize opium as acceptable, partly because the effects it produces on people are not particularly admired here; in fact, Americans would be likely to observe, and quite correctly from their point of view, that opium makes people docile, relaxed and even somnolent; Americans probably would use words like "lazy," "shiftless," "worthless," "unreliable," etc. to describe opium smokers.

On the other hand, Americans tend to admire a vigorous, aggressive, ambitious type of personality of the go-getter stamp. While opium will not bring out these qualities in most users, alcohol seems to emphasize them or at least to magnify or release the personality traits already present. Therefore, in America, where people believe mainly in getting things done, the per capital consumption of alcohol is very high; while the use of alcohol is by no means universal in America, nor is it approved by all groups, it is socially acceptable among the vast majority of the population, and alcoholism is fast becoming a major national problem. To the Oriental, Americans who use alcohol must appear as boisterous, aggressive, unmannered people incapable of dignity and lacking in the reserve which is the mark of a gentleman. In Japan, coincidental with the stimulation of aggressiveness by the influence of Western civilization, alcoholism has been prevalent and opiate drug addiction slight. Dr. Wikler has observed that among orthodox Jews alcoholism is low. There is also the relationship of opiates to the very different concepts of sexual behavior between East and West which will be discussed later on.

While it must be understood that not all Orientals approve the use of drugs any more than all Americans use or approve the use of alcohol, it should be clear that the status of the drug user depends largely upon the degree of social acceptability which the practice enjoys. Furthermore, there appears to be some difference in races and cultures with regard to resistance to drugs, although this difference has not been fully explored scientifically. Many opium smokers have observed, however, that Orientals keep their opium habits under much closer control than do non-Orientals and that the moderate use of opium is much more common among Orientals than it is in the West. In addition to this possible racial difference, there is at present in the Orient an awakening to the need for closer control of the use of drugs. Also, we are all familiar with the disastrous effects which a new drug may have when introduced into a culture which is unprepared for it, or where the people have not had an opportunity to establish social pressures for its control. For example, the effect of whiskey on the American Indian is well known, and, although many Indian groups have learned to use alcohol with some moderation, the sale of it to Indians is still prohibited in some western areas of the United States. The sudden introduction of opium into the United States had a similar demoralizing effect, although the results were not so obvious since opiates do not release the violent impulses which are characteristics of alcohol, especially when alcohol is used by people unaccustomed to consuming it.

While the authors wish to make it clear that they certainly do not recommend the unsupervised use of opium for non-medical purposes in any culture, they believe that the reader must be prepared to view the problem broadly and to integrate the element of social acceptance into any equation evaluating the use of any drug. This is essential if we are to meet the problem sensibly and objectively. Many of our past mistakes in dealing with drugs have stemmed from a national tendency toward morality and sentimentality in matters in which those qualities can only obscure the fundamental problems of education, cultural adaptation and the adjustment of the individual to life. Our own Prohibition Amendment was a monument to the confusion of morals with manners and self-restraint.

In the United States, the social distribution of drug addiction varies with the type of drug used and with different types of social organization. Today, the smoking of opium is not common and has been on the decline since the 1930's. At that time opium smokers included the upper crust of the underworld, as well as a liberal representation from the socialite class, theatrical people, professional men, brokers and financiers and sporting people. The statement of a successful professional thief, for many years an opium smoker, is interesting in this connection:

> Pipe smokers in the days when I first started to smoke were considered the tops or the best, and the most capable people of the underworld. Mostly those who lived by their wits—the slick article, con-guys, prowlers, card-cheaters of the top bracket, night-men, peter-guys (safe-crackers), boosters (store thieves), penny-weighters (swindlers), big-time pimps, madams, etc. However, there were a legion of others I have met around a lay-out—business and professional people (men and women), attorneys, bondsmen, doctors, brokers, storekeepers, butchers, cooks and chefs, waitresses, dietitians, opticians, department store buyers and the like who smoked in varying degrees—some only pleasure-smokers, others with habits. Also a large percentage of the sporting element. Show people were, in great numbers, smokers—musicians and orchestra leaders too. You would be surprised at some of the big names in show business who smoked. . . .

In the main, opium smoking was, and still is, considered a gentleman's vice, and a few diehards still pursue it, despite the difficulties of transporting the elaborate equipment and finding a safe place to smoke. Twenty-five years ago in Paris, many of the first names among the arts—writers, artists, musicians and intellectuals—used opium in moderation, with occasional periods of "disintoxication" when their habits got out of bounds. This use of opium was considered a sort of intellectual and physical discipline and was pursued as a ritual. Many of these people believed that it prepared them mentally for work, increased the quality as well as the quantity of their productions and to a large extent freed them from the necessity for sexual relationships. One very famous French writer, still producing vigorously, made a trip around the world about 1935 and took with him not only the entire opium smoking *layout,* but a supply of high grade smoking opium as well. Apparently, he had no difficulties going through the customs anywhere in the world. Opium smoking apparently continues to be practiced in Bohemian circles abroad.

In Europe, and especially France, there is a more tolerant attitude toward individual idiosyncrasies than we find in the United States, and opium smoking is still practiced there with less interference from the law than is the case in this country. However, smoking is still done here, although the so-called "opium dens" are a thing of the past; pipe-smokers now smoke alone or gather in groups at the home or apartment of one of their own kind. Smoking today is entirely surreptitious, and, because of the noticeable odor of opium, windows and doors are often sealed with masking tape, and sheets soaked with oil of wintergreen or some other aromatic substance are hung up to prevent the odor from becoming obvious. Although popular opinion associates opium smokers with the underworld—and with some justification—the fraternity of opium smokers includes some very complex and gifted mentalities, among them people who can in no way be classed as criminals, although some of them, of course, would be considered by psychiatrists as unstable personalities.

As the use of opium by pipe grew more difficult, other substitute opiates (morphine, heroin, codeine) were taken up by opium users, and the needle became the accepted method of administration. The development of these "hard" drugs, along with widespread use of the hypodermic, made drug addiction an even more vicious habit. There was, and still is to some extent, a distinct class line between the smokers and those who took opium by mouth or who took other drugs by needle. Opium smokers still feel superior to needle-addicts. Today, because of the tendency for drug addicts to turn to crime to support their habits, the use of the needle is regarded by legitimate people as a form of depravity; there is also a general psychological revulsion at the idea of using a needle. Even alcoholics look down on needle-addicts, although many morphine or cocaine addicts are simply alcoholics who have "cured" their alcoholism by substituting another drug. This social attitude is often resented by drug addicts, who feel that they are persecuted by a middle-class society which tolerates alcoholism; furthermore, they feel that this persecution is unjustified, since opiates do not generally predispose the individual to violence, while alcohol frequently does so. Reichard[5] has described the different effects of alcohol and opiates by saying that the alcoholic gets drunk, comes home and beats his wife while the morphine or heroin addict gets high, comes home, and his wife beats him. There is a tendency among addicts to rationalize their own weakness by pointing out this comparatively severe criticism. The social ostracism suffered by the drug addict today is intensified by the rather lurid popular misconceptions of the nature of drug addiction which have been disseminated through literature, the movies and gossip.

The opium addicts of the past, then, associated because they found pleasure in one another's company; those who were criminals were professionals first and addicts second. They belonged to a fraternity of people who either smoked occasionally for pleasure or cultivated a regular habit. The expense of smoking was very little, and no one interfered. Today, most users of heroin or morphine are forced by the demands of their habits into crime, usually some form of thievery and are driven into mutual association by several strong forces. For several reasons they developed a kind of synthetic subculture which became parasitic on the dominant culture. First, their supply now comes almost exclusively from the underworld, and they must maintain contact with sources of supply; this fact tends to cause addicts to gather in certain places near which or at which a contact with the peddler is possible; the places which sell drugs or harbor addicts often have police protection, which means that they are probably tied in with other rackets. Second, addicts like to be in contact with other addicts, since, in the event the peddler is not available, other users are likely to have drugs and will often share them with known addicts, either gratis or for a price. Third, while some individual physicians have attempted to handle the addict as a medical problem in sanitaria or otherwise, the medical profession as a whole has never attacked the problem of addiction as they attacked venereal disease or tuberculosis; most physicians simply want to get the addict out of their offices as quickly as possible, which is understandable. On the whole, medical men tend to accept addiction as a police problem rather than a medical problem, largely because they do not have the facilities or even the knowledge at the present time to handle it otherwise, although there are indications of a growing acceptance of responsibility. Furthermore, the law in the main justifies this medical attitude. However, there is no doubt that this medical indifference directs thousands of addicts toward the underworld as their only source of supply and leaves those who might be reclaimed by proper treatment without local medical supervision. Fourth, narcotic addicts are clannish even beyond the degree motivated by maintaining contact with their supply. There are several psychological factors involved here, the dominant ones perhaps being a feeling of inferiority in the company of non-addicts, a compensatory mechanism in associating with other addicts and a seeking of others who have the same problems; it is significant that the foremost topic in the conversation of most addicts is the consumption and effects of narcotics; furthermore, the desire of one addict to be with another is often strong enough to motivate his introducing a companion to drugs, either directly or indirectly. There is also an element of self-interest here, since an addict who introduces several prosperous people to drugs and then leaves them without a supply may be able to use this situation to his advantage.

Because of the social stigma attached to opiate addiction, then, the vast majority of addicts tend to seek the companionship of their own kind and to avoid, on the whole, personal and social ties with non-addicts in favor of relationships with other addicts. There are exceptions to this which deserve mention, and many otherwise legitimate persons, sometimes in the professions or in business, keep their addiction secret and never establish contact either with the underworld or with other addicts.

The users of marihuana have, until very recently, been unacceptable to the users of opium as well as to needle-addicts generally; in fact, as late as the 1930's, opiate addicts scorned and rejected marihuana smokers as socially inferior. Recently, however, since the cycle of marihuana to heroin and/or, occasionally, cocaine has been established in youthful addicts, many heroin addicts were formerly marihuana smokers and retain associations from those times. Also, the heroin addict-peddler knows that marihuana users readily switch to heroin, and he is always interested in more customers. Therefore, today there is a tendency for these two groups of addicts to merge, especially in the lower age-groups, although many old-time morphine and opiate users still refuse to accept marihuana smokers as social equals. Marihuana smokers, incidentally, have a rather broad and loose but nevertheless recognizable social organization which seems to center about the production of and preoccupation with swing music and its derivatives. It should be noted that the boisterous and drunken behavior of the marihuana user is objectionable to the more reserved opiate addict; the same is true of cocaine users, although today the use of cocaine alone as a drug of addiction is rare; most addicts mix it or alternate it with opiates *(speedballs)* or barbiturates in order to reduce the extreme anxiety which cocaine, taken straight, creates in the user.

Within the past decade a new group of addicts has appeared; they are those who use the so-called "dangerous" drugs—the barbiturates, the amphetamines and tranquilizers. While they are addicts in the sense that they develop both physical and emotional dependence, and in that withdrawal of the drug may cause a severe abstinence syndrome, they have little else in common with opiate addicts. These barbiturate addicts do not, as a rule, depend so heavily on underworld contacts for drugs and they do not appear to be as well organized as the other types of addict, although, in some subcultures of entertainment and artistic groups, the taking of barbiturates has become somewhat of a social behavior which is talked and joked about more or less openly. Stimulants, including Benzedrine, Methedrine, and other drugs of the amphetamine group, all of which belong to the so-called "dangerous" drugs, are also being used in increasing amounts by truck drivers, students and others who often start to use these drugs to stay awake for long periods of time or to give them the stimulating effect which they desire to make them feel competent to meet the frustrations of modern life. They are also used to counteract the effects of large doses of sedatives and barbiturates. In some cases, these two types of drugs are taken in increasingly large doses in an alternating manner until a serious toxic mental behavior results. Addicts frequently tell of taking large quantities of stimulants in the morning to meet the day and large quantities of sleeping pills in the evenings to relax and sleep, in a futile effort to strike a satisfactory balance.

Their behavior-pattern, generally speaking, resembles that of the solitary-drinker type of alcoholic; they seldom become violent, but like to maintain a constant state of intoxication in which they escape reality. While addicts using other sedatives, chloral hydrate, paraldehyde and the bromides can be classed with barbiturate addicts, this is only a convenient grouping; there appears to be little if any social organization among these people compared to that existing among the users of opiates and their synthetic equivalents or among marihuana smokers. As mentioned above, Benzedrine is also used in increasing amounts by truck drivers, students and others who must, on occasion, stay awake for long periods of time. As long as this use is strictly limited to small dosage, is sporadic and not habitual, we would hardly consider such users addicts.

Until recently, the incidence of addiction to Benzedrine, Methedrine and related stimulants was observed largely in institutions and in the Armed Forces, with some heavy usage in certain occupational groups, such as truck drivers and musicians, and there was no such social organization among these addicts. They were not accepted readily by opiate addicts or marihuana users, but now "pill dropping" of stimulants and barbiturates is acceptable behavior in groups where heroin and other hard narcotics are also used. In the San Francisco area especially, many heroin addicts have willingly shifted to Methedrine as a more desirable drug, although the physical effects should be opposite, one being a stimulant and the other being a narcotic. Methedrine apparently was introduced to the addict group there by several physicians who substituted it for heroin in the course of withdrawal of the latter drug. Some addicts claim that heroin withdrawal is avoided by the substitution of Methedrine and that a definite physical dependence with subsequent withdrawal illness occurs from the prolonged use of Methedrine (see page 156). There is no scientific evidence that Methedrine can prevent heroin withdrawal illness or that a withdrawal illness follows the prolonged use of Methedrine, but many addicts insist that this is true. Methedrine is also used to considerable extent in the New York area, but very little in other sections of the country. The chemical name for Methedrine is methamphetamine hydrochloride, which is also marketed as Drinalfa and Desoxyn. It is reported that this drug

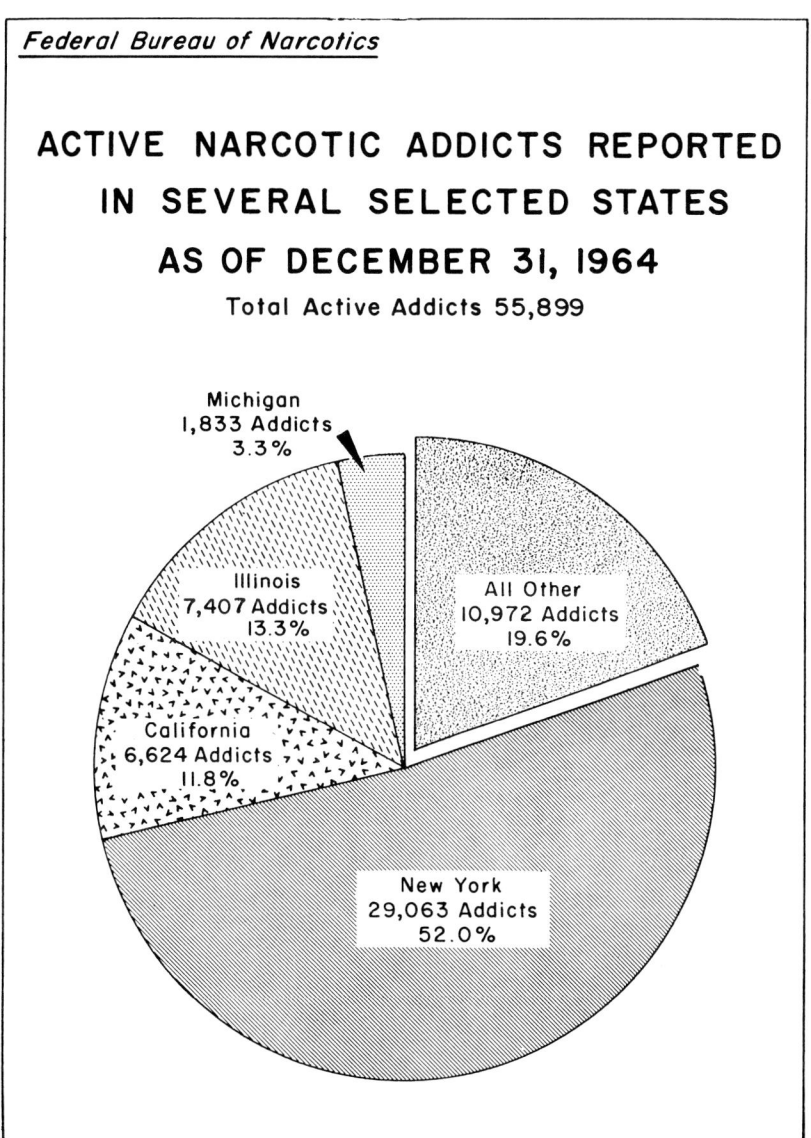

FIGURE 2. Addicts by states.

is recovered in crude crystals from certain poultry feeds which contain it as an egg-laying stimulant; it is also reported that large supplies of methamphetamine hydrochloride crystals are sometimes obtained from wholesale chemical companies and peddled to addicts in small lots after being adulterated four or five times.

In the United States, three of the states—New York, California, and Illinois—account for approximately 77 per cent of known opiate addicts, most coming from the large cities of those states, New York alone accounting for more than one half the addicts known to the Federal Narcotic Bureau (see Fig. 2).

Only about 28 per cent of the known addicts are native-born whites. Negroes constitute about 53 per cent, while Puerto Ricans, Cubans and Mexicans together make up the rest (see Fig. 3). The heavy preponderance of nonwhites and Latin Americans in northern population centers indicates a trend over the years and may reflect the socioeconomic conditions under which these races live. Although the majority of Negroes still live in the South, relatively few Negro addicts are reported in the South, with the exception of those in urban centers like New Orleans, Atlanta and Norfolk.

In New York, with increasing immigration, Puerto Ricans in 1964 made up 12 per cent of the addicts, compared with 8 per cent in 1960. In California, almost one half of the known addicts are of Mexican descent, with 12 per cent being Negroes, compared to 53 per cent for the country as a whole. Forty-two per cent of the addicts in California are white, compared to 28 per cent for the nation (see Fig. 3).

However, the proportional distribution of addicts according to race and national origin is constantly in flux. The reader should remember in this connection that, since the exact number of addicts is simply not known, all statistics tend to be unreliable. For example, Federal statistics show 6,624 known addicts in California (December 31, 1964), while that State officially lists some 17,109 addicts (June 30, 1964), and about 150 names are being added each month. The California Department of Corrections reported in 1965 that 10,000 addicts are actually under the control of that Department; neither State or Federal figures include

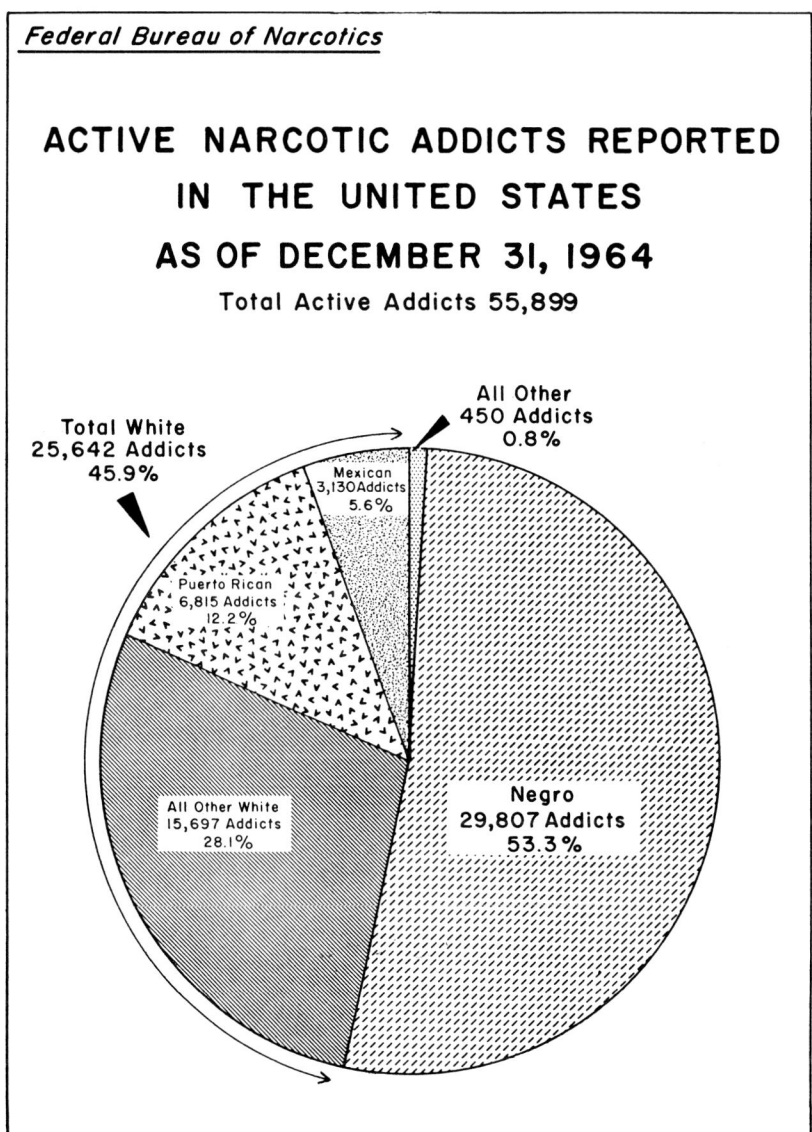

FIGURE 3. Addicts by race.

marihuana users exclusively. Since similar discrepancies exist in other states as well, it is obvious that we badly need a more realistic census of addicts.

A review of addict admissions to the Lexington and Fort Worth Federal Hospitals from 1937 through 1963[17] showed a rough parallel with the number of addicts reported by the Federal Bureau of Narcotics with a peak in 1950. The Federal Hospital figures also show a decrease in the median age from thirty-nine years in 1937 to thirty-two years in 1963. The proportion of nonwhites increased from 11.6 per cent in 1937 to 35.5 per cent in 1963.

In general, it would seem that the use of drugs creates a fraternal spirit which may lead to social organization and which, in turn, is reenforced by the rejection of the addict by legitimate society. This organization is further strengthened by economic and psychological factors and constitutes one of the most serious obstacles to reduction or eventual elimination of the drug traffic. The taboos placed on the use of drugs may, to some extent, make their consumption more attractive, especially to youngsters, who get a false sense of status from admission to the fraternity of drug-users. Also, the predominantly puritan background against which human behavior is evaluated in the United States may tend to heighten the emotional factors in the rejection of the addict from legitimate society, thereby stimulating counter-forces which strengthen the social organization of the addict and especially the criminal addict.

A report of the Sub-committee on Narcotic Addiction of the Medical Society of the City of New York describes very well the sociologic conditions which give rise to the big city problems of drug addiction:[14]

> Finally, it is always well to emphasize that narcotic addiction is in its inception predominantly a sociologic problem. The prejudice, slums, unemployment, substandard housing and inadequate education which plague our cities provide the undesirable milieu in which frustration, anger and consequent antisocial behavior flourish, one manifestation of which is the illicit use of narcotics and other drugs. No program is either balanced or potentially successful unless a vigorous attack is

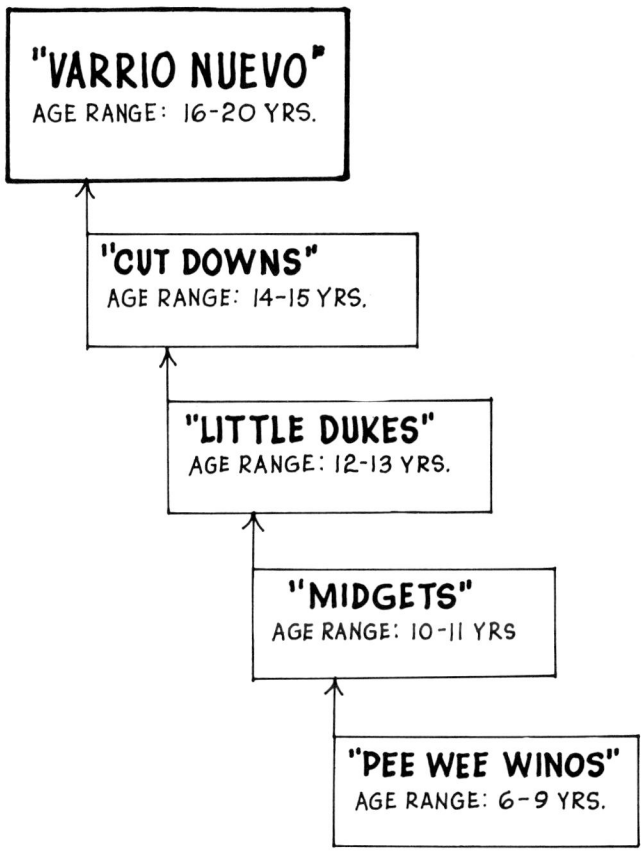

STRUCTURE OF "VARRIO NUEVO" GANG IN LOS ANGELES

FIGURE 4. *(Courtesy, Martin Ortiz.)*

made on not only the symptom, in this case abuse of drugs, but simultaneously on the underlying malady, in this case the sociologic and economic problems plaguing our urban centers.

The present trend toward the civil type of commitment and treatment of addicts supports the growing concept that addiction is a disease and that criminal behavior is best minimized by treatment of the addiction. Although addiction is thus generally considered to be a disease, it might be better considered as a symptom of a disease—a symptom of the social disease in a community where minority groups are underprivileged socially and economically, where the pattern is for juveniles to drop out of school and become identified with community juvenile delinquent gangs, with inadequate housing and less-than-equal job opportunities, without normal development in a competitive and capitalistic community. The juvenile who leaves school and becomes identified with the neighborhood gang, acquiring the tatoo marks and dress characteristic of his peers, is following the norm of behavior in his community. In one Los Angeles area, he has been prepared for this by progress through various levels of junior gangs as naturally as Cub Scouts become Boy Scouts and Boy Scouts become Eagle Scouts. In a East Los Angeles neighborhood today, there is a gang of "peewee winos" where the six- to nine-year-old members beg and steal money which they promptly spend for wine at the neighborhood grocery and are on the streets in a state of intoxication much of the time (see Fig. 4). Treatment of the individual is important, of course, but more significant treatment must be directed toward the community of which addiction is but a symptom.

It is, in our opinion, a reflection on modern social intelligence that control of so vital a problem as narcotic addiction should have been initiated in the form of a tax law. It is still so written, although everyone concerned understands that its primary purpose is the control of human behavior and not the production of revenue.

THE NATURE OF ADDICTION

The action of the opiate drugs (and their synthetic equivalents) upon the human being is still imperfectly understood. This fact is striking when we consider that opium has been used generally for thousands of years and that few medicines are more useful or more generally used by physicians than the modern opium derivatives and opiate-like synthetics. It is even more striking when we recall that no other type of medication has been the center of such violent and lengthy controversy during the entire history of medicine. The volume of writing about it in all civilized languages—historical, pharmacological, medical, psychological, psychiatric and legal—is almost staggering. Certain fundamental questions are still unanswered; many peripheral or incidental problems remain to be solved. With some of the basic reactions of opiates upon the human physiology and neurology are still obscure, it is not surprising that the nature of addiction to drugs of the opiate series, and, for that matter, to drugs in general, should still be a controversial matter. The nature of narcotic addiction is not yet fully understood.

Up until the seventeenth century, opium was regarded as possessing certain supernatural or God-given powers to relieve pain, to exalt the individual, to remove him from the conflicts and sufferings of human existence. This attitude persisted even beyond the seventeenth century and is reflected to some extent in the very descriptive modern phrase coined by Sir William Osler to describe morphine: "God's own medicine." However, with the beginnings of scientific medicine, opium was used more and more as a palliative for intolerable suffering and less and less as a treatment or remedy for specific diseases. The opiate series today are without equal as analgesics. At the same time, addiction has been recognized under various names and attributed to various causes since earliest historic times. The withdrawal syndrome has been known to all the peoples who used opium, but its relationship to the use of opium or opiates is not clearly understood even at the present time.

During the late eighteenth century and well into the nineteenth century, narcotic addicts were regarded as the victims of slow "poisoning," and both symptomatology and pathology were confused and vague. It may be said today, after some years of organized research, that medical science, while able to classify and recognize symptomatology more accurately than formerly, is still in the dark about some phases of the physiology of addiction. During the last quarter of the nineteenth century and the first quarter of the twentieth century, there was much controversy over whether drug addiction was a disease or a vice, and the inhumane treatment often given addicts—extending even into the present time—reflects the attitude of the public and law enforcement officers that narcotic addiction is a vice from which the addict can be broken if he is treated severely enough. However, by about 1925, the medical profession, as a result of much discussion in the medical journals and in the medical societies, generally accepted the theory that a drug addict is a sick person, and that addiction *per se* does not mean that the individual is necessarily either vicious or criminal. The Federal law, for all practical purposes, until recently made it a crime to be a narcotic addict, and some of the recent severe state laws seem to ignore more enlightened medical opinion and revert to the punitive action as the sole treatment for addiction—confinement to jail or prison. However, there is a current trend toward civil commitment and medical therapy for addicts. With California leading, New York, New Jersey and the Federal Government appear to be moving in a similar direction.

Many private physicians and medical organizations have taken little active interest in the present near-hysteria over drug addiction, despite the fact that most medical men recognize that a drug addict is sick and needs medical treatment as does a victim of syphilis who may have violated the law in acquiring the disease. (Specific relations between addiction and crime are discussed in Chapter VIII.)

Present-day thinking about the nature of addiction is by no means unanimous; in fact, there are so many different points of view, some of them diametrically opposed, that we can only conclude that there are still some key factors which have not been clarified. Medical thinking is still confused and hampered by legal restrictions, and many writers feel impelled to include in the list of addicting drugs all those proscribed by law and then write a definition of addiction which includes these drugs. An interesting problem of this sort is posed by the inclusion of apomorphine among those drugs of addiction controlled by Federal laws, apparently because of the presence of the word *morphine* in the name and the fact that it is derived from morphine, although, as every physician knows, apomorphine has no properties of addiction but is a valuable expectorant and emetic. Nalline is another example of the opium series which has no attraction for addicts but is under Federal narcotic control.

In spite of this problem, however, the authors realize the need for a working definition, or at least description, of addiction and will attempt to describe the nature of addiction in terms of the most recent medical, pharmacological and psychiatric research, as well as in the light of their own observation of addicts.

First, in considering addiction, several points should be borne in mind. While most of the drugs of addiction do have pharmacological properties which make them addicting not only to man, but, as has been shown many times experimentally, to animals as well, these drugs must always be considered in relationship to human personality. Furthermore, there are many degrees of addiction as well as several marked personality types which seem to determine the degree, the duration and the tendency to relapse involved in addiction.

The authors like the concept that some people who feel inadequate to meet the demands of society are addiction-prone, while others have adequate strength to meet the demands upon them, perhaps with minor psychoneurotic adjustments but without becoming addicted to the use of chemicals or drugs. Addicts to stimulants may feel superior to their problems, while those using sedatives or narcotics may be indifferent. Hallucinatory drugs such as LSD, peyote, mescaline or perhaps to some extent marihuana and alcohol may help users to withdraw from reality in a state of intoxication.

Much has been written by addicts of their subjective experiences while under the influence of these drugs, and the authors do not attempt to review this literature.[15] Probably no one can understand the effects of narcotic drugs if he has not been an addict himself. With the marihuana smoker, the most common description is that everything seems funny and all is right with the world. The opiate addict feels that peace has descended upon him. A girl recently described it thus: "Taking a shot of heroin is like putting on an expensive mink coat." The LSD or peyote dilettante is lost in a world of color and fantasy.

Much has been written by psychiatrists on the classification of addicts, and a great variety of explanations have been advanced from involved Freudian theories through various types of non-Freudian psychoneurotic behavior. Some writers regard the addict as a constitutional psychopath born with a character disorder for which nothing can be done. At times, it seems that the addict is the hedonistic, selfish, pleasure-seeker. At other times, it seems that he is a masochistic person, and the high incidence of death from "accidental" overdoses of heroin or barbiturates may represent an unconscious drive towards self-destruction. More than anything else, the common denominator in addicts is immaturity. The fact that many addicts seem to "burn out" during their fourth or fifth decades may represent a delayed maturity. The more successful treatment programs are designed to bring about a maturity long overdue.

There is every danger—and little benefit—in accepting a narrow or arbitrary definition of addiction, because such a definition not only tends to harm many people by stigmatizing them wrongly as addicts, but further obscures the nature of the problem. Last, it is important that we do not permit the element of social acceptance or social disapproval of certain phases of behavior to influence our concept of addiction unduly. There is always the semantic danger of assuming that because we have a term, *addiction*, there must be a specific and absolute referent for that word, which must necessarily fulfill our cultural preconceptions with regard to the use of drugs; such thinking has obscured medical problems before. The authors, therefore, will not attempt to isolate or identify any referents for the word *addiction* (which has already been both generalized and specialized freely by ordinary usage) but will attempt to describe the special conditions which are present when the use of various drugs reaches a state which is commonly identified as addiction.

A host of writers have attempted to define addiction, and there is no point in recapitulating the history of those attempts here. The reader will find much of this material abstracted by Terry and Pellens in *The Opium Problem*,[3] which appeared in 1928. Within our own generation, although some still vary widely, researchers have come closer to agreement. A cross-section of very modern views can be obtained by surveying the work of Wolff,[6] Himmelsbach and Small,[7] Krueger, Eddy, and Sumwalt,[8] Vogel, Isbell and Chapman,[9] Reichard,[5] Felix,[10] and, more recently, John B. Williams.[13] Additional concepts of addiction will be found stated throughout most of the bibliographical items referred to during the course of this book.

Himmelsbach and Small, writing in 1937, give a very concise

The Nature of Drug Addiction

definition which makes an excellent point of departure for any consideration of the nature of addiction; however, they were thinking mainly of the opiate series, and their definition should be considered in that light. They say:

> Addiction to opium and similar drugs embraces three intimately related but distinct phenomena: (1) Tolerance; (2) Physical dependence; and (3) Habituation.
>
> *Tolerance* is defined as a diminishing effect on repetition of the same dose of the drug, or, conversely, a necessity to increase the dose to obtain an effect equivalent to the original dose when the drug is administered repeatedly over a period of time. *Physical dependence* refers to an altered physiologic state, brought about by the repeated administration of the drug over a long period of time, which necessitates the continued use of the drug to prevent the characteristic illness which is termed abstinence syndrome. *Habituation* refers to emotional, psychologic, or psychical dependence on the drug—the substitution of the drug for other types of adaptive behavior. Habituation is closely related to the drug's euphoric effect, i.e., relief of pain or emotional discomfort.

In passing, we should note that this definition stresses the reaction of the individual to drugs rather than any absolute pharmacological properties of the drugs themselves. Also, as will be indicated later on, this definition does not cover fully some drugs which are considered either narcotics or other drugs of addiction, or both, by the law. However, on the whole, it represents a very clear concept of three of the principal factors in addiction.

The complexity of the problem of developing a comprehensive definition of addiction can be understood better if we recall that for more than twenty years the Expert Committee on Drugs Liable to Produce Addiction, now a subdivision of the World Health Organization, labored to produce such a definition. In 1950 they agreed upon the following:[11]

> Drug addiction is a state of periodic or chronic intoxication, detrimental to the individual and to society, produced by the repeated consumption of a drug (natural or synthetic). Its characteristics include:
> (1) an overpowering desire or need (compulsion) to continue taking the drug and to obtain it by any means;

(2) a tendency to increase the dose;
(3) a psychic (psychological and sometimes physical) dependence on the effects of the drug.

In considering this definition, we should remember that the Committee was under the necessity of having to include all the drugs previously brought under consideration by international protocols and treaties; hence, they were forced to operate on a rather broad base and could not be as specific as if they had been able to confine themselves to the opiate series.

Habituation (including emotional or psychological dependence) is not easy to define so that it excludes all non-deleterious acts and includes all deleterious ones; it is even more difficult to define with regard to specific substances, unless those substances produce the definite physical dependence known to be characteristic of opiates or their synthetic equivalents. While habituation is one of the factors in addiction, it may or may not be the determining factor. Great difficulty has been experienced by writers on the subject in distinguishing between *habit-forming drugs* or the *drug habit*, and *addicting drugs* or *drug addiction*. Habit-forming drugs are taken by most of us in one form or another, for instance, the caffeine taken in coffee; that caffeine is habit-forming can be easily established by talking to any number of coffee drinkers. However, no one would contend that coffee is an addicting drug, even though some individuals develop a considerable emotional dependence on it, especially early in the morning. Until recently, the World Health Organization distinguished drugs which are merely habit-forming but not addicting rather vaguely as follows:[11]

> A habit-forming drug is one which is, or may be, taken repeatedly without the production of all the characteristics outlined in the definition of addiction and which are not generally considered to be detrimental to the individual and to society.

Habituation, it will be noted, indicates a repetitive act, the performance of which is facilitated by repetition, often at a regular time; often there is a decreasing resistance to the temptation to repeat the act. Habits may be either beneficial or harmful, and all normal human beings have cultivated a host of both kinds in connection with their daily lives. Addiction, on the other hand, carries with it a certain stigma which is not unjustified; it suggests the connotation of a pernicious or harmful repetitive act which gets out of the control of the individual. Addiction emphasizes the elements of compulsive use as well as the harmful effects upon the individual or upon society.

If we are to differentiate between definitely harmful drugs, then, and such relatively harmless substances as coffee, tea, soft drinks, etc., we must be careful to avoid *compulsion* alone as a valid criterion, since millions of people feel a compulsion to use harmless or even beneficial substances. Care must also be exercised in determining what is harmful and what is beneficial, for there are many conflicting points of view on this subject; fanatics are always ready to inveigh against some form of human behavior which meets their disapproval, without being able to show any objective evidence that such acts are harmful either to the individual or to society. On the other hand, even the medical profession has, now and then, made some startling evaluations of human behavior.

Many of us can remember when constipation was universally deplored by physicians and when cathartics were liberally prescribed—even in cases of undiagnosed appendicitis. The echoes of the wholesale evangelism of the open bowel are still with us, and advertisements still ring with the virtures of "keeping regular" with chemicals which have already played havoc with the intestinal tracts of half the nation. The dental profession has contributed its share of pious habits, some of which have been exploited by the purveyors of dentifrices; "a clean tooth never decays" is a truism to most of the public because the dentists have permitted and even encouraged that lucrative slogan to be used in educating our youth; just what causes dental decay is not known, but it is known that brushing the teeth is not of paramount importance in preventing it. And so, to mention only two instances, we still see millions of people compulsively brushing their teeth and emptying their bowels because they have been taught that these are ways to preserve the health. The intentions behind these acts, their instigation and their perpetuation, are not relevant; the fact is that they are compulsive and that people have become habituated to them. Yet we must recognize that people have a certain right to behave as they wish—so long as they do not harm others in the process. Most courts feel that society can go only so far in trying to outlaw either habit-forming laxatives or phony dentifrices, even to protect the uninformed individual. The answers to these problems are educational rather than legal; and the term *compulsion* must be considered here only in relationship to definitely dangerous drugs, as well as in connection with the other components of addiction.

The phrase *physical dependence* must also be used with qualifications, but of a different kind. There has been a notable tendency, especially on the part of pharmacologists, to characterize addicting drugs as those which may not be used consistently over a long period of time without developing in the user a state of physical dependence. In the light of what is now known about addiction, this distinction is too narrow, or at least too narrow for the purposes of this study. Certainly it can now be shown that some of the drugs used compulsively and with very definite harm to the individual and to society are lacking in the power to produce true physical dependence in the user. Cocaine is a good example of this. Therefore, while physical dependence is one of the identifying characteristics of addicting drugs, it is not the sole one; nor do all addicting drugs produce physical dependence.

In connection with the early definition offered by the Expert Committee of the World Health Organization, one further point should be noted: It is stated there that the addict experiences an overpowering need to continue taking the drug and "to obtain it by any means." The compulsion to take—and consequently to secure—addicting drugs is great to be sure, but to say that addicts feel a compulsion to "obtain it by any means" seems to the authors to be too strong a statement. However, police reports show an increasing number of addicts involved in violent crime to obtain drugs, although most addicts resort to petty thievery, forgery or other forms of nonviolent crime to secure either drugs or money with which to purchase them. Furthermore, when addicts are under the influence of opiates, they lack the drive, the initiative and the sense of aggression necessary to carry out a planned crime of violence. When they do not have opiates, they are undergoing some degree of withdrawal illness and are too sick to be effective in carrying out any crime of violence. Addicts who take other drugs which do not result in physical dependence have even less compulsion to obtain the drug "by any means," for they do not fear withdrawal distress. It has been the experience of the authors, in the course of observing addicts for a number of years, that a very high percentage of addicts simply purchase their drugs through well-established retail channels, both legal and illicit. The use of drugs by holdup men, racketeers and other professionals who use violence is rare, although in recent years a few holdup mobs in which one or more members are addicted have come to our attention. Also, during and after World War II there was a marked increase in the robbery and burglary of pharmacies, hospitals and other legitimate storage places for narcotics; however, it would seem that many of these large robberies were conducted by non-addicts who could sell medical narcotics for a very high price on the bootleg market and not simply by addicts in need of drugs.

The authors prefer the definition of drug addiction stated by Vogel, Isbell and Chapman:[9]

> Drug addiction may be defined as a state in which a person has lost the power of self-control with reference to a drug, and abuses the drug to such an extent that the person or society is harmed.

It should be noted that addiction implies a compulsive and repetitious use of the drug and that the harm done the user varies with the degree of personality disorder which characterizes the addict. In addition, one or more of the following related but distinct phenomena are always present:
1. *Tolerance;*
2. *Physical dependence* with resulting abstinence illness when the drug is withheld;
3. *Habituation* or *emotional dependence.*

By this definition, alcohol would be a drug of addiction if the individual loses self-control, or if his use of alcohol is injurious to himself or others, as frequently happens.

Even coffee and, particularly, tobacco can be considered addicting in cases in which the individual suffers from an ailment which is aggravated or caused by these drugs and in which the user cannot stop taking them, even though he realizes the harmful effect. A patient with arteriosclerotic heart disease or with emphysema of the lungs who cannot stop smoking—although his health is in danger—would be an example. Here, of course, values become relative, since arteriosclerotic heart disease is usually fatal sooner or later.

Tobacco in cigarette form falls more and more into the class of addicting drugs as we learn more about the serious harmful effects in people who cannot or will not stop smoking.

The World Health Organization in 1964 decided to replace the terms "drug addiction" and "drug habituation" with a single term—"drug dependence," which is defined as a state arising from repeated administration of a drug on a periodic or continuous basis. Its characteristics will vary with the agent involved, and this must be made clear by designating the particular type of drug dependence in each specific case—for example, drug dependence of morphine type, of cocaine type, of cannabis type, of barbiturate type, of amphetamine type, etc.[15] The authors agree that there is much to be said for a term which applies to each type of drug abuse and avoids the awkward distinction of habituation and addiction as well as a definition which attempts to coincide with the "narcotic" laws of various nations but instead draws attention to the common feature of the harmful effect to the user or to society.

In applying this definition of addiction, reliance on responsible opinions is implied, especially where the reputation or even the freedom of an individual is involved. The question of harm resulting from any drug, or from its manner of use, is a decision for medical authorities. The harm done to society should be decided by judicial opinion, based on an examination of the individual case as well as a familiarity with reliable data when it is available; a real question is: How much deterioration on the part of the individual can the society tolerate without also suffering? Psychiatric opinion should be used to establish the presence of the kind of personality disorders which characterize the addiction-prone individual. In the main, the same procedures and the same safeguards should be used in handling drug addiction which are generally used by judges and medical men in handling cases of mental derangement or the commitment of individuals to mental institutions.

Because of the stigma attached to the term "addiction," it should not be used loosely to the damage of any individual or class of individuals. Furthermore, patients who are suffering from painful or incurable diseases or who, for any other legitimate reason, are taking addicting drugs under medical supervision, should not be stigmatized by the label of "drug addict," even though they may be addicted in fact. In all cases, drug addicts (although some may at the same time be criminals) are sick people and should be handled as such. Anyone tempted to rely upon a very narrow or arbitrary definition of addiction should remember that, in a very strict sense, food produces not only tolerance, but emotional dependence and physical dependence as well; we are all familiar with the withdrawal syndrome resulting from failure to eat at the habitual time.

Legally, the controls on so-called "narcotic drugs" do not cover all true narcotics and include some drugs which are not narcotic in nature, that is, depressant and sleep-producing. In the United States, the present Federal narcotics law rigidly controls principally the following drugs listed as narcotic or addicting:

1. Opium and all its derivatives including:
   Morphine and   Dilaudid
     Apomorphine   Paregoric
   Heroin   Laudanum
   Codeine   Metopon
   Pantopon
2. The synthetic equivalents of opiate drugs including:
   Demerol   Numorphan
   Dromoran   Pentazocine
   Methadone   Percodan
   Leritine   Prinadol
   Nalline
3. Cocaine
4. Marihuana
5. Peyote (while peyote is not controlled, peyote users are eligible for treatment in Federal narcotics hospitals; the authors

do not know of any instances where peyote users have been treated.)

At the present time, Congressional action is not necessary to put a drug under Federal control, but this can be done easily and promptly by Presidential Proclamation, upon the recommendation of the Commissioner of Narcotics, which is based on the exhaustive tests carried under the auspices of the U. S. Public Health Service. If a new drug is shown to be addicting, it can be placed immediately under Federal control.

In addition to those drugs listed above as presently controlled by the narcotics law, the authors consider the following drugs potentially dangerous. It should be emphasized, however, that none of the drugs in this table is addicting if taken as prescribed or in accordance with labels on the bottles.

Sedatives
1. *Barbiturates*, including:
   - Alurate
   - Alurate sodium
   - Butisol sodium
   - Delvinal
   - Dial
   - Evipal, evipal soluble
   - Ipral
   - Luminal, phenobarbital
   - Amytal, amobarbital
   - Barbital, veronal, barbiton
   - Mebaral
   - Nembutal, pentobarbital sodium
   - Neonal
   - Nostal
   - Ortal
   - Pentothal
   - Pernoston
   - Phanodorn, cyclobarbital
   - Sandoptal
   - Seconal
   - Tuinal

   and the more than 250 other barbiturate preparations now on the market
2. *Bromides*, including:
   - Bromidia
   - Bromobarb
   - Bromoseltzer
   - Potassium bromide
   - Sodium bromide
   - Monobromic camphor
   - Nervine
   - Neurosine
   - Triple bromides
3. *Paraldehyde*
4. *Chloral Hydrate*
5. *Alcohol*

Stimulants

1. *Amphetamine and similar drugs,* including:

   Benzedrex Drinalfa
   Benzedrine Methedrine
   Desoxyn Tuamine
   Dexedrine Vonedrine
   Desyphed

Hallucinogenic, Psychedelic or Psychotomimetic drugs:

Peyote and Mescaline Morning Glory seeds
Psilacybin Dimethyltryptamine (DMT)
Lysurgic acid diethylamide
 (LSD)

All these drugs, except alcohol, including those now controlled by Federal narcotic laws, are discussed in detail, including their physiological and psychological effects in Chapters 2, 3 and 4.

From a public health standpoint, probably the most important drug of addiction in the United States today is alcohol. Its significance lies in the rapidly increasing per capita amount consumed, its accessibility and its statistical relationship to crime and antisocial behavior. It is also important that in the United States, as contrasted to Europe, the public has not yet learned to use alcohol wisely. Excessive consumption, the use of high-proof liquors before and between meals and the tendency to compensate for the tensions and strains of modern living by drinking liquor habitually and in large quantities all contribute to the problem. While the authors do not wish to class moderate social drinkers with alcoholics (who are simply addiction-prone personalities who have lost control over their use of alcohol), the similarity between the problems of drug addiction and alcoholism are striking. With alcohol, of course, both tolerance and emotional dependence (habituation) develop; there is conflicting evidence that tolerance occurs; it is possible that the more spectacular phases of alcoholism, such as delerium tremens, alcoholic "epilepsy," attributed to the toxic effects of alcohol, are in reality part of a withdrawal syndrome based on physical dependence on the drug.[12] While rigid legal control of alcohol, on much the same basis as that employed for other addicting drugs, has proved to be both ineffective and unpopular, as seen during the Prohibition era, there is every indication that we are in need of a sound educational program, perhaps instituted in the schools, to teach both young people and adults the importance of substituting moderate and controlled use of liquors for excessive consumption; addiction-prone persons should be advised against any consumption of alcohol, if possible before they have begun to use it. At present, it should be noted, beverage alcohol does not even come under the labeling provisions of the Food, Drug and Cosmetic Act covering sale of substances which may be poison or habit forming.

Alcohol, however, constitutes a very large problem separate from other drugs of addiction; its detailed consideration does not fall within the scope of this study.

METHODS OF TAKING DRUGS

In the course of medical practice, most of the drugs just listed (with the exception of raw gum opium, prepared opium for smoking and heroin in the United States) are prescribed for legitimate medical purposes. They are usually administered by mouth or by hypodermic injection; details will be found in Chapters 2, 3 and 4, where the individual drugs are discussed. If drugs are given orally, the opiates are given in solution or in tablets of rigidly controlled dosage. When the relief of pain is important and quick action is needed, hypodermic injection is preferable; subcutaneous, intramuscular and, in certain emergencies only, intravenous injections are used. However, neither opiates nor any addicting drug should ever be self-administered by hypodermic needle, as this is courting addiction. The barbiturates and other non-opiate sedatives are usually administered orally in the form of tablets or capsules, but some are prepared for hypodermic injection where quick and powerful sedation is indicated. It seems quite safe to permit self-administration of the barbiturates by mouth under medical supervision. Cocaine is almost never injected today, but is applied to the mucous surfaces where local surface anesthesia is desired; procaine, Novocain and similar local anesthetics are generally given hypodermically and are not considered addicting.

On the whole, there is little danger of addiction in the use of any drug when it is properly supervised by a competent physician who knows his patient well. However, the drugs of addiction should be used sparingly, generally speaking, and for relatively short periods of time. Of course, in incurable cases, addiction is often inevitable and is the comparatively cheap price paid for the relief of severe pain. It should be noted that relatively few persons actually become addicted as a result of medical practice, although many addicts claim to have started their habits this way in order either to rationalize their own weakness or to cultivate sympathy for their condition.

In non-medical administration (that is, the use of drugs solely to satisfy physical or emotional dependence), a considerable variety of methods are used. Most drugs are self-administered, although some are given by attendants in *joints* or places where narcotics are sold to addicts. The attendant is particularly useful in opium smoking, as well as in the administration of heroin or morphine by needle, when the addict is *needle shy* or when he has not learned the technique of self-administration.

Whereas opiate addicts formerly commonly started by oral dosage, swallowing tablets or caps of the drugs, most addicts are now "turned on" by friends who give the first dose as an intravenous "fix."

Narcotic addicts often start by oral dosage, swallowing tablets or capsules of the drug. Morphine, Dilaudid, gum opium, heroin, codeine, Pantopon, Metopon, Demerol and, rarely, methadone among the opiates or synthetics are taken this way; cocaine is rarely taken orally. All the bromides can be taken orally and are rarely taken any other way. All the barbiturates can be taken by capsule or tablet, orally. Benzedrine and Benzedrine-like drugs are taken by tablet or, when extracted from inhalers, chewed or ingested from the paper or fabric strips impregnated by the drug. While most of the drugs just named can be taken in solution, by mouth, the most common ones so taken are paregoric (containing opium), laudanum (opium tincture), codeine (in cough syrups), cannabinol (the active principle of marihuana and hashish), the bromides, paraldehyde, the barbiturates and chloral hydrate.

While there are, of course, many degrees of addiction and many kinds of addict the general rule is that, as tolerance develops, the addict needs more and more of the drug to give him the same effect he originally obtained from a small dose. If this dose was taken by mouth first, the increasing dosage becomes both expensive and difficult to purchase; therefore, it is natural to start using the hypodermic needle because of the greater potency of small amounts of drug taken that way. A small proportion of addicts succeed in remaining on drugs taken orally (barbiturate addicts often swallow almost incredible numbers of capsules) but most of them eventually adopt the needle, especially those who use opiates.

Among addicts there are several significant aspects of the use of the hypodermic. First, while a few addicts still use the regulation hypodermic syringe—these naturally include physicians, dentists, nurses and other types of addict who are familiar with the instrument and have easy access to it—most addicts, especially of the underworld type, do not use standard surgical equipment. The favored apparatus for injecting drugs is a medicine dropper to which is attached a hollow needle (usually standard); in emergencies, any type of sharp, needle-like instrument such as a safety pin, a sewing machine needle, a small nail or any other sharp object is used to puncture the skin or the vein so that the tip of the medicine dropper can be inserted. Usually, however, the standard hollow needle is attached to the medicine dropper by inserting the end of the dropper into the hollow shank of the needle, the joint having been made air tight with a small gasket (*gee rag*) of cigarette paper, cloth, thread or other material (see Fig. 5).

The apparatus is set up and laid aside, ready for use. Most addicts make some attempt to keep their equipment clean, and some sterilize it religiously. Others take little care with cleanliness, while many addicts, even those who keep their equipment clean, run the needle through their hair several times before each injection, on the presumption that the oil on the hair supplies lubrication, making insertion of the needle easier. The drug to be injected is then measured out (as accurately as possible, since bootleg drugs in capsules or *bindles* are often of varying strength) and put into solution with a small amount of water held in a teaspoon, a bottle cap with wire handle, or other type of *cooker*. A match is

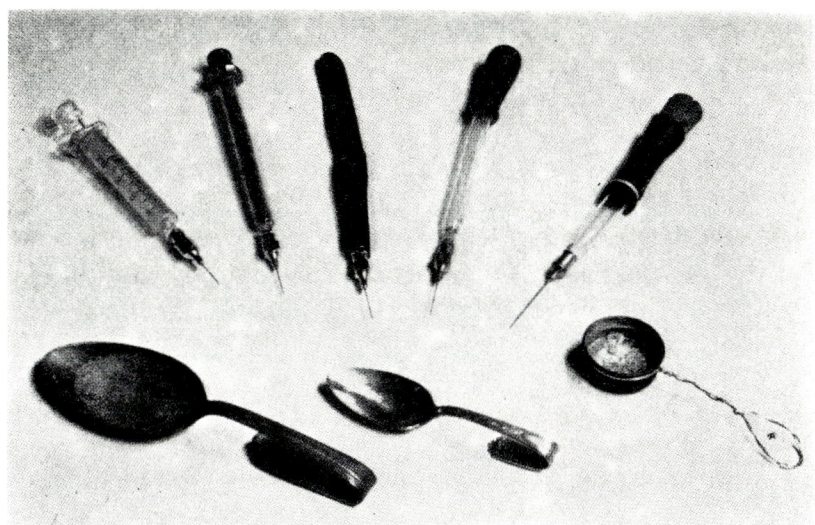

FIGURE 5. Types of hypodermic equipment and cookers used by needle-addicts. *Courtesy, U.S.P.H.S.*

then held under the *cooker* until the solution boils or reaches the desired temperature, at which point the solution is taken up into the syringe or medicine dropper, with a wisp of cotton usually employed as a filter to keep out foreign matter which might be in the drug. The solution is now ready to inject.

If the addict is a *skin popper,* he inserts the needle under the skin in a convenient area—usually the forearm, the upper arm, the thigh, the back of the hand, the calf of the leg or almost any accessible place, and injects the drug; the effect of the drug so taken, while more rapid and potent than when taken orally, is relatively mild and somewhat delayed; also, the extreme euphoria or thrill, often described as resembling a sexual orgasm of considerable duration, is not so pronounced as when the solution is put into the vein. Therefore, most skin-shooters eventually take up vein-shooting in order to compensate for tolerance and in an attempt to recapture the ecstasy characteristic of their earlier days of addiction, a chimera which is especially attractive to addiction-prone individuals. One site for skin shooting, in order to avoid leaving telltale needle marks, may include the wrinkled skin of the scrotum or the mucous membrane of body cavities—see Figure 17 for the photo of an addict who used the inner aspect of his lip. Girls and women who wish to avoid disfiguration sometimes raise the skirt and put the needle into the crease under the buttock. The most common site of intravenous injection is one of the large veins in the hollow of the elbow *(main lining)*. In order to distend this vein and make the injection easier, the addict first applies a tourniquet which may be any kind of a cord knotted or twisted above the elbow so that the vein shows firm and blue. He may use a woman's stocking knotted so that it may be released easily. He may slap or massage the surface of the forearm until the blood builds up in the vein. When this distention was reached the maximum, he punctures the vein wall with the needle; many addicts at this point apply a slight suction to the dropper to see if blood shows; if so *(verification)*, they know they have hit the vein; if not, they try again; then the addict injects the entire contents of the dropper and instantly releases the end of the cord held in his teeth. This permits the concentrated solution to move directly into the circulation. The impact of the drug taken this way is terrific. If the addict has a large habit (usually measured by the number of *caps* (heroin) he takes a day), he may need to repeat in order to get the required amount.

Some drugs such as paregoric and Methedrine are very irritating to the veins resulting in early formation of scar tissue (see illustrations) so that addicts frequently use large veins in the groin and in the neck to minimize the sclerotic effect and maintain an available intravenous route for as long as possible. The fragile veins on the back of the hand are "burned out" quickly by irritating injections.

The vein-shooter is always troubled about finding new veins to use as one *burns out*—that is, becomes sclerotic from repeated puncturings and from the abscesses resulting from infections at the point of injection. When one vein is unusable, he hunts another close to the surface in another part of the body and uses it.

After an addict starts vein-shooting, no other method of taking drugs interests him, and, if possible, he will continue that method as long as he lives or as long as he is on drugs, which often amounts to the same thing. He may have trouble, however, because medicines intended for oral use are frequently very irritating when injected because they contain inert substances.

While most drugs of addiction may be taken hypodermically, either in the skin or in the vein, the most commonly used are morphine, heroin, Dilaudid, Demerol. Cocaine or Methedrine is used in combination with morphine or heroin *(speedball)* and the barbiturates. In so-called *panics,* when the normal source of supply is interrupted by arrests or by lack of drugs, all sorts of makeshifts are in order, and addicts accustomed to the needle will try almost any drug, including aspirin, in an effort to ward off withdrawal distress. The authors have known addicts to boil out the *gee rags* or small cloth patches used as packing in an opium pipe and inject the resulting solution into the vein, even though they know that this will probably cause a painful abscess. Some addicts are ingenious at recovering opium or a concentrate of opium derivatives from medicaments not ordinarily considered addicting, as for example, paregoric; they inject the residue when their drug of choice is not available.

Some addicts *sniff* or *snort* their drugs, especially cocaine or heroin. They do this either by inhaling directly from the little paper or cellophane *bindle* in which the drug is sold or by placing the powdered drug on the back of the hand and inhaling it from there. The drug is absorbed by the mucous membranes of the nose and throat and enters the bloodstream from there. The effect is delayed and weak compared to intravenous injection, and most addicts who start inhaling drugs, or go to inhalation from oral dosage, eventually take to the needle and the veins.

Recently, addicts have combined a boiled-down residue of paregoric with dissolved oral tablets of Pyribenzamine. This mixture is known as "blue velvet" because of its color. It is injected intravenously—usually in the jugular vein—because of its irritating effect. It may be taken by several addicts at "stew parties." Sniffing is also employed with glue containing various volatile solvents, such as gasoline, cleaning fluid, carbon tetrachloride and lighter fluids. The fumes of saturated rags held in the hands or placed in paper bags are sniffed. Some of these agents have a dangerous toxic effect on the body, especially the liver, which may be damaged permanently.

Some drugs are eaten in a solid or semi-solid form. These include opium, hashish, barbiturates, bromides and Benzedrine. Usually, both opium and hashish are imbedded in or mixed with some sweet substance to help disguise the disagreeable taste; strips from inhalers may be covered with mineral oil or some other gelatinous covering to protect the mouth and throat from the irritants usually found in inhalers and calculated to discourage ingestion. Peyote (although the authors doubt that it is an addicting drug) is usually eaten; however, it may be made into an infusion and taken as a tea. Its taste is very disagreeable by either method, and nausea precedes and frequently overshadows its rather spectacular and colorful visual hallucinations.

Smoking is, of course, an ancient method of taking drugs, and today two drugs immediately suggest smoking as a method of introducing them into the body. These are hashish and opium. While both drugs are much more widely smoked in other parts of the world than in the United States, they are both still smoked here to some extent. Marihuana, which is only a dilute form of hashish, is very widely smoked in the United States, as well as in the South and Central American countries. It is smoked in the form of cigarettes, which are usually inhaled down to the shortest possible stub; hashish is smoked, mostly in the Orient and the Mediterranean area, in water pipes *(narghilé)* of special construction. Sometimes in this country, and regularly in the orient, heroin is smoked in a foil trough held over a flame. In Hong Kong this is called *chasing the dragon.*

Opium, once smoked extensively in this country, requires a set of special equipment and considerable knowledge of the handling of the drug if the addict is to get the full pleasure from the smoke. Formerly, most of the places in the United States where opium was sold and consumed furnished an attendant or *chef* to assist the smokers; this is still true in Europe and the Orient. Many smokers, however, are quite adept at handling the drug themselves and some of the old-timers, especially Orientals, can prepare their own smoking opium directly from raw gum opium, a rather complex process. It is described here in some detail because it does not appear in the literature.

The equipment necessary to smoke opium can be simple or very elaborate, but the essentials are always the same. The care and maintenance of this equipment is a matter of great pride among old-timers and Orientals; before smoking, the opium user

The Nature of Drug Addiction

sets out his equipment in careful order and is sure that he has everything at hand so that he will not need to move about once he lies down to smoke.

Opium smokers may smoke alone, but usually prefer to smoke with several friends, with a professional attendant or, usually, with one of the group serving as *chef*. The largest convenient number of smokers is four if one *layout* is being used, but as many as ten may be served from two *layouts*. All the smokers lie down on the floor, including the *chef*, and each smoker places his head on another's hip—called *laying on the hip*—although actually the head is placed on another's belly, just about at the belt-line. The smokers all turn on their sides, and the *chef* uses a Chinese pillow made of a paving brick wrapped in a piece of cloth or matting. They form a sort of circle about the *layout* which is assembled on a large tray on the floor. Most smokers do not like a mattress or pad, but prefer the hard floor; the bunks where opium is served to smokers sometimes have thin mattresses or pads. Before the smokers lie down, all the equipment is checked, the pipes are assembled, the lamp is lit and trimmed, the opium tried, smelled and tested, and the *chef* is ready to prepare the *pills* and warm the pipe for the smokers.

At this point, it might be helpful to describe each item which will be used so that the reader will follow the process of smoking without confusion. The *layout* described here is the type used by old-timers; other kinds will be described later on. The entire equipment, including the opium, is kept on a tray, often made of teakwood or mahogany, skillfully recessed to hold each item and often elaborately carved or decorated with semiprecious stones (see Figs. 6 and 7).

The *stems—yen cheung*—(kept separate from the *bowls*) are made of bamboo or cherry-wood and carved or decorated. They vary in length up to 24 inches or more. At least two and often more are kept in grooves in the *layout*.

The *bowls—yen dow*—(of which four to six are kept in special recesses) are made in many forms, often designed to resemble the heads of birds or animals or made plain in round, hexagon, octagon or diamond shapes. While some are made of silver or pewter, the preferred type is made from fine pottery clay or clay and

FIGURE 6. An opium-smoker's *lay-out*. Quality grade. *Courtesy, United Nations.*

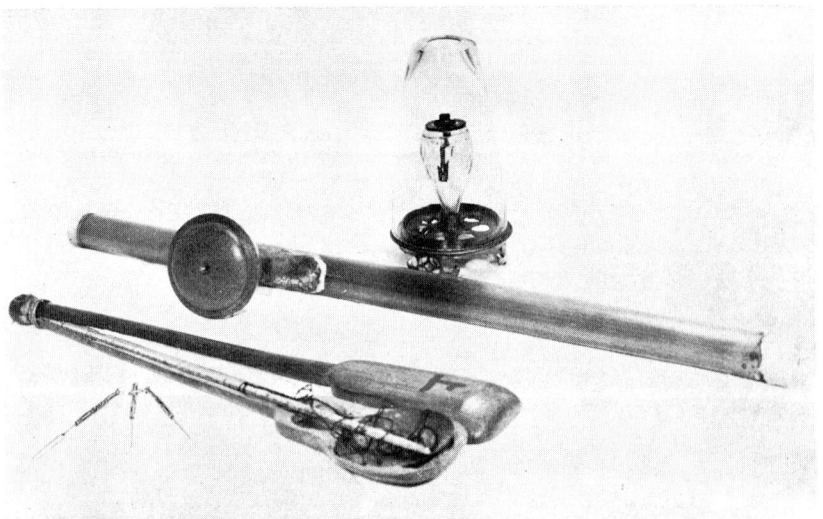

FIGURE 7. An opium-smoker's layout. Average grade.

cherry-wood combined, with the clay top fitted permanently to the cherry-wood base. The top—*yung chee*—where the heat is greatest, is of pottery and has a small hole in the center (the eye). The entire bowl is hollow with a larger hole in the *shank* or *butt*—*dow gerk*—which is fitted into the top side of the *stem*. The plain, round pipebowl roughly resembles a flattened half-sphere or truncated cone, with the *eye* in the slightly concave top surface, and the *butt* protruding like a small, short tube from the curved undersurface, passing through the *saddle*—*tong how*—of metal or bamboo to make the connection between the *bowl* and *stem*. Bowls are made with great skill and are handled with care. After each smoke, or whenever the pipe gets hot, the bowl is cooled and wiped off with a *suey pow*, which is a damp pad about the size and shape of a small powder puff, and kept in a *suey pow* well or box made for that purpose. There are many other types of pipes which will not be described here.

When the pipe is assembled, the joint between the bowl and the stem is made airtight by pushing the *shank* through a small square of linen or cotton cloth in the center of which a small round hole has been cut. The shank fits into this hole; the bowl is then pushed into the hole in the stem, with the cloth forming a tight gasket between stem and bowl. This is called a *gee rag* and a supply of fresh ones is kept in a box on the tray, while the old ones are often saved for an emergency, when a small amount of opium may be boiled out of them for smoking, injection or making *yen shee suey* to drink during a *panic*.

Included also in the *layout* is the *hop toy* (a small silver or pewter box) for smoking opium, a metal container for the *yen shee*, or residue of the burned opium which is frequently reworked with fresh opium, and one or two *yen shee gows* for scraping the bowl and the stem where opium residue may collect; *yen shee gows* vary widely in form but generally are shaped something like the letter "z" with a handle on one end and a small, sharp blade on the other; they are inserted through the shank of the bowl and twisted about inside the hollow interior to loosen the *yen shee*, somewhat as the cake is cut out of a tobacco pipe. Pipes increase in value with age and the absorption of *yen shee*. There is also a pair of small scissors, dulled all along the blades except at the points, which are used to trim the lamp-wick *(yow sum)*, while the dull portions are used to pull the wick up as needed.

The lamp—*yow dung*—is an essential part of the *layout*. There are two general classes of lamps: those used in *hop joints* or *lay down joints* (the term "opium den" belongs to romantic fiction and is not used by smokers) and those used by private smokers. Both are small oil lamps burning peanut oil—*yow*—and other vegetable oils—never petroleum-base oils—and some occasionally use alcohol. They resemble a child's toy lamp, when compared in size to a table lamp. Those used by private smokers are smaller than those used in *joints*, with smaller shades; so-called "traveling lamps" are of the collapsible type, with the base—*dung gerk*—folding over the shade to make a compact and safe package, and the entire lamp made of beaten brass, copper or gold. The lamps used in *joints* are generally larger, and have a taller glass shade—*dung jow*—resembling a small lamp chimney, often decorated with paintings or darkened a little, for the lamp gives ample light for smoking even when shaded. Both types of lamps are used to *cook* the opium for smoking, the heat being concentrated in the opening at the top of the shade.

When the *layout* is ready and the smokers recline with the *chef* about the lighted lamp, smoking begins. The pipe or pipes are *lipped* (tested by the *chef* by sucking on the stem) to be sure that they are airtight and working properly. The *hop toy* or other container is opened, and the *chef*, as well as the smokers, may smell it and test a bit of it by trying it on the *yen hok*. The *chef* then begins to *cook*, dipping the *yen hok* into the opium and pulling out enough for two or more pills; he holds both the bowl and the opium over the top of the lamp and begins to *tchi* the opium, that is, working the heated opium like taffy, pulling it with the *yen hok* and working it on the flat top surface of the pipe bowl until the color, the consistency and the feel on the *yen hok* suits the *chef* exactly. Good *chefs* usually *tchi* enough opium for six or eight *pills* in one *bundle*, then roll the *pills* for smoking. The *pills* are not conventionally-shaped, but are small, cylindrical segments with a hole through the center where the *yen hok* pierces them. The *chef* cuts out enough opium for each smoker, with the *pills* varying in size according to the smoker's specifications; small *pills* are *bird's eyes,* medium-sized ones are *buttons,* and large ones are *high hats.* The *chef,* whether a paid attendant or one of the group who is expert enough to do the work, customarily takes the first two or three *pills* in order to warm up the stem and the bowl. He smokes these by impaling the *pill* on the *yen hok* and holding it, along with the bowl of the pipe (turned slightly sidewise), over the top of the lamp-chimney; at the moment the *pill* becomes volatile, he places it deftly into the *eye* of the pipe and simultaneously inhales deeply. The hole left by the *yen hok* coincides exactly with the hole in the *yung chee,* so that air can be drawn slowly through the bubbling *pill* and into the pipebowl. When a *pill* is smoked properly, one long puff should consume it, leaving only *yen shee.* Some smokers, however, use a series of short puffs. After the *chef* has smoked, he passes the pipe to the next smoker, selects the size *pill* desired and cooks it over the lamp on the *yen hok* as he did for himself, except that the smoker holds the pipe and the *chef* manipulates the *yen hok* unless the smoker wishes to do so himself. The pipebowl is wiped and cooled with the *suey pow* as often as necessary, since each smoker uses it in turn; it is important to keep the bowl at the right temperature and to avoid burning or scorching the *pills* so as not to ruin the flavor or the effect, or both; the large hollow space inside the closed pipebowl permits the volatile opium gases and smoke to mix liberally with air so that an optimum mixture can be inhaled into the lungs. When all the smokers have been served, the *chef* smokes again himself, and starts another round; anyone wishing to skip a smoke says "By me," and the round continues, each smoker taking as many *pills* of the preferred size as are necessary to *take his habit off,* to make him comfortable.

When opium smokers do not have access to a standard *layout,* they sometimes construct a makeshift arrangement which would outrage the esthetics of any old-time smoker to whom smoking is a ritual. This makeshift is made with a small glass bottle of two- or three-ounce capacity; a small-sized ink bottle is very satisfactory for the bowl. A small hole is drilled in the bottom or the bottom edge of the bottle to serve as an *eye,* and a long glass or rubber tube is put through a cork, which is then set tightly into the bottle. Adhesive tape is often used to make the connection airtight. A lamp is made from a small can or jar filled with oil and fitted with a rag wick; the shade is provided by scraping thin the peeling of half an orange or even half a lemon and cutting a small hole in the top from which the concentrated heat escapes when the shell is turned over the lamp. A knitting needle, a large darning needle with a cork for a handle, or a piece of steel wire may serve as a *yen hok* and the *pill* is *tchi'd* and rolled on the side of the bottle. After the bottle becomes coated inside with *yen shee* from the smoke, it makes a fairly palatable smoke, but nothing like the skillfully made and meticulously maintained bowls used with a standard *layout*. There are other makeshifts, too, but they hardly have a place here. It might be mentioned, however, that in prisons and elsewhere, an ordinary tobacco pipe may be made to serve as an opium pipe by drilling a hole into a coin and then sealing the coin tightly into the top of the pipebowl; the *pill* is then *tchi'd* on the surface of the coin, which is very close quarters.

The amount of opium smoked, as well as the frequency of smoking, varies greatly with the individual. A steady smoker may take ten medium-sized pills at a smoking and find it necessary to smoke three times each twenty-four hours to satisfy his habit. This, however, is not considered a large habit, and the amount of opium consumed by heavy smokers may range up to enormous amounts. On the other hand, some opium smokers hold their habits down to a minimum for many years, and some so-called *pleasure smokers* smoke infrequently and irregularly without becoming thoroughly enslaved by physical dependence; nevertheless, if opium smoking is continued for any length of time, even on an irregular basis, both physical and emotional dependence develop, and, as tolerance increases, the addict is forced into a regular routine of smoking. Opium addicts differ from other drug users, however, in that some of them develop habits which must be satisfied at longer intervals than could possibly be managed by users of the needle; some opium smokers feel the need of smoking once a day and continue to do so for a long time before increasing their frequency; others smoke every other day, or every third day; some smoke once a week *(Saturday night habit)*, and the authors have heard of addicts who smoke every two weeks *(every other Saturday night habit).*

On the contraband market, crude opium is known as *gum* (smuggled in as balls or bricks wrapped in poppy leaves, in cans, etc.) and must be processed before it can be smoked; after it is prepared for smoking, it is called *grease, black stuff, mud.* Raw opium is usually handled on the wholesale market (contraband) in pounds, and a pound of raw opium when worked up for smoking by dealers or smokers should yield about 1,200 *fun* not including the *dog,* or residue which goes to the bottom of the cooker after the smoking opium has been strained off; this *dog* is saved and eventually re-cooked. Sometimes the quantity is increased by adding a solution of boiled banana skins, which resembles the cooked opium; the strength may be increased by adding morphine or heroin.

Smokers usually measure opium by *fun* a Japanese weight pronounced in the United States as *foon,* although in Canada, England and on the East Coast of the United States (excepting New York City) one hears *foong;* the singular and plural forms are the same. One *fun* equals 5.79 grains, and an ounce of opium is roughly considered to be 100 *fun.*

Smoking opium is sold in sealed cans under various brand names; the contents of the cans vary, with the most common type (of Chinese origin) containing 480 *fun;* another type (Japanese) is put up in four small tins sealed within one large tin, the entire contents amounting to about 600 *fun;* also, the Japanese, around 1930, produced prepared pills about the size of a five-grain aspirin tablet, red in color, known to the underworld as *red smokers;* they probably contained a mixture of opium and heroin. There are many different ways of packaging opium for sale, especially in these days when the price is high and large quantities are not so frequently moved in the retail contraband market.

Up to about 1930, the prices on smoking opium were quite stable and reflected a steady wholesale supply. At that time, opium smoking, while kept closely under cover, was not inordinately expensive. Then raw gum opium could be bought by the pound at $40 in Canada or $65 in the United States. The standard cans of prepared smoking opium (480 *fun*) sold for $25 to $50, depending on quality and locality. One hundred *fun* (packaged) cost $10 to $15, and a fifty *fun* package cost about $7.50. *Packages* were often put up in English walnut shells, later in cellophane, because these containers could be emptied completely and every trace of opium scraped from them by the smoker. Twelve- to fifteen-*fun toys* (small metal boxes) sold for $2.50. The above prices, of course, applied to prepared opium for private consumption; smokers in *hop joints* paid from 50 cents to $4.00 to *lay down* which entitled them to smoke about eight *fun*. This was usually served on a playing card and was referred to as a *card of hop*. Prices varied with the class of *hop joint*, the lower prices for cheaper places where the smoker usually *cooked* his own *pills*, the higher prices for better places where the services of a *chef* were included; self-servers were assigned the upper bunks, while those receiving *chef*-service occupied the lower bunks; group smoking on the floor as described earlier applied (and still does) only to private smokers.

Today opium prices have skyrocketed. In eastern United States, raw gum opium (Chinese or Near Eastern origin) is priced at $750 per pound; cans (480 *fun*) cost $450, and the very small *toys* $35 to $40. On the West Coast, raw gum (of Mexican origin, largely) sells for $550 per pound, or $350 per can. Very little opium is available in small amount *(packages* or *toys)* in the West, and these sell for a minimum of $7.50 to $10. While a private smoker in 1930 could consume about 30 *fun* per day for $4.00 or less (if he bought it by the can), or a patron of the better class *hop joints* could smoke the same amount, with *chef* furnished, for $6.00 to $12 per day, today the same amount would be much more expensive. If he bought it in 480 *fun* cans, he would spend $35 to $45 per day at least, and if he bought in smaller quantities, or by the *pill*, he would spend from $75 to $90 per day to support the same habit.

Of course, the size of habits varies with individuals, and there are private smokers who today spend $100 or more per day for opium. The *hop joints* in the United States are, for all practical purposes, a thing of the past, although here and there one may operate for select patrons. Since it is very difficult for the ordinary smoker to buy his opium in small quantities, most of the smoking is done in private homes, some of them very fine homes.

The Nature of Drug Addiction 57

FIGURE 8. Crude opium from the contraband trade. Origin: Turkey. *Courtesy, United Nations.*

Only persons with high incomes, either from licit or illicit sources, can afford to support even a mild opium habit today.

Opium smoking, while still common in the Orient and practiced widely in Europe among certain classes, has been steadily on the wane in the United States since the Harrison Act was passed in 1914. It is estimated that at present one in every thousand drug addicts is an opium smoker, although this ratio will run higher in large urban centers—perhaps one in every 500 users in places like Los Angeles, New York, Detroit, Cleveland, San Francisco and New Orleans, not to mention smaller places like Salinas or Martinez, California, where there are small private circles of smokers.

Because of the ancient origin of this form of taking opium, and because of the sentimental traditions which surround it, there is no reason to believe that it will ever entirely disappear; in fact, if channels for the importation of illicit raw opium should be forced open more widely—and the restrictions being imposed by the United Nations on the amounts necessary for medical use, as well as the development of synthetic drugs, are putting a severe strain on some countries whose chief export is opium—the use of opium could increase substantially.

REFERENCES

1. NEGLIGAN, A. R.: *The Opium Question, with Special Reference to Persia.* London, 1927. Quoted in: Terry, C. E., and Pellens, M.: *The Opium Problem.* Camden, N. J., The Haddon Craftsmen, 1928.
2. MACHT, D. I.: The history of intravenous and subcutaneous administration of drugs. *Journal of the American Medical Association, 66*:856 (Mar.), 1916.
3. TERRY, C. E., and PELLENS, M.: *The Opium Problem. For the Committee on Drug Addiction, in Collaboration with the Bureau of Social Hygiene, Inc.* Camden, N. J., The Haddon Craftsmen, 1928.
4. WIKLER, A.: Psychodynamic study of a patient during self-regulated addiction to morphine. *Psychiatric Quarterly, 26*:270 (Apr.), 1952.
5. REICHARD, J. D.: Narcotic drug addiction. A symptom of human maladjustment. *Diseases of the Nervous System, 4*:275 (Sept.), 1943.
6. WOLFF, P. O.: The treatment of drug addicts. A critical survey. *Bulletin of the Health Organization, League of Nations, 12*:455, 1945-46.
7. HIMMELSBACH, C. K., and SMALL, L. F.: *Clinical Studies of Drug Addiction. II "Rossium" Treatment of Drug Addiction. With a Report on the Chemistry of "Rossium."* Supplement No. 125 to the Public Health Reports. Washington, D. C., U. S. Government Printing Office, 1937.
8. KRUEGER, H., EDDY, N. B., and SUMWALT, M.: *The Pharmacology of the Opium Alkaloids.* Parts 1 and 2. Supplement No. 165 to the Public Health Reports. Washington, D. C., U. S. Government Printing Office, 1941.
9. VOGEL, V. H., ISBELL, H., and CHAPMAN, K. W.: Present status of narcotic addiction. With particular reference to medical indications and comparative addiction liability of the newer and older analgesic drugs. *Journal of the American Medical Association, 138*:1019 (Dec. 4), 1948.
10. FELIX, R. H.: An appraisal of the personality types of the addict. *American Journal of Psychiatry, 100*:462 (Jan.), 1944.

11. EXPERT COMMITTEE ON DRUGS LIABLE TO PRODUCE ADDICTION. *Second Report:* World Health Organization Technical Report Series No. 21. Geneva, Switzerland, World Health Organization, 1950.
12. JELLINEK, E. M.: *Effects of Alcohol on the Individual. A critical Exposition of Present Knowledge. Alcohol Addiction and Chronic Alcoholism.* New Haven, Yale University Press, 1942, Vol. 1.
13. WILLIAMS, JOHN B. (ed.): *Narcotics.* Dubuque, Iowa, Wm. C. Brown & Company, Publishers, 1963.
14. EBIM, DAVID (ed.): *The Drug Experience.* New York, The Orion Press, 1961.
15. WORLD HEALTH ORGANIZATION EXPERT COMMITTEE ON ADDICTION-PRODUCING DRUGS. *Thirteenth Report,* World Health Organization Technical Report Series No. 273. Geneva, Switzerland, World Health Organization, 1964.
16. BALL, JOHN C., and COTTRELL, B. A.: Admissions of narcotic addicts to public health service hospitals. *Public Health Reports, 1936-63, 80*:6 (June), 1965.

Chapter 2

OPIATES AND THEIR SYNTHETIC EQUIVALENTS

DRUGS which have the power of addiction are commonly classified as sedatives or stimulants. This classification is somewhat artificial since some drugs, particularly the opiates, have a sedative effect on the nervous system and at the same time have a stimulant action on other phases of physiological processes. However, the distinction between sedative and stimulant drugs is so well established that it will be retained for practical purposes. For instance, the apparent stimulating action of a sedative drug may actually result from its depressant effect upon an inhibitory function of the central nervous system.

In considering the question of addiction, there are three well recognized phenomena which are sometimes considered criteria of addiction. These are: *physical dependence,* followed by abstinence illness upon withdrawal of the drug; *psychic* or *emotional dependence;* and the development of *tolerance.* Incidentally, these are characteristic of all opiates although they do not apply strictly or uniformly to all sedatives. As has been pointed out previously, however, the authors do not accept the strictly limited concept of addiction as determined by the presence of the withdrawal syndrome. In order to consider the entire problem of addiction, it has been necessary to extend the concept of addiction, and that concept has been given in detail in Chapter 1.

While retaining, then, the traditional classification of drugs, it has seemed convenient to group all the drugs discussed as: first, *The Opiates and Their Synthetic Equivalents;* second, *The Addicting Non-Opiate Depressant or Sedative Drugs;* and third, *The Stimulants.*

This chapter is concerned with that group of sedative drugs derived from opium or made synthetically with opium-like characteristics.

OPIUM

Technical or scientific names:
   Opium (U.S.P.)[1]
Argot names:
   Black stuff, tar, mud, hop, yen shee, yenshee suey, pen yen, gee yen, O., gow, grease, gonger, canned stuff, card, pill, red smoker, san lo, yen pok, yet lo, ah pen yen, fi do nie, sook nie, hock for, dai yen, shong nie, gee nie, green ashes, green pill, high hat, button, bird's eye, p.g., lem kee, black jack—all with specialized meanings. (See Glossary for details.)

Legitimate opium contains not less than 9.5 per cent of anhydrous morphine. All of it used in the United States is imported. The opium poppy can be grown in most parts of the world between the latitudes of 56° North and 56° South, although the production may be neither profitable nor legal. In Central Europe, the opium poppy is grown for its seeds, from which a commercial non-narcotic oil is extracted. The residue of the seeds after oil extraction is frequently used as stock food. The narcotic drugs derived from opium, chiefly morphine, heroin and codeine, may also be obtained in lesser quantities from the straw of the plant. Recently a refinement of the method for processing the entire poppy plant in Hungary has resulted in a spectacular increase in the quantity of morphine produced in that country.

Of the many species of poppies, only *Papaver somniferum* produces morphine or commercially valuable seeds. Gum opium is collected from these poppies by scoring the seed-pods with a specially constructed knife at exactly the right time. A gum exudate results, which is laboriously collected by skilled workers.

The Mesopotamia area is probably the original home of the opium poppy, where the drug was known at least four thousand years ago. The Sumerian ideogram for opium was *hul gil*,[2] meaning plant of joy. It was apparently cultivated and used by the pre-Semitic peoples of the lower Euphrates valley in prehistoric times. Today, the principal producers of opium are India, Turkey, Iran and Yugoslavia, with smaller amounts also being produced by

Bulgaria, Hungary, Greece, Macedonia, Afghanistan, Kashmir, Pakistan, China, Burma, Thailand, Indo-China, some parts of the USSR, Mongolia, North Korea, Mexico and Argentina.[3]

For thousands of years, opium has been used as a drug of addiction and as an anesthetic by drinking it as an infusion. The smoking of opium, first a major problem in China, is only some hundreds of years old. Opium culture reached Japan about five hundred years ago, but since the American occupation of Japan following World War II it has become almost nonexistent. Apparently, the smoking of opium originated in India and was spread from there to China, being reenforced in the mid-nineteenth century by the British via the so-called "opium war," which provided a market for Indian opium in China.

The production of opium in several of the major producing countries is a large source of national income and is frequently operated as a national monopoly, thus contributing substantially to financing the government. Accordingly, attempts at international control have proceeded rather slowly. As Henri Laugier, Assistant Secretary-General in Charge of Social Affairs of the United Nations, reviews the subject,[4] six international conventions and agreements, designed to limit production and distribution of opium, were concluded between 1912 and 1936, followed by two international protocols through the United Nations in 1946 and 1948. Seventy-one countries are parties to one or more of these agreements designed to seek a method of absolute control of production and distribution of opium. The Single Convention on Narcotic Drugs of 1961 was a further step in the right direction. At this time the final solution has not yet been found, chiefly because of the economic disturbance which limitation of production would create in the several principal producing countries.

It has been proposed in the United Nations Committee on Narcotic Drugs to establish an international monopoly which will support the price of opium in order to assure a continued reasonable income to producing countries in the face of diminished production. Under such an agreement, total world production would be cut to that needed for legitimate medical purposes, estimated to be about 750 metric tons a year instead of the present production amounting to about 10,000 tons a year, the difference, of

Opiates and Their Synthetic Equivalents 63

course, going into contraband channels. This problem is further complicated by the recent development of synthetic narcotic drugs, which will further diminish the need for legitimate opium production.

When gum opium is fresh, it is rubbery, soft and light colored; later it becomes harder, tougher and brown or almost black in color. The odor is characteristic and the taste very bitter. Crude commercial opium is usually shaped in rounded or flattened masses of hard gum from ten to fifteen centimeters in diameter. A cross section of this opium may vary from smooth to coarse and range from black to mottled brown in color. It frequently includes fragments of leaves and dirt. It may be wrapped in dried poppy leaves, cloth, newspaper, oiled paper or packed in tin cans.

Where opium is produced under government control, the quality and strength are standardized. Various batches or crops of opium are mixed so as to provide a consistent morphine strength of 12 to 14 per cent, usually prepared in standardized shapes or packages, for example, the *sticks* of Iranian opium.

The United Nations supports a laboratory in the United States for the identification of opium samples according to country of origin,[6] thus simplifying the investigation of opium in contraband channels. It is frequently possible from microscopic examination and from the chemical determination of the relative concentration of the various alkaloids of opium to state the country of origin. For instance, Turkish opium shows few crystals on microscopic examination and is relatively low in codeine content but high in morphine content. Opium of Iranian origin shows many crystals, including few rods, with low porphyroxine-meconidine content, but is high in codeine content. Indian opium shows many crystals with many rods but with high porphyroxine-meconidine, high codeine content and low morphine content.

In some countries of production, opium is used extensively much as alcohol is used in the West; this unsupervised use has spread to some extent to Europe and America. It is drunk in the form of an infusion, smoked or taken orally with some other substance such as sugar or coffee. Most frequently in Europe and the Americas it is smoked in a specially constructed pipe.

It is used as the source material for production of purified forms of opium and narcotic alkaloids, of which the most important are morphine, heroin and codeine. The legal conversion of opium usually occurs in the country of eventual consumption, but clandestine laboratories for the processing of opium for contraband world markets are located in various parts of the world, including France, Italy, Germany, Mexico and Turkey. Recent information leads to the conclusion that some of these illicit factories are operating in the United States and Canada. The sale of crude opium is prohibited in the United States except to five ethical pharmaceutical manufacturers for processing. Twelve companies are at present authorized to produce synthetic narcotic drugs in the United States. The reader is referred to an official annual publication of the Bureau of Narcotics for a complete list of controlled drugs and the activities of the Bureau in controlling them.[5]

Preparations of Opium, Including Its Derivatives

"Prepared" Opium. This is a boiled-down aqueous solution of raw opium for the use of opium smokers. "Prepared" opium is not prescribed medically, but is used throughout the world for smoking. The possession of opium prepared for smoking is illegal in the United States.

The technique and apparatus needed to prepare smoking opium are not highly complex, although the process is kept carefully secret by Chinese who convert much of the raw gum into prepared smoking opium. The conversion must be made where the inevitable fumes will not be too noticeable and where the operator can work in a leisurely fashion, for the process takes time. The equipment needed is very primitive: two or three cooking pots and plenty of filtering material such as cheesecloth will suffice. The pots may be small iron, tin or aluminum cooking utensils, or they may be large stainless steel or aluminum vats where opium is prepared on a large scale.

The brick-gum, or raw opium, is first heated in a small amount of water and boiled until it goes into solution with the hot water; then it is filtered through several layers of cheesecloth into a second vessel; the residue caught in the cheesecloth is called *dog* and consists of various impurities such as leaves, fragments of poppy pods, stems, etc. which were taken up when the crude gum was collected. This *dog* is put through several more boilings (with some water added) in order to extract all the opium possible from the residue, and each boiling is filtered into the pot containing the original filtration. Then the entire filtrated solution is cooked very slowly over a low fire and carefully stirred to prevent scorching. When the maximum water has been boiled off, the resulting thick, sticky paste is ready for smoking. While this process requires some skill and experience, it is not the highly secret and mysterious process that Chinese processors usually make it out to be.

When the opium cools somewhat, it is put up in quantities for the retail market, some of which are known as *gee bow* or *fi gee* (decks), *fung* (jars), *toy* (small box) or *gorn* (a sealed tin ranging from 1 to 5 taels in weight, and containing up to 6½ to 7 oz). (The prices of these various measures of opium on the retail bootleg markets have been discussed in Chapter 1.)

Granulated Opium. This is an approved medical drug which is air-dried opium reduced to a standard-sized granule yielding between 10 and 10.5 per cent of anhydrous morphine. Granules are brown in color. Fragments of poppy leaves and straw occur as in the crude opium. The action of opium in the body closely resembles that of morphine. Average dose is 60 mg (approximately 1 grain) occasionally prescribed for dysentery and diarrhea; administration is by mouth.

Powdered Opium. This is the same as granulated opium except that it is reduced to a very fine powder. The sale of both granulated and powdered opium in the United States is restricted by Federal narcotic laws. However, neither granulated nor powdered opium is much used by the addicts, because they are prepared only by controlled processors and stocked by dispensing druggists only in small quantities.

Tincture of Opium, Laudanum. This is an approved medical drug, an alcoholic solution of opium containing approximately 10 per cent of opium or 1 gm of morphine to each 100 cc of alcohol. Taken by mouth, the average dose is 0.5 cc. During the past century addicts commonly drank laudanum; DeQuincey has described the effects in a classic work which is perhaps too often taken as a general picture of opium addiction.

Camphorated Tincture of Opium, Paregoric. This is an approved medical drug, containing about 4 per cent tincture of opium or 40 mg of morphine per 100 cc, together with camphor, benzoic acid and anise oil. Taken by mouth, it is used especially to relieve gastrointestinal distress, particularly that associated with diarrhea in infants. It is used by some addicts who drink it and others who are skilled at reclaiming the opium content for injection. The average medical dose is 4 cc, containing 1/14 grain of morphine.

Paregoric is considered to be an "exempt" drug under the Harrison Narcotic Act because it has less than 2 grains of opium or less than 1/4 grain morphine per fluid ounce. Although prescriptions from physicians registered by the Act are not necessary for the purchase of paregoric, druggists are required to keep a record of sales and to sell it for medical purposes only. Most state narcotic laws further restrict the amount of paregoric which may be sold to any one customer at any one time. It is increasingly used by addicts, who take it by mouth and by intravenous injection.

Powder of Opium and Ipecac, Dover's Powder. This is an authorized medical preparation containing 10 per cent opium as well as powdered ipecac and milk sugar. Taken by mouth, it is dispensed in capsules, in average doses of 0.5 gm containing 1/2 grain of morphine. A generation ago, Dover's powders were widely used by addicts; a few, largely in rural areas, still use them. Dover's powders, incidentally, constitute one of the oldest "proprietary" medicines. The editors of *Remington's Practice of Pharmacy*[7] report that the powders were originally prepared in 1709 by Dr. Thomas Dover who rescued Alexander Selkirk (the original of DeFoe's Robinson Crusoe).

Pantopon. This is a proprietary preparation containing all of the alkaloids of opium in about the same proportion in which they occur naturally in gum opium, but free from impurities and inert ingredients. It is sold as tablets for oral use or as ampules for hypodermic use. It has the same medical uses as morphine and the same addiction liability.

DERIVATIVES OF OPIUM

Morphine

Technical or scientific names:
  Morphine Sulfate (U.S.P.)[1]
Argot names:
  M, white stuff, morph, junk, lent, white nurse, Dr. White, cotton morphine, mojo, cotics, cube, emsel, fix, shot, geezer, gunk, piece, ixey, medicine, paper, bindle, o z, poison, quarter piece, half piece, short, uffi, unkie—all with specialized meanings. (For details, see Glossary.)

Morphine, an opium derivative, is prepared as morphine sulfate, morphine hydrochloride, morphine acetate and morphine tartrate. Morphine is prepared from opium in legal or illegal factories located widely throughout the world.

Morphine sulfate, the most common form, occurs as white feathery crystals, sometimes in cubical lumps or as white crystalline powder. It is odorless and darkens on prolonged exposure to light. Its taste is very bitter. It deteriorates very slowly if kept airtight. (A presumptive test for morphine and other alkaloids of opium is given in Chapter 5.)

Morphine is probably the most valuable drug used by physicians because it relieves suffering which often cannot be treated by removing the cause. It has a specific pain-relieving or analgesic action on the central nervous system. It has a generally depressant action on the entire central nervous system, including the center controlling respiration. It consistently produces constipation. Small doses result in relief of pain; larger doses may in addition cause narcosis, except in tolerant individuals. Occasionally, individuals show a preliminary reaction of stimulation, followed by the usual depressant action. This reaction is almost universal to some degree among narcotic addicts. Nausea and even vomiting may occur among unconditioned users.

Morphine slows heart action, and its depression of respiration threatens life following an overdose. Morphine characteristically causes a marked constriction of pupils. The drug is generally believed to cause a constriction of smooth muscle fibers and thus is contraindicated in cases of asthma. It should not be used in conditions such as skull fracture, where alleviation of the pain may obscure the diagnosis, nor should it be used medically for the relief of pain in chronic conditions unless the calculated risk of addiction is accepted; terminal cancer cases are always justified, although some of the newer synthetics may, in some cases, be preferred. It should not be used unless absolutely necessary for the relief of complaints in neurotic individuals who may be addiction-prone. Morphine should not be used as a sedative, but only for the relief of pain which cannot be controlled by other medication. Its relief of pain and emotional tension when administered hypodermically is almost immediate. In addiction-prone individuals, there is a positive pleasure sensation, or euphoria, which is usually absent in the normal individual who often feels a little uneasy after the administration of morphine, experiencing only the relief of pain, without euphoria.

Morphine sulfate, the most common preparation, is sold legally in tablets containing the following amounts: $\frac{1}{12}$, $\frac{1}{8}$, $\frac{1}{6}$, $\frac{1}{4}$ and $\frac{1}{2}$ grain (5, 8, 10, 15 and 30 mg); twenty tablets are ordinarily packed in a glass tube for hypodermic use; large quantities of tablets are packed in bottles for dispensing for oral use. Morphine may be given subcutaneously or intravenously, although the latter is unusual, except in self-administration by addicts.

The average medical dose of morphine sulfate is $\frac{1}{6}$ to $\frac{1}{4}$ grain (approximately 10 to 15 mg). A fatal dose may be as low as 1 grain (64 mg) if the individual has developed no tolerance. The self-administered dose for a tolerant addict may be 10 grains or more, repeated several times a day and taken intravenously. The average addict takes 2 to 10 grains per day, usually in four self-administered injections.

Morphine is also prepared in collapsible tubes containing $\frac{1}{4}$ to $\frac{1}{2}$ grain with attached needles for hypodermic use, known as "syrettes" for field use, particularly by the military. Morphine sulfate is sometimes combined with atropine sulfate in tablets, usually containing $\frac{1}{4}$ grain of morphine (15 mg) for the purpose of counteracting the depressant action of morphine without interfering with its pain-relieving action.

Morphine from clandestine factories may be transported and marketed as bulk powder or in cubes, ranging from 10 grains to an ounce in size, or for sales to consumers in small gelatin capsules containing about 1 grain per capsule. Bootleg morphine is frequently impure, in which case it may be brownish in color rather than white and may contain varying amounts of diluents such as milk sugar or starch. Often it contains much less morphine than is represented.

Of the other alkaloids of opium, narcotine and thebaine, like apomorphine, are not considered to be narcotics or to have addiction liability, but all are controlled by Federal law.

Heroin

Technical or scientific names:
Di-acetyl-morphine
Argot names:
H, sometimes any word beginning with *H*, often a proper name, *Horse, Harry;* also such words as *medicine, shot, stuff, junk, white stuff, shit, flea powder*, etc. which are generic and apply to any of the opiates and sometimes to cocaine as well.

Heroin is a white crystalline powder closely resembling morphine, from which it is prepared by acetylation. It was first produced in 1898 and sold as a substitute for morphine and codeine; it was even promoted as a cure for morphine addiction! Although it was formerly much used in the United States as a sedative in cough mixtures and to relieve pain, it has been banned by law since 1925 because of its dangerous addiction liability. It is questionable whether it has greater addiction liability than morphine, but it is about twice as potent in any given quantity and is preferred by many addicts; its elimination as an unnecessary duplication of morphine makes enforcement of anti-narcotic laws somewhat simpler. The World Health Organization recommends that the entire world follow the action of the United States in making heroin illegal, on the grounds that its complete suppression would help all officials working to reduce drug addiction.[8]

Heroin appears in relatively large quantities in contraband trade as white powder. Sometimes contraband heroin is off-white or tan, especially that of Mexican origin. It is the most common narcotic drug of the opiate series in contraband trade. Large dealers and smugglers may handle it in relatively pure form with little or no adulteration. It is sold to the retail trade (usually heavily cut) in capsules, folded in tissue paper *(decks* or *bindles)* or in cellophane envelopes or in rubber balloons or condoms which contain *pieces* or *half pieces* (1 oz or ½ oz). Occasionally it appears in tablet form.

Heroin may be used the same as morphine, by mouth or hypodermically and intravenously. In addition, addicts may take heroin alone or with cocaine by sniffing it up the nose where it is absorbed through the nasal mucous membrane. This is often an initial phase of addiction preceding intravenous injection; heroin and cocaine are also taken, mixed, by needle. Today, heroin is overwhelmingly the drug of choice for addicts; the Federal Narcotics Bureau reports that 82 per cent of the known addicts use it.

Dionin

Technical or scientific names:
Ethylmorphine Hydrochloride
Argot names:

No argot names since it is not used by addicts.

Dionin is a white crystalline powder derived from morphine. Its effects closely resemble codeine but are weaker, causing intense irritation of mucous membrane, for which purpose dionin is used in the treatment of chronic inflammatory conditions of the eye where the resulting hyperemia is beneficial. For this purpose, dionin is used in solution of from 2 to 10 per cent or as 10 per cent ointment. Although it is not used by addicts because it is weak and causes local irritation, it is controlled by Federal law.

Dilaudid

Technical or scientific names:
Dihydromorphinone Hydrochloride
Argot names:

D; no other specific argot names encountered, but generic terms like *junk, white stuff,* etc., include Dilaudid.

Dilaudid is a fine white crystalline powder, prepared from morphine, having the same general actions and uses. Since the duration of analgesia is somewhat shorter than morphine, doses for the relief of pain are required at shorter intervals. Its sedative action is equal to that of morphine. Medically, it is given by mouth, by hypodermic injection or by rectal suppository, the average dose being 1/20 grain (3 mg). After the production of Dilaudid in Germany in 1923, it was claimed by some that it was a non-addicting substitute for morphine, and much addiction was unknowingly caused by the prescription of Dilaudid until it was definitely shown by King, Himmelsbach, and Sanders[9] in 1935 that Dilaudid was an addicting drug in every sense of the word. It is very popular with addicts who inject it intravenously; however, it is not generally available in contraband traffic, and is obtained directly or indirectly from medical or pharmaceutical sources. It is controlled by Federal law.

Apomorphine

Technical or scientific names:
Apomorphine Hydrochloride
Argot names:
No argot names encountered since it is not used by addicts.

Apomorphine is prepared as a hydrochloride from morphine. In small doses apomorphine is used to stimulate expectoration, and in larger doses as an emetic to produce vomiting. It is usually given hypodermically. The average emetic dose is 1/12 grain (5 mg). It is a dangerous drug, producing severe depression of the nervous system, but is not considered either a narcotic or an addicting drug; as a derivative of morphine, however, it is under Federal control.

Metopon

Technical or scientific names:
Metopon Hydrochloride (New and Non-Official Remedies)[10] 7-Methyl-dihydromorphinone Hydrochloride
Argot names:
No specific argot names, but covered by such generic terms as *junk, white stuff*, etc.

Metopon is a white crystalline powder, produced as a hydrochloride, soluble in water, closely resembling morphine in structure, but is derived from thebaine, another alkaloid of opium. Its medical uses are similar to morphine, with a greater analgesic effect combined with less sedation of mental activity. It is highly effective by mouth, with a low incidence of side reactions, but is used hypodermically also. The average dose is 3 mg. It is used in preference to morphine for the relief of chronic pain, such as terminal cancer. Its addiction liability is definite, but somewhat less than morphine insofar as the development of tolerance is concerned, according to Eddy.[11] It is used by narcotic addicts in the same way as heroin or morphine when it is obtainable, usually from medical sources. It is controlled by Federal law.

Codeine

Technical or scientific names:
Codeine Methylmorphine
Argot names:
No specific argot names encountered but covered by such generic terms as *junk, white stuff*, etc.

Codeine appears as white crystals or powder obtained from opium or prepared from morphine. Commercially, it is prepared in tablets for oral use or for hypodermic injection. It may be taken either way prepared as codeine phosphate or codeine sulfate. The average dose is ½ grain (30 mg) for medical use. It was first isolated from opium in 1832. Its effects are similar to morphine but about one sixth as strong in the relief of pain and in the support of addiction, and it is used widely for the medical relief of less severe pain and for the suppression of coughing. Codeine does not occur in contraband traffic except for small quantities diverted from legal medical supplies. In adequate doses it causes addiction and supports addiction originally established by other opiate drugs, although very large quantities are necessary to support a full-fledged morphine habit. However, addicts do seek to obtain codeine by deceit on prescriptions from physicians. The elixir of terpin hydrate and codeine, a cough syrup, is given in an average

4 cc dose, containing 8 mg codeine. As such, its retail sale is exempt from the Harrison Narcotic Act but it may be controlled by state law. Sufficient elixir of terpin hydrate and codeine may be taken to establish and maintain addiction. A naive addict may become addicted to this preparation without realizing that it contains an opiate; the sophisticated addict may seek and take large quantities of terpin hydrate and codeine as a substitute for a stronger opiate. Alcoholics sometimes become addicted through the use of elixir of terpin hydrate to sober them up. This elixir contains 40 per cent alcohol and, it has been observed, may be used by some addicts for the alcohol as well as for the codeine content.

Himmelsbach[12] definitely showed codeine to produce tolerance, as well as psychic and physical dependence, although some countries, notably France, still do not recognize its addiction liability. Codeine is combined with papaverine and sold as a cough and cold remedy, copavin or with coal-tar analgesics such as A.P.C. tablets or capsules (aspirin, phenacetine and codeine), not to be confused with the non-narcotic A.P.C. tablets containing caffeine. Codeine is also combined with white pine cough syrup and calcidine, but is not used in this form by addicts.

DERIVATIVES OF CODEINE

Eukodal, Eucodal, Percodan

Technical or scientific names:
Dihydrohydroxycodeinone Hydrochloride
Argot names:
No argot names encountered.

Eukodal is a white crystalline powder derived from codeine, used widely in Europe. It is used similarly to codeine and morphine, but is much stronger than codeine therapeutically (dosage 3 to 5 mg) as well as in addiction liability. It is controlled by the Federal narcotic law. In the United States, this drug is sold as Percodan, which combines the narcotic with homatropine, aspirin, phenacetin and caffeine. Percodan is available as yellow tablets which contain 4.5 mg of the narcotic or pink tablets which contain one half that amount. The manufacturer states this drug has less addiction liability than morphine but more than codeine. Addicts may either swallow Percodan tablets or dissolve and ingest them. Percobarb capsules are a combination of Percodan and a barbiturate. These are blue and yellow or blue and white in color.

Dicodide, Hycodan

Technical or scientific names:
Dihydrohydrocodeinone Bitratrate
Argot names:
None

Dicodide is a white powder derived from codeine. It bears the same chemical relationship to codeine that Dilaudid does to morphine. It is equal to morphine in potency, used chiefly as a cough remedy. Dosage is 5 to 15 mg. Widely used by addicts in Europe and in the United States. It is controlled by Federal narcotic law.

In the United States, Hycodan is an ingredient in Hycodan Syrup and Hycodan Tablets and Hycomine and Hycomine Compound Tablets.

Papaverine

Technical or scientific names:
Papaverine Hydrochloride
Argot names:
No argot names encountered. Not used by addicts, or at least rarely used.

Papaverine is a white crystalline powder, prepared as papaverine hydrochloride from opium or manufactured synthetically as an opiate alkaloid which relaxes smooth muscles. It has a feeble sedative and pain-relieving action through its capacity to relieve smooth muscle spasm. Frequently it is prescribed (orally or hypodermically) to dilate coronary arteries for the relief of angina pectoris. The average dose is 1½ grain (0.1 gm). Although an alkaloid derived from opium, papaverine belongs to an entirely different chemical series than morphine or heroin, and no cases of addiction have been reported. It is controlled by Federal narcotic law. Papaverine combined with codeine is sold as a cough and cold remedy, copavin.

N-Allylnormorphine Hydrobromide, Nalline, Nalorphine

Technical or scientific names:
N-Allylnormorphine Hydrobromide
Argot names:
Eleanor, Babo (because it "takes the user to the cleaner").

This drug, a white crystalline powder, was recently prepared in the United States from codeine but it is more closely related to morphine in molecular structure. It has been shown at the Lexington hospital to be a very effective, often dramatic antidote for poisoning from other opiate drugs (see Chapter 6). Research there also shows that N-allylnormorphine intensifies the abstinence illness resulting when morphine, heroin, methadone, and, perhaps, Demerol, are withheld from addicts (see Chapters 5, 6 and 7). It provides a useful means of diagnosing addiction to these drugs because it precipitates clinical or subclinical withdrawal symptoms. This new drug has not been fully tested yet for its usefulness in poisoning or addiction to other drugs of the opiate series. When given to active morphine, heroin and methadone addicts it has a dysphoric effect; it is unpleasant to addicts because it cancels the euphoric effect of the opiate drug of addiction. In the non-addict it may produce, in small doses, euphoria, the sensation being similar to that caused by the use of alcohol. With repeated use or larger doses, the euphoria is displaced by dysphoria; hence the addiction liability of this drug is probably slight. Although a derivative of opium, it is antagonistic to the other opiates in action and is now exempt from Federal narcotic law control. The argot names given are those used by the addict-patients in the research laboratory at the Lexington hospital. Because of recent publicity given the drug, most addicts know it well by a trade name, Nalline. Levallorphan is a related drug with similar action.

SYNTHETIC EQUIVALENTS OF OPIATE DRUGS

Demerol

Technical or scientific names:
Meperidine Hydrochloride (N.N.R.)[10]
Argot names:
No argot names encountered, but the drug is covered by such generic terms as *junk, white stuff,* etc. The drug is used by addicts.

Demerol, also known as *perthidine, meperidine, dolantin, dolantol, isonipecaine,* is a white crystalline powder prepared synthetically, resembling morphine in its use and, to some extent, atropine in that it decreases secretions and dilates the pupils. It is an analgesic and sedative with a depressant action on smooth muscle.

Demerol is marketed in ampules and disposable syringes of various sizes; a banana-flavored elixir; 50 mg and 100 mg white tablets; pink mottled tablets; white, green and pink layered tablets; and yellow tablets combining Demerol with other drugs. Usually it is given medically by mouth or by intramuscular injection. When originally introduced, this drug, like others, was at first believed by some to possess the analgesic action of morphine without the addiction liability, a claim which received wide publicity in both professional and lay journals, resulting in numerous cases of addiction. Its addiction liability was definitely established by Himmelsbach[13] and Wieder,[14] among others. It is controlled by Federal narcotic laws.

Methadone

Technical or scientific names:
Methadone Hydrochloride (N.N.R.)[10]
Argot names:
No specific names encountered, but the drug is used by addicts.

Methadone, also known as *methadon, amidone, adanon, Dolo-*

phine and *10-8-20,* is a fine white powder. It was developed during World War II in Germany, and released for sale under Federal control in 1947. Its effects generally are those of morphine, except that they develop more slowly and persist longer. Although methadone is addicting, the abstinence syndrome is slower in onset and milder in severity than that of morphine. This latter characteristic makes it useful in the treatment of withdrawal distress from other opiates inasmuch as it can be substituted for the opiate of addiction with subsequent milder withdrawal. It has been successfully used in withdrawing addicts both at the Lexington and Fort Worth U. S. Public Health Service Hospitals. Methadone is prepared for sale in powder form, tablet form and ampule form. It may be taken by mouth or hypodermically. The average dose is 5 mg. It is also sold as Dolophine in a cough syrup.

Methadone is attractive to the addict and supports opiate addiction. Addicts taking it experimentally often identify it as either heroin or morphine.[15]

Proposals that methadone be given addicts after discharge from an institution, as a "non-addicting, continuing substitute" for heroin can only lead to disaster, repeating the tragic introduction of heroin as a "non-addicting" substitute for morphine. To whatever extent it may be synthesized illegally or diverted from legal channels, it will appear in contraband trade. Methadone is under the control of the Federal narcotic laws.

Dromoran, Levophan

Technical or scientific names:
DL 3-hydroxy-N-methylmorphinan
Argot names:
None

Dromoran is a synthetic drug of the morphine series and resembles morphine closely in its action, although it is somewhat more potent. The dosage is 6 mg, which equals in action about 15 mg of morphine. The length of action is somewhat longer than morphine. The addiction liability is equal to that of morphine. It is controlled by Federal narcotic law.

Phenazocine, Numorphan, Prinadol, Narphen, Winthrocine

Technical or scientific names:
14-hydroxydihydromorphinone
Argot names:
None encountered.

This new drug, synthesized by Man and Eddy at the National Institute of Health, is a more powerful analgesic than any opiates now in clinical use. Physical dependence develops more slowly and is less intense, so that it can be used over longer periods of time than morphine in cases of chronic pain. It has fewer side effects than morphine, but reports that there is no respiratory depression, thus making it an ideal drug for obstetrical use, have been questioned. It is a narcotic drug, has addiction liability and is regulated by Federal narcotic laws. It is sold in ampules in solution for hypodermic injection, and in the form of rectal suppositories. The dose is 1 to 2 mg by injection, or 2 to 5 mg by suppository. Numorphan is also sold as 10 mg blue tablets for oral use. This drug may appear soon under other trade names.

Leritine

Technical or scientific names:
Anileridine
Argot names:
None encountered.

This synthetic drug ranges in between Demerol and morphine in analgesic potency. It is reported to have fewer side effects, including respiratory depression, than morphine and to have greater spasmolytic action. It is supplied in tablets for oral use and in solution for injection. The dose is 25 to 50 mg.

Numerous synthetic drugs related to Demerol and methadone have been produced and subjected to experimentation. Isbell[16] has reported on the addiction liability of five new compounds in the meperidine series: bemidone; keto-bemidone; Nu-1196; Nu-1779; and Nu-1932. Keto-bemidone, which has become available for medical purposes in Europe since it has some advantages over Demerol, has been brought under Federal narcotic regulation by

Presidential Proclamation, as has iso-methadone, a drug related to methadone. Keto-bemidone is one of the most addicting drugs ever discovered and will probably never be authorized for sale in the United States. Levo-methadone,[17] a constituent of methadone, has been shown to be responsible for both the analgesic and addictive effects of methadone; it may eventually be manufactured and offered as a replacement for methadone. It is probable that many more synthetic drugs with opiate-like action will be produced and studied experimentally and that a few of these will eventually be authorized for medical use under Federal narcotic law control. Synthetics available now are adequate to take the place of the natural opiate drugs (except codeine) for medical purposes in a country which might be cut off from supplies of opium by war or economic barriers. In 1958, for instance, the United States produced seventeen times as much pethidine (Demerol) as morphine, clearly indicating the trend away from natural narcotics and toward synthetics.

Since opium and its derivatives have for centuries been the most valuable group of drugs in the doctor's armamentarium, it is not surprising that Remington's Practice of Pharmacy[7] lists, in addition to the official preparations, forty-eight unofficial preparations of opium alkaloids and derivatives, as well as forty-four specialty medicines containing opium alkaloids and derivatives.

There is always the hope of discovering a drug which is a good analgesic for the relief of pain, but which is not addicting. So far, no such drug is known, and every physician must weigh the value of pain relief against any possible danger of addiction, especially in the case of individuals known or suspected to be addiction-prone. Recently, however, a new drug, Pentazocine (phenozocine hydrobromide), has been introduced experimentally as a non-addicting analgesic with approaches morphine in effectiveness. Unpleasant side effects will probably prevent its wide use, but this is one step toward producing a potent non-addicting analgesic.

Figures 9 and 10, based on the work of Vogel, Isbell and Chapman,[18] show in condensed form the comparative analgesic efficiency and the relative addiction liability of the most commonly used opiate drugs or synthetics resembling opium derivatives.

FIGURE 9

TABLE SHOWING THE COMPARATIVE EFFICACY OF SINGLE AVERAGE DOSE OF SEVERAL ANALGESIC DRUGS*

Drug	Effectiveness in Relief of Pain	Sedation or Sleep Production	Duration of Clinical Relief of Pain-Hours
Dilaudid	5	5	3
Heroin	5	5	4
Morphine	4	5	4
Metopon	5	3	4
Demerol	3	4	3
Methadone**	2	2	4-10
Codeine	1	1	4

* The numeral 5 indicates the most effective of all the drugs in producing the effect noted; the numeral 1 indicates the least effective of all the drugs.

** Applicable only to single doses of methadone, which in repeated doses becomes as effective as morphine in the relief of pain.

FIGURE 10

TABLE SHOWING THE COMPARATIVE ADDICTION LIABILITY OF SEVERAL ANALGESIC DRUGS

Drug	Physical Dependence Liability	Psychic or Emotional Dependence Liability	Rapidity of Tolerance Development	Points Total
Morphine	4	4	4	12
Heroin	4	4	4	12
Dilaudid	4	4	4	12
Metopon	3	4	3	10
Demerol	2	3	2	7
Methadone	1	4	1	6
Codeine	2	1	2	5

The numeral 4 indicates that the particular drug has the greatest liability of all the drugs with respect to the particular addiction characteristic shown; the numeral 1 indicates the lowest liability; the sum of the three characteristics gives the total addiction liability, the highest possible addiction liability score being 12 and the lowest being 0.

Thus dilaudid, while very effective in the relief of pain, and high in sedative value, also ranks among the highest in addiction liability. Codeine, while least effective as an analgesic, is also very low in addiction liability.

PHYSIOLOGICAL AND PSYCHOLOGICAL EFFECTS OF OPIATE DRUGS

While the opiate drugs differ in their individual effects upon addicts, there is considerable similarity among all of the opiate derivatives or synthetic opiate-like drugs; therefore, it is possible to generalize on the physiological and psychological effect of these drugs if we note exceptions as they occur.

Authorities on drug addiction recognize several classes of addicts. These have been discussed in detail in Chapter 1. In any event, one must recognize at least two psychological classes of addicts, even though there may be no difference between these two groups in the basic physiology of addiction. These two groups are those which might be considered "normal" at the time of addiction, on the one hand, and those which would be classed as addiction-prone, on the other. However, in both groups certain identical phenomena are observed. These are the development of physical dependence on the drug, the development of tolerance to the drug and habituation.

Among "normal" individuals—that is those individuals with stable personalities—the reaction to drugs is usually negative. To this type of individual the first experience with opiate drugs, usually encountered during medical treatment, is distasteful, except insofar as they relieve pain. He does not experience the intense pleasure or euphoria which the addiction-prone personality seeks. However, the normal person will become physiologically addicted to opiates just as truly as the addiction-prone personality if he is exposed sufficiently to the drugs, except that his emotional dependence is not so marked, being chiefly related to the distress of withdrawal rather than to the positive pleasure effect. The normal personality, however, cooperates readily, as a rule, in withdrawal treatment and shows a lesser tendency to revert to drugs than does the addiction-prone individual.

Persons considered to be addiction-prone usually experience intense pleasure on their first contact with opiates, and whether their first experience with drugs is under medical supervision or whether it occurs as a result of experimentation or the suggestion of addicted acquaintances, the results are usually dramatically pleasurable. Pleasure may be intense, despite accompanying nausea or the nervousness attending the event. Sometimes the addict begins by smoking opium, although that is a rare occurrence today. Usually he begins with a hypodermic needle, and his first shot is taken subcutaneously or intramuscularly. The pleasure that he receives from this initial contact he does not forget, and even though the may not continue with the use of drugs at that time, he reverts to them on the strength of his memory of the initially pleasurable experience. Very shortly, if not immediately, he begins to inject morphine or heroin directly into his veins so that the full effect of the drug in solution is felt almost instantaneously throughout the body. The result of this injection is a very intense pleasure often described by addicts as of several minutes' duration, sometimes centered in the abdomen. With an addiction-prone personality, the initial stages of addiction appear to be indescribably pleasurable, with the individual repeating the pleasurable climaxes almost at will or at his regular periods of self-administration. Among conditioned adult addicts, these administrations occur about four or five times daily, usually at intervals of four or five hours, although the number of shots and the time intervals may differ considerably among individuals. It has been observed that adolescents and young adults using heroin are not so inclined to take their rations of drug in regular amounts on a regular schedule, but inject the drug when they have it, taking as much as they are able to secure and enjoying full pleasure briefly with each injection.[20]

Intensity of the pleasure from opiates seems to vary with the degree to which the individual may be called a neurotic or a psychopath, and Dr. Kolb[19] has described in detail the types of abnormal personality which seem to be highly susceptible to addiction; however, eventually the addiction-prone individual ceases to get from the drug the intense pleasure he formerly experienced, and even rapidly increased doses of the drug fail to recapture the ecstasy which he experienced during the early stages of use. Little by little, the pleasure of opiates gives way to the driving necessity to take drugs in order to avoid withdrawal distress, and the addict's chief occupation becomes the securing of a regular supply of drugs. At this point, many chronic addicts like to break the habit and undergo the withdrawal syndrome chiefly for two reasons: first, the habit which they have built up has become very expensive; and second, they would like to recapture the pleasurable sensation which they recall from the beginning of addiction. Therefore, they remain off drugs for a period of several months or more, but almost inevitably return when circumstances permit them to secure drugs or when they take a single *joy pop* with friends or acquaintances. While it cannot be said certainly that the normal individual does not experience any of the euphoria or intense pleasure registered by the addiction-prone person, it is certain that the "normal" person does not get pleasure in any great degree, nor does he feel the high degree of compulsion to return to drugs which characterizes the addiction-prone personality.

A long-time addict describes this cycle quite vividly:

> It's hard for ordinary people to sympathize with a drug addict—nearly impossible for them to understand him. The addict is a self-made outcast who has renounced humanity before it could renounce him. Yet he can go nowhere; so he continues to lurk in the shadows, an unwanted spectre, a mocking reminder of the colossal errors that can be made by the combined forces of nature and man.
>
> Emotionally a child, though physically an adult, this enigma is forced to live in a world where he does not really belong. He lacks the spirit, if not the ability, for everyday competion; so he erects a protective wall between himself and those "outsiders" who might help him. Safer, he feels, to loll in the anesthetized realm of euphoria, soothed by the gentle hand of Morpheus. There he can shed the problems and pains of living. . . . There he can encourage the gratifying dreams of pleasure and power that were so reassuring as a child. . . . There he can stand alone and undaunted, self-sufficient and free from care. Freedom in a fleecy cloud—soft and warm and so easily maintained by a marvelous, omnipotent medication.
>
> But an addict's synthetic pleasures are short-lived. Soon he must pay for his sojourn in the wispy land of Nod. The cloud disintegrates. Warmth turns cold. Peace is gone and reality wrenches the soul. Problems and pains erupt again. Fears and doubts emerge to resume control. Misery, a hopeless, empty

ache, and the frantic race begins! How quickly can he find the way to make the means to take the trip back into oblivion? He must have money for drugs! Then more money for more drugs— ever more and more and more, for there's no end to the sick addict's perilous pursuit of peace. Panic! No time for morals. No time for decency. No time for self-respect. There's no time for anything in this headlong plunge toward disaster!

No, the addict, while using narcotics, does not present a pleasant picture, nor a hopeful one. He's like a blind man staggering toward inevitable doom. Like Samson helplessly shackled to the millstone, he must travel ever around, unable to escape the circular route that will be his eventual destruction. Whipped by a tormenting need, urged on by unquenchable longings, he will gradually be ground into dust by the sheer weight of his affliction. But he stumbles passively on, unable to give up the unequal contest.

All individuals when exposed to opiates or their equivalents tend to develop similar symptoms, including physical dependence, tolerance and habituation. The opiates are, in general, depressant drugs; however, it has been observed that while they depress certain parts of the nervous system, they serve as a stimulant to others with the secondary stimulative effects of morphine, Dilaudid and heroin probably being greater than those of opium and other opiate derivatives. It is understood that *depressant* and *stimulant* are used here in a neurophysiological sense which has no direct correlation with pleasurable effects.

Rare individuals appear to have an allergic reaction to opiates, resulting in severe illness or death. The authors believe that at least some of the deaths attributed to an overdose of drugs may actually be a result of this anaphylactic reaction. See Fig. 11 for the photograph of an addict who died before he could release the tourniquet or put down the syringe. We have reports from addicts who indicate that they have taken heroin, without any ill effects, from the same batch used by another addict who died suddenly.

Regardless of the type of personality involved, every human being who takes opiates over a period of time also develops certain changes in his physiology which might be called characteristic of addiction. Not all individuals develop these symptoms in the same degree, and in some individuals certain symptoms may fail to appear or appear in a very mild form, but physiological reaction as well as the pyschological behavior of the addict falls into a characteristic and recognizable pattern. The reactions of the so-called normal individual in this respect are no different from those of the addiction-prone type.

The general effect of the opiate drugs is to reduce all physiological activity; the principal effects involve depression of the central nervous system with secondary effects upon the peripheral nervous system.[28, 34, 35] The metabolic rate is decreased, the blood pressure is lowered, and the respiratory rate goes down; in fact, opiates become fatal at the point where respiration is reduced below the level compatible with maintaining the oxygen needs of the body.

While the individual is on drugs the entire digestive tract is strongly affected. The digestive fluids, including the saliva, are reduced in quantity. In general, there is a loss of appetite and the reduction of intestinal fluids, along with other factors, produces severe constipation. Because of loss of appetite caused by drugs, opiate addicts are often underweight, a condition which is to be ascribed to the failure to maintain a proper intake of food rather than to any qualities of the drug itself. In some cases, the intake of food is undoubtedly reduced because the addict conserves all his money for drugs. The loss of weight often affects the general body health, and large dental caries are often present; however, it has not been possible to demonstrate that opiate drugs in themselves actually destroy tissue or are directly the cause of tissue deterioration.

It is recognized that during addiction the reproductive system generally tends to become inactive, although this condition is not universal and the mechanism involved is not fully understood. Among human addicts, the sexual secretions diminish. While the female addict is consuming considerable quantities of opiates, the menstrual cycle is frequently disrupted; however, during addiction, ovulation may continue and pregnancies do sometimes occur.[29, 30]

Recently, Dr. Gaulden has shown that large doses of heroin given seventy-two women suppressed ovulation and menstruation in 64 per cent, heroin with amphetamine or marihuana in 29 per cent and heroin with barbiturates in 76 per cent. In another group of seventy-four women, he found that the libido was decreased in 61 per cent, increased in 4 per cent and unchanged in 35 per cent. Fifteen per cent of this group reported a nipple discharge.

In both males and females, opiates have a general tendency to reduce or obliterate sexual desire, although there are many individual exceptions to this. The use of opium, especially by smoking, appears to enable some men to maintain erections for several hours, and although sexual relations may take place after smoking, orgasm is usually absent. Similar effects are reported from heroin, and cases are known where women encourage their men to use heroin for this reason. At the same time, most male addicts do not feel an active desire for intercourse, although they may indulge in it to please their companions. Many opium smokers have noticed that it is possible to have orgasm before smoking, and so far as is known, the opiates have no direct effect on the fertility of the male. All the secretions of the reproductive system tend to diminish, including that of the seminal vesicle and the prostatic fluids.

This reduction of body fluids reflects the general dehydration of the tissues which accompanies the chronic use of opiates. There is frequently a spasm of the vesical sphincter, leading to distention of the bladder and a constant but ineffective desire to micturate.[19] The intestinal secretions diminish, and the sweat glands are partially inactive. The skin of addicted persons is usually dry and the nails rather pale and brittle.

The most commonly used and the most useful of the opiate drugs is morphine; the effects of codeine resemble those of morphine except that both the analgesic effect and the addiction liability are reduced, the latter so considerably reduced that in some European countries codeine is not considered a drug of addiction; however, in this country its addiction liability is well established. It is widely used, and medical preparations containing less than 1 grain codeine per ounce are not presumed to be dangerous enough to be under Federal control. The relatively low solubility of codeine compared to morphine makes it difficult for an addict to take large quantities of it hypodermically.

Both the physiological and psychic effects of drugs differ with their method of administration; certain differences should be noted between the medical application of drugs and self-administration by addicts. In the case of morphine-like drugs, medical administration may, where a mild and not-too-rapid analgesic effect is required, be administered orally in relatively small doses. Where rapid relief of severe pain is indicated, opiate drugs are injected by nurses or doctors subcutaneously in small quantities.

The addict, however, primarily uses self-administration, and although he may go through a stage where the morphine, heroin or codeine is injected subcutaneously (and some addicts remain in this stage for a long period of time or permanently), eventually he usually adopts intravenous injection as the method of choice. His technique for intravenous injection differs from recognized medical techniques (medically intravenous injection of an opiate is rarely indicated) in that he tries to deliver a concentrated dose of morphine, heroin or codeine abruptly to the whole body through the bloodstream. (The method by which this is done is described in some detail in Chapter 1.) The effect of opiates taken in this way differs dramatically from medical administration subcutaneously, and in the addiction-prone personality produces a degree of euphoria which is probably unequaled in human experience. Eventually, of course, the euphoria diminishes, and the addict injects increasing quantities of opiate largely for the purpose of allaying withdrawal distress. When his habit becomes too expensive or his euphoria diminishes sufficiently as tolerance develops, he may "kick the habit" voluntarily and start over in an effort to recapture the early ecstasy which he experienced from opiates used intravenously.

Psychological tests administered by Mario Levi *et al.*,[31] showed that morphine increased the anxiety response to the Rorschach and TAT test. A study of the effect of drugs on driver performance showed, as any policeman knows, an impairment of the various elements of driver skills in handling an automobile.[32]

The physical and psychic effects of methadone differ considerably from other opiates and opiate synthetics, and a discussion of its properties along with a comprehensive description of the action of the drug has been published by Isbell, *et al.*[15] Already it is being used by addicts, as is evidenced by the fact that some are being sentenced to the Federal hospitals for treatment. Probably most methadone at present is stolen or diverted from legitimate channels; however, sooner or later it will probably be manufactured illicitly.

Heroin is without medical use and has been outlawed in the United States for some years; opium is used medically in various preparations such as laudanum, tincture of opium, etc. but prepared smoking opium is contraband and is used only by opium addicts for smoking. Crude opium is imported legally for the manufacture of opiate drugs under license by three pharmaceutical manufacturers: Merck; Mallinkrodt; and the National Quinine Company. Five companies are licensed to package the opiates after manufacture and sell them to numerous wholesale drug houses for distribution to registered pharmacists. Gum opium as contraband has two principal uses—first, the preparation of smoking opium, which has been described earlier in this chapter, and second, the ilicit refinement of morphine or heroin.

Under some circumstances, narcotic addicts will inject opium or take it by mouth. These alternates are used when smoking opium is not available or when some other opiate drug cannot be obtained. Also, addicts are very ingenious at recovering opium from medical preparations which contain too small an amount to be considered normally addicting. Law enforcement officers and physicians should be familiar with methods of such recovery. For instance, the temperature of paregoric may be reduced by refrigerating it or putting it in ice water to crystallize the camphor; the remaining solution, consisting largely of alcohol and opium, is then boiled until the alcohol evaporates. The residue, which is a thick viscous gum, is then diluted and filtered through cotton. It can then be injected hypodermically. In the contraband traffic it is known as *black jack*.

Laudanum (tincture of opium) is simply boiled down and the gummy residue diluted sufficiently to inject after filtering. When opium obtained from either paregoric or laudanum is injected, a chill results, and if the vein is missed an abscess usually forms.

Rectal suppositories containing opium and belladonna may also be treated to remove the belladonna and leave the opium. The suppositories, usually with a cocoa butter base, are melted, then chilled suddenly so that oil in the suppository solidifies, leaving a liquid core. The top of the wax capsule is then broken and the liquid drawn out with a medicine dropper, filtered and injected, with abscesses frequently developing as a complication.

Sometimes addicts who cannot get the drug of choice will boil out the *gee rags* from opium smoking, or re-work the ashes or dilute the gum so that it can be cooked up and injected. (This solution is sometimes taken orally when smoking opium cannot be obtained. It is called *yen shee suey*.) Again, this method of injecting opium is dangerous because abscesses so frequently follow; sometimes there is a long time lapse between the injection and the abscesses (perhaps as much as two years) after which a chronic inflammatory mass begins to form and progresses until it becomes a large fibrous knot. This may break down into a boil-like abscess; the discharge from it may contain black particles remaining from the original injection of opium; if it does not break down, it may leave a fibroma which will remain until removed surgically; the original inflammation may also subside and recur later as a chronic reaction.

The constipation resulting from opiate addiction is sometimes extreme; a hard, difficult bowel evacuation is sometimes called a *yen shee baby*.

Tablets containing a combination of morphine and atropine may be processed by addicts in order to remove most of the atropine by placing the tablet on a blotter and applying a drop or two of water which dissolves the atropine and carries it into the blotting paper. Some addicts hold a match under the damp spot on the blotter just long enough for the steam to aid in this crude method of separating the drugs. This treatment will sufficiently reduce the atropine content so as to preclude the unpleasant effects of injecting the two drugs simultaneously; if enough of the untreated tablets are injected to get the desired effect from the morphine, the atropine taken simultaneously may cause severe illness. The methods for reclaiming opiates just described are, of course, used by addicts, as a rule, only in an emergency.

Sooner or later, most opiate addicts develop abscesses if they use the needle. These develop in the areas most used for injection of the drug and, while some addicts avoid them for years, most develop them as a result of infection concomitant to use of the needle. Those who are careless have a much greater tendency to develop infection than those who are not. In addition to abscesses, those addicts who share their equipment with others or sterilize it inadequately may acquire or transmit syphilis, hepatitis with jaundice, malaria or other infectious diseases.

The abscesses are both primary and secondary. The primary abscesses appear at the site of injection—the crook of the elbow is the most common, but if the addict uses the hollow of the knee, the back of the hand, the veins of the neck, the instep or other areas, these may also become infected. The primary abscess is painful and exudes pus usually containing very large numbers of staphylococci or streptococci. Several abscesses may develop at the same point, and they may become confluent. Superficially, they resemble large boils or carbuncles.

The secondary abscesses appear from one to three weeks after the beginning of withdrawal and are usually of no serious consequence. They are painful and exude serous pus, usually without bacterial content. Both types of abscess tend to leave long scars which are characteristic of addiction to opiates by needle; in some addicts, these scars constitute large elongated masses of scar-tissue over the sites of injection.

In addition to abscess scars, most addicts tend to develop sclerosis of the veins from repeated puncturing; that is, the normal veins are partially or completely replaced by cords of scar tissue.

Drug addicts follow a rather well-defined behavior pattern. They differ from alcoholics largely in the nature of the drug they use; it should be understood that no drug possesses mysterious powers to subjugate a human being; the drug becomes dangerous only when it comes into contact with the human personality and especially with the addiction-prone type of personality. The opiates have an analgesic action and the capacity to quiet mental distress. They relieve mental and physical tension. They differ from alcohol chiefly in that they decrease the urge toward physical action and, in general, inhibit all activity. When a person with psychological conflicts which he cannot resolve in some practical way, or with chronic physiological or organic distress, comes into contact with opiates, he may feel that he has found an attractive solution for his difficulty. If he has an unstable personality as well as a low tolerance for either physical or mental discomfort, and if opiate drugs relieve this discomfort to the degree of ecstasy and a complete sense of well-being, he will probably become a drug addict.[18, 21] While these characteristics of personality are not the complete cause of drug addiction, they are typical of the personality types found among addicts. Kolb[22] classified these in 1925 and, a little later, in conjunction with Ossenfort,[19] modified his classification to include six personality types. Subsequently, Felix[23] reduced this list to three types; psychoneurotics; psychopaths; and individuals with psychoses who are addicted to drugs.

All the research done on drug addiction within the past two generations indicates that addiction itself is not a disease, but rather a symptom of personality defects which, if they did not lead to drug addiction, would lead to difficulties of other types. The opiates, however, have the capacity of reducing the individual's sensitivity to external stimuli and thus exclude much that is somatically or psychologically unpleasant. While there is much more to drug addiction than simply classifying addicts as poorly adjusted people who seek a compensation for their own weaknesses, the personality defect is clearly manifest in those who are inveterate addicts, and the capacity of opiates to give the individual the illusion that he has mastery over life situations about which he can do little or nothing, coupled with the power these drugs have of giving intense physical and emotional pleasure, may make them irresistible to addiction-prone people.

On the other hand, normal or well-adjusted people can be given opiates under medical supervision, even to the point of developing strong physical dependence, and, once the physical dependence is broken through withdrawal, these individuals do not feel the need to return to drugs; in fact, the use of drugs is usually unpleasant to them, and the development of tolerance and physical dependence frightens them. While normal people can become addicted to the point where they must have the help of others to break the habit, their addiction need not recur. There is no reason why any well-trained physician should hesitate to administer opiates as indicated, for they are useful and, at present, irreplaceable drugs; however, prescriptions and administration should be always in the hands of the physician, who should have some experience in identifying the addiction-prone personality. There is a widespread popular belief that most drug addicts are made by prolonged use of opiates during a painful illness, and this story is often used by addicts who try to justify their condition, but, as a matter of fact, very few of the addicts seen by the authors are known to have started addiction as a result of medical treatment, although many give histories of medical addiction to "save face." Five per cent of 1,000 admissions to the Lexington hospital were considered medical addicts.[24]

Two generations ago, when prescription practices were much looser than today, and when patent medicine could contain opiates, there was a good deal of justification for the theory of so-called "medical" addiction. Now, the only substantial percentage of such "medical" addicts are those who have been treated for alcoholism with opiates, usually morphine, and who simply shifted drugs. Every year, hundreds of thousands of bona fide medical and surgical cases are given opiates under supervision, and the number of addicts so produced is small.

In California in 1963, sixty-six of 331 reported deaths from poisoning were due to narcotics, 104 were due to barbiturates, and two were due to glue sniffing.[33] A high proportion of known narcotic fatalities were young people with Spanish surnames. None of these was known to have occurred with suicidal intent.

One half of the persons dying from barbiturates had also been drinking alcohol; it was characteristic of this group that they included a high proportion of females of the non-Mexican Caucasian group and that they were middle-aged instead of young adults as with the narcotic fatalities. A considerable but unknown proportion were with suicidal intent.

A study in New York indicated that about 120 of 200 cases of hepatitis seen at a large municipal hospital in New York City were due to narcotic usage. In addition, fifty cases of endocarditis occurring in narcotic addicts, most of them fatal, were reported annually.

In New York it was estimated that one per cent of the addict population dies each year from overdose. A high death rate for addicts by narcotic overdose is understandable when contraband narcotics on the market vary from zero to 77 per cent heroin (10 per cent of samples purchased contained no heroin at all).

Figure 11 shows an addict who died from an overdose of heroin with the eye-dropper syringe still in his hand before he could remove the nylon stocking tourniquet.

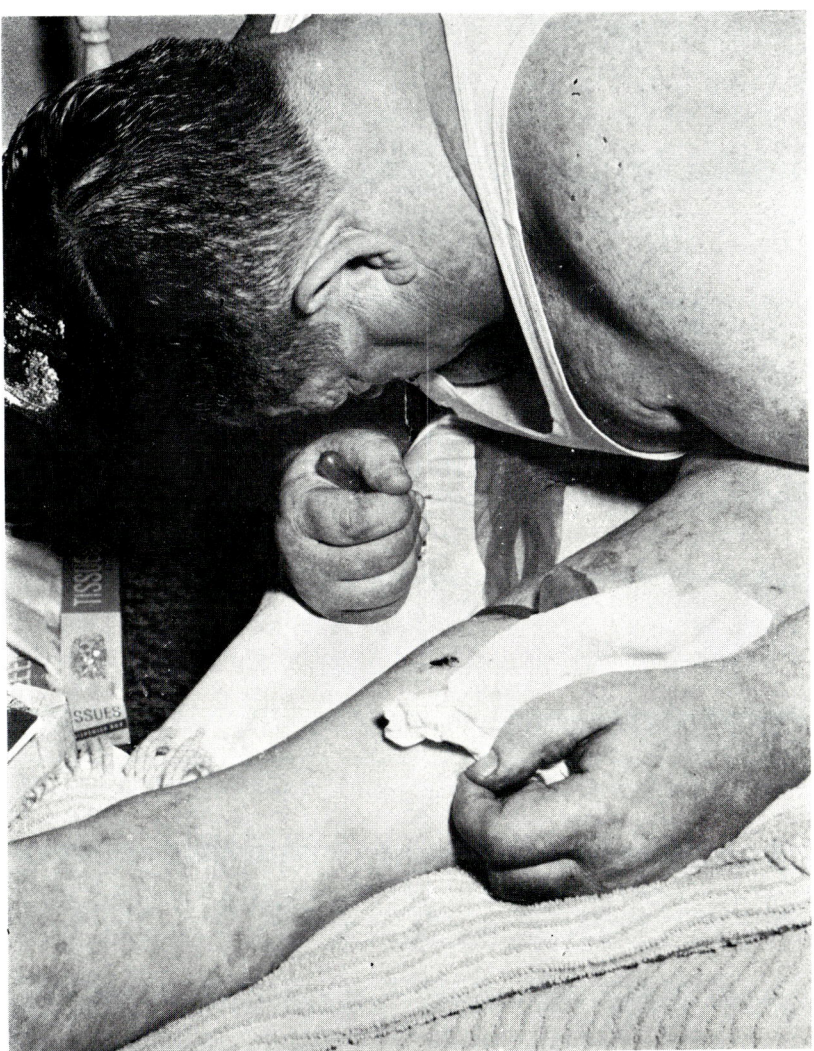

FIGURE 11. This addict died of an overdose of heroin with the eye-dropper syringe still grasped in his hand and before he released the nylon stocking tourniquet.

WITHDRAWAL ILLNESS

No discussion of opiates would be adequate without some mention of the withdrawal syndrome, since most people who come into contact with addicts will have to deal with this phenomenon and will gain their knowledge of addiction rather from the effects of the absence of drugs than from their direct effect on people. In fact, as long as the customary amount of drugs is taken by an addict at regular times, even those with wide experience in dealing with addiction might not be able to determine by observation that the individual is an addict. When the proper quantity of drug is used regularly, it compensates somewhat for the personality defect and maintains the addict at what he feels is a "normal" level; he is sufficiently stabilized by the drug that it is difficult to identify him as an addict until the drug is withdrawn. The only dependable signs are the characteristic abscess scars (or blue-black tattooing when the individual has been taking the drug subcutaneously) and fresh needle marks or the very rapid constriction of the pupils of the eyes immediately after injection of some drugs, with dilatation of the pupils to normal when the effect of the drug has worn off. The diagnosis of drug addiction is not to be undertaken by amateurs, and, except in cases where the individual admits addiction, the police or other untrained persons should not proceed on unwarranted assumptions. Needle marks may be from authorized medication or may be resembled by insect bites; burns may resemble abscess scars, and pupils may be constricted for other reasons. (See Chapter 5 for diagnosis of addiction.)

The effects of withdrawing opiates have, of course, been known for time immemorial, but it is only within our own century that they have been studied scientifically, and only within the last decade that Kolb,[25] Himmelsbach,[26] Isbell[17] and others at Lexington, Kentucky, have put the measurement of the withdrawal syndrome or abstinence syndrome on a partially objective basis. While withdrawal from opiates is never a pleasant experience, its terrors have probably been exaggerated considerably in the minds of addicts; certainly fear of recurring withdrawal distress is not a very strong factor is discouraging recidivism. The syndrome varies somewhat in intensity with individuals, as well as with the drug being used at the time of withdrawal and the quantity being used. However, the pattern for the opiates and their commercially available synthetic equivalents is clearly established, and the syndrome for some non-opiates will be discussed in the following chapter.

When an addict misses his first shot, he senses mild withdrawal distress ("feels his habit coming on"), but this is probably more psychological than physiological, for fear plays a considerable role in the withdrawal syndrome. At this stage, a placebo may give relief. During the first eight to sixteen hours of abstinence, the addict becomes increasingly nervous, restless and anxious; close confinement tends to intensify these symptoms. Within fourteen hours (usually less) he will begin to yawn frequently; he sweats profusely and develops running of the eyes and nose comparable to that accompanying a severe head cold. These symptoms increase in intensity for the first twenty-four hours, after which the pupils dilate, and recurring waves of goose flesh occur. Severe twitching of the muscles (the origin of the term "kick the habit") occurs within thirty-six hours, and painful cramps develop in the backs of the legs and in the abdomen; all the body fluids are released copiously; vomiting and diarrhea are acute; there is little appetite for food, and the addict is unable to sleep. The respiratory rate rises steeply, both systolic and diastolic blood pressure increase moderately to a maximum between the third and fourth day; temperature rises an average of about one degree, subsiding after the third day; the blood sugar content rises sharply until the third day or after; the basal metabolic rate increases sharply during the first forty-eight hours. These are the objective signs of withdrawal distress which can be measured; the subjective indications are equally severe, and the illness reaches its peak within forty-eight to seventy-two hours after the last shot of the opiate, gradually subsiding thereafter for the next five to ten days. (See Chapter 6 for a system of objective rating of withdrawal signs.) Complete recovery requires from three to six months, with rehabilitation and, if needed, psychiatric treatment. The withdrawal syndrome proper is self-limiting, and most addicts will survive it with no medical assistance whatever (this is known as kicking the habit "cold turkey"). Abrupt withdrawal is inhumane, but with the development of such drugs as methadone, it is possible to reduce the distress of withdrawal very considerably.

The symptoms described above vary with the individual, the

length of time he has been addicted and the quantity of drugs he has been taking. As a rule, the more opiates he has been taking, the more severe his withdrawal illness, and the less he has been taking, the lighter will be the distress. In no event is the illness to be taken lightly, and allowing addicts to go through it unassisted in jails or prisons is not only unnecessarily brutal, but may endanger the life of the individual; certainly some assistance is desirable if the individual is to have any hope of staying off drugs once he is withdrawn, as will be shown in the chapter dealing with the treatment of addiction and withdrawal.

Some addicts will show a light touch of the symptoms described if they miss a shot or two, then will return to normal immediately when they get their drugs; if they get bootleg drugs which have been heavily cut, they may develop light withdrawal distress even though they are taking regular dosage; if they get a slight overdose or space their shots a little too close together, they tend to become drowsy or even comatose. The fear of withdrawal distress is undoubtedly one of the very strong factors in sustaining addiction and eventually apparently supersedes the desire for pleasure which the addict originally felt on taking opiates; nevertheless, as tolerance develops, most addicts cannot support the large habits which they build up and must withdraw themselves or be withdrawn so that they can start over on a smaller dosage.

It is a peculiar fact of opiate addiction that individuals will continue to take—and apparently to need—much larger amounts of opiates than the maximum shown to be utilized by the human organism, which is probably about 20 grains of morphine in twenty-four hours.

This apparent need of the addict to take more opiates than his system can utilize is not fully understood, but there appears to be an emotional need to consume increasing amounts of the drug, over and above the increase accounted for by the development of tolerance. Cases are known in the United States in which addicts have taken as high as 78 grains of unadulterated morphine by needle every twenty-four hours and as high as 100 grains of morphine daily administered orally; there are possibly higher rates of consumption unrecorded. There are also undoubtedly many instances in which the addict either believes that he consumes more than he does because of the dilution to which bootleg drugs are often subject or claims to take more than he actually does because he hopes that he may be tapered off on a heavier ration than he might otherwise get in institutions where gradual reduction is practiced. At any rate, whatever the beliefs of the addict may be, it is definitely established that a maximum of 10 grains per day will prevent the development of withdrawal distress, regardless of the size of the habit. In the underworld, a certain status goes with a large habit, together, of course, with the means to support it. However, this tendency to build up the habit is not restricted to underworld characters. Wolff[27] reported a rich Harbin merchant who smoked 350 grains of opium a day for some time, then reduced his habit voluntarily. A generation ago, large opium habits were common in the United States and England, but at present the scarcity of smoking opium, together with the complicated apparatus needed, the time consumed and the danger of detection because of the odor, all combine to reduce both the number of smokers and the size of their habits. The typical heroin or morphine addict takes from 2 to 10 grains of the more or less pure drug a day, by needle.

Although the authors have developed their own concepts of opiate addiction, mainly agreeing and often anticipating those articulated by the World Health Organization's Expert Committee on addiction-producing drugs in 1964,[36] that Committee's findings are reproduced here. This is done not only because they present some minor divergences from our thinking, but mainly because they represent international agreement on concepts of addiction by over 100 countries who subscribed to the Single Convention on Narcotic Drugs of 1961.

> Drug dependence of morphine type is described as a state arising from repeated administration of morphine or an agent with morphine-like effects on a periodic or continuous basis. Its characteristics include:
> 1. An overpowering desire or need to continue taking the drug and to obtain it by any means; the need can be satisfied by the drug taken initially or by another with morphine-like properties;
> 2. A tendency to increase the dose owing to the development of tolerance;
> 3. A psychic dependence on the effects of the drug related

to a subjective and individual appreciation of those effects; and

4. A physical dependence on the effects of the drug requiring its presence for maintenance of homeostasis and resulting in a definite, characteristic and self-limited abstinence syndrome when the drug is withdrawn.

The abstinence syndrome is the most characteristic and distinguishing feature of drug dependence of morphine type. It appears within a few hours of the last dose of drug taken, reaches peak intensity in 12 hours or more, and subsides spontaneously, most often within a week, the time course varying with the duration of action of the specific morphine-like agent involved. The abstinence syndrome may also be precipitated in a matter of minutes and made to take a more rapid time course by the administration of a specific antagonist while continuing the administration of the agent responsible for the dependence. The complex of symptoms which constitute an abstinence syndrome includes: yawning, lacrimation, rhinorrhoea, perspiration, mydriasis, tremor, gooseflesh, anorexia, anxiety, restlessness, nausea, emesis, diarrhoea, hot flushes, rise in body temperature, increase in respiratory rate and in systolic blood pressure, abdominal or other muscle cramps, and dehydration and loss of body-weight.

With morphine, the harm to the individual is in the main indirect, arising from preoccupation with drug-taking; personal neglect, malnutrition and infection are frequent consequences. For society also, the harm may be related to the preoccupation of the individual with drug-taking; disruption of interpersonal relationships, economic loss, and crimes against property are frequent consequences.

REFERENCES

1. *Pharmacopoeia of the United States of America (The United States Pharmacopoeia)*, Seventeenth Revision U. S. Pharmacological Convention, 1965.
2. TERRY, C. E., and PELLENS, M.: *The Opium Problem. For the Committee on Drug Addiction in Collaboration with the Bureau of Social Hygiene, Inc.,* New York. Camden, N. J., The Haddon Craftsmen, 1928.
3. ANONYMOUS: Opium production throughout the world. *Bulletin on Narcotics,* 1(1):6 (Oct.), 1946. Lake Success, New York.

4. LAUGIER, H.: International control of narcotic drugs. *Bulletin on Narcotics,* 1(1):4 (Oct.), 1949.
5. ANONYMOUS: *Traffic in Opium and Other Dangerous Drugs.* (Released by the U. S. Bureau of Narcotics.) Published annually.
6. ANONYMOUS: Determining the origins of opium. *Bulletin on Narcotics,* 1(1):14 (Oct.), 1949.
7. COOK, E. F., and MARTIN, E. W.: *Remington's Practice of Pharmacy* (10th ed.). Easton, Pa., The Mack Publishing Company, 1951.
8. WOLFF, P. O.: Some aspects of drug addiction. *Journal of Pharmacy and Pharmacology,* 3:1, 1951.
9. KING, M. R., HIMMELSBACH, C. K., and SANDERS, B. S.: *Dilaudid (dihydromorphinone), A Review of the Literature and a Study of Its Addictive Properties.* Supplement No. 113 to the Public Health Reports. Washington, D. C., U. S. Government Printing Office, 1935.
10. THE COUNCIL ON PHARMACY AND CHEMISTRY OF THE AMERICAN MEDICAL ASSOCIATION: *New and Non-Official Remedies,* 1957. Philadelphia, Lippincott.
11. EDDY, N. B.: Metopon hydrochloride, an experiment in clinical evaluation. *Public Health Reports,* 64:93 (Jan. 28), 1949.
12. HIMMELSBACH, C. K.: The addiction liability of codeine. *Journal of the American Medical Association,* 103:1420, 1934.
13. HIMMELSBACH, C. K.: Studies of addiction liability of demerol (D-140). *Journal of Pharmacology and Experimental Therapeutics,* 75:64 (May), 1942; and Further studies in the addiction liability of demerol (1-methyl-4-phenylpiperidine-4-carboxylic acid ethylester hydrochloride). *Journal of Pharmacology and Experimental Therapeutics,* 79:5 (Sept.), 1943.
14. WIEDER, H.: Addiction to meperidine hydrochloride (demerol hydrochloride). *Journal of the American Medical Association,* 132:1066 (Dec. 28), 1946.
15. ISBELL, H., WIKLER, A., EDDY, N. B., WILSON, J. L., and MORAN, C. F.: Tolerance and addiction liability of 6-dimethylamino-4-4-diphenyl-heptanone-3 (methodone). *Journal of the American Medical Association,* 135:888 (Dec. 6), 1947.
16. ISBELL, H.: The addiction liability of some derivatives of meperidine. *Journal of Pharmacology and Experimental Therapeutics,* 97:182 (Oct.), 1949.
17. ISBELL, H.: Methods and results of studying experimental human addiction to the newer synthetic analgesics. *Annals of the New York Academy of Sciences,* 51:108 (Nov. 1), 1948.

18. VOGEL, V. H., ISBELL, H., and CHAPMAN, K. W.: Present status of narcotic addiction with particular reference to medical indications and comparative addiction liability of the newer and older analgesic drugs. *Journal of the American Medical Association, 138*:1019 (Dec. 4), 1948.
19. KOLB, L., and OSSENFORT, W. F.: The treatment of drug addicts at the Lexington hospital. *Southern Medical Journal, 31*:914 (Aug.), 1938.
20. ZIMMERING, P., TOOLAN, J., SAFRIN, R., and WORTIS, S. B.: Heroin addiction in adolescent boys. *Journal of Nervous and Mental Diseases, 114*:19 (July), 1951.
21. REICHARD, J. D.: Narcotic drug addiction. A symptom of human maladjustment. *Diseases of the Nervous System, 14*:275 (Sept.), 1943.
22. KOLB, L.: Types and characteristics of drug addicts. *Mental Hygiene, 9*:300 (April), 1925.
23. FELIX, R. H.: An appraisal of the personality types of the addict. *American Journal of Psychiatry, 100*:462 (Jan.), 1944.
24. PESCOR, M. J.: *A Statistical Analysis of the Clinical Records of Hospitalized Drug Addicts.* Supplement No. 143 to the Public Health Reports. Washington, D. C., U. S. Government Printing Office, 1943.
25. KOLB, L., and HIMMELSBACH, C. K.: *Clinical Studies of Drug Addiction: III. A Critical Review of the Withdrawal Treatments with Method for Evaluating Abstinence Symptoms.* Supplement No. 128 to the Public Health Reports. Washington, D. C., U. S. Government Printing Office, 1938.
26. HIMMELSBACH, C. K., and SMALL, L. F.: *Clinical Studies of Drug Addiction: II. "Rossium" Treatment of Drug Addiction; with a Report on the Chemistry of "Rossium."* Supplement No. 125 to the Public Health Reports. Washington, D. C., U. S. Government Printing Office, 1937.
27. WOLFF, P. O.: The treatment of drug addicts. A critical survey. *Bulletin of the Health Organization of the League of Nations, 12*:455, 1945-46.
28. FRASER, B. E., *et al.*: Effect of a cycle of addiction to intravenous heroin on certain physiological measurements, from the National Institute of Mental Health, Addiction Research Center, PHS Hospital, Lexington, Ky., U. S. A. *Bulletin on Narcotics,* Vol. *XVI:* No. 3 (July-September, 1964), United Nations, New York.

29. GAULDEN, E. C., et al.: Menstrual abnormalities associated with heroin addiction. *American Journal of Obstetrics and Gynecology* (in press, May, 1964).
30. GAULDEN, E. C., et al.: Some observations on the effects of heroin on the female reproductive organs. A paper presented to the American Medical Association, Annual Meeting, San Francisco, June 24, 1964, Section on Obstetrics and Gynecology.
31. LEVI, MARIO, et al.: The effect of drugs on responses to the Rorschach and Buss-Durkee Tests. A paper given at the California State Psychological Convention, Los Angeles, December 11, 1964.
32. GAULDEN, E. C., et al.: The effects of drugs on driver performance. A paper given at the American Automobile Association, Los Angeles, June 4, 1964, Driver Rehabilitation Conference.
33. *California's Health*, 22:18 (March 15, 1965), California State Department of Health.
34. MARTIN, W. R., and FRASER, H. F.: A comparative study of physiological and subjective effects of heroin and morphine administered intravenously in post-addicts. *Journal of Pharmacology and Experimental Therapeutics, 133*:388-399, 1961.
35. FRASER, H. F., JONES, B. E., ROSENBERG, D. E., and THOMPSON, A. D.: Effects of addiction to intravenous heroin on patterns of physical activity in man. *Clinical Pharmacology and Therapeutics*, 4:188-196, 1963.
36. WORLD HEALTH ORGANIZATION EXPERT COMMITTEE ON ADDICTION-PRODUCING DRUGS: *Thirteenth Report*, World Health Organization Technical Report Series, No. 273. Geneva, Switzerland, World Health Organization, 1964.

Chapter 3

ADDICTING NON-OPIATE SEDATIVES

THERE is a large group of sedative and depressant drugs which are not derived from opium and do not have opium-like characteristics, but still have the power to addict individuals who use them regularly in quantities larger than would be prescribed medicinally. While addiction to non-opiate drugs differs considerably from addiction to opiate drugs, there is no question in the minds of the authors that addiction to certain non-opiate drugs can be demonstrated. This can be just as dangerous as opiate addiction, although in some cases the addict does not appear to develop physical dependence, and the withdrawal syndrome, as in the case of marihuana, may be absent; however, many non-opiate drugs produce a high degree of intoxication followed by severe withdrawal illness. Probably the most important of the non-opiate group are the barbiturates. In the number of illicit users, however, marihuana probably surpasses all other non-opiate drugs; in fact, marihuana probably leads all the types of addicting drugs in the number of delinquently oriented persons who use it.

BARBITURATES

Technical or scientific names:
   All are derivatives of barbituric acid.
   See Table III for official names (New & Non-Official Remedies).[1]

Argot names:
   Blue heaven (sodium amytal), *Christmas tree* (Tuinal), *candy* (any barbiturate), *cap* (a capsule of barbiturate), *goof ball, nimbie* (Nembutal), *red devil* or *red bird* (seconal), *yellow jacket* (Nembutal).

The barbiturates are a group of sedative and sleep-producing drugs derived from barbituric acid, which, according to Remington,[2] was given its name because it was first synthesized in 1863 in Germany on Saint Barbara's Day. The first hypnotic barbiturate drug was prepared in 1882 under the name "Barbital." More than a score of barbiturates have been synthesized since that time and sold under a variety of chemical and proprietary names. With a few exceptions, the distinguishing feature of the names of the barbiturate drugs is that they end with the suffix "al." The barbiturates in pure form occur as colorless or white crystals, odorless but with a somewhat bitter taste.

The barbiturates are widely used in a great variety of diseases and disorders where sedation or sleep is needed; used under proper medical supervision, they are very valuable drugs with no dangerous implications. Consequently, the barbiturates are frequently prescribed in cases of nervousness, emotional anxiety or tension when it is desired to lessen or deaden somewhat the reaction of the body to external stimuli and to disturbing emotional conflicts or tensions from within. They are widely used to relieve menstrual discomforts and during the menopause. In somatic disorders, where emotional tension is combined with physical malfunction, as in gastric ulcer, thyroid dysfunction or cases of asthma and hay fever, the barbiturates are frequently combined with ephedrine-like drugs or with anti-spasmodics such as atropine or belladonna and with the analgesic drugs of the aspirin or coal tar series.

The barbiturates in themselves are not strong analgesic drugs, but when combined or taken with the coal tar analgesics such as phenacetin, the combined effect may be greater than from taking one type of drug alone. Quick-acting drugs of the barbiturate series are frequently used to control convulsive manifestations of a variety of diseases; phenobarbital and Mebaral are effective in the control of epilepsy. Barbiturates are used widely in anesthesia, either as a pre-anesthetic sedative or in quick-acting forms prepared for intravenous injection or for complete general anesthesia, particularly for short operations where complete muscular relaxation is not important. Evipal and Pentothal are used in this way for anesthetics. The barbiturates are not substitutes for narcotic drugs, nor can they be used for the relief of pain, except as anesthetics, but they are very useful drugs to the physician.

Pentothal and Amytal when used intravenously in proper dosage may, in the hands of a skilled physician, result in a semiconscious state where a patient's conscious (as well as unconscious)

FIGURE 12
BARBITURATE DRUGS

Name	Usual Form	Onset	Duration of Action
Barbital (veronal, barbitone)	White tablets	Delayed	Long
Luminal (phenobarbital)	White tablets; pink fluid elixir ("pink lady")	Delayed	Long
Amytal (amobarbital)	White tablets; blue capsules ("blue heavens," "blue angels")	Intermediate	Intermediate
Butisol sodium (butabarbital sodium)	Lavender, green, orange and pink tablets; lavender capsules; green fluid elixir	Intermediate	Intermediate
Delvinal sodium (vinobarbital sodium)	Brown, orange, orange and brown capsules; brown fluid elixir	Intermediate	Intermediate
Ipral (probarbital)	White tablets; yellowish-brown fluid elixir	Intermediate	Intermediate
Nembutal (pentobarbital sodium)	Yellow capsules ("yellow jackets"); yellow tablets; reddish-orange fluid elixir	Intermediate	Intermediate
Neonal (butethal)	White tablets	Intermediate	Intermediate
Ortal sodium (hexethal sodium)	Purple capsules	Intermediate	Intermediate
Mebaral (mephrobarbital)	White tablets	Intermediate	Intermediate
Phanodorn (cyclobarbital)	White tablets	Intermediate	Intermediate
Alurate sodium (aprobarbital sodium)	White tablets; red or green fluid elixir; red-white capsules	Intermediate	Intermediate
Dial (diallylbarbituric acid)		Intermediate	Intermediate
Sandoptal (allybarbituric acid)	White tablets	Intermediate	Intermediate
Pernoston (butallylona)	White tablets	Intermediate	Intermediate
Seconal (secobarbital sodium)	White tablets Red capsules (red birds, red devils); light amber fluid elixir	Quick	Short

FIGURE 12—*Continued*

Name	Usual Form	Onset	Duration of Action
Evipal	White tablets	Quick	Short
Evipal sodium (hexobarbital sodium)	Ampules for intravenous use	Short	General Anesthetic
Pentothal sodium (thiopental sodium)	Ampules for intravenous use	Short	General Anesthetic
Tuinal (amytal sodium and secobarbital sodium)	Blue and orange capsules "Christmas trees"	Quick	Long

inhibitions and deceptions may be somewhat diminished, with the result that questions may be more truthfully answered than otherwise. When used in this manner in the course of legal investigations, it is known as "truth serum." However, its efficiency is dubious, and results obtained with it are usually not acceptable to the courts. Its use must be sanctioned by the accused in most states. Similar use is frequently made by psychiatrists in the course of investigations of the unconscious factors in connection with some psychiatric disorders.

The manufacture of barbiturates in the United States has increased at an astounding rate. In 1959, the production was 819,000 lbs, with a wholesale value of about $40,000,000, which gives some idea of the size of the market. In 1962, a survey showed a national output of 654,000 lbs equivalent to 4½ billion 1 grain doses. As in the case of amphetamines, however, two major producers of barbiturates, accounting for approximately one half the national production, refused to supply figures. Therefore, we can estimate the total 1962 production at a much higher figure than that given above. By 1966 the estimated annual production of amphetamines was 8 billion doses.

There is every indication that both production of the drugs and their consumption is still increasing. Acute intoxication with barbiturates now accounts for about 25 per cent of all patients admitted to general hospitals for treatment of acute poisoning. More deaths are caused by barbiturates, either accidentally or deliberately ingested, than by any other poison.[3] According to Robie[4] the number of deaths caused by barbiturates in New York City increased more than 375 per cent in seven years; in Los Angeles, barbiturate deaths increased 670 per cent in three years; while in Cook County, Illinois, a 1,300 per cent increase in barbiturate deaths is reported over an eight-year period.

Barbiturates are classified in Figure 12 by the duration of their clinical effects. In general, there is a direct ratio between the duration of clinical effects and the time interval between the administration of a dose and the beginning effect; that is, the quicker the drug produces relaxation, the shorter the duration of its effect, while the slower the onset of the drug, the longer the duration of the effect. Figure 12 shows the barbiturate drugs in most common use, but there may be additions to this list or to the names under which drugs are sold, inasmuch as these products are a rapidly increasing source of profit to the pharmaceutical manufacturers. One company markets a barbiturate preparation in six different dosage forms in four different colors. It is not possible to give all the names of the various preparations in which barbiturate drugs are combined with other drugs and sold.

Barbital and phenobarbital, which are relatively slow-acting drugs of this series, may require thirty to sixty minutes after ingestion for the effect to be noted, and the sleep which results may last four to six hours or longer and leave a moderate "hangover." The drugs in Figure 12 which show intermediate onset, and duration may produce effects in fifteen to thirty minutes and cause a sleep of only two to four hours with less "hangover." The drugs with prompt onset of action also have a relatively short duration of effect; nevertheless, the barbiturates with relatively short action are likely to be most popular with addicts because of the sudden transition from normal state to abnormal state which intensifies the euphoric effect for the addict personality. However, addicts do not use barbiturates to produce sleep, but for the intoxication resulting from very large doses, taken either orally or intravenously.

Barbiturates are compounded with sodium to form soluble compounds which may be used medically for intramuscular or intravenous injection. Powder or solution for this purpose is often prepared and sold in glass ampules. The most common form in which these drugs are dispensed, however, is tablets or capsules for oral use, the latter frequently appearing in distinctive colors to identify a particular manufacturer's product in the mind of the consumer. Figure 12 describes the most common form in which each drug is sold.

The various barbiturate preparations, if used in greater than the therapeutically prescribed doses, cause acute intoxication or chronic intoxication, depending on the amount consumed and the frequency with which the dose is repeated. Abuse of this type is widespread among addiction-prone individuals. Addict users may pay little or no attention to medical instructions concerning the mode of administration and dose; preparations intended for oral use may be indiscriminately injected intravenously by the addict.

Addicts to the various opiate drugs may take barbiturates coincidentally with narcotics, or as a substitute of necessity when the opiate drug of choice cannot be obtained. The chronic alcoholic may at times take intoxicating doses of barbiturates periodically instead of alcohol, or he may shift more or less permanently from alcohol to barbiturates, taking them in large quantities either orally or intravenously, feeling that it is a form of intoxication which may not be so obvious or reprehensible as alcohol intoxication, which carries with it the obvious odor of alcohol on the breath. The emotionally depressed patient who is taking properly prescribed barbiturates may by his own action increase the dose to dangerous levels, seeking to obtain greater relief from his own emotional conflicts or anxieties.

Barbiturates are often taken in combination with other drugs; opiate addicts sometimes use barbiturates to mitigate withdrawal distress when the drug of choice is not immediately available, but do not otherwise voluntarily substitute barbiturates. Cocaine users almost always combine (intravenously) cocaine with an opiate or a barbiturate to reduce the anxiety and emotional tension resulting from the use of cocaine alone. The most frequent combination encountered, however, is that of alcohol taken orally with the barbiturates, taken either orally or intravenously. The barbiturates intensify the effect of the alcohol and reduce the expense of continued intoxication somewhat. It should be noted that when the barbiturates are taken in large quantities by the addict, they do not produce sleep; in fact, research subjects taking fifteen to twenty capsules a day complained of insomnia during their chronic intoxication. One patient (a physician) receiving treatment for morphine addiction died during withdrawal because he failed to tell the physician in charge of his case that he had been maintaining a constant state of intoxication with Nembutal taken orally, the quantity being later estimated by his wife as about fifty capsules a day. (Chapter IV includes a discussion of the abuse of amphetamines (stimulants) combined with barbiturates.)

Many deaths reported as suicide from the ingestion of barbiturates, while self-administered, are not suicide in the sense of the word that the fatal dose was taken with deliberate intent to produce death. Rather, they represent the irresponsible act of intoxicated persons who, while intoxicated, continued to take more and more of the drug until a fatal result ensued. This is more likely to happen in the case of intoxication with barbiturates than in the case of intoxication with alcohol, where greater motor coordination is required to continue to ingest the larger amounts of a bulkier liquid drug necessary to cause death.

Cases are known of self-medication where persons take excessive amounts of barbiturates combined or alternating with Benzedrine. Too much Benzedrine is taken with the result that the subject becomes tense and jittery; he then tries to balance his condition by taking barbiturates. The result is that the subject gives himself alternate "handfuls" of Benzedrine tablets and barbiturate capsules until he develops a toxic psychosis; finally, a fatal dose of barbiturates may be taken.

In correctional institutions, narcotic addicts may find it possible to obtain from institutional physicians barbiturates for the relief of simulated or deliberately misrepresented symptoms. In such places, barbiturates take on a definite value and are used as a medium of exchange among the prisoners. They may be accumulated and taken orally or by improvised syringe, intravenously, in order to attain a state of intoxication.

There is a greater margin of safety between the therapeutic dose and the addicting dose of barbiturates than there is in the case of opiate drugs. There is little doubt that a patient can continue indefinitely to take, on prescription, one or even two capsules of a barbiturate nightly for the relief of nervous tension or insomnia without developing a state of physical dependence. On the other hand, there is equally little doubt that the patient who, by self-prescription may increase the dose to ten or fifteen capsules a day, can escape chronic intoxication and the consequences of physical dependence followed by serious withdrawal illness when the drug is stopped.

Until 1965, except for the limitations of the Food, Drug and Cosmetic Act, which designates barbiturates which move in interstate commerce as habit-forming drugs to be sold on prescription only, barbiturate drugs were not controlled by Federal law. In that year, a more effective law gave regulatory powers for barbiturates and other dangerous drugs to the Food and Drug Administration. All manufacturers are licensed, and marketing is controlled through careful records which will reveal illegal diversion of drugs. Possession without prescription is a crime.

Most states now have adopted the Uniform State Barbiturate Act or other legislation to limit the sale of barbiturates to persons for whom they are medically prescribed, but there is wide latitude in the detailed provisions of these laws regarding refilling of the prescriptions, lack of control of wholesale sales, or facilities for law enforcement. The status of barbiturate regulation was reviewed in detail in 1946 by Fishelis.[5]

In 1951, a bill was introduced into Congress which would bring the sale of barbiturate drugs under Federal control by the Bureau of Narcotics. The Chief of the Bureau of Narcotics testified against the bill, favoring state control instead. In testifying against the bill, he compared the task of controlling barbiturates with that of trying to enforce prohibition, and there was certainly some logic in his argument. Unfortunately, a very general attitude has grown up that the rather liberal use of sleeping pills is without great harm; many physicians until recently believed that barbiturates, while habit-forming, were not addicting in the full sense of the word, until the work of Isbell and his group[3, 6] at the U. S. Public Health Service Hospital in Lexington, Kentucky, definitely established contrary facts. Unfortunately, some physicians still prescribe barbiturates rather loosely, and unscrupulous or uninformed druggists sell large quantities of barbiturates for self-administration without knowledge of or regard for the great addiction liability which exists.

Under the 1965 law, pharmacists are forbidden to refill a prescription more than five times, and possession without a prescription is a crime.

Although the authors have developed their own concepts of barbiturate addiction, mainly agreeing and often anticipating those articulated by the World Health Organization's Expert Committee on addiction-producing drugs in 1964,[17] that Committee's findings are reproduced here. This is done not only because they present some minor divergences from our thinking, but mainly because they represent international agreement on concepts of addiction by over 100 countries who subscribed to the Single Convention on Narcotic Drugs of 1961.

> Drug dependence of barbiturate type is described as a state arising from repeated administration of a barbiturate or an agent with barbiturate-like effect on a continuous basis, generally in amounts exceeding therapeutic dose levels. Its characteristics include:
>
> 1. A strong desire or need to continue taking the drug; the need can be satisfied by the drug taken initially or by another with barbiturate-like properties;
>
> 2. A tendency to increase the dose, partly owing to the development of tolerance;
>
> 3. A psychic dependence on the effects of the drug related to subjective and individual appreciation of those effects; and
>
> 4. A physical dependence on the effects of the drug requiring its presence for maintenance of homeostasis and resulting in a definite, characteristic, and self-limited abstinence syndrome when the drug is withdrawn.
>
> The abstinence syndrome is the most characteristic and distinguishing feature of drug dependence of barbiturate type. It begins to appear within the first twenty-four hours of cessation of drug taking, reaches peak intensity in two or three days, and subsides slowly. There is at present no known agent that will precipitate the barbiturate abstinence syndrome during continuation of drug administration. The complex of symptoms which constitute the abstinence syndrome, in approximate order of appearance, are: anxiety, involuntary twitching of muscles, intention tremor of hands and fingers, progressive weakness, dizziness, distortion in visual perception, nausea, vomiting, insomnia, weight loss, and a precipitous drop in blood pressure on standing; convulsions of a grand mal type and/or a delirium resembling alcoholic delirium tremens may occur.

With the barbiturates, the detrimental effect on the individual stems in part from his preoccupation with drug taking, but more particularly from persistent effects of the drug—ataxia, dysarthria, and impairment of mental function, with confusion, loss of emotional control, poor judgment, and occasionally a toxic psychosis. The harm to society is related to both the individual's preoccupation with drug taking and the drug's effect on interpersonal relationships.

CHLORAL HYDRATE

Technical or scientific names:
Chloral Hydrate (U. S. Pharmacopoeia)[7]
Argot names:
Knockout drops, Mickey Finn. (See Glossary for details.)

Chloral hydrate is a synthetic drug occurring as colorless or white crystals, with bitter, unpleasant taste and aromatic, penetrating odor. It is a drug with sedative and sleep-producing effect. When given in therapeutic doses of 10 grains (640 mg), it produces drowsiness which passes into a condition resembling natural sleep lasting five to eight hours, unless the patient is deliberately aroused earlier. It usually has no unpleasant results or "hangover." It should not be used for the relief of pain, inasmuch as its analgesic value is slight. It is useful in the treatment of insomnia and is sometimes given to assist in the control of convulsive symptoms of such diseases as tetanus, although it is not as useful for this purpose as the barbiturates used intravenously. Larger quantities of around 75 grains or 5 gm produce very prolonged sleep of ten to fifteen hours, leading perhaps to coma; in still larger doses it may produce a state of general anesthesia. Therapeutic use as an anesthetic agent is not justified because the anesthetic dose approaches the fatal dose, causing death from respiratory failure. Therapeutically, the administration of chloral hydrate with alcohol should be avoided, inasmuch as the latter drug acts in some way with chloral hydrate to greatly increase its narcotic action; unconsciousness, and death may rapidly ensue. Chloral hydrate is employed for its sedative action in the management of alcoholic patients from whom the alcohol has been withdrawn. This potentiated action of chloral hydrate and alcohol accounts for the administration of chloral hydrate in alcohol by criminals in *clip joints,* where it is known as *knockout drops,* sometimes said to be used for the purpose of robbery. In popular literature, it is common to confuse *knockout drops* with the so-called *Mickey Finn,* and to use the terms synonymously. The *Mickey Finn* is, strictly speaking, not a sedative but rather a very fast cathartic (usually croton oil) mixed with whiskey and used to discourage undesirables around a hangout. The unskillful or criminal use of chloral hydrate to render an individual unconscious may result in the death of the victim.

Addiction to chloral hydrate may occur chiefly in persons who carry on self-administration in increasing doses, following acquaintance with the drug through medical prescription. The opiate addict may take chloral hydrate as a temporary substitute for morphine or heroin if those drugs are not available. Addicts to the opiate drugs who change to the habitual use of chloral hydrate as the drug of choice are not known. Psychic dependence occurs with chloral hydrate, and tolerance develops; the German literature describes withdrawal illness similar to that following use of the barbiturates.

Except for limitation of sales to medical prescription by some state laws, chloral hydrate is not under formal narcotic control. It is not widely used, having been replaced in medical use and for addiction purposes by the barbiturates. With excessive consumption of chloral hydrate, the sleep-producing effect may be replaced by a condition resembling acute alcoholic intoxication, an effect which is of course sought after by the addiction-prone individual. Chloretone, or chlorobutanol, is a similar drug to chloral hydrate.

PARALDEHYDE

Technical or scientific names:
Paraldehyde (U.S.P.)[7]
Argot names:
None encountered.

Paraldehyde occurs as a clear, colorless liquid with a disagreeable burning taste and a most unpleasant characteristic odor. It is one of the oldest and best hypnotic drugs, with a low degree of toxicity. Its disagreeable taste and odor (somewhat reduced by giving it in cold fluids or with cracked ice) prevent its being more widely used therapeutically. Because it is poorly soluble in water, it is frequently prescribed in combination with alcohol. It is usually taken by mouth, but is also absorbed through the rectum when given as a retention enema.

The most common use is for patients undergoing withdrawal therapy for alcoholism, particularly delirium tremens. If delirium tremens represents a withdrawal illness caused by physical dependence to alcohol, the successful use of paraldehyde in this treatment may be explained by the existence of a cross-tolerance between paraldehyde and alcohol. The usual medical dose is 10 cc. Paraldehyde is frequently used by the addiction-prone individual in much the same manner as alcohol is used to bring about chronic intoxication, which closely resembles that due to alcohol, followed by withdrawal distress similar to delirium tremens. The use of the drug can usually be determined by the characteristic odor of paraldehyde on the breath of the user. There is no Federal control on the sale of paraldehyde and in most areas no limitation by state or local law.

BROMIDES

Technical or scientific names:
Sodium Bromide, Potassium Bromide, Ammonium Bromide, Triple Bromides, etc.
Argot names:
None encountered.

Sodium bromide, the most commonly used, occurs as white, odorless crystals or granular powder. It has a direct depressant action upon the central nervous system and is used as a sedative and sleep-producing drug. Formerly it was much used for the control of epilepsy, but now has largely been replaced by drugs of the barbiturate series. After prolonged administration, the concentration of bromides becomes too high in the body, and intoxication occurs. This toxic state is sometimes called bromism and is characterized by an acne-like eruption of the skin, loss of appetite, drowsiness with impairment of mental function, slow, stammering speech, difficulty in remembering words and mispronunciation of words. The memory is definitely impaired. There may be a slow pulse and lessened reflexes.

The mental symptoms may be very striking, including delirious behavior, with complete loss of contact with reality. Hallucinations and delusions, frequently of a paranoid nature, are encountered. In 1,000 consecutive patients admitted to the Colorado Psychiatric Hospital[8] it was found that 7.7 per cent of the mentally disturbed admissions had been taking bromides, many during the course of treatment for other mental disorders, and in seventeen of seventy-seven cases there was a fatal outcome. Some of these patients had refilled their prescriptions without authority or had taken doses larger than those prescribed. Others were taking bromides without prescription or in patent medicines in which either the bromide content or the significance of bromide content was not realized.

Nervine, Neurosine and Bromoseltzer are bromide preparations frequently taken by the public, which may, over a period of time, result in bromide intoxication if not taken according to instructions. Acute intoxication from single doses of bromide practically never occurs. Sleep produced by bromide is a restless, disturbed state, resulting from a general dulling of perception which is more of a stupor than natural sleep. The toxic picture previously described occurs only as a result of excessive ingestion of bromide medications. Chronic intoxication may be manifested by the delirious reaction mentioned, or less frequently by a dull, stuporous, almost comatose condition which may alternate with periods of excitement. All these symptoms may occur in addiction-prone individuals who like the sedative effect of bromides, usually without realizing that they may be addicting.

Other preparations of bromides, alone, in proprietary form, or in combination with other drugs are numerous, including Bromidia, Bromobarb, ammonium bromide, lithium bromide, strontium bromide, calcium bromide, monobromic camphor and triple bromides.

Addicts to the opiate drugs may take bromides in excess if unable to obtain the drug of choice. No case is known of an addict to an opiate drug willingly substituting bromides for opiate drugs.

In institutions, addicts should be prevented from access to bromide drugs, or, if prescribed, drugs should be strictly limited. Bromide chemicals as well as bromide medicines in institutions should be carefully safeguarded. In one hospital for the treatment of drug addicts, a patient employed in the photographic and x-ray department took bromide developing powders to the point where chronic intoxication occurred which nearly resulted fatally.

The diagnosis of a delirious patient suffering from chronic bromide intoxication may be difficult to differentiate from the other acute deliria unless routine blood bromide tests are made or unless a history of bromide ingestion is elicited. Unfortunately for the protection of the public, there is no legal limitation on the sale of some bromide drugs, nor in some states on the renewal of prescriptions written by physicians. Several bromide "nerve medicines" are sold on the market completely without restriction or warning as to dangerous content. The average medical dose of sodium bromide is 15 grains or 1 gm. Sodium bromide is also prepared as fluid elixir. Potassium bromide is sometimes used, but possesses no advantage and has some disadvantages over sodium bromide.

Older people and others with arteriosclerosis and diseases of the kidney may excrete bromides at slower than the normal rate, with consequent accumulation of bromides in the body and more likelihood of developing chronic bromide intoxication. The administration of bromides should be supervised closely by physicians, and prescriptions should not be refilled without the physician's knowledge. Bromides may result in psychic or emotional dependence, but not physical dependence. Tolerance is not developed to any appreciable degree. On the contrary, bromide accumulates in the body with increasing likelihood of toxic effect. If physical dependence with subsequent withdrawal illness occurred, of course the picture of the accumulative toxic effect would not be seen. If the picture of acute intoxication, on the contrary, represented withdrawal illness, relief would be obtained by the further administration of bromides, but such is not the case. On the contrary, the treatment consists of abruptly stopping the intake of bromides and of stimulating the excretion of accumulated bromides.

Acute unexplained psychotic behavior may represent bromide

poisoning. Persons handling patients with acute delirium should be alert to recognize this condition, which may come to the attention of police, ambulance attendants, nurses and doctors seeing emergency cases.

MARIHUANA

Technical or scientific names:
Cannabis indica, Cannabis sativa
Argot names:
Griefo or greefo, love weed, muggles, Texas tea, tea, ea tay, fu, Indian hay, Mary Jane, Mary Warner, mezz, mutah (moo tah or mooter), joy smoke, loco weed, laughing grass, eedway, eed waggles, reefer (or stick), bambalache, Doña Juanita, Maria Johanna, hierba, la mota, la bareta, marijuana, roach, many with specialized meanings. (See Glossary.)

The products of several varieties of the Indian hemp plant have been used by millions of people as an intoxicant from ancient China, India and Africa to Harlem or Chicago over the last four or five thousand years. Walton[9] gives a list of almost 200 word equivalents in almost every language known for the hemp plant or the crude drug, indicating worldwide use over past centuries. Walton also gives a list of about 150 terms in various languages for folk preparations of the hemp drug. According to Taylor,[10] the Indian hemp plant was described in a book on pharmacy written for the ancient Chinese by Emperor Shen Nung in 2737 B.C. About 800 B.C., the plant was introduced into India, where it has been cultivated on a large scale, and since then has been accepted widely also in Japan, Russia, the Mediterranean area, the United States, part of Africa and much of Central and South America.

In fact, there are few inhabited areas of the globe where hemp cannot be grown successfully. In many areas, once introduced, it grows more or less wild. Depending on the soil and the degree of cultivation, this weed-like annual plant may reach a height of from one to twenty feet. It is more or less useful as a source of fiber, seed and the narcotic resin, which is the basis of its use as an intoxicant. The resinous content of the plant varies widely with the climate and quality of the soil. This variation in strength may, in part, explain some of the widely differing reports covering human reaction to the drug in various parts of the world.

In the United States Department of Agriculture Year Book for 1913, Dewey[11] has given a very fine description of the cannabis plant.

Because of the strong current interest in marihuana, and because it is so widely grown throughout both the Americas, some notes on its cultivation are pertinent. Cannabinol, the resin of the cannabis plant which is responsible for its potency as an intoxicating drug, is found in the flowering tops of the female plant. It is extracted from cultivated plants in relatively pure form, known as *charas* in India, and used for smoking or eating. *Hashish* is a powdered and sifted form of this resin. A less potent preparation is made from the cut tops of the uncultivated female plant and contains a relatively low content of resin, which is known as *bhang* and is used either for drinking as a tea or as a smoking mixture. Marihuana is a Mexican name for the equivalent of *bhang*. The purer grades of *hashish* are not commonly used by smokers in the United States, and the commercial smoking marihuana examined by the authors has not been relatively very potent. *Ganja* is a preparation of cut tops of specially cultivated grades of the female plant of the Indian hemp used for smoking and for eating. This preparation is more potent than *bhang* but does not approach the potency of *charas*, which is relatively pure, unadulterated resin.

The hemp plant, cultivated for its fiber, was one of the earliest crops of the American colonies, reported here as early as 1632. The first crop in Kentucky was planted in 1775, according to Dewey,[11] and constituted a major source of income there for many years. It is remarkable that traffic in the drug did not develop very early in Kentucky and other colonies; if it did, there is no indication of it, and the smoking of marihuana on a large scale seems to have come in from Mexico since about 1910. Since about 1920, the acreage planted in hemp in the United States rapidly diminished until it was entirely dropped with the passage of the Marihuana Control Act in 1937. With the interruption of imports during World War II, licenses were granted to farmers in Kentucky to again cultivate hemp commercially for fiber, a practice which has again been stopped with the resumption of imports following the termi-

FIGURE 13. A cannabis plant grown in the United States. *Courtesy, Los Angeles City Police Department.*

nation of the war. The cultivation of hemp was introduced early to South America also, but there it was brought in by Negro slaves from Africa for use as an intoxicant and, as Wolff[12] points out, those provinces of Brazil to which the Africans originally imported hemp have long been and are still active productive centers for cannabis. Some of the names for the plant in Brazil are of African derivation, notably *diamba* and *maconha*. It is also probable that the American Indians, especially of the Caribbean area, knew and cultivated the hemp plant for its intoxicating resins.

Cannabis indica is the scientific name given the flowering tops of the female plants of *Cannabis sativa*. The various preparations of Cannabis indica are or have been smoked either alone or mixed with tobacco or other leaves in cigarettes, cigars, pipes, water pipes, drunk as infusions or concoctions or mixed with sugar or honey as a confection.

Cannabis has been used medically as a sedative and as an analgesic, but its effects is erratic, and it is practically never prescribed at the present time. It is sometimes used as an ingredient in corn remedies, but probably has no value in this respect. Medically, then, this is an unimportant drug, but its importance lies entirely in the fact that it is the object of widespread self-administration for its intoxicating effect; it has become the subject of a very great continuing controversy as to its addiction liability and as a cause of crime.[12, 13, 14]

The authors believe that marihuana is addicting in the sense that it is a dangerous intoxicating drug, but its use does not result in physical dependence, followed by withdrawal illness. It is not an important criminogenic drug, although many criminals use it as an intoxicant in the same way they use alcohol.[18]

At present, the importation, production, preparation for sale, prescription or dispensation of marihuana is controlled in the United States by the Marihuana Tax Act of 1937. Transactions may be legally performed only by licensed persons. The legal prescription of cannabis by physicians has diminished to practically nothing in recent years; at the present time no licenses are being issued for the cultivation of hemp in the United States except to approximately six farmers in Kentucky for the production of seed. Hemp seed remains fertile only several years. Therefore it is nec-

FIGURE 14. Close-up of the seed-pods of the *cannabis* plant from which the concentrated hemp resin is obtained. Grown in the United States. *Courtesy,* U.S.P.H.S.

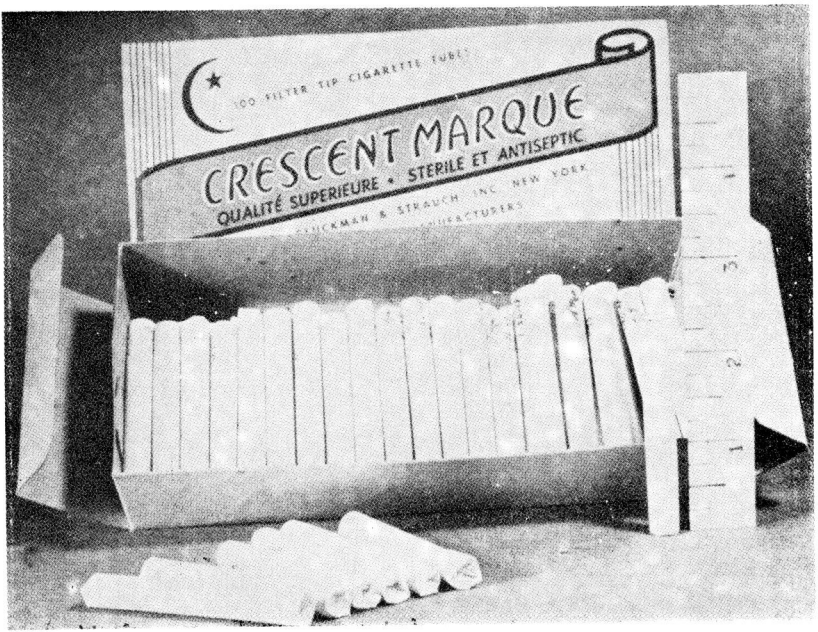

FIGURE 15. Marihuana cigarettes intercepted in contraband traffic. Hand-rolled with ends tucked in to prevent spillage. *Courtesy, United Nations.*

essary to raise a little to maintain a supply of seed in case war makes it necessary to again raise hemp for rope making in this country. The agents of the Federal Bureau of Narcotics, which is responsible for enforcing this Act, devote their efforts to the suppression of the illegal traffic in marihuana, which has become very extensive in recent years. Insofar as this law is concerned, the term marihuana means "all parts of the plant Cannabis sativa L., whether growing or not; the seeds thereof; the resin extracted from any part of such plant; and every compound, manufacture, salt, derivative, mixture or preparation of such plant, its seeds or resin; but shall not include the mature stalks of such plant, fiber produced from such stalks, oil or cake made from the seeds of such plant, any other compound, manufacture, salt, derivative, mixture or preparation of such mature stalks (except the resin extracted therefrom), fiber oil or cake or the sterilized seed of such plant which is incapable of germination."

A synthetic substance called *pyrahexyl compound* has been

produced by Professor Roger Adams at the University of Illinois, which for all practical purposes appears to be identical with the active principle of Cannabis indica.

PHYSIOLOGICAL AND PSYCHOLOGICAL ASPECTS OF ADDICTION TO NON-OPIATE DRUGS

The barbiturates are useful depressants of the central nervous system; taken in small quantities under medical supervision they are neither intoxicating nor addicting. However, taken in large quantities they produce chronic intoxication which is very attractive to the addiction-prone individual and may be equally dangerous to the normal person who habitually takes large doses. Barbiturates are commonly but not always taken by opiate addicts in combination with morphine, heroin, etc.

Although the German scientists recognized the danger of barbiturate intoxication prior to 1940, in the United States most of the medical interest has centered on acute barbiturate poisoning, until recently when Isbell and others[3] made a very comprehensive study of the effects of intoxication, addiction and withdrawal on human beings. The dangers of abuse of barbiturates are now being recognized by various state legislatures, but until 1966 these drugs were not under Federal control.

Addiction to barbiturates (which constitutes habitual use of large quantities either by mouth or by needle to maintain a chronic state of intoxication) manifests itself in general as resembling alcoholic intoxication without any odor of liquor being present. The addict may appear drowsy and confused. He cannot coordinate his muscular actions, and this is especially obvious in the way he walks and stands. Some addicts lose motor control to the point of collapse; they may remain partly conscious or black-out entirely. While they are able to move about, they show severe tremors of the hands, lips and tongue. Their eyes roll about in characteristic movements; they have great difficulty in speaking clearly or become quite inarticulate. Occasionally, they develop psychoses and register unorganized delusions of a paranoid type. Their emotional control is unstable; they become hostile to the point of physical assault, although their highly intoxicated condition usually renders them relatively harmless. They regress toward childhood behavior-patterns. Because of impaired motor coordination, they tend to fall frequently; for instance, those being studied by Isbell and his group fell and injured themselves to the extent of broken bones while living under controlled laboratory conditions. People even mildly under the effects of barbiturates are great safety hazards if they drive cars.

Physiological symptoms differ widely from those manifested by persons addicted to opiates, in which the general effect of the drug is to induce calmness and quiet. The barbiturates, on the other hand, produce sleep in small doses administered properly, but in large doses produce intoxication. When a person is chronically intoxicated, there is a cumulative effect of the drug, and even small amounts, especially taken on an empty stomach, may produce a marked effect. There is evidence of the development of some tolerance, though not so obvious as with opiates. During intoxication, there may be very slight depression of rectal temperatures, especially during the early weeks, after which fluctuations of temperature may be greater than when the individual is not on barbiturates. The pulse rate is elevated slightly (about 10 beats per minute in those addicts examined by Isbell), while respiration and blood pressure do not vary significantly. Neither do any significant changes appear in the urine, in the blood count or in the blood composition. There is consistent increase in the amplitude of all the waves registered on the electroencephalogram, with slow or delta waves diminishing almost to the vanishing point, while the percentage of beta waves increases noticeably after the first thirty days of intoxication. The Kohs Block Test, the Bender Gestalt Test, the "Draw A Man" Test and the Rorschach Test showed impairment of both sensory and motor functions, a decrease in the ability to organize, accentuation of pathologic features already present in the personality, regression to more primitive emotional levels and a slight decrease in contact with reality.

Mario Levi et al.[19] have reported the effect of Seconal responses to the Rorschach, TAT and Buss-Burke tests. Among other reactions, they reported increased indirect aggression, negativism, suspicion and a lowering of defenses.

The Babinski and ankle clonus reflexes were occasionally observed. During a period of intoxication, the addicts closely studied by Isbell did not become psychotic, were always oriented in time, place and person and had no hallucinations or delusions, though weird dreams were reported. However, during chronic intoxication they became irritable and quarrelsome and often staggered noticeably.

The withdrawal syndrome for barbiturates differs markedly from that produced by opiates. During the first twelve to sixteen hours of withdrawal, barbiturate addicts seem to improve. Confusion diminishes along with neurologic manifestations, although the addicts tend to be depressed and moody. After this, anxiety, tremors, weakness, insomnia and nausea appear and increase until, after twenty-four hours, these symptoms become severe and the addict wants to be in bed. Cardiovascular changes on changing posture are similar to those in a patient recovering from a severe febrile illness, with elevation of the pulse rate, a decrease in systolic blood pressure and either decrease or increase in diastolic pressure when the addicts sits down or stands up. Within thirty-six to seventy-two hours there are usually convulsions resembling epileptic seizures. Delirious states resembling delirium tremens occur. Within about ten days, withdrawal symptoms usually subside, but weakness persists for some weeks. Isbell's experimental addicts recovered completely in from sixty to ninety days, and he reported that no residual damage could be detected either physically or psychologically.

While there may be some differences in the addiction liability as well as the severity of physical dependence followed by the withdrawal distress, according to the particular barbiturate used, no specific research results differentiating the effects of various barbiturates are available as yet. It would appear that all barbiturates are addicting in every sense of the word. Says Isbell:[3] "Prolonged use (in quantities) causes great harm to the user and to society. Although the degree of tolerance is less in barbiturate intoxication, and the manifestations of physical dependence on barbiturates are different from those of dependence on morphine, the phenomena characteristics of addiction to the opiates—habituation, or emotional dependence, tolerance and the appearance of signs of abstinence after withdrawal of the drug—are all present in chronic barbiturate intoxication." All in all, it would seem that in the United States we are tardy in recognizing that the barbiturates are just as dangerous as the opiates and perhaps more so, since barbiturate intoxication impairs not only mental ability and emotional control, but reduces motor coordination beyond the state usually found in opiate addiction. The tolerance to opiates developed in the addict reduces such impairment of control as may occur; barbiturates develop little tolerance, and, therefore incoordination may be serious. The withdrawal from barbiturates is usually much more severe than that from opiates.

The physical and psychological effects of smoking marihuana are not so clearly defined as those of the barbiturates. They seem to vary with the part of the world in which Cannabis sativa is grown and smoked and with the social pattern within which the addicts live. Highly concentrated hashish resin, when smoked or eaten, seems to have a much more violent effect than the chopped pods and leaves of the plant which, when mixed with tobacco, constitute the marihuana smoked in the United States at the present time. However, it is consumed by thousands of smokers who usually do not consider themselves drug addicts and are not accepted as drug addicts by the fraternity of opiate users. Nevertheless, marihuana is an addicting drug by our definition; although it does not cause physical dependence comparable to the opiates, users do develop some tolerance.

Marihuana smokers notice a lightness, a feeling of power and distortions of time, space and kinesthetic sensations which are usually regarded as pleasurable. Some smokers describe a sensation that the arms and legs are longer than they really are, that the head is much larger than it could possibly be, etc. Usually the smoking of marihuana is accompanied by a good deal of laughter and characteristic mild inebriation. Some smokers believe that it excites the sexual desires and habitually use it preceding sexual activity. In fact, Dr. Bouquet[15] concludes that the primary objective leading to addiction in India, Asia and Africa is the maintenance or improvement of sexual potency. However, it is not a true aphrodisiac. One of the characteristic physical symptoms is that immediately after smoking the addict develops a voracious appetite for food. This symptom is unique to marihuana and is just the reverse of the effect produced by opiate drugs. Marihuana tends to release inhibitions, to increase suggestibility, to increase auditory sensitivity and to produce pleasurable intoxication. While it is popular with jazz musicians and with fans of the more frenetic variety, its beneficial effects on the musical understanding and performance have been shown by Aldrich[16] to be largely the result of self-deception.

The inebriating qualities of marihuana make it particularly dangerous when used by someone driving a car. Police have become increasingly alert to check for its use when a driver appears intoxicated but does not smell of alcohol. The drug leaves a characteristic smell of burned hemp on the breath of a user.

In the United States, there is little published scientific evidence linking the use of marihuana with violent crime, although enforcement officers both here and in Canada feel that there is a close relationship; however, in Asia and South America the reverse is reported, and the late Dr. Pablo Wolff[12] believed that there was a high incidence of violent crime among marihuana users. The problem of its relation to crime will be discussed fully in later chapters. The drug is particularly vicious in that it does not appear on the surface to be addicting because its withdrawal produces no abstinence syndrome. Addicts deprived of the drug experience only a strong desire to consume the drug when it is available, but this is not accompanied by distress, and mildly addicted persons can usually take marihuana or reject it at will. However, in the United States, it is characteristically the first step to heroin addiction, especially among the youngsters who become habituated to marihuana. They then pass readily on to heroin or to cocaine mixed with heroin and may eventually become underworld addicts. Munch[22] gives data on marihuana and crime.

In the Americas, the full effect of hemp addiction has not yet been felt, even though there is widespread use of the drug, and in some Latin American countries there have been reports of its effects upon crime of a violent nature. The exact number of users in the United States is not known, but most people who are familiar with drug addiction agree that marihuana addicts far outnumber the combined total of the users of all other addicting drugs with the exception of alcohol. As a result of a survey sponsored by the United Nations in 1950, it has been estimated that some 200,000,000 people throughout the world now use cannabis in one or several forms as an intoxicant. The bulk of these, of course, are in Asia and Africa, but the speed with which cannabis is spreading into previously uncontaminated areas is indicative of its universal attractiveness as an inebriant. Already such staid societies as Britain, Australia and New Zealand are reporting concern. There is every reason for its strict control, insofar as that is possible.

Although the authors have developed their own concepts of marihuana addiction, mainly agreeing and often anticipating those articulated by the World Health Organization's Expert Committee on addiction-producing drugs in 1964,[17] that Committee's findings are reproduced here. This is done not only because they present some minor divergences from our thinking, but mainly because they represent international agreement on concepts of addiction by over 100 countries who subscribed to the Single Convention on Narcotic Drugs of 1961.

> Drug dependence of cannabis type is described as a state arising from repeated administration of cannabis or cannabis substances, which in some areas is almost exclusively periodic, in others more continuous. Its characteristics include:
>   1. A desire (or need) for repeated administration of the drug on account of its subjective effects, including the feeling of enhanced capabilities;
>   2. Little or no tendency to increase the dose, since there is little or no development of tolerance;
>   3. A psychic dependence on the effects of the drug related to subjective and individual appreciation of those effects;
>   4. Absence of physical dependence so that there is no definite and characteristic abstinence syndrome when the drug is discontinued.
>
> With cannabis, lasting disturbance of mental function has been alleged but not proven. Distortion of perception, one of the effects of the drug, may lead to disruption of interpersonal relationships, and abuse of the drug to criminal behavior

TRANQUILIZERS

In 1966 an increasing number of the so-called tranquilizer drugs were shown to be capable of producing physical dependence and serious withdrawal illness when taken in amounts in excess of medical prescription. Bakewell and Wikler[20] and Essig[21] reported that Miltown, Equanil, Valmid, Placidyl, Librium, and Valium, as well as the non-barbiturate sedative drugs Doriden and Nolu-dar were dangerous in this manner. It was also reported that there was a cross-tolerance between these drugs and the barbiturates, i.e., the withdrawal illness resembled that of the barbiturates and was relieved by the administration of barbiturates. As with the barbiturates, disorientation, illusions, hallucinations and convulsions were encountered.

It was reported that 6.8 per cent of 132 consecutive admissions to the psychiatric service of the University of Kentucky Medical Center were dependent on tranquilizers or non-barbiturate sedatives. It appears that the increasing liberal use of tranquilizers is fraught with serious hazards.

Nutmeg, in the ground variety of this spice, is sometimes used by addicts in institutions for its intoxicating effect, which is described as similar to marihuana, which explains its inclusion here, though nutmeg *per se* can hardly be considered an addicting drug. It is customarily measured in a safety match box—one boxful being swallowed and washed down with warm water. To avoid the unpleasant taste it is sometimes wrapped in a piece of bread or a piece of tissue paper and swallowed. The onset of the action comes one to two hours after ingestion, lasts for several hours and fades slowly. This amount of nutmeg, when it does take effect, has been compared to about two sticks of marihuana with a feeling of intoxication and silliness, accompanied by a floating sensation. No cases of repeated use or addiction outside of institutions are known. Although the effect is similar, marihuana is preferred if both substances are available. There is a need for medical research to investigate this intoxicating effect of nutmeg. There are unconfirmed reports that ground mace is used similarly.

REFERENCES

1. COUNCIL ON PHARMACY AND CHEMISTRY OF THE AMERICAN MEDICAL ASSOCIATION: *New and Non-Official Remedies.* Philadelphia, Lippincott, 1957.
2. COOK, E. F., and MARTIN, E. W.: *Remington's Practice of Pharmacy* (11th ed.). Easton, Pa., The Mack Publishing Company, 1956.
3. ISBELL, H., ALTSCHUL, S., KORNETSKY, C. H., EISENMAN, A. J., FLANARY, H. G., and FRASER, H. F.: Chronic barbiturate intoxication, an experimental study. *Archives of Neurology and Psychiatry,* 64:1 (July), 1950.
4. ROBIE, T. R.: Treatment of acute barbiturate poisoning by non-convulsive electrostimulation. *Post-Graduate Medicine,* 9:253 (March), 1951.
5. FISCHELIS, R. P.: A review of the present status of barbiturate regulation. *Journal of the American Pharmaceutical Association, Scientific Edition,* 35:193 (July), 1946.
6. ISBELL, H.: Addiction to barbiturates and the barbiturate abstinence syndrome. *Annals of Internal Medicine,* 33:108 (July), 1950.
7. *The Pharmacopoeia of the United States of America (The United States Pharmacopoeia),* Seventeenth Revision. U. S. Pharmacological Convention, 1965.
8. STRECKER, E. A., and EBAUGH, F. G.: *Practical Clinical Psychiatry for Students and Practitioners* (4th ed.), Chapter V. Philadelphia, P. Blakiston Company, Inc., 1935.
9. WALTON, R. P.: *Marihuana, America's New Drug Problem.* Philadelphia, Lippincott, 1938.
10. TAYLOR, N.: *Flight from Reality.* New York, Duell, Sloan and Pearce, 1949.
11. DEWEY, L. H.: Hemp. In *Yearbook of the U. S. Department of Agriculture,* pp. 283-346. Washington, D. C., U. S. Government Printing Office, 1913.
12. WOLFF, P. O.: *Marihuana in Latin America. The Threat It Constitutes.* Washington, D. C., The Linacre Press, 1949.
13. WILLIAMS, E. G., HIMMELSBACH, C. K., WIKLER, A., RUBLE, D. C., and LLOYD, B. J. JR.: Studies in marihuana and pyrahexyl compound. *Public Health Reports,* 61:1059 (July 19), 1946.
14. WALLACE, G. B.: *The Marihuana Problem in the City of New York.*

Mayor's Committee on Marihuana, Sociological, Medical, Psychological and Pharmacological Studies. Lancaster, Pa., Jacques Cattel Press, 1944.
15. BOUQUET, J.: Cannabis. Parts III and IV. *Bulletin on Narcotics,* 3(1):22 (Jan.), 1951.
16. ALDRICH, C. K.: The effect of a synthetic marihuana-like compound on musical talent as measured by the seashore test. *Public Health Reports,* 59:431 (March) 1944.
17. WORLD HEALTH ORGANIZATION EXPERT COMMITTEE ON ADDICTION-PRODUCING DRUGS: *Thirteenth Report,* World Health Organization Technical Report Series, No. 273. Geneva, Switzerland, World Health Organization, 1964.
18. ANDRADE, DR. OSWALD MORAES: The criminogenic action of cannabis (marihuana) and narcotics. *Ban Narcotics,* Vol. XVI: No. 4, p. 23.
19. LEVI, MARIO, *et al.:* The effect of drugs on responses to the Rorschach and Buss-Durkee Tests. A paper presented to the California State Psychological Convention, Los Angeles, December 11, 1964.
20. BAKEWELL, W. E., JR., and WIKLER, ABRAHAM: Nonnarcotic addiction: Incidence in a university psychiatric ward. *Journal of the American Medical Association, 196*:710 (May), 1966.
21. ESSIG, C. F.: Newer sedative drugs that can cause intoxication and dependence of barbiturate type. *Journal of the American Medical Association, 196*:714 (May), 1966.
22. MUNCH, JAMES: Marihuana and crime. *Bulletin on Narcotics, 18*:15 (April-June) 1966.

Chapter 4

STIMULANT DRUGS

STIMULANT drugs induce sleeplessness and increase nervous irritability. Drugs of this class discussed here are cocaine, Benzedrine, Dexedrine, Methedrine and related drugs, peyote, including mescaline, LSD, Psilacybin, and DMT.

COCAINE

Technical or scientific names:
  Cocaine Hydrochloride (U.S.P.[1])
Argot names:
  Burnese, bernice, bernies, coke, C., happy dust, dust, Heaven dust, Cecil, star dust, snow; also included in such generic terms as *mojo, Old Steve, bow sow, hocus, goods, merchandise.* (See Glossary.)

Cocaine is a white crystalline powder, odorless with a bitter taste. It was first prepared from the leaves of a bush, *Erythroxylon coca,* of Brazilian origin, by Gaedkin in 1844. It is now prepared chiefly from Peruvian and Columbian coca leaves. Cocaine was first used as a local anesthetic, and its present legitimate use is chiefly in that field. It is not effective as an anesthetic on the intact skin, but does cause anesthesia when applied to denuded areas or to mucous membranes or when it is injected subcutaneously or into nerves.

It is a strong stimulant of the central nervous system, but it is not employed clinically as such. It is used by addiction-prone individuals, both here and abroad, however, for its systemic effect as a stimulant drug. Legitimately, cocaine is sold as cocaine hydrochloride in powder form, in solution for injection or in tablet form for the preparation of solutions. In contraband channels, it is sold as the more or less pure powder and in such channels it arrives in quantity from South American sources. For sale to the ultimate addict-consumer, it is frequently sold in small papers of powder, cellophane packets or gelatin capsules, containing about 1 grain.

Its pleasurable effect is of relatively short duration; hence, the addict may take doses at frequent intervals in order to obtain a sustained effect. It may be used in this way for sprees or binges, either by sniffing it up the nose, whence it is absorbed through the nasal mucous membrane, or by intravenous injection. As a stimulant it produces in the addiction-prone individual an intense feeling of euphoria or exultation, but its use for this purpose is frequently followed by a feeling of strong anxiety or fear, with hallucinations and delusions of a paranoid nature. To counteract this fear or anxiety, cocaine is frequently taken in combination with depressant drugs of the opiate series, either sniffed in conjunction with heroin or taken intravenously with drugs of the opiate series.

As an illustration of the lengths to which addicts will go to get the drug, patients at a narcotic hospital on one occasion were detected in the practice of reclaiming cocaine swabs which had been used for applications in the treatment of diseased conditions of the nose, soaking the cotton in water and injecting the solution intravenously.

Cocaine is a harmful drug in its effect on the personality, and is under the control of the Federal narcotic laws. While tolerance does develop, physical dependence with ensuing withdrawal illness does not occur when the drug is discontinued. The habitual use of cocaine alone does not occur frequently, although some years ago it was very common. The reason for its decrease is the unpleasant, anxious reaction which follows the period of euphoria or pleasure; opiate drugs do not produce this type of reaction and are currently used with cocaine to reduce the unpleasant effects.

The paranoid delusions and excitement which occur following the use of cocaine sometimes result in unpremeditated and unjustified acts of violence by cocaine users. It should be understood that addicts who become violent do so as a reaction to hallucinations which they cannot distinguish from reality; they are desperately "defending" themselves against attackers, when in reality they are committing aggressive crimes upon persons who have no intent to harm them.

Taylor[2] writes that Peruvians habitually chewed the coca leaf for centuries before Pizarro reported their doing so in the sixteenth century. It continues to be chewed by Indians of Peru, Ecuador and Bolivia for its relief of fatigue and alleviation of hunger. Its effect in increasing the endurance of South American Indians in the performance of incredible feats of burden-bearing and work in high altitudes with inadequate food has been reported many times, without adequate explanation. Its reputed effect under these conditions is probably due to the cocaine content, although Taylor calls attention to the fact that the amount of cocaine contained in the average amount of leaves chewed during the day is a very small dose compared with that taken by cocaine habitués in more civilized situations. He believes that there may be other alkaloids in the coca leaf which account in part for its effect on the South American Indian and perhaps sufficient nutritious value to provide some substitute for food. This latter is difficult to understand, however, since the native is reported to chew on the average only about 2 ounces of the leaf daily. The exact nature of the effect of the leaf on primitive peoples is apparently not yet fully understood.

Its use is so widespread in the high altitudes of South America that it corresponds to the use of tobacco or coffee or tea in other areas. Its beneficial effects are so respected that it is revered as a kind of divine agent. Its widespread use by underprivileged laboring classes has been compared to the use of betel nut in India; both betel nut and coca leaves are chewed with an alkali substance (lime) to enhance the effect.

The name of the popular beverage Coca-Cola stems from the fact that the formula contains an extract of coca leaves as flavoring. All cocaine, of course, is carefully removed from the extract. At one time a wine, *Vin Coca Mariani* containing an infusion of coca leaves, was extremely popular in Europe.

Several synthetic preparations with a power to induce local anesthesia similar to cocaine are in use. The most common of these are procaine, Novocain, phenacaine (holocaine), tetracaine, pantocaine, eucaine and stovaine. These are neither habit forming nor addicting.

In 1950, a United Nations Commission on Inquiry on the coca leaf reported to the Economic and Social Council of the United

Nations that the coca leaf chewing had been found to be harmful, although it was considered to be more habit forming than addicting in view of the fact that physical dependence was not established. The Commission reported specifically that when coca leaf was chewed, cocaine entered the blood stream and that it reduced the appetite and led to physical exhaustion as well as malnutrition —this despite the widespread belief that coca leaf chewing increases the capacity for work and in some ways acts as a substitute for food. The Commission recommended a gradual suppression of coca leaf chewing over a period of fifteen years. The steps to bring this about were to be a limitation of production, a legal prohibition of its chewing in the armies of certain countries and the prohibition of payment for work with coca leaves, a practice which exists in several of the countries prominent in coca leaf production.

The United Nations representatives of Bolivia and Peru previously objected to the conclusions that coca leaf chewing is necessarily harmful as practiced by the laboring natives in high altitude areas of their countries, requesting reconsideration of the Commission's report. This is an interesting example of the power of social acceptance in any community where certain drugs are commonly used.

By 1962,[10] all countries in South America agreed that the chewing of coca leaf is undesirable and were taking vigorous steps to restrict the culture of the coca plant to the amount necessary for the production of legitimate cocaine. However, that same year Boliva reported about 50,000 acres were devoted to coca growing with an annual crop of 12,000 to 18,000 tons of leaf only one half of which was for the production of cocaine for legitimate export.

Although the authors have developed their own concepts of cocaine addiction, mainly agreeing and often anticipating those articulated by the World Health Organization's Expert Committee on addiction-producing drugs in 1964,[11] that Committee's findings are reproduced here. This is done not only because they present some minor divergences from our thinking, but mainly because they represent international agreement on concepts of addiction by over 100 countries who subscribed to the Single Convention on Narcotic Drugs of 1961.

Drug dependence of cocaine type is described as a state arising from repeated administration of cocaine or an agent with cocaine-like properties, on a periodic or continuous basis. Its characteristics include:

1. An overpowering desire or need to continue taking the drug and to obtain it by any means;

2. Absence of tolerance to the effects of the drug during continued administration; in the more frequent episodic use, the drug may be taken at short intervals, resulting in the build-up of an intense toxic reaction;

3. A psychic dependence on the effects of the drug related to a subjective and individual appreciation of those effects; and

4. Absence of a physical dependence and hence absence of an abstinence syndrome on abrupt withdrawal; withdrawal is attended by a psychic disturbance manifested by craving for the drug.

With cocaine, the individual detrimental effect may be indirect, resulting from the individual's preoccupation with drug taking, again with malnutrition and infection as frequent consequences, or direct, a severe toxic reaction accompanying rapid and repeated administration in episodic drug use. The harm to society is related to preoccupation with drug taking by the individual, with economic loss and crimes against society as consequences. When drug dependence of cocaine type is brought about through chewing of coca leaves, anorexia, a change in working habits, and loss in weight are additional characteristics.

AMPHETAMINES: BENZEDRINE, DEXEDRINE, METHEDRINE

Technical or scientific names:
Amphetamine Sulfate, Dextroamphetamine Sulfate, Methamphetamine Hydrochloride
Argot names:
Bennies, pep pills.

These closely related synthetic drugs, which are closely related to ephedrine and epinephrine (Adrenalin), are discussed together.

Benzedrine is sold in pink, heart-shaped tablets of 5 mg or 10 mg size and maroon and clear capsules containing 15 mgs of multicolored pellets.

Dexedrine is prepared in brown and clear capsules containing 5, 10 or 15 mg of multicolored pellets.

Methedrine is marketed as white, 5 mg tablets and glass 1 cc ampules, each containing 20 mg. This drug, as Desoxyn, is sold in white tablets of 5 mg, pink tablets of 10 mg and yellow tablets of 15 mg. Methedrine is particularly popular in the San Francisco area where it is on the illicit market also in bulk and in capsules.

Taken orally or injected, they have a direct stimulating effect on the central nervous system and a local constricting effect on the nasal mucous membrane.

The effects of these drugs on the central nervous system usually include feelings of euphoria, or well-being and confidence, and some heightening of alertness and initiative, the total effect of which is to reduce or prevent sleepiness and fatigue to some extent.

One of the outstanding effects of these drugs is to reduce appetite. For this purpose they have been prescribed in the treatment of obesity, although they are not usually recommended for this purpose, and most people who take them do so by self-prescription and administration, a practice which may lead to increased doses with the danger of toxic effects.

"Desyphed," for instance, has been advertised for obesity as "a tablet of concentrated will-power."

Other reducing preparations containing this type of stimulant drugs are: Tenuate, green and white oval tablets; Preludin, salmon-colored square and round tablets; Ionamin, gray and yellow capsules; Desbutal, orange or yellow and blue tablets; Dexamyl, dexedrine combined with a barbiturate, is a green heart-shaped tablet. Daprisal, a yellow oval tablet, is a combination of Dexedrine with a barbiturate used as an analgesic.

Benzedrine is frequently prescribed by physicians for the control of narcolepsy and several other disorders of the central nervous system. It is sometimes used as an antidote for poisoning with depressant drugs of the opiate series. Persons taking Benzedrine therapeutically should be under the frequent observation of a physician, who may detect early signs of toxic action.

Vonedrine, Drinalfa and Tuamine are used similarly to benzedrine in inhalers. For inhalation, the drug is used to saturate paper strips or cotton through which air is drawn for local action on the nasal mucous membrane. In addition to local action, a certain amount is absorbed and to a slight extent gives the systemic effect of Benzedrine sulfate taken orally.

Addiction-prone individuals find considerable satisfaction in the intoxicating effect of the amphetamines when taken in larger than therapeutic doses. As with other types of intoxicants, the inebriating action is considerably modified by the personality of the user. Benzedrine, along with related drugs, has come into increasing use by self-administration for the purpose of reducing sleepiness by truck drivers and others who have to keep awake during long periods of time or during the course of monotonous duty. Students have used Benzedrine when faced with the necessity for long hours of study in preparing for examinations. Of 147 medical students who were given small doses of the drug for three days,[3] 113 reported increased "peppiness," 72 exhilaration and 61 greater power of concentration. Thirty-eight of these students said they would like to continue using the drug. Thirty-eight of the total group of 147 were considered to be addiction-prone. One study[12] indicated a slight increase (about 4 per cent) in athletic performance after the use of amphetamines, but deplored this practice as dangerous on both ethical and physical grounds.

Monroe and Drell[4] studied the use of amphetamines by military prisoners. The most common effect reported by their subjects was that the drug seemed to make time go faster. Other effects frequently reported were a feeling of euphoria or happiness, talkativeness and a feeling that they forgot their troubles.

Amphetamines, particularly in the form of inhalers, have been extremely common as a contraband item for introduction into prisons and correctional institutions. Prisoners and persons involuntarily in military service, and persons under conditions of confinement, seem to find the euphoria, and particularly the feeling that time goes faster, of great satisfaction. In this connection, it is interesting to note that the effect of amphetamines on the time-sense is exactly the opposite of marihuana which, it is generally agreed, gives the illusion that time passes more slowly than it actually does. Because inhalers are so widely used and sold without prescription, institutional guards and employees sometimes regard selling them to inmates as an innocent way to make a little money. The use of amphetamines in some prisons has reportedly become very widespread.

Chewing the strips of drug-saturated paper or cotton removed from the inhaler is the simplest method of administration, although concoctions may be made by soaking the strips in water, tea, coffee or alcohol. The strips themselves are frequently incorporated into bits of food and swallowed whole in order to insure full utilization of the drug.

Benzedrine and Benzedrex inhalers contain folds of saturated paper, each of which is known as a *strip*. The average dose for self-administration by addiction-prone persons is from one half to two strips chewed or swallowed several times a day. One strip equals 30 mg, the maximum recommended therapeutic dose, so it is quite easy for users to take sufficient amounts of the drug to cause intoxication beyond that possible with controlled therapeutic doses.

Addiction-prone persons frequently make solutions of either amphetamine tablets or the active principle recovered from inhaler strips and inject it intravenously, a route of administration which is not recommended therapeutically.

Each amphetamine inhaler contains about twenty-five times the amount of amphetamine in one tablet, and inhalers are sold freely in drug stores without thought or requirement of prescription, whereas the purchase of an amount of amphetamine tablets equivalent to several inhalers might be quite conspicuous and in some instances contrary to state or local law.

In an effort to reduce the abuse of Benzedrine inhalers, the manufacturers have replaced Benzedrine inhalers on the market with Benzedrex inhalers. Observations in a penal institution indicate that addiction-prone persons who previously used Benzedrine inhalers could also get the desired effect from Benzedrex inhalers, although larger doses were necessary. One experiment of the manufacturers of Benzedrine inhalers involved the saturation of the cotton filler with a strong irritant which is not volatile and hence had no local effect on the nasal mucous membrane when used as an inhaler, but when ingested caused intense irritation of the mucous membrane of the mouth and throat. Experienced addicts in the research ward of the Lexington hospital found by experimentation that if the cotton from these inhalers was soaked in mineral oil which was then ingested, the gastrointestinal tract was protected from the irritating effect of the adulterant, while the decided systemic stimulating effect of the Benzedrine was unimpaired. Consequently this experimental inhaler was not marketed.

Illicit sales of amphetamine drugs now constitute contraband traffic of some importance. During a campaign to stop it, the Food and Drug Administration undertook 126 criminal prosecutions in 1960. In eight of these actions, almost 2,000,000 tablets and capsules were confiscated. One defendant drove a delivery route offering as many as 25,000 tablets in bulk drums. Sadusk[20] of the Food and Drug Administration reported in 1966 that enough amphetamines are produced in the United States each year to provide each man, woman and child with thirty-five doses. Of the 8 billion tablets produced each year, 50 per cent were estimated to find their way into illicit channels. The profits were enormous, considering that tablets or capsules are sold wholesale for less than $1.00 per thousand, resold in bulk in illegal traffic for $30 to $50 per thousand, and finally sold at retail for five to ten cents a dose. In May 1966, in California, the first illicit plant for manufacturing amphetamines was discovered, which adds a new dimension to the problem of illegal diversion from legal producers.

Benzedrine and similar stimulants, at least in California, are customarily sold in tinfoil rolls of ten tablets at $1.00 per roll. Until 1965, under Federal laws, it had to be proven that the drugs were sold without prescription after having moved illegally in interstate commerce. In that year, however, a new law brought the amphetamines and the barbiturate drugs under strict inventory control from manufacturer to consumer with a limit on the number of times a prescription could be filled. Consequently, it is expected that abusive use of these drugs will materially decline.

In 1962, the Food and Drug Administration attempted a survey on the quantity of amphetamines and accounted for an annual output of 102,000 lbs (4½ billion 10 mg doses). However, since two of the largest producers refused to give figures on their production, we may speculate that the actual output was then probably somewhat greater than the amount referred to above. Authorities estimate that at least half of total production finds its way into illicit use.

Symptoms of intoxication with drugs of this class can include agitation, restlessness, sleeplessness and talkativeness. The skin is flushed, there is profuse perspiration, the pupils are dilated. Blood pressure increases, the reflexes become hyperactive and the startle-response is heightened. Sometimes a tremor of the hands is noted, and occasionally a toxic psychosis ensues in which there are paranoid ideas and vague hallucinations. When this psychosis develops, the user may become very anxious and so fearful of danger that he seeks protection. Many acute toxic psychoses have been reported in which there are paranoid ideas, hallucinations and dangerous aggressiveness.[13, 14, 15, 16]

The valid uses of amphetamines are small, even for weight reduction, where diet is the logical approach. Vast quantities of amphetamines are used illegally and by unwise prescription. There is a rising demand for restrictive legislation for "dangerous drugs" at both the Federal and state level. Referring to the addiction liability of amphetamine habituation or psychic dependence undoubtedly occurs in addiction-prone individuals. Tolerance occurs more often than previously thought with reports of daily intake of 700 to 1,200 mg daily compared to the therapeutic dose of 5 to 15 mg.

Monroe and Drell[4] listed certain complaints following the cessation of administration of Benzedrine which they mention as withdrawal symptoms. This matter has not been critically studied, however, and it is doubtful if withdrawal, according to the criteria set up by Himmelsbach,[5] accompanies the use of this group of drugs. The most common effects reported by Monroe and Drell following cessation of Benzedrine were feelings of fatigue and sleepiness. (Similar symptoms follow the withdrawal of cocaine.) Of the military prisoners studied by Monroe and Drell, about 15 per cent reported that they took Benzedrine prior to their military service, and 65 per cent used Benzedrine prior to the time they reached the disciplinary barracks. About 25 per cent of all

Stimulant Drugs 141

the prisoners in the barracks reported the use of Benzedrine at one time or another. Diagnosis of amphetamine intoxication is made by a history or evidence of amphetamine use, by the characteristic signs mentioned above, or by laboratory examination of the urine.

Amphetamines may, if taken in overdose by the addiction-prone individual, cause very serious illness or death. Several such cases have been reported.[6, 7] The antidote for amphetamine poisoning is one of the barbiturate drugs. In less acute cases, barbiturates by mouth are effective, and in cases of acute poisoning or intoxication, one of the barbiturates intravenously usually gives prompt relief.

Addiction-prone individuals who fall into the excessive use of amphetamines or of barbiturates sometimes alternate an amphetamine with a barbiturate, hoping to find an emotional equilibrium with no unpleasant effects. The quantities of both drugs may be increased in an effort to keep them in balance. The intoxicating effect of the drug reduces a patient's judgment in this matter, and in psychiatric practice, one sometimes finds a person who takes alternately large quantities of first one drug and then the other. He may take the barbiturate for sedation and then, disliking the unpleasantness of the excessive drowsiness, take amphetamines to counteract it. If he takes too large a dose of the stimulants he becomes unpleasantly nervous and jittery and takes more barbiturate to counteract that. So he alternates between excitement and depression. Patients may take barbiturates in the evening to insure sound sleep and the next morning, disliking the residual drowsiness or hangover, take amphetamines to clear their minds in preparation for the day's work.

Unfortunately, there is an increasing amount of facetious material in fiction and on the air concerning the use of Benzedrine as a means of increasing the work output or heightening the capacity for pleasure. The unfortunate connotation is, as with barbiturates, that this is a drug which has no inherent danger of consequence.

Although the authors have developed their own concepts of amphetamine addiction, mainly agreeing and often anticipating those articulated by the World Health Organization's Expert

Committee on addiction-producing drugs in 1964,[11] that Committee's findings are reproduced here. This is done not only because they present some minor divergences from our thinking, but mainly because they represent international agreement on concepts of addiction by over 100 countries who subscribed to the Single Convention on Narcotic Drugs of 1961.

> Drug dependence of amphetamine type is a state arising from repeated administration of amphetamine or an agent with amphetamine-like effects on a periodic or continuous basis. Its characteristics include:
> 1. A desire or need to continue taking the drug;
> 2. Consumption of increasing amounts to obtain greater excitatory and euphoric effects or to combat more effectively depression and fatigue, accompanied in some measure by the development of tolerance;
> 3. A psychic dependence on the effects of the drug related to a subjective and individual appreciation of the drug's effects; and
> 4. General absence of physical dependence so that there is no characteristic abstinence syndrome when the drug is discontinued.
>
> The amphetamines tend to cause anorexia, persistent and exaggerated psychomotor disturbances, and disruption of mental function, even to the occurrence of toxic psychosis. For society, the harm is related in part to the drug's psychomotor effects (involvement in accidents, for example).

HALLUCINOGENIC, PSYCHEDELIC OR PSYCHOTOMIMETIC DRUGS

From time immemorial man has used hallucinogenic drugs to alter his perception, his state of consciousness, his image of the world and himself. Often these drugs were taken in connection with his attempt to achieve detachment, selflessness, and the sensation of having made contact with divine sources of energy. Sometimes they were taken to prepare warriors for battle, and we are now fairly certain that the "berserk" state which made the Danes and other Scandinavian tribes such terrible foes within early historic times was induced by these drugs. While the chief source of many of these primitive drugs was—and still is—certain mushrooms which reach back into pre-historic times both in the New World and the Old, there were other plants in Asia and Africa which produced them also. One immediately thinks of the hallucinatory stages through which a hashish user passes, and the homicidal mania which that drug produces when used heavily and continuously for some time, though of course hashish is an addictive drug, different in other respects from the true hallucinogens.

Until very recently in the modern world, the hallucinogens were used by a relatively small number of primitive and semi-primitive tribes in religious rites. Peyote and mescaline, along with a number of lesser known fungi, were, and still are, so used by Indians in both North and South America. Some varieties of morning glory seeds also contain active hallucinogenic agents. However, a small number of non-primitives also experimented with these primitive drugs during the late Nineteenth and early Twentieth Century, including some distinguished researchers. Their interests were largely philosophic and psychological, and their reports are probably the source of an experimental interest, especially in peyote, which flourished in Bohemian circles during the 1940's and 1950's in the United States. Some use of peyote appeared on university campuses, first on the West Coast, then in the East. However, neither the religious use by scattered Indian tribes nor this occasional experimental use caused any serious social problems. In fact, the ordeal of taking crude peyote is so severe that one must be either a devout religionist or a dedicated experimenter if he feels a compulsion to repeat the experience. And of course these drugs are not addicting in that they produce tolerance, physical dependence, and a withdrawal syndrome, so that there is not the compulsion to repeat their use which we have observed in addictive drugs.

In the 1960's the most powerful of the known hallucinogens became easily available in concentrated form in this country. This was LSD (lysurgic acid diethylamide), discovered by Dr. Albert Hofmann in Switzerland in 1943. At first it was cautiously used by European psychiatrists as a device to explore the nature of various psychoses, which it produced artificially under controlled conditions, and as an experimental shock treatment for patients suffering from severe mental illness. It is unlikely that any of the professional experimenters with LSD anticipated that it would be widely used by thrill-seekers just for "kicks."

Glowing reports by Alpert and Leary in the Harvard Crimson and the Harvard Review in 1963, and an article by Gordan, "The Hallucinogenic Drug Cult," in the *Reporter* in August 1963, concerning the "consciousness-expansion" effect of LSD have led to a rising tide of experimentation which has become a great concern to law enforcement officers and psychiatrists who must deal with the altered behavior of people under the influence of this powerful drug which is readily available from illegitimate sources in various Bohemian and campus communities.

PEYOTE AND MESCALINE

Technical or scientific names:
  Lophophora Williamsii
Argot names:
  None encountered.

Peyote is a small spineless cactus, *Lophophora williamsii*, occurring chiefly in northern Mexico and southern Texas. The peyote plant is not yet classified botanically. It is also referred to as *Anhalonium lewinii*. The peyote or peyotl is one of the least impressive of the family of cacti. It has a large root, but above the ground it appears as clusters of small button-like growths frequently mistaken for mushrooms. These, when dried, are known as peyote buttons or mescal buttons. The latter is a confusing name because it bears no relationship to mescal, which is an alcoholic beverage widely used in Mexico. The chief alkaloid found in peyote buttons is mescaline, which has also been synthetically prepared. The synthetic preparation is usually used for laboratory purposes because the concentration of the active principle in the natural source is extremely variable. According to Taylor,[2] Francisco Hernandez described peyote and its intoxicating effect in 1576. Numerous references to the use of this drug by Mexican Indians appear in early Mexican church history. The gathering and consumption of the peyote buttons have been closely associated with religious ritual both before and since the introduction of Christianity into Mexico; peyote played a prominent role in ancient Aztec rites. It continues to be used by Mexican Indians and in the United States by the Apaches, the Omahas, the Kiowas, the Comanches and other tribes.

Limited surreptitious traffic in peyote buttons goes on between Indians who live in areas where the peyote cactus grows and Indians in other parts of the country. It apparently has never been used habitually, but only in connection with rather sacred ritual practices of periodic religious ceremony. Several hours after the ingestion of peyote, the subjects experience hallucinations and delusions of perception, taste, odor and visions, the latter frequently of brilliant and exciting intensity. To the ignorant Indian, these are impressive religious experiences. The observations of a number of scientists who have subjectively reported on the experiences of peyote mention particularly the brilliant visual hallucinations of indescribable color and beauty, frequently resembling fields of brilliant colored jewels, associated with hallucinations of beautiful perfumes, all making an impressive experience. The details of peyote intoxication are reported by Dr. S. Weir Mitchell,[8] a well-known psychiatrist and writer.

Havelock Ellis also reported that peyote caused an artificial paradise, and enthusiastically recommended it to several of his friends. William James[8] tried peyote at the suggestion of Dr. Mitchell, hoping to reproduce the fairyland of glorious and jeweled splendor described by Mitchell, but reported that it caused considerable gastric distress and subsequent hangover, but no visions. Nausea and vomiting are frequent preliminary effects of the drug. A prominent modern composer told the authors that some thirty years ago, while a student at Harvard, he was introduced to the experimental use of peyote as a device for exploring religious experience. He reported a series of brilliant color visions, some of which he recalled vividly even after the passage of many years. He reported no compulsion to use the drug and no bad effects except the initial nausea, which he attempted to avoid by boiling the cactus buttons down into a strong tea which could be drunk very quickly.

Dr. Paul H. Hoch[9] and other psychiatrists have used mescaline experimentally to produce emotional states for comparison with the behavior found in psychotic persons. Some authors have noted the similarity of the experiences under peyote to those manifest by mental patients suffering from schizophrenia or dementia praecox. It appears likely that the effect of the drug enhances or aggravates such symptoms in persons predisposed to schizophrenia or in the early stages of that disorder. Hoch describes with scientific detail the variety of hallucinations and delusions, with the apparent disintegration of personality which occurs in experimental subjects under the influence of mescaline. He noted that formal intelligence does not appear to suffer while under the effect of mescaline, and that the psychotic symptoms occur in a state of clear consciousness, although amnesia subsequently is often found for the period of intoxication.

Results similar to Hoch's were observed in experimental subjects taking mescaline at the U. S. Public Health Service Hospital in Lexington, Kentucky, by Dr. Isbell and his group. While Dr. Hoch gave mescaline intravenously with apparent safety, Dr. Isbell gave it by mouth and intramuscularly. It was found here that although most of the patients experienced some more or less brilliant type of visual hallucinations, the stimulant effect of the drug on the central nervous system caused unpleasant physical distress, sweating, tremors, elevation of the blood pressure, flushing of face and, frequently, a general anxiety resembling that experienced from the administration of cocaine. Many of the hallucinations and delusions were of a paranoid nature and associated with fear.

It was noted in this research that intravenous barbiturates are most effective in counteracting the effect of an overdose of mescaline or abolishing signs and symptoms of mescaline intoxication. Except for experimental use of mescaline in investigations of the nature of mental conditions, there appears to be no present medical or scientific use of mescaline, and it is not prescribed by physicians. Although by law, peyote or mescaline users are eligible for treatment at the U. S. Public Health Service Hospitals for narcotic addicts, there has been no instance of a patient applying for treatment. There is no authentic record to show that the habitual or addictive use of peyote occurs either by Indians or others who use it periodically or experimentally. It is likely that the unpleasant physical effects of the drug, including the anxiety it produces, would prevent it from being a habit-forming or addicting drug of

Stimulant Drugs

consequence. Inasmuch as apparently little or no tolerance is developed, it is not an addicting drug in that sense of the word. The dose of peyote buttons appears to be from one to three, and the dose of the synthetic alkaloid mescaline for experimental use is reported as 0.4 to 0.6 gm, intravenously by Hoch, or 5 to 6 mg per kilogram of body weight orally.

Peyote differs from marihuana in that the former usually causes wakefulness and does not produce the type of delusions or behavior of merriment found characteristically with marihuana. Furthermore, it has never been identified with criminal behavior.

Doctors Rinkel and Schultes have studied peyote, coca, teonanacatl, coapi in a transcultural framework, with qualifications regarding their addiction liability. LSD (lysergic acid diethylamide) is an interesting drug in psychiatric research, being hallucinogenic but without serious addiction liability, although some small groups have been known to play with the drug for the sake of the bizarre reactions it produces.[18] It is beginning to appear on the contraband market in the form of sugar cubes on which the liquid drug has been dropped. Attempts are current to exempt it from legal controls by establishing it as a religious sacrament.

PSILACYBIN

Technical or scientific names:
   Psilocybe mexicana, Teonanacatl
Argot names:
   None

Psilacybin is the active principle of a Mexican mushroom with effects similar to LSD and peyote.

LSD OR LSD 25

Technical or scientific names:
   Lysurgic acid diethylamide or d-lysurgic acid diethylamide tartrate.
Argot names:
   Acid, sugar, sugar cubes.

LSD is a tasteless, odorless, white powder prepared from ergot, a fungus growth on rye grain, or prepared synthetically. The natural and synthetic forms are indistinguishable by inspection or chemical tests. LSD has not yet been approved by the Food and Drug Administration for other than medical research by specifically approved doctors and institutions, numbering fewer than 75. It appears on the illegitimate market as sugar cubes treated with LSD solution; as powder in capsules; and in vials of solutions of 1 cc each for individual doses, selling for $5.00 to $10 a dose.

Serious psychiatric researchers believe that the study of psychotic behavior caused by these powerful drugs may give a clue to the causes of slower developing psychoses occurring more naturally. There is also some hope to believe that the use of these drugs as sort of a shock treatment may be useful in modifying for the better the psychotic behavior of some mentally ill people but it is too soon to reach any conclusion concerning this. The current furore over uncontrolled use is reducing legitimate production to the point where legitimate researchers have difficulty in obtaining it.

Meanwhile a substantial black market has developed for LSD, and various laws are now being passed to control the drug very rigorously. However, the real damage is done only by the uncontrolled or unsupervised use of the drug which, in its bootleg form, may vary widely in quality and strength of dosage (50 to 400 micrograms, with a microgram being equivalent to one ten-thousandth of a gram, being the average medical dose) because of the loose laboratory methods by which the drug is produced and packaged for sale, usually on sugar cubes. While the persons most susceptible to personality damage from unsupervised use of the drug are psycho-neurotics, psychopathic types, incipient schizophrenics, and those with latent paranoid tendencies, anyone may develop psychotic behavior from the drug, even at periods beyond its initial onset. Although the popular assumption is that the brain is directly affected, it has been shown that only an infinitesimal amount of the hallucinogenic agent is present in brain tissue, with most of the doses concentrating in the kidneys, the liver, and the small intestine. The entire metabolism is disrupted, and the results range from prolonged ecstatic trances comparable to the rather brief experiences of mystics and religious zealots to hours of pure, concentrated horror such as is not experienced by man in his natural or undrugged state. It cannot be too often repeated that the drug should not be taken except under medical supervision, with an experienced physician at hand during the entire duration of the effect.

This is a valuable drug, the implications of which are not yet known. Research on it should continue under controlled conditions, and in some cases such as a painful and terminal disease, or in certain types of psycho-therapy, it appears to have great value in the hands of conservative physicians. It is not addictive in the commonly accepted sense of the word, although some compulsion toward frequent self-administration has been observed. Sensible legal regulation is desirable, though the ease of manufacture and the miniscule amounts needed to produce dramatic effects may make effective regulation difficult if not impossible. The effects on persons who are given the drug without their knowledge are traumatic and dangerous; parties are now reported at which a neophyte is given a dose for the amusement of more experienced users. The effect of the drug on groups of persons taking it unknowingly is disorganization and chaos. There is no doubt that various nations are already manufacturing the drug in quantities with a view to possible psychochemical warfare, for the drug could be disseminated effectively in food supplies, in central water supplies, or as mist or dust in the air; a mere handling of the drug and then touching the fingers to the mouth can give a heavy dose. One man could carry enough of the drug in a briefcase to reduce any great city in the world to a shambles if it were properly disseminated.

This is not the place for anything like a full discussion of LSD, but the reader is referred to Dr. Sidney Cohen's recent book, *The Beyond Within*,[18] for what is probably the best discussion of the drug and its effects yet available.

At the present time, irresponsible and unregulated use of LSD is becoming a major problem for law enforcement officers in cities where some university campuses and Bohemian communities are located, particularly New York, Los Angeles and San Francisco. LSD users refer to experiences with LSD, which usually include vivid hallucinations in colors, as "taking a trip." Users refer to themselves as "acid heads." Meetings of "acid heads" for the purpose of "going on a trip" are openly advertised in newspapers in Los Angeles and San Francisco.

Dr. Sidney Cohen[18] has described three periods of LSD use. The first, or Scientific, covered the years after discovery of the drug during which cautious medical research was carried on. The second, or Psychedelic phase, during which there was rapidly expanding more or less serious but non-medical experimentation by university faculty members. The third period, or Acid Head phase, was marked by an alarming spread of LSD use by both academic and non-academic groups who used it excessively for kicks and sensual satisfaction. There was little or no pretense of research by addiction-prone people who usually had used other types of dangerous and narcotic drugs and who sometimes combined other drugs, particularly the amphetamines, with LSD for maximum sensation. Use of LSD by such people created an atmosphere in which it became very difficult for serious research to continue so that, in 1966, the only legitimate manaufacturer of LSD withdrew it from the market, leaving only mushrooming, clandestine manufacturers to supply the growing demand of psychopaths and psychoneurotics.

Summaries of cases reported by the Los Angeles County Sheriff at hearings on bills introduced by the California Legislature to control LSD traffic follow:

> The Police Department of a local well-to-do beach community reported that a 19-year-old boy who was under the influence of LSD was apprehended while completely nude in an apparent burglary-rape attempt. The startling facts of the case revealed that the boy admitted consuming LSD and subsequently had an overwhelming desire to commit rape. The subject then got into his automobile and drove a few blocks from his home where he observed lights in the window of a home.
>
> The subject disrobed and then went to a window where he observed a 15-year-old girl and a 9-year-old boy in the home. The subject entered the home through an unlocked rear door and was confronted by the children. Subject appeared bewildered and wandered in the home. The girl succeeded in placing a telephone call to a next door neighbor who came to the rear of the home with a shotgun. The subject, upon seeing the neighbor, began walking towards him. The neighbor commanded the subject to stop, however, the subject appeared

oblivious to the situation and kept proceeding until the neighbor fired a warning shot.

Questioning of the subject, a college student of the "beatnik" type complete with "beatle" haircut and handlebar mustache, disclosed that he had taken LSD on approximately ten occasions. The subject admitted having the same urge on at least three of the prior experiences and entering three homes in other parts of the county. Subject could not recall what had happened during those situations.

Deputies responded to a call regarding a suspicious person in a vehicle and found suspect slumped over the wheel of his vehicle which had the rear wheels over the curbing on the sidewalk. Suspect who was intoxicated was aroused and became violent and had to be restrained.

A father found his 17-year-old son in a semi-coma in his bedroom. Upon being aroused the boy began clawing motion with both hands at his own eyes. As the son continued to act strangely and could not be brought to his senses, the father took him to a doctor. Subsequent investigation by Deputies of the Narcotic Detail disclosed that the boy had taken a small amount of LSD powder which had been given to him by a friend as payment for a $20 debt. The boy related that during his hallucinogenic state he knew that he was dead and that he was also aware of being under water. The boy recalled that at one time he was unable to see and tried to pull his eyes out of the sockets to enable his eyes to see.

Narcotic Deputies assisted a State Parole officer in the apprehension of a parole violator who had a narcotic background. The suspect attempted to close the door on the officers who were standing in the open doorway. One of the officers had his hand caught in the door jamb and it was necessary to force the door open to gain entry. As the officers were gaining entry the suspect lunged for a large Bowie knife nearby, but the officers prevented him from reaching the knife. The suspect then ran to a sword which was hanging on a wall. One of the officers tried to keep the suspect away from the sword and the suspect struck the officer with his elbow breaking his nose. The suspect then succeeded in grabbing an open pocketknife which was on a table and attempted to stab the officer in the stomach. The suspect was subsequently restrained.

An 18-year-old female, an associate of an outlaw motorcycle club, and wearing a motorcycle club type jacket bearing the letters "LSD" across the back, was being taken into custody on a traffic warrant, when she attempted to pass the sugar cubes to a friend.

Deputies investigating a young hitchhiker found 97 sugar cubes containing LSD in his bedroll. This hitchhiker who was heavily bearded, extremely nervous and trembled visibly, explained that he was living on the cubes as an experiment.

A 17-year-old boy appeared at an emergency hospital in a highly disoriented and intoxicated state seeking medical attention. Further investigation disclosed that the boy had taken one capsule of LSD two days prior and took one-third of a capsule of LSD the previous day. Subject stated that he feared he was going to die and went to the hospital for medical aid.

An 18-year-old student was found wandering aimlessly by Deputies. Investigation disclosed the student to be in a highly intoxicated state. The student was alternately violent and then docile. It was necessary to use restraining straps to prevent injury to himself or others. Interrogation by Deputies of the Narcotic Detail disclosed that the student had been given an LSD capsule by a student acquaintance during an experiment at his friend's home. Subject could only recall that his experience was very "weird" and that his thoughts became uncontrollable and he fled from the house. Narcotic Deputies proceeded to the house where they were admitted and the evidence seized was found in the dining room and bedroom.

Deputies received a call that an all night LSD party was being held at a given location and that the sponsoring group had previously been in San Francisco. The group reportedly worked their way to Southern California arranging LSD parties along the way. Deputies checked the address and reported that the location was an automobile repair shop rented for the occasion.

There were approximately eighty to ninety people in various eccentric dress and appearance attending the party. The people were painting mannequins and themselves, including their faces, bodies, and clothing, with various colored paints, most of which glowed under the ultra-violet lights. Some were in costume, others wore animal skins on their heads, several wore clothing which was caked with dirt. There was a phonograph playing weird, abstract music and someone was showing color slides that were pictures of walls, sand, and different paints and colors. People arrived in groups, usually consisting of four to ten persons. A large bus was parked in front of the location. The bus bore a sign asking, "Can you pass the Acid Test?" The bus was painted with various colors in geometric shapes.

At 4:00 A.M., Deputies were contacted by a neighboring police dept. who informed them that a person whom they had previously thought to have been an assault victim was not a victim at all but merely under the influence of LSD. Questioning of this subject disclosed that he had attended the party. The subject stated that shortly after the party started, someone brought in a punch bowl filled with some kind of punch to which another person added about three handfuls of LSD pills which were stirred in and dissolved. Everyone had a drink of the potion. The subject was still suffering hallucinations and was staggering about when the officers talked to him. The suspect had an advertisement from a small local newspaper in his pocket. The article titled "Acid Test" and listed a date, time, location (the same as reported to the Deputies) and an admission charge of $1.00. The newspaper was a specialty tabloid devoted to "free expression." At 8:00 A.M. a person dressed in garish attire was observed staggering on the sidewalk a short distance from the party. The person was extremely intoxicated, appeared to be in a trance, and made strange gestures in the air with his hands. The person was unable to care for himself and was taken into custody.

A youth on a California airplane recently attacked the stewardess in an effort to force his way into the pilot's cabin. He explained later to the police that he had taken a dose of LSD the day before and that he wished to enter the pilot's cabin "so that he could get a better view of the pretty rainbows."

Several university students were taken into protective custody by the police after the neighbors phoned them because the students were observed to be crawling on a lawn eating grass.

In another instance, police who were called to an apartment by neighbors who objected to the noise found two young men hacking at one another with knives in order to get blood to draw "beautiful pictures" on the wall.

It has been reported that one-third of the people taking LSD subsequently report unpleasant emotions and sensations and of these about one-half experience panic and fear that they are becoming insane. Two-thirds of the subjects report some degree of pleasurable experience—some ecstatic and of mystical, religious nature. Artists and writers sometimes feel that they are more creative after taking LSD but this appears to be purely a subjective feeling since most sober observers report deterioration of ability.

In 1966, Dr. Lipinski of the Student Health Service of Stanford University was reported in the press as saying that twenty students had been brought to the university psychiatric services for treatment of acute psychiatric emergencies following ingestion of LSD. Eight of the twenty were plagued with visual distortions for days or weeks and six were so disturbed that they had to drop out of school.

Mental hospitals in the areas where LSD is popular report increasing admissions of acutely disturbed people following the use of LSD. At this time it can not be said who are most likely to respond to LSD with prolonged or permanent mental damage, but it would appear that it is the element of the population with borderline emotional adjustment which is attracted to the use of psychedelic drugs. In other words, those most likely to be seriously or permanently damaged by LSD are those most likely to experiment with it.

It is uncommon for persons to take LSD frequently over a considerable period of time such as the case with opiates, barbiturates or amphetamines, but cases are known who have remained under the influence for three days by repeated doses, while others are reputed to have taken the drug on literally hundreds of separate occasions. The duration of effect is unpredictable. The onset is likely to be within one-half hour and to last for several hours but there are cases where a single dose has caused profound disturbances as long as a year after apparent recovery from a single dose. Except for the regulatory authority of the Food and Drug Administration which prohibits unauthorized physicians from prescribing the drug until it is found safe by approved research physicians, there is little or no control over the manufacture, distribution, sale, possession, and use of this dangerous drug. Steps are being taken to include it under the Federal

Dangerous Drug law enacted in 1965, but the ease of clandestine manufacture will make enforcement very difficult.

The precise nature of its action on the human body and mind and possible organic damage to body organs are unknown at this time. It seems apparent that LSD should be brought under strict control at an early date to prevent further spread of its abusive use. Its ultimate usefulness should be determined by cautious, careful medical research conducted only in institutions. Dr. Cohen reports the remarkable finding that mental and emotional disturbances occur with unusual frequency among the relatively small number of psychiatrists and physicians who do extensive experimental work with patients who take the drug.

DMT

Technical or scientific names:
  Dimethyltryptamine
Argot name:
  None

This is a synthetic drug with effects like LSD, but quicker and shorter. May be smoked by soaking tobacco in the drug, or sniffed in ether or other solvent.

Physiological and Psychological Effects of Stimulant Drugs

Cocaine was originally thought to be a non-addicting and relatively harmless substitute for the opiates. It is now well known, of course, that this is not true and that cocaine is a dangerously addicting drug. It is a stimulant and never causes sedation like the barbiturates or alcohol or the stupor comparable to morphine or heroin. Cocaine is an antidote for both alcohol and for the opiates and is sometimes used in the treatment of alcoholism. The pleasurable stimulation caused by injecting cocaine subcutaneously or intravenously is occasionally registered to some extent by normal persons, but is strong and pronounced in the addiction-prone type of personality. Psychopaths who take the drug usually develop great anxiety and fear; some psychopaths experience a calm comparable to that produced by opiates, with the drug eliminating worries and conflicts and at the same time stimulating both intellectual and physical activity. The drug is probably a sexual stimulant; however, if used over a period of time it decreases the appetite, brings on rapid emaciation and causes nervousness and anxiety which ultimately develop into delusions of persecution; the continued physical stimulation may ultimately result in convulsions.

While a few persons use cocaine exclusively, either sniffing it in crystalline form or injecting it hypodermically, most addicts ultimately use cocaine in combination with other drugs, especially morphine and heroin. Combination shots of cocaine with morphine or cocaine with heroin or all three drugs mixed are known as *speedballs,* and cocaine is commonly used in large, frequently repeated doses much as alcohol might be used on a spree. Cocaine produces a degree of physical and mental deterioration not found in connection with the use of opiates. Many addicts find that the combination of cocaine with the opiates reduces the undesirable mental and physical effects concomitant with the use of cocaine alone, while it seems to emphasize the pleasurable effects of the opiates.

Amphetamine is a stimulant which acts directly on the central nervous system and produces psychic dependence along with very great tolerance. In some individuals, physical dependence comparable to that of opiates or the barbiturates has not been observed. The general effect (if used in small doses) is one of severe intoxication modified by the personality of the user. Excessive doses of amphetamines taken by addiction-prone persons may cause serious illness or death. The barbiturates constitute an antidote for the amphetamines. Methedrine, which is widely used intravenously by addicts in the San Francisco area, causes such violent behavior that the term *methmonster* is used to describe it. One of several boys shooting Methedrine became psychotic while with addict friends, suddenly jumped from a moving car and ran wildly down the street calling for police protection from his companions. This behavior resembles that found in cocaine users.

Until very recently, peyote was not considered a drug of addiction, but recently unverified press reports indicate that it may be so used in Southwestern United States. It produces neither physical nor psychic dependence, and the pleasurable effects found by addicts in the opiates and barbiturates are not reported; however, the drug provides a type of escape from reality which might be attractive to addiction-prone persons and may become a problem if its use is extended beyond the religious rituals celebrated by American Indians, or the occasional experimental use by the curious.

REFERENCES

1. *Pharmacopoeia of the United States of America (The United States Pharmacopoeia),* Seventeenth Revision. Easton, Pa., Mack Publishing Company, 1965.
2. TAYLOR, N.: *Flight From Reality.* New York, Duell, Sloan and Pearce, 1949.
3. IVY, A. C., and KRASNO, L. R.: Amphetamine (Benzedrine) sulfate: A review of its pharmacology. *War Medicine,* 1:15 (Jan.), 1941.
4. MONROE, R. R., and DRELL, H. J.: Oral use of stimulants obtained from inhalers. *Journal of the American Medical Association,* 135:909 (Dec. 6), 1947.
5. HIMMELSBACH, C. K.: Studies of certain addiction characteristics of (a) dihydromorphine ("Paramorphan"), (b) dihydrodesoxymorphine-D ("Desomorphine"), (c) dihydrodesoxycodeine-D ("Desocodeine"), and (d) methyldihydromorphinone ("Metopon"). *Journal of Pharmacology and Experimental Therapeutics,* 67:239 (Oct.), 1939.
6. GERICKE, O. L.: Suicide by ingestion of amphetamine sulfate. *Journal of the American Medical Association,* 128:1098 (Aug. 11), 1945.
7. SMITH, L. C.: Collapse with death following use of amphetamine sulfate. *Journal of the American Medical Association,* 113:1022 (Sept. 9), 1939.
8. JAMES, W.: *The Letters of William James* (edited by his son Henry James). Boston, Atlantic Monthly Press, 1920, Volume II, pp. 36-37.
9. HOCH, P. H.: Experimentally produce psychoses. *American Journal of Psychiatry,* 107:607 (Feb.), 1951.
10. AVALOS JIBAJA, DR. CARLOS: Consultative group on coca leaf problems. *Bulletin on Narcotics,* Vol. XVI: No. 3 (July-September 1964), United Nations, New York.
11. WORLD HEALTH ORGANIZATION EXPERT COMMITTEE ON ADDICTION-PRODUCING DRUGS: *Thirteenth Report,* World Health Organiza-

tion Technical Report Series, No. 273. Geneva, Switzerland, World Health Organization, 1964.
12. AMERICAN MEDICAL ASSOCIATION: Pep pills and sports. *The AMA News,* June 29, 1959, Editorial Viewpoint.
13. PROUT, CURTIS T.: Reactions to use of amphetamines as observed in a psychiatric hospital. *New York State Journal of Medicine,* May 15, 1964.
14. RICKMAN, E. F., et al.: Amphetamine medication as cause of acute psychiatric reactions. *Medical Digest,* 1961.
15. RICKMAN, M. D.: Acute toxic psychiatric reactions related to amphetamine medication. *Medical Annals of the District of Columbia, XXX*:4, April, 1961.
16. McCONNELL, W. B.: Amphetamine substances in mental illnesses in Northern Ireland. *British Journal of Psychiatry, 109*:218-224, 1963.
17. LEIGHTON, ALEXANDER H.: *Transcultural Significance of Magic Plants.* Cambridge, Massachusetts, Harvard University, 1965.
18. COHEN, SIDNEY: *The Beyond Within: The LSD Story.* New York, Atheneum Press, 1965.
19. CONNELL, P. H.: Amphetamine type of dependence. *Journal of the American Medical Association, 196*:718 (May), 1966.
20. SADUSK, J. F., JR.: Size and extent of the problem. *Journal of the American Medical Association, 196*:707 (May), 1966.
21. RINKEL, MAX, and SCHULTES, RICHARD EVANS: *Transcultural Significance of Magic Plants.* Boston, Botanical Museum, Harvard University, 1965.

Chapter 5

IDENTIFICATION OF DRUGS AND PROOF OF ADDICTION

THE NEED FOR PROOF OF ADDICTION

FORTUNATELY, the diagnosis of drug addiction can usually be made on the basis of admission by the addict, supplemented by such obvious signs as withdrawal illness, fresh needle marks, etc. However, there are some situations in which additional objective evidence is necessary to establish either addiction or absence of addiction and to identify the drugs of addiction. For instance: an individual may deny addiction, and the courts may have reason to prove that he is an addict; or a prisoner may be charged with addiction and need to establish proof that he is not addicted; or a person may claim to be a drug addict, and the courts or a physician may have to substantiate that claim or disprove it. In cases of suspected murder or suicide, identification and proof may be decidedly pertinent. There are now methods available to establish reasonable proof of addiction or lack of addiction in many cases, as well as to identify, under conditions to be described shortly, most of the drugs used by addicts. However, at the outset the following should be noted: the individual may be addicted to either illicit drugs or to those not covered at present by state or Federal laws; addiction, although established, may be due to medical treatment and does not necessarily imply any criminality; tests for drugs in the human system must be repeatedly positive in order to confirm addiction; and these tests must be carried out under highly controlled conditions by persons qualified to run the tests. Also, there is no single laboratory test which will, of itself, establish addiction.

As an indication of the types of situation which make identification of drugs and proof of addiction desirable, over and above any weight attached to statements made by the individual either confirming or denying addiction, a few illustrations might be cited. In the handling of insurance applications or insurance claims, the addictive use of drugs may need to be established, the nature of the drugs established and the presence of addiction or the extent of addiction proved. In the investigation of thefts or mishandling of legal drugs in legitimate commerce, it may be important to eliminate suspects who are not addicted and to identify suspects who are addicted. It may be necessary to identify drugs found on a criminal suspect or a dead body; also, it is frequently necessary for narcotics agents or customs officials to identify contraband. In Selective Service cases in which addiction is claimed or denied, objective proof may be needed. In litigation involving wills, estates, criminal or civil liability, etc., it may be pertinent to establish whether or not an individual is an addict and to what drugs he is (or was) addicted. In the investigation of suspected smuggling and use of contraband drugs in public or private institutions (hospitals, prisons, etc.), it may be necessary to identify the drugs and prove that certain individuals are using them. In coroners' inquiries for the determination of cause of death, objective evidence of the use of drugs and the identification of the drugs may be most significant. In evaluating character for purposes of accepting or rejecting testimony, the presence of addiction is important; the same implications are present in questioned applications for visas, applications for certain types of employment, cases involving suspected drunken driving, etc. Last, addiction may bear directly upon certain types of criminal cases in which the accused asks leniency because he is (or claims to be) addicted to certain drugs, thereby not infrequently influencing both judges and juries; the same may be true in reverse, when addiction may be charged and prejudice the court or the jury unduly. There are, of course, many other situations in which identification and proof are essential, but there is no point in enumerating them here.

Research workers experimenting with the addiction liability of various drugs have need of very precise methods of identification and evaluation of results; furthermore, in the laboratories where attempts are now being made to modify the molecule of alkaloids of opium or otherwise synthesize drugs, in the search for an effective analgesic material without addiction liability, or very low in addiction liability, there is need for accurate identification

Identification of Drugs and Proof of Addiction 161

of drugs and proof of their addicting properties; the delicate chemistry involved in this type of research is beyond the purview of this book. It is sufficient to say that need for recognition and proof often exists and that there are now rather precise methods available for determining both the fact of addiction and the drugs used.

Identification procedures fall into two categories: first, the identification of drugs or substances suspected of being addicting drugs in body fluids; second, the identification of these substances outside the human body. The identification of drugs in a relatively concentrated form outside the body is much simpler and more reliable than their identification in body fluids. Proof of addiction involves showing that an individual uses drugs known to be addicting, that he uses them consistently over a period of time and that his behavior is or has been characteristic of habitual drug addicts. Since addicting substances are found in the body fluids only in minute concentrations, and since the diagnosis involves agreement by all parties on a definition of addiction, there is no laboratory test which will effectively establish addiction as compared to the use of a single or occasional doses of addicting drugs. No laboratory test will, by itself, prove addiction, though it will show the presence or absence of a given drug in the body at the time of the test. No single chemical test on body fluids will indicate the time of the dose or the intervals at which doses may be taken. Furthermore, chemical analyses of body fluids, while they may give rather accurate qualitative results, do not yield very accurate quantitative data. This chapter will present certain reasonably accurate criteria for establishing addiction, along with the techniques by which drugs can be identified when adequate laboratory facilities are available. Some of these tests are presumptive only and might not be sustained in the courts; however, the procedures for preparing evidence for court presentation are described in some detail.

Police officers, teachers, social workers, physicians, institutional personnel and others may have an interest in the identification of drugs and proof of addiction. The first advice to such people is to pass along any gross or crude observations they have been able to make to people technically trained and competent to render an opinion. Especially during times when a great deal of publicity attends addiction, and when sensationalism is rampant, there is a marked tendency for lay persons to suspect addiction in others. Irresponsible or badly informed newspaper writers give out criteria for the identification of addicts, or casual references in their articles are taken as reliable generalizations by the public. For example, teachers have been told that a constriction of the pupils of the eye indicates use of drugs; while it is true that opiates cause constrictions of the pupils, other medicines do so too, and the cause may be as simple as exposure to bright light; furthermore, there is a wide range in the size of normal pupils. Parents have been advised that a change in the mood of children or adolescents indicates addiction; while it is true that there may be abrupt changes of mood varying with the stage of euphoria or withdrawal in the case of some drugs, normal individuals, and especially adolescents, may also manifest abrupt shifts of mood.

When the press reports statements by excited witnesses to the effect that certain criminals seemed "doped" or "under the influence of some drug," these statements are sometimes interpreted to mean that addicts are consistently violent criminals on the one hand or, on the other, that criminals who operate with great calm are drugged. The general public, as a rule, entertains some very fantastic ideas of what the symptoms of addiction are, and these false beliefs often extend to responsible persons like police officers and even physicians, if they have not had the opportunity to observe various types and kinds of addicts. The newspapers in Louisville, Kentucky, once carried stories of a "dope scare" of considerable proportions in a large suburban high school; investigation by narcotics agents showed that there was simply a fad among high school youths of chewing or sucking toothpicks dipped in cinnamon; this reflected both hysteria on the part of the public and lack of sound information on the part of school officials.

At the same time, all those who deal with addicts must to some extent depend upon superficial observations, and observations made by untrained laymen are often useful in locating and dealing with the use of contraband drugs. Therefore, it is important to know what symptoms are significant—always keeping in mind

Identification of Drugs and Proof of Addiction 163

the fact that such observations must always be supported by other evidence, preferably objective evidence, in order to make a presumption of addiction. And, again, it is important to distinguish between medical addiction and criminal addiction, for the one may be humanitarian and useful, while the other is not. Before listing the symptoms characteristic of addiction, it should be emphasized that, despite sensational claims to the contrary, there are no criteria by which a narcotic addict may be recognized on

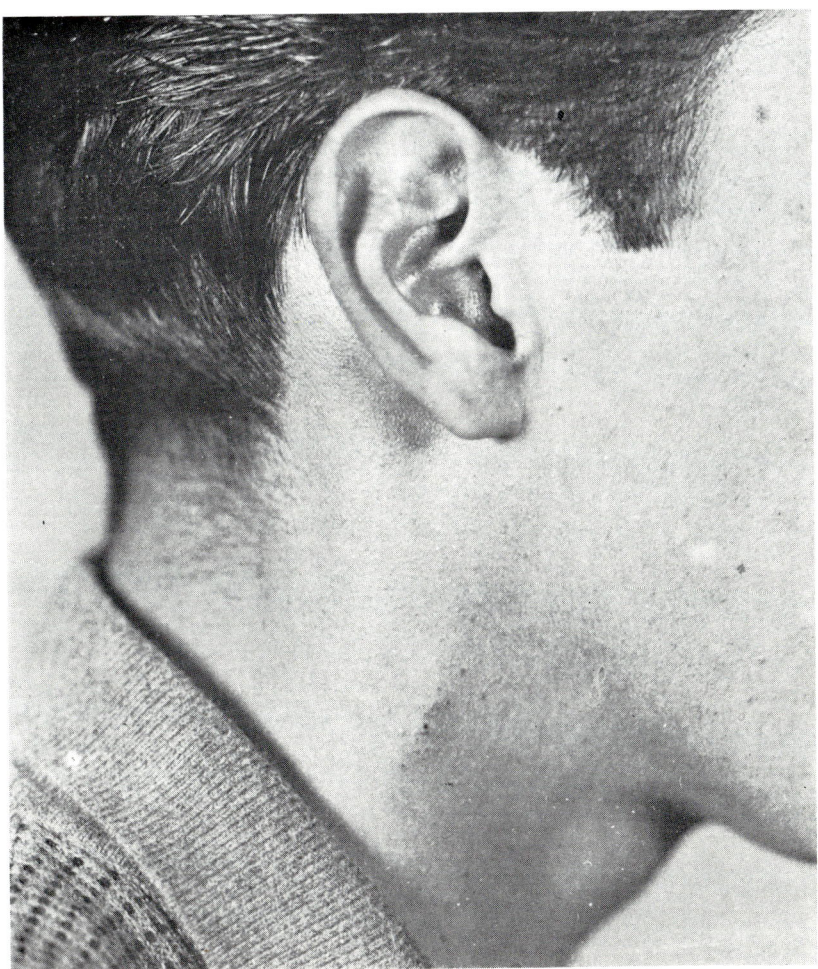

FIGURE 16. Needle marks over jugular vein of a Methedrine user.

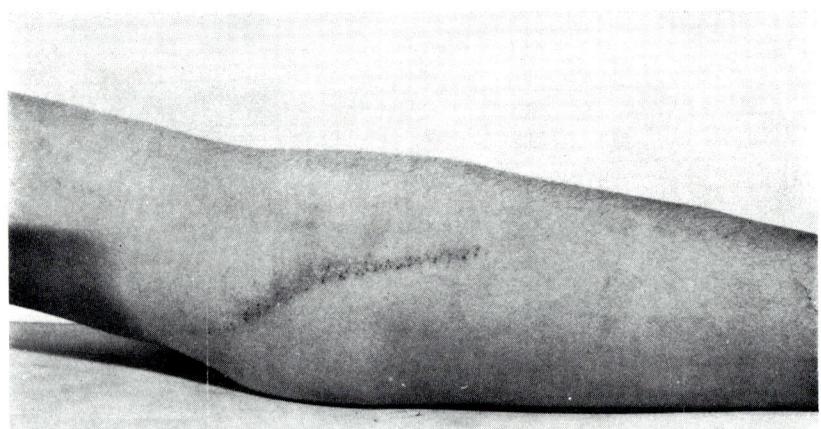

FIGURE 17. Needle marks over an arm vein of a heroin user.

sight; in fact, thorough medical examination may on occasion fail to reveal addiction, provided the addict is getting his regular dosage and does not show fresh abscesses or needle marks. There are cases known to the authors in which individuals used opiates or other addicting drugs discreetly over a period of many years without anyone suspecting that they were addicts.

The most significant signs which may (when supplemented by further objective evidence) indicate addiction are the following.

1. A statement by the individual that he is an addict.

2. The possession of addicting drugs (either medical or contraband) without adequate medical explanation.

3. A tendency on the part of the suspect to hide or conceal these drugs.

4. The presence of needle marks in the form of black or blue spots resembling tattooing; these may indicate skin-shooting and will usually appear on the arms and legs or even on the backs of the hands. Fresh needle punctures, sometimes topped by minute scabs or crusts, are especially significant (see Figs. 16, 17).

5. The presence of elongated scars (frequently of tattooed appearance) over the veins, especially those of the forearms (see Fig. 18), the insteps or the lower legs; however, these may have a medical explanation unrelated to addiction.

Identification of Drugs and Proof of Addiction

6. The presence of boil-like abscesses over the veins or near the sites where veins approach the surface (see Figs. 19, 20).

7. An appearance of drowsiness, sleepiness or lethargy ("on the nod"), especially if accompanied by a tendency to scratch the body as if itching. This sometimes indicates a slight overdose of opiates or their synthetic equivalents.

8. The tendency to develop withdrawal symptoms (described in detail in Chapter 6) if isolated completely and observed constantly for a period of twelve to twenty-four hours. (This applies only to the opiates and barbiturates.)

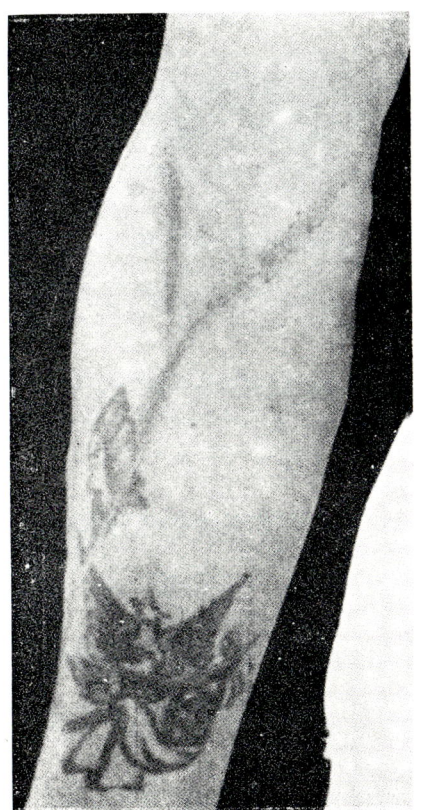

FIGURE 18. Characteristic V-shaped scars over the arm-veins of an addict who habitually injects narcotics into the veins. *Courtesy, U.S.P.H.S.*

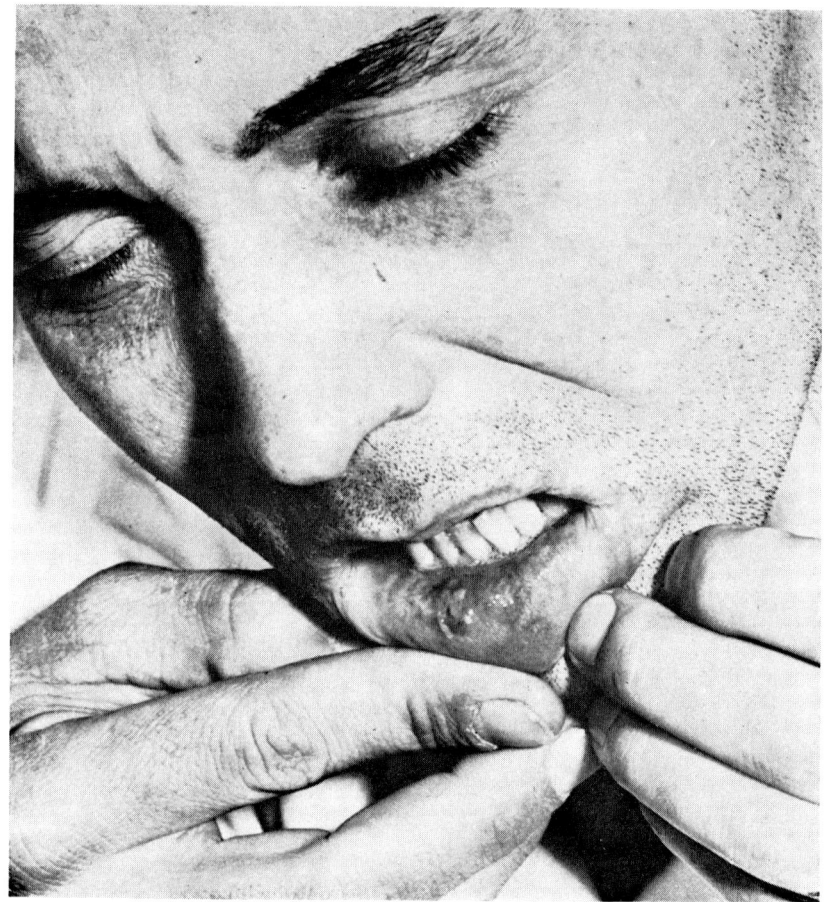

FIGURE 19. Ulcer following injections into lip vein.

9. Wide fluctuations in the size of the pupils of the eyes, with the pupil reaching a maximum of constriction immediately after the suspect may have taken an injection. (This applies only to opiates.) Amphetamines, marihuana, and LSD cause dilation.

10. The possession of equipment for smoking opium, unless, of course, this equipment has only a curiosity value or is owned by a collector. If it is freshly or currently used, the odor will be characteristic (see Figs. 6, 7).

11. The possession of hypodermic equipment, excepting those

Identification of Drugs and Proof of Addiction 167

persons with a legitimate need for such equipment, such as medical addicts or diabetics who must take regular injections of insulin. However, the legitimate user will invariably possess a standard medical syringe and needle, while the addict usually (but not always) tends to prefer the homemade syringes described elsewhere (see Fig. 4).

12. An appearance of intoxication, but with no odor of alcohol present; this may indicate the use of marihuana, chloral hydrate or the barbiturates. Marihuana *tends* to produce the hilarious type of intoxication, while the barbiturates *tend* to produce stupor when used in intoxicating quantities, but there are also all ranges of intoxication encountered. Persons who have recently smoked marihuana will have a characteristic "cubeb" or "weedy" odor of the breath. Marihuana tends to cause the impairment of judgment without impairing motor control in proportion, or at least to the extent that intoxicating doses of alcohol would impair motor control.

13. A tendency for the individual to sit looking off into space, known to young addicts as "goofing"; this may indicate the use of heroin or barbiturates, or both.

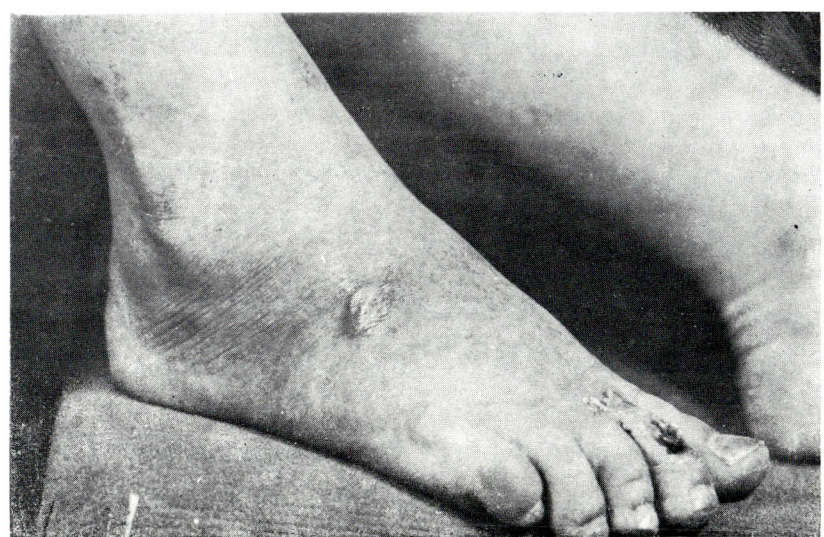

FIGURE 20. Abscess following injections into toe vein.

14. The possession of a *cooking spoon* with handle characteristically bent backward or a *cooker* made from a metal bottle cap with a wire handle; small glass vials are also sometimes used. They are all characteristically blackened from being held over a lighted match (see Fig. 4).

15. A tendency to laugh excessively or to laugh at things which others do not think funny; a tendency for the metaphors used to reflect a distortion of time and space. This may be indicative of mild intoxication on marihuana, but is not observed among opiate users.

16. A knowledge of the argot of the underworld narcotic addict (see Glossary). While some addicts who secure their drugs exclusively from medical sources never learn any of the argot, these addicts are decidedly in the minority; most addicts will know or respond to terms from the argot of the underworld addict, and especially to terms employed predominantly by users of the type of drug which the addict takes.

17. A tendency for the suspect to isolate himself at regular intervals (about four or five hours apart) in order to take hypodermic injections.

18. An obvious discrepancy between the amount of money the suspect earns and the amount he spends for the necessities of life; if he makes $200 a week and is always broke, with no obvious expenditures for necessities, he may be supporting a drug habit.

19. The tendency for a person who has previously been reliable to resort to thievery, embezzlement, forgery, prostitution, etc. This may indicate that he or she needs the large amounts of money necessary to support a drug habit.

20. Addicts, at least on the West Coast, have a high incidence of tattoos, frequently in the nature of juvenile gang identification marks, including daggers and mystical symbols on the hands. Particularly common are blue "beauty mark" dots on the face. In one study of an institutional population of 235 females, fifty-six facial tattoos and eighty others below the elbows and below the knees were counted.

21. The Nalline test. During research on the drug N-allylnormorphine at the Lexington Hospital several years ago, it was

Identification of Drugs and Proof of Addiction   169

shown that this drug (nalorphine, Nalline), administered hypodermically to opiate addicts, would immediately precipitate withdrawal distress expected in from twenty-four to forty-eight hours when opiates are abruptly withdrawn.

Subsequently, Dr. James Terry of the Alameda Rehabilitation Center, Pleasanton, California, developed and refined the Nalline test so that it is now a useful diagnostic device for opiate addiction. It is now widely accepted in law enforcement as well as in parole and probation supervision. More than 10,000 tests have been given in Alameda County, and a special law now provides for state-wide use of the test, which is also now being introduced in other sections of the country.

In one California study, parolees with a history of opiate use had 28 per cent fewer jail sentences and prison returns at the end of one year when they were assigned to Nalline testing programs rather than to regular parole caseloads without Nalline testing.

The usefulness of the Nalline test lies in the fact that a small dose (3 mg) will produce in opiate users a diagnostic dilation of the pupils of the eye, without precipitating the other drastic and even dangerous symptoms of withdrawal.

The size of the pupils is measured before and from fifteen to twenty minutes after the injection of Nalline. Comparison is made with black dots on a "pupillometer." If the pupils increase more than 1.25 mm in diameter, the recent use of opiates is indicated; if the diameter decreases by .25 or more or remains constant, the test is considered negative, although a "no change" indicates probable use. Demerol is an exception in that it never gives a reaction stronger than "no change." Eighty-five per cent of known addicts give positive readings within these limits, and 99 per cent show some dilation if the pupils are examined with a slit lamp. A deviation of pupil size from that observed in past tests makes the Nalline test more sensitive than observation of a single test. Any margin of error is almost always in favor of the subject, but the authors believe that false-positive results do occur very rarely.

When confronted with positive test results, addicts almost always admit use, show recent needle marks or both. In the rare

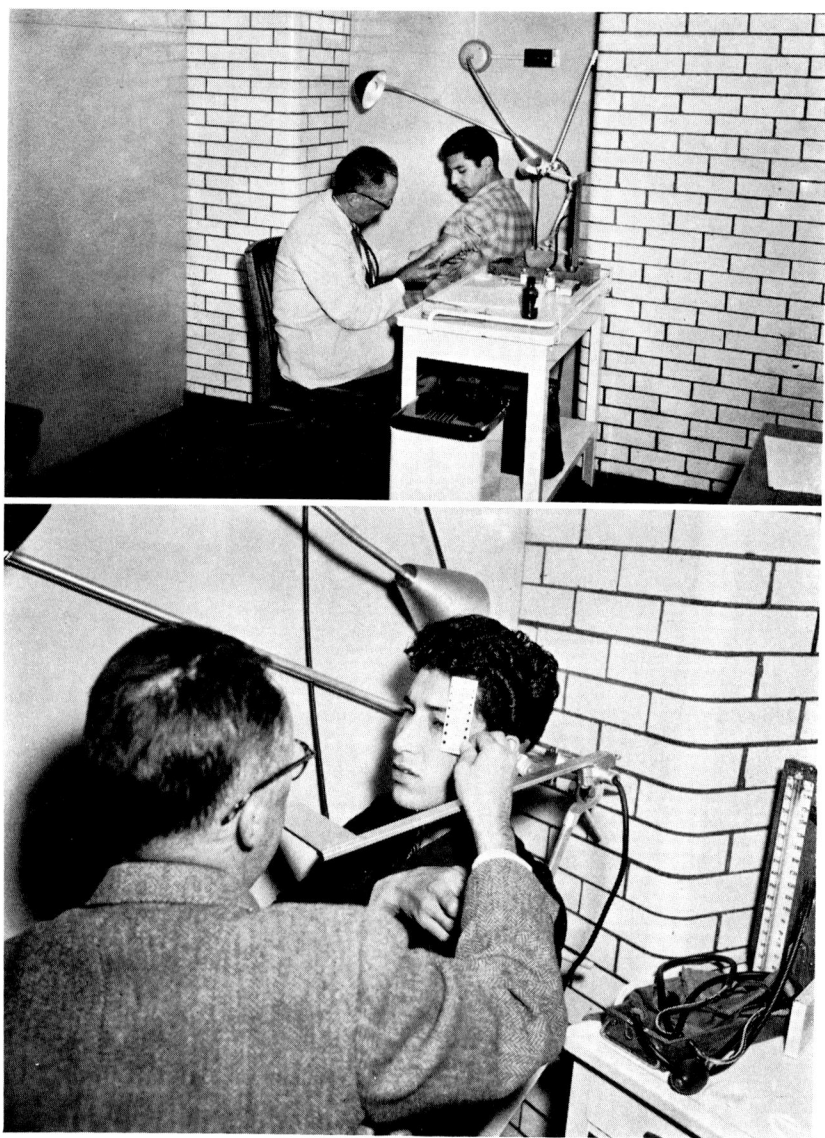

FIGURE 21. *(Above)* Injection of Nalline. *Courtesy Dr. James Terry, Alameda Co., Cal.*

FIGURE 22. *(Below)* Observation of Pupil Size Using Pupillometer. *Courtesy Dr. James Terry, Alameda Co., Cal.*

case in which there is no confirmatory evidence of addiction with a positive Nalline test, a supplementary urine test should be made.

California investigation found that a 3 mg dose of Nalline would give positive results after a subject had taken as little as 40 mg of morphine a day for one week prior to testing. Larger dosages of Nalline may show positive results after four 40 mg of morphine per day for two days. Two or three days after the last intake of opiates, the test is negative.

Some direct effects of Nalline are observed in from 3 to 5 per cent of the subjects. These may include respiratory depression, nausea, pallor, perspiration, dizziness or mental reactions, including confusion, anxiety, feelings of intoxication or fear of death. These temporary reactions should not be confused with withdrawal illness and do not suggest positive results. Although there have been more than 100,000 Nalline tests in California without a fatality, subjects being tested should be kept under close observation for about thirty minutes, and antidotes as well as resuscitative facilities should always be at hand. Those contemplating a Nalline testing program should refer to the literature on the subject and to the Department of Corrections in California.

For a discussion of the legal and constitutional issues involved (possible self-incrimination and cruel and inhuman punishment) the reader is referred to an article by Coleman.[30] Since Coleman's paper appeared, a California law specifically authorized the Nalline test for probationers and parolees. Some of the provisions of this law are:

    a. Only a licensed physician who holds a Federal Narcotics Stamp and who is approved by the local health officer may give the test;

    b. The test is to be given in accordance with a guide provided by the State Department of Public Health in conjunction with the State Bureau of Narcotic Enforcement;

    c. The test will be administered only upon request of the agency having supervision of the subject to which agency the test result must be furnished on a form provided by the State with copies to the Bureau of Narcotic Enforcement and to the local Health Officer;

d. The results shall not be open to public inspection.

22. Thin Film Chromatography urine test. The most practical urine test is by Thin Film Chromatography analysis.[8, 9, 31] This is an ingenious test of great accuracy, but occasional false positives are reported. Only 10 cc of urine are necessary, and about six hours are required to run the test, but, of course, the laboratory technician can run a large number of tests during the same period.

The test depends on the principle that different substances in solution have characteristic rates of climb up a porous surface. Laboratory procedures are described in the literature.

Morphine, Percodan, Dilaudid, metopon, Demerol, opium and cocaine can be specifically identified. Heroin is always converted to morphine in the body and reported in the test as morphine. Codeine is partially converted to morphine, so codeine use may be reported as codeine or morphine or both. Fortunately, Nalline appears as Nalline, so the validity of the urine test is not affected by a Nalline test preceding the urine test. A positive urine test confirms a positive Nalline test. A positive urine test after a negative Nalline test is significant because of the greater sensitivity of the former, which may reveal as little as 0.025 mg of a narcotic. The urine test becomes positive about thirty minutes after a single dose and remains positive up to thirty-six hours for a single dose or seventy-two hours after repeated doses, whereas the Nalline test may be positive as long as five days after the last dose of a series.

Because of the time differential, not all positive Nalline tests will be followed by positive urine tests, but a positive urine test is always confirmation of a positive Nalline test. The urine test can be adapted to detect amphetamines which addicts may take to mask the Nalline test or as substitutes for opiates by addicts on parole. The test may be useful in enforcing the "dangerous drug" laws as concerns the various amphetamines. The urine test, not requiring the services of a physician, may be useful in situations in which only occasional or small numbers of tests are required or for tests outside of usual office hours (see Fig. 23).

FIGURE 23

SUMMARY OF THE ADVANTAGES AND THE DISADVANTAGES OF THE PUPIL AND THE URINE TESTS

(From Parker et al.[31])

Pupil Test Advantages
(1) Has had wide use in California and is acceptable to the addict
(2) Is positive with many natural and synthetic narcotic drugs
(3) Result is immediately available
(4) Encourages contact of subject with parole officer and physician
(5) Is inexpensive

Pupil Test Disadvantages
(1) Involves administration of a drug with occasional unpleasant side-effects
(2) Must be administered by a physician at a specific location
(3) Surprise testing is frequently difficult to arrange and can be done only when a physician is available
(4) Is relatively insensitive depending on the drug
(5) Equivocal tests are common, leading to uncertainty in interpretation
(6) Congregation of a large number of narcotic users occurs in one place at the time of test
(7) Does not detect occasional codeine use

Chemical Test Advantages
(1) Detection of small amounts of narcotic is possible
(2) False positives or doubtful results unlikely to occur
(3) The most commonly abused narcotics are detected
(4) A physician, clinic and emergency equipment are not required
(5) Specimen can be obtained at any time by parole officer
(6) No need to assemble parolees in the same area
(7) By expansion to include Test B almost all of the abuse drugs used by addicts are detected (e.g., methadone, pethidine, amphetamine, methamphetamine and cocaine)

Chemical Test Disadvantages
(1) Both Tests A and B are required if most of the commonly used narcotic and dangerous drugs are to be detected
(2) Delay in obtaining results
(3) Greater unit cost (approximately 1.5 times) compared to the pupil test
(4) Loss of influence of physician in testing program
(5) Labor and inconvenience of collecting and handling urine specimens

In conclusion, a satisfactory anti-narcotic testing service should provide both the Nalline or Thin Layer Chromatography urine tests, although it should be emphasized that no one of these criteria is in itself indicative of addiction; when several are present, additional objective evidence should be collected in an effort to confirm or disprove addiction if this is important for any reason. On the whole, unless there is some justifiable reason for inquiring into the personal life of some other person, amateur sleuths and investigators should be discouraged from invading the privacy of individuals who might, by the manifestation of one or more of the above signs, be suspected of addiction. In fact, both of the authors might well manifest two or three of the signs enumerated above, yet neither of them has ever used drugs. Proof of drug addiction in the last analysis boils down to the establishment, through evidence, of the following facts: that the individual uses a drug of addiction and that he uses it regularly and compulsively. These facts are not always easy to demonstrate, as for instance in the cases of addicts who have successfully simulated illnesses requiring the application of medical opiates; the fact that many experienced and ethical physicians have been deceived by addicts only shows the difficulty of differentiating a true medical need from addiction.

THE IDENTIFICATION OF DRUGS

When it is necessary to identify drugs, either in pure or adulterated form outside the human body or in solution in body fluids, it is always wise to call on Federal or state laboratories which are especially equipped with facilities and personnel. These laboratories not only give accurate identification within very narrow limits, but frequently turn up additional evidence from the drugs themselves pointing to violations of the Federal or state narcotic laws. Specifically, interested persons are referred to the city toxicological laboratory usually found in large urban centers, often operating in conjunction with the coroner's office. State toxicological laboratories are usually both reliable and available. In addition, Federal laboratories, located on a district basis, are often available as adjuncts of the U. S. Alcohol Tax Unit. In addition to chemical tests, it is sometimes useful to make close observations of the form and appearance of the drug. It is valuable to record the appearance of an unknown drug, both gross and microscopic, the taste and the smell. However, the macroscopic or microscopic examination of crystalline materials will identify them only to the experienced observer. Crude opium has a characteristic appearance and smell—but again, only to the experienced observer. The alkaloids of opium all have a characteristically bitter taste—but so do many other alkaloids. The derivatives of opium

Identification of Drugs and Proof of Addiction 175

do not have any characteristic odor, and, if they are pure, all appear as white powders or tablets. Marihuana can easily be identified by appearance and burnings smell, as well as by chemical identification described later on. The odor of paraldehyde is so characteristic that it is easily identified by experienced persons. The barbiturates and amphetamines can often be tentatively identified by the characteristically colored capsules and tablets which the manufacturers use to prepare them for the retail trade, but absolute identification of specific barbiturates is difficult, except by infrared spectrophotometry or x-ray diffraction analysis; however, there are simple chemical tests which serve to identify the barbiturate family.

Also, it is always imperative to collect any drug bottles found in the immediate vicinity being investigated and to note their contents, labels, source, name of the prescribing physician, etc. These data may not only bear upon violations of the drug laws, but in some cases, such as acute poisoning from an unknown drug, may make possible an immediate and probable identification of the drug so that antidotes may be given. At the same time, it must be remembered that addicts often carry drugs in containers which are mislabeled or not labeled at all. When drugs are found concealed in body cavities, sewed into the clothing or hidden about the room or in a car, there is immediately a strong presumption that they may be illicit narcotics.

On the whole, however, gross examination is not very helpful unless it is supplemented by precise chemical testing. Following is a description of the tests and procedures which may be useful in identifying drugs and, in part, establishing the fact of addiction. When testing is being done with a view to using the results in court, special care must be taken to follow the instructions given later on in some detail.

LABORATORY TESTS FOR OPIUM, ITS DERIVATIVES AND SYNTHETIC EQUIVALENTS

Presumptive tests exist for the general identification of the alkaloids, to which group the opiates belong, as well as for the more positive identification of individual drugs of the opiate series.

Procedures also exist for the identification of most opiate drugs in the body fluids of drug users. Since most opiate drugs are white crystalline powders, macroscopic and even microscopic identification is not dependable, nor is there any characteristic odor of the purified derivatives of opium.

More or less pure forms and simple solutions can be analyzed relatively easily and without special equipment. Such identification is made by characteristic color reactions occurring when the powder or dried residue of the solution is brought into contact with a special chemical reagent. It is possible to differentiate between most drugs of the opiate group by using various combinations of these spot tests. This section therefore concerns itself with chemical testing procedures. The Physicians' Desk Reference[10] found in almost every doctor's office, has a useful section of colored photographs of various drugs in actual sizes.

TESTS FOR POWDERS AND SIMPLE SOLUTIONS

Following is a general nonspecific test for alkaloids known as *Mayer's*. This test gives positive reaction with most alkaloids, including cocaine, caffeine, strychnine, atropine and others, in addition to the opium alkaloids. It is useful as a field test in examining substances suspected of being opiates by eliminating nonalkaloid substances. Substances which give positive results must be examined further before positive identification can be made. *Reagent Used:* Mayer's reagent. *Preparation:* 13.55 gm mercuric chloride and 50 gm potassium iodide in water to make 1 liter. *Testing Procedure:* Take a pinch of the suspected powder or the residue of the solution evaporated to dryness, place it on a porcelain spot plate, apply one or two drops of the reagent and a drop of hydrochloric acid. An amorphous white or pale yellow precipitate occurs within a few seconds if the substance being examined is an alkaloid.

SPECIFIC TEST FOR OPIUM AND ITS DERIVATIVES

There is a group of tests giving characteristic color reactions which provide for the specific identification of opium and various drugs of the opiate series. Each test is generally known by the

Identification of Drugs and Proof of Addiction

name of the reagent used, that is, *Froehde, Marquis, Nitric Acid* and *Ferric Chloride*. The reagents are prepared as follows:

Froehde's solution as modified by Buckingham: 2.5 gm ammonium molybdate in 25 cc of concentrated sulfuric acid. Between uses the bottle containing this reagent should be sealed from the air with melted paraffin.
Marquis' solution: forty drops formaldehyde (40 per cent) in 60 cc of concentrated sulfuric acid.
Nitric Acid: Concentrated reagent grade.
Ferric Chloride: 10 per cent solution in water.

The procedures for carrying out these "spot" tests are as follows: If the opium is in crude or prepared form, it is ground up with a small amount of warm water. This aqueous extract must be carefully evaporated to dryness. Dry residues of aqueous extracts of opium, paregoric, tincture of opium (laudanum), powdered or granulated opium, Dover's Powder, Pantopon (reconstituted opium, 60 per cent morphine), may then be tested as opium according to Figure 24.

FIGURE 24

TABLE SHOWING SPOT TEST REACTIONS FOR OPIATES AND SYNTHETIC EQUIVALENTS

	Froehde	*Marquis*	*Nitric Acid*	*Ferric Chloride*
Opium*	Blue-violet	Red-violet	Red-orange	Blue-green
Morphine	Blue-violet	Red-violet	Red-orange	Blue-green
Heroin	Blue-violet	Red-violet	Green	O
Dilaudid	Blue-violet	Red-violet (slow)	Red-orange	Blue-green
Metopon	Blue-violet	Red-violet (slow)	O	Blue-green
Codeine	Olive-green	Red-violet	Weak red-orange	O
Dionin	Olive-green	Red-violet	Weak red-orange	O
Dicodide	Khaki→ green	Red-violet (slow)	Yellow (slow)	O
Eukodal	Greenish-brown	Brown-violet (slow)	Yellow	O
Dromoran	Prussian blue	Dirty brown	Red-orange	Yellow-green
Papaverine	Violet→ yellow → O	Violet→ red → orange	Yellow	O
Apomorphine	Green	Blue-violet	Violet→ red-orange	Red-orange

* Opium gives same reactions as morphine because morphine overshadows other constituents. See text for differentiation of morphine and opium.

Figure 24 shows the characteristic color obtained by each of the opiates listed according to the reagent used. It will be seen that various combinations of these tests provide for the differentiation of the opiates. For example, morphine and heroin both show the same color reaction to the Froehde and Marquis reagents, but the differential identification may be made by using nitric acid, which results in a red-orange color with morphine, but gives a green color with heroin. With ferric chloride, morphine shows a blue-green color, whereas heroin does not react with any color formation.

Testing Procedure: A very small pinch (a barely visible amount) of the drug or residue to be tested is put on a porcelain spot plate, and one drop of the indicated reagent is added. (Too large an amount of test material gives a color reaction too dark to read.) The characteristic color appears immediately unless otherwise indicated in the Figure. In using the Froehde reagent, the color must be read immediately because the reagent itself rapidly becomes blue on exposure to air. The color with the Marquis reagent increases in intensity up to one minute, and the reaction should be read within that period. It should be noted that in using the reagents according to the Figure, it is not possible to differentiate between opium and morphine, the former being in fact tested for its morphine content in order to make the identification. In the case of crude opium, of course, the gross appearance, texture and odor, in addition to the reaction, make the identification.

Prepared or refined opium may be distinguished from morphine by its gross appearance and by extracting codeine in accordance with the procedure outlined below, the codeine then being identified by appropriate spot tests. When codeine and morphine are both present, as in opium, the reaction from morphine, being of much greater concentration, determines the color reaction, any reaction from codeine being masked. If, after extraction, an unknown substance is determined to contain both morphine and codeine, the presumption is that it was opium.

A test has been described for meconic acid[1] which, when accompanied by a positive test for morphine, is presumptive of opium. It is strongly suggested that any person unfamiliar with the preparation and interpretation of these spot color reactions first become thoroughly familiar with the procedures and resultant colors by testing known pure substances until he is thoroughly familiar with the characteristic colors. If this precaution is observed, these identification procedures are quite reliable.

IDENTIFICATION OF SYNTHETIC EQUIVALENTS OF OPIATES

There are no characteristic color reactions for methadone and Demerol, the most common of the synthetic narcotics.

Demerol

Identification of powders or simple solutions. Demerol can best be identified by the crystals it forms with common reagents.[2]

Procedure: One drop of a 0.1 per cent solution of the test powder or 1:50 dilution of test material from a fluid ampule is placed on a microscope slide (magnification x 100). One drop of the appropriate reagent is then added. With saturated picric acid, feathery rosettes are obtained. If the slide is roughened by scratching, these crystals will appear in X-shaped figures. With potassium-dichromate-hydrochloric acid (5 per cent $K_2Cr_2O_7$ in HCl 50 per cent by volume), delicate yellow needles in sheaf formation are obtained. Scratching the slide does not affect their form. With 20 per cent potassium iodide, very long needles, singly or in sheaves, are slowly formed. If the slide is scratched, short blunt rods of uniform length appear. Excellent illustrations appear in the Levine reference noted above. If the article is not available, practice slides with known Demerol solutions are suggested.

Methadone

Identification of powders or simple solutions. Determination is most easily accomplished by characteristic crystals formed with various reagents: *Potassium Ferrocyanide* (5 per cent aqueous solution). The substance to be identified should be prepared in about 1:50 dilution. A sample drop and a reagent drop are placed next to each other on a microscope slide. The two drops are allowed to flow together. After about one minute, the slide is examined under the microscope (magnification x 100). Crystals appear first as bundles of needle-like rods curving outward at the end, resembling sheaves of grain. Later, rosettes of plates appear.[3]

Bromine Water (Saturated). The drug should be prepared in 1:200 to 1:1000 dilution. One drop of saturated bromine water is placed on the slide next to one drop of test material plus one drop of dilute HCl. The drops are then permitted to flow together. Numerous small crystals of various shapes appear: short matched plates; bow-knots; and rosettes of narrow plates. The more dilute bromine water described in the Watson and Bowman article[3] is less satisfactory as a reagent.

Potassium Bromobromide Reagent. (Two gm of potassium bromide plus 10 cc of saturated bromine water.) One drop of test solution (1:200) is placed on a slide next to a drop of the reagent. The two drops are then drawn together with a glass rod. Since crystals form slowly, a cover glass is used to prevent evaporation. Crystals and rosettes appear. The individual crystals are flat with key-like structures at each end.[4] For illustrations of the crystals, see the reference articles. If references are unavailable, the test samples can be compared with known methadone crystals.

TESTS FOR OPIATES IN BODY FLUIDS AND COMPLEX SOLUTIONS

See paragraph 22, page 172 for discussion of Thin Film Chromatography, a simple and reliable test for opiates in urine and other solutions. The article by Parker, *et al.*, describes the technique of this test.[31]

CERTIFICATION OF LABORATORY PROCEDURES FOR COURT PURPOSES

If a laboratory analyst anticipates the possibility of being called upon to testify in court regarding identification of drugs in either unknown drug samples or in body fluids, special precautions must be taken if the evidence is to be accepted. Every step of collection or receipt and analysis of the specimen should be witnessed by the analyst and a second party. Seals should be placed on envelopes or bottles containing specimens, which seals are subsequently broken only in the presence of two persons when a portion of the specimen is removed for analysis, after which the envelope or other container is resealed. An account of the time the seal is broken, the amount of specimen removed and the time the container is resealed is placed on the container and signed by both the analyst and the witness. If possible, the same person should witness each step of the procedure.

The specimen container and any unused portion of the specimen, as well as the analyst's records, must be preserved for presentation in court as evidence. If a positive result is obtained, the analysis should be repeated at least once or preferably twice. At the Lexington hospital, when body fluids are being examined, two additional specimens are analyzed if the first proves positive.

In the collection of urine for analysis, the analyst must be prepared to show beyond all possible doubt that a specimen was actually from the subject named and could not have possibly been contaminated by the use of unclean laboratory equipment or confused with other specimens. Actual passage of the urine specimen should be observed by two persons who are able to identify the subject and to swear that no addition of any kind was made to the sample and that contamination or substitution did not occur. Specimen bottles should be closed with sealed screw tops which should be removed only in the presence of the subject as well as the witnesses.

Specimen bottles should then be sealed or closed in a heavy envelope, preferably of the locked type, sealed and signed by both witness and the subject (if he can be persuaded to sign), giving the time of passage and stating the name of the person from whom the specimen was obtained. The sample must be carried to the laboratory by one of the witnesses, and the analyst should acknowledge receipt of the container, noting thereon the time and the name of the messenger. This receipt should also be signed by a second witness on the laboratory staff. A case is known to the authors where laboratory evidence was thrown out of court because it was not possible to prove beyond all possible doubt that the laboratory glassware was clean and that it had not been possible for someone in the laboratory to have confused or substituted specimens during the analysis. There was also some confusion in the testimony as to how the specimen bottle was closed and delivered to the laboratory.

LABORATORY TESTS FOR BARBITURATES

It is not easily possible in the laboratory to distinguish one barbiturate from another. However, there is a rather simple qualitative test for the identification of the barbiturates as a group, and there is a satisfactory procedure for the extraction of barbiturates from the urine and other solutions so that the qualitative test can be applied. Turfitt[11] has published a scheme for differentiation.

QUALITATIVE TEST FOR BARBITURATES IN POWDER FORM AND SIMPLE SOLUTIONS (KOPPANYI ET AL.[12])

Reagents Used: Cobaltous actetate, 1 per cent in absolute methyl alcohol;
Isopropylamine, 5 per cent in absolute methyl alcohol.

Procedure

The capsule or coating of the suspected powder is removed, and a pinch is dissolved in 2 cc of absolute methyl alcohol. If a solution is being tested, a pinch of the residue is obtained after evaporating the solution to dryness. After 0.1 cc of cobaltous acetate is added, the solution is shaken, and 0.6 cc of isopropylamine is added. The appearance of a pinkish color indicates the presence of barbiturates. The color is read at about five minutes, after which time it will fade.

TESTS FOR BARBITURATES IN URINE AND IN COMPLEX SOLUTIONS

Reagents Used: Sodium bicarbonate U.S.P., powdered;
Ethylacetate, C.P.;
Cobaltous acetate, 1 per cent in absolute methyl alcohol;
Isopropylamine, 5 per cent in absolute methyl alcohol.

The reaction described above using cobaltous acetate is preceded by extraction: 25 cc of urine is saturated with sodium bicarbonate, filtered and extracted with three 25 cc portions of ethyl acetate, each in a separatory funnel, for three minutes each. At the end of each extraction, the funnel is swirled to permit sodium bicarbonate to settle and be drawn off. The combined extracts of ethyl acetate are filtered through a retentive filter paper, such as C.S.&S. No. 602 into a flask, and evaporated to dryness. The residue is dissolved in 2 cc of absolute methyl alcohol and examined for color as in the Koppanyi test above. If the solution is clear, the next step of sublimation can be omitted. If the solution has a straw color, it is necessary to place it in a sublimation tube and sublime it at 300° C. The crystals are washed from the finger of the sublimation tube with 2 cc of absolute methyl alcohol into a 15 cc conical-shaped centrifuge tube. If the amount of barbiturate present is very small, it may be lost during the sublimation process. Unless the extraction residue is very highly colored, the sublimation process is omitted in the Lexington hospital laboratory.

Liquid pharmaceutical preparations of barbiturates are also tested in this manner. It has *not* been possible to extract sodium alurate, Seconal or pentobarbital from the urine, after its administration, by using this method.

At the Lexington hospital, no successful method for the qualitative analysis for barbiturates in blood has been found. No successful quantitative analysis for barbiturates in urine and other solutions has been used. Several methods have been advanced, none of which has proved completely satisfactory in the laboratory available to the authors. Since these methods all require special apparatus, including an ultraviolet spectrophotometer, and trained personnel, we merely offer several references.[13, 14, 15, 16, 17]

The minimum time necessary to accomplish this extraction and test for barbiturates is five hours; if possible, the evaporation phase should be allowed to proceed spontaneously overnight, but it can be shortened somewhat by the application of gentle heat. It will be seen that the procedure requires approximately the same amount of time as the test for opiates in body fluids, and frequently both tests are carried on simultaneously. As with the tests for opiates, this test should be performed by a skilled technician, preferably by one experienced in this particular procedure. A positive reaction should be confirmed by running at least one additional specimen. There is no simple urine test for barbiturates comparable to the Thin Film Chromatography analysis. Blood analysis is the best laboratory test to confirm the use of barbiturates.

CHLORAL HYDRATE QUALITATIVE TEST (GETTLER)[18]

Procedure: To 1 cc of solution, six drops of a saturated aqueous solution of resorcinol and 1 cc of saturated sodium carbonate solution are added. A rich rose to ruby-red color results. This is allowed to stand for thirty minutes, then 10 cc of water are added. A green fluorescence results when viewed with the light source at the back of the observer, and the specimen held against a glossy background. Observations should be made within thirty minutes after the addition of water.

Chloral Hydrate in Body Fluids

·After administration of the drug, it remains in the blood stream for several days. It may be determined by the method of Adams.[19] A small fraction appears unchanged in the urine, but most of it is excreted in the conjugated form within eighteen hours after ingestion. A nonspecific test, invalid when glycosuria is present, is the reduction of Fehling's solution by the conjugate.

Quantitative Assay: Directions for quantitative determination can be found in any edition of the Pharmacopoeia of the United States.

PARALDEHYDE

This drug is most easily distinguished by its characteristic (fusel oil) odor. By warming it with several drops of concentrated sulfuric acid, it is converted into acetaldehyde, recognizable by its unpleasant odor.

BROMIDES

Inorganic

Sodium, potassium, ammonium and zinc bromides, singly or in combination (Triple Bromides, Nervine, Neurosine, Bromoseltzer, etc.), respond to tests for inorganic bromides.[20]

Procedure: Silver nitrate solution containing a little nitric acid is added to a solution of the powder to be tested. A white precipitate indicates chloride, a pale yellow one bromide or iodide. The solution is centrifuged and the supernatant fluid removed. The precipitate, if bromide, will be soluble with difficulty in ammonium carbonate solution, which distinguishes it from silver chloride, which is easily soluble.

Organic

If bromide is incorporated into an organic molecule or combined with organic substances, the compound must be ignited with sodium carbonate.

Procedure: Place the powder or dried material in a crucible with an equal amount of anhydrous sodium carbonate. With a Bunsen burner, the crucible is heated to red heat until the mixture is melted. It is then allowed to cool. This will convert the bromide to sodium bromide, and it can be tested as described above for inorganic bromides.

Bromides in Blood

Qualitative tests are not significant, since blood may show up to 75 mg per cent of sodium bromide without indicating bromidism.

Quantitative Test for Bromides in Blood[20, 21]

The color produced by the reaction of bromide with gold chloride is measured colorimetrically.

Reagents Used: Gold chloride, 0.5 per cent;
Trichloracetic acid, 5.0 per cent;
Sodium chloride-trichloracetic acid solution:
To 0.12 gm NaCl in a 100 cc cylinder add 70 cc of the trichloracetic acid. Dilute to 100 cc;
Stock standard: An accurate 1 per cent solution of NaBr (1 cc = 10 mg);
Dilute standard: Pipette 5 cc of the stock standard into a 100 cc volumetric flask. Dilute to the mark with the sodium-chloride-trichloracetic acid mixture (1 cc = 0.5 mg);

Procedure:

1. In an Erlenmeyer flask, 16 cc of trichloracetic acid solution is shaken, while 4 cc of serum is slowly added. After it is well mixed, it is allowed to stand for thirty minutes, and is then filtered.
2. Ten cc of clear filtrate is poured into a test tube.

3. Four cc of dilute standard is poured into another test tube, and 6 cc of sodium chloride-trichloracetic acid mixture is added.

4. Eight cc of dilute standard is poured into a third tube, and 2 cc of the same diluting fluid is added.

5. One cc of gold chloride solution is added to each tube and the contents mixed.

6. The observer should compare the resulting color in the visual colorimeter with the nearest standard.

Calculation: Using the equivalent of 2 cc of blood serum, the first standard is equivalent to 100 mg and the second standard to 200 mg of sodium bromide per 100 cc. The standard is set at 10; then mg per cent of sodium bromide is:

$$\frac{1000}{\text{Reading of unknown}}$$

or

$$\frac{2000}{\text{Reading of unknown}}$$

Note: Normal: up to 75 mg per cent, because the blank for this method is high, owing to the faintness of the color at low concentrations.

If the sodium bromide exceeds 250 mg per cent, the test should be repeated with smaller amounts of sample.

MARIHUANA

Walton[22] gives an extensive bibliography of references concerning tests for recognition and determination of various stages of growth and activity of the cannabis plant.

Chemical Test

The Federal Bureau of Narcotics uses the following test for marihuana, which is a modification of the Beam test.[23]

A test tube is filled to a depth of about one inch with the suspected material. If necessary, crush the material to a coarse powder. Marihuana reagent (100 cc of 95 per cent ethyl alcohol and 2 gm of potassium hydroxide) is poured over the material until it is covered. About one fourth teaspoonful of Darco (activated charcoal) is added, and the tube is shaken and the mixture filtered into a second test tube. A violet color in the filtrate denotes the presence of marihuana.

For a satisfactory response to this test, the material should be fairly fresh. It may be dry, but some of the green color of the fresh plant should be present. After about two months, when the plant turns brown, the reaction is equivocal. Faint violet overtones in a brown background may appear in three to five minutes, after which fading occurs. When the material is fresh, a brilliant lasting violet color is produced immediately, even with very small quantities of the drug.

Microscopic Examination

The microscopic appearance of marihuana is very useful in identification. Small fragments of leaf such as those extracted from a marihuana cigarette will suffice for microscopic examination.

The gross appearance of the plant has been shown previously. Detailed descriptions of the plant are given by Walton[22] and by the U. S. Treasury Department Bureau of Narcotics.[23]

A piece of leaf is moistened and placed on a slide and flattened under a cover glass. At a magnification of x 100, non-glandular hairs with pointed ends may be observed. These appear green and fresh when the leaf is from a newly plucked plant, but are somewhat desiccated in older specimens. On addition of a drop or two of concentrated hydrochloric acid, effervescence can be noted as the acid reacts with the characteristic calcium carbonate deposits in the leaf. These microscopic tests have been used effectively on specimens up to eight years old, provided any leaf fragments are still uncrushed. Further descriptions of the microscopic appearance of the marihuana leaf are given by Turner[24] and Merrill.[25]

No test is known by the authors which is satisfactory for application to urine or other body fluids to indicate the introduction of marihuana into the human body.

COCAINE

Test for Powders and Simple Solutions

A good tentative preliminary test for the powder or evaporated residue is to place a granule on the tip of the tongue. Cocaine produces temporary local anesthesia.

A small portion of the powder or dried residue is dissolved in two drops of dilute hydrochloric acid. One drop is put on a microscope slide, and one drop of 5 per cent gold chloride solution is added. Characteristic crystals are formed at 1:1000 dilution and appear as a series of fine projections at right angles to *one* side of a long axis.[20]

BENZEDRINE AND OTHER AMPHETAMINES

Tests for Powder and Simple Solutions

One to 2 mg of powder or residue from evaporated solution is put on a microscope slide. One drop of 5 per cent aqueous gold chloride is stirred in, and the cover slip is put on preparatory to examination under the microscope (magnification x 100). Benzedrine crystals are distinct yellow square plates of various sizes.[26]

Thin Film Chromatography, paragraph 22, page 172, is a good test for amphetamines in urine and other solutions.

PEYOTE AND MESCALINE

Tests for Powder or Simple Solutions

The best method of identification of mescaline is by conversion to the picrates and the determination of its melting point, 217°-220° C.[27] Unfortunately, this is a fairly long process.

Potassium hydroxide is added to the test material to pH 9, and it is extracted twice with an equal volume of toluene-isobutyl alcohol (1:1) mixture. The solvent is evaporated *in vacuo*. The resulting brown residue is treated with hot water, and the undissolved material is filtered off. The mescaline will be in the filtrate, which is then evaporated and dried (both processes *in vacuo*) and dissolved in 3 cc of toluene. To this is added 0.1 cc picric acid (2 per cent in chloroform) and 3 cc of chloroform. This mixture is filtered and the crystals are retained. They can be purified by repeatedly dissolving in acetone and precipitation with petroleum ether, and the melting point determined for identification.

To test crude material suspected of being peyote, it is ground in a mortar. Potassium hydroxide is added, and the procedure described above is followed.

Test for Body Fluids

A good but rather technical extraction method is presented by Woods et al.[28] The extract can be used for qualitative or quantitative determination of mescaline. For qualitative identification, convert to the picrate as described above. For quantitative estimation, the drug is combined with a dye and read on a Beckman spectrophotometer.

Woods and his co-workers have used this method to determine mescaline in blood and urine of dogs[29] at Michigan and human subjects at the Lexington hospital. Some of the mescaline is metabolized, but he removed from 28 to 56 per cent of the administered dose in twenty-four hours in humans. Small amounts appear in blood up to four hours. It has not yet been determined whether mescaline will appear in urine after ingestion of peyote buttons. The presumption is that it would so appear, since Woods (personal communication) has isolated mescaline from ground peyote buttons. He found that it comprised 30 per cent of the total alkaloid.

LSD

Thin Film Chromatography and the spectrograph will detect this drug in concentrated form but can not be used for testing body fluids. Early reports indicate that vitamin B_3 may act as an antagonist just as Nalline does for opiates.

REFERENCES

1. AUTENREITH, W. (translated by WARREN, W. H.): *Laboratory Manual for the Detection of Poisons and Powerful Drugs* (6th American ed.). Philadelphia, Blakiston, 1928.
2. LEVINE, J.: Microchemical identification of Demerol. *Industrial and Engineering Chemistry,* Analytical Edition, *16*:408 (June), 1944.
3. WATSON, R. C., and BOWMAN, M. I.: Microchemical identification of Amidone. *Journal of the American Pharmaceutical Association,* Scientific Edition, *38*:369 (July), 1949.

4. SCHULDINER, J. A.: Identification of Amidone. *Analytical Chemistry,* 21:298 (Feb.), 1949.
5. TERRY, J. G., and BRAUNSOELLER, F. L.: Nalline: An aid in detecting narcotic users. *California Medicine,* 85:299, 1956.
6. HURLEY, C. T.: Anti-narcotic testing: A physician's point of view. *Federal Probation,* June 1963.
7. ELLIOTT, H. W., et al.: Comparison of the Nalorphine test and urinalysis in the detection of narcotic use. *Clinical Pharmacology and Therapeutics,* 5:405, 1964.
8. COCHIN, J., and DALY, I. W.: Rapid identification of analgesic drugs in urine with thin-layer chromatography. *Experientia,* 18:294, 1962.
9. TRUTER, E. V.: *Thin Film Chromatography.* New York, Interscience Publishers, 1963.
10. *Physicians' Desk Reference.* Oradel, New Jersey, Medical Economics, Inc. Published annually.
11. TURFITT, G. E.: Identification of clinically important barbiturates. *Quarterly Journal of Pharmacy and Pharmacology,* 21:1 (Jan.), 1948.
12. KOPPANYI, T., DILLE, J., MURPHY, W. S., and KROP, S.: Studies on barbiturates. Contributions to methods of barbiturate research. *Journal of the American Pharmaceutical Association,* 23:1074, 1934.
13. BORN, G. V. R.: The quantitative determination of barbiturates in tissues by ultraviolet absorption spectrophotometry. *Biochemical Journal,* 44(4):501, 1949.
14. RAVENTOS, J.: Method for the estimation of barbituric and thiobarbituric acids in biological materials. *British Journal of Pharmacology and Chemotherapy,* 1:210 (Sept.), 1946.
15. GOULD, T. C., and HINE, C. H.: A modified ultraviolet spectrophotometric method for quantitative determination of barbiturates. *Journal of Laboratory and Clinical Medicine,* 34:1462 (Oct.), 1949.
16. GOLDBAUM, L. R.: An ultraviolet spectrophotometric procedure for the determination of barbiturates. *Journal of Pharmacology and Experimental Therapeutics,* 94:68 (Sept.), 1948.
17. WALKER, J. T., FISHER, R. S., and McHUGH, J. J.: Quantitative estimation of barbiturates in blood by ultraviolet spectrophotometry. I. Analytical method. *American Journal of Clinical Pathology,* 18:451 (June), 1948.
18. GETTLER, A. O.: The detection of small amounts of chloral in

the presence of chloroform and formalin in embalming fluid. *Proceedings of the Society for Experimental Biology and Medicine, 16*:110 (Apr.), 1919.
19. ADAMS, W. L.: The determination of chloral hydrate, chloroform and related substances in blood. *Journal of Pharmacology and Experimental Therapeutics, 74*:11 (Jan.), 1942.
20. SCOTT, W. W.: *Standard Methods of Chemical Analysis.* New York, D. Van Nostrand Company, Inc., 1925.
21. DIETHELM, O.: On Bromide Intoxication. *Journal of Nervous and Mental Diseases, 71*:151 (Aug.), 1930.
22. WALTON, R. P.: *Marihuana, America's New Drug Problem.* Philadelphia, Lippincott, 1938.
23. BUREAU OF NARCOTICS, U. S. TREASURY DEPARTMENT: *Marihuana, Its Identification.* Washington, D. C., U. S. Government Printing Office, 1938.
24. TURNER, R. F.: *Forensic Science and Laboratory Technics.* Springfield, Illinois, Charles C Thomas, Publisher, 1949.
25. MERRILL, F. T.: *Marihuana, the New Dangerous Drug.* Washington, D. C. Opium Research Committee, Foreign Policy Association, Inc., 1938.
26. KEENAN, G. L.: Crystal Tests for Benzedrine. Report on Microchemical Tests for Alkaloids and Synthetics. *Journal of the Association of Official Agricultural Chemists, 25*:830 (Oct.), 1942.
27. SALOMAN, K., GABRIO, B. W., and THALE, T.: A study of mescaline in human subjects. *Journal of Pharmacology and Experimental Therapeutics, 95*:455 (Apr.), 1949.
28. WOODS, L. A., COCHIN, J., FORNEFELD, E. J., MCMAHON, F. G., and SEEVERS, M. H.: The estimation of amines in biological materials with critical data for cocaine and mescaline. *Journal of Pharmacology and Experimental Therapy, 101*(2):188, 1951.
29. COCHIN, J., WOODS, L. A., and SEEVERS, M. H.: The absorption, distribution, and urinary excretion of mescaline in the dog. *Journal of Pharmacology and Experimental Therapy, 101*(2): 205, 1951.
30. COLEMAN, A. H.: Nalline: Some legal implications of its use. *Journal of Forensic Sciences, 3*:4 (Oct.), 1958.
31. PARKER, KENNETH D., CRIM, M., HINE, C. H., NOMOF, N., and ELLIOTT, H. W.: Urine screening techniques employed in the detection of users of narcotics and their correlation with the Nalorphine Test. *Journal of Forensic Sciences, 11*:No. 2 (April), 1966.

Chapter 6

TREATMENT OF NARCOTIC ADDICTION

DRUG ADDICTION AS A SOCIAL DISEASE

ALTHOUGH we commonly speak of drug addiction as a disease, it is more properly a symptom of disease which is rooted in social and economic conditions that tend to create dissatisfaction, unhappiness, conflict, tension and strife in the minds and souls of human beings. When the fundamental emotional stability and equilibrium of the individual is not equal to these environmental stresses, some persons consciously or unconsciously seek the psychological or chemical means which may be available for a measure of relief, even though that relief is overshadowed by involvement in greater conflicts and tensions, which may be of a permanent nature.

Psychological relief may occur with the onset of neurosis or psychosis; that is, there may be a more or less complete withdrawal from reality or the development of a psychoneurotic state in which motives, responses and values are disturbed and rearranged in order to provide the emotionally sick individual with more acceptable explanations of his deficiencies. Psychoneurotic escape mechanisms may be manifested by the multiple physical complaints of the hypochondriac, the compulsive actions or the obsessions which characterize the psychoneurotic or in periodic amnesia or conversion hysteria; here there is major withdrawal from normal function without loss of contact with reality.

If chemical means are at hand and the individual becomes cognizant of their action, even accidentally, he may find refuge in the lulling and deadening curtain which drugs of the narcotic series lower over the facts of reality, or he may seek the effects of the stimulant drugs, which temporarily seem to increase his ability to meet and overcome his difficulties. Eventually, victims of addiction become totally preoccupied with supporting their habit and live in the inner world which is fashioned more to their liking than the real world all about them.

Superficially, at least, there is nothing mysterious or obscure about the nature of the conflicts and tensions which appear to influence the narcotic addict. We all live with them continually. Sometimes they are the frustrations induced by poverty and unhappy homes; sometimes they are tensions arising from having too much money to spend; then, again, there are frictions and repressions when certain racial or religious groups are segregated or discriminated against; sometimes unsolved problems in developing satisfactory sexual relations are used to explain addiction. It is the opinion of the authors that one cannot underestimate the effect of the general deterioration of character, the shifting of what should be individual responsibility to some vague authority, the imperfections of our school system in developing people who know how to live richly and fully and the general unrest and human dissatisfaction which besets a civilization wherein human beings are, to a large extent, losing touch with the cycles of nature, the sun and the soil, and substituting for fundamentals a very synthetic way of life. It is no accident that narcotic addiction flourishes best in the large urban centers.

As has been said, most of us live with similar tensions and adjust to them; the addict or the potential addict does not or cannot make the adjustment. Therefore he uses drugs in an effort to achieve "normalcy"—that is, to make up the difference between what he has and what he needs to live with himself and with others.

A very small proportion of adult addicts are essentially normal people addicted accidentally by medical prescriptions during illness. A somewhat larger proportion of addicts seem to be essentially normal individuals inadvertently addicted because of association with some addict friend or, less frequently than generally believed, a peddler.

Treatment of these emotionally normal accidental addicts may be relatively simple, requiring only an initial treatment without subsequent relapse—without the necessity for retreatment which is characteristic of the chronic addict. The chronic relapsing addict possessing an addiction-prone personality, which type makes up the preponderance of addicts, is the one with which we are chiefly concerned in this chapter. However, we are dealing with human beings and not with absolutes. It is not a question of black and white. There is the intermediate group with minor personality difficulties who, although tending toward addiction of one kind or another as a refuge, may, with proper instructions and guidance, be able to understand that the disadvantages of addiction as an adjustment mechanism far outweigh its transient advantages. Many of this borderline group can be reclaimed.

PREVENTION OF ADDICTION

As the late Dr. P. O. Wolff of the World Health Organization said: "It is scarcely a paradox to say that the best way to be cured of addiction is not to become an addict, and the best weapon against addiction is the possession of a normal psyche."[1] This places the emphasis on psychiatry and mental hygiene for the elimination of the addiction-prone individual from our population. Others place emphasis elsewhere, saying: "Prevent the addict from getting his drug and he will cure himself and, if unable to get the drug, he will stay cured."[2]

Truly, drug addiction results from the interaction of the addicting drug and the human being who desires the drug. Eliminate the drug completely and ergo—addiction stops. Eliminate the desire for the drug and addiction stops, except, of course, for a few individuals who become accidentally addicted in the course of an illness.

While we do not as yet know all the answers to the question of the prevention of addiction, we believe that there are certain fundamental procedures which, if followed out simultaneously, will reduce addiction considerably. These involve, first of all, an education program designed to reach all potential addicts, but concentrated on youth in the schools. (This has been explained in some detail in Chapter 9.) The authors believe that if people are conditioned early against the dangers of drugs, they are not so vulnerable to the persuasion of some addict or a peddler who has a selfish interest in getting them to use drugs. However, there is some disagreement on this point. For instance, as late as 1951 a resolution opposing education was recommended by the United Nations Commission on Narcotic Drugs. However, the Economic and Social Council did not approve the recommendation. For years, the Federal Bureau of Narcotics opposed narcotic information programs in the schools and to the general public on the grounds that such programs would cause more addiction by arousing curiosity than was prevented. However, the official attitude now is unquestionably in favor of such education and information. Almost without exception, areas where addiction is a serious problem now have preventive educational programs in the schools.[23, 34]

The second procedure involves vigorous law enforcement, with state and local enforcement agencies concentrating on smaller individual violations of the law, thereby freeing more of the rather limited resources of the Federal Bureau of Narcotics for investigation and prosecution of large-scale smuggling and wholesale operations.

The third method for reducing addiction is attack on the international production of narcotics through the United Nations; this body has already made notable progress in the formulation of international treaties, but there is still the knotty problem of how to limit opiate production to medical needs without seriously disrupting the economies of those countries where opiates constitute a major export product. Further development of such synthetics as methadone and Demerol may also eventually supplant opiates partially or even totally, with consequent forcing of the natural opiates into the contraband trade as the only profitable outlet. Until a pain-relieving drug is developed which is not addicting, physicians should use great caution and prescribe opiates only where absolutely needed for the relief of severe pain. Opiates should not be used for mild pain or to induce sleep.[3, 4]

Fourth, there must be a gradual and long-range attack on the social and economic conditions which break down the individual personality and bring about the substitution of drugs and alcohol for the healthy functioning of the individual within his culture.

The best treatment of the individual addict is prevention, because addiction spreads from one victim to others. Most addicts report that they became addicted from association with other drug users.

Of course, the ideal answer to the problem of medical addiction would be a drug as pain relieving as morphine or heroin, without the pleasurable effects desired by the addict. It may be that the relief of physical pain (the nature of which is as yet imperfectly understood) is so closely associated with relief of emotional distress or anxiety that such an ideal drug will never be found. This association may not be inherent in the structure of the molecule and may not be inseparable pharmacologically. Intensive efforts have been made for years and are continuing in the synthesis of new drugs related to the opiates. As such drugs are prepared either by the chemists of the Public Health Service or by commercial drug houses, they are tested in the research department of the Lexington hospital for addiction liability. Many interesting drugs have been so tested, but none approached the ideal product. If this drug could be developed, addiction-prone individuals who make their initial acquaintance with drugs in the course of medical treatment might go for years or perhaps indefinitely without feeling the desire for drugs. Of course, the emotionally normal individual who has to have drugs during the course of an illness in amounts necessary under present conditions to produce physical dependence and withdrawal illness, would be spared that ordeal if such a drug were available.

TREATMENT OF THE OPIATE ADDICT

The treatment of the individual opiate addict falls into five parts: first, the treatment for physical dependence, that is, the withdrawal illness; second, convalescence from withdrawal, with concomitant treatment for medical and surgical defects; third, treatment for psychic or emotional dependence on the drug and its withdrawal; fourth, continued rehabilitation; fifth, community cooperation and follow-up after the patient's discharge from medical treatment.

Management of Withdrawal

Should withdrawal be undertaken in all cases? This question must, of course, be decided on an individual basis each time withdrawal is contemplated. It is our opinion that the vast majority of addicts should be withdrawn. Possible exceptions fall into the following three categories.

1. Patients who are undergoing medical and surgical treatment

in which pain can be controlled only with opiates. Some such cases are self-limited in time, and withdrawal may be accomplished after recovery from the illness; in some, the illness is progressive, or of a malignant nature, so relief of pain may become increasingly necessary until death occurs, and opiates should be used freely in the relief of such cases. Withdrawal is medically contraindicated in less than one case per thousand admissions to the Lexington hospital. The rare exceptions are reported to their family physicians with the recommendation that they be continued on drugs after their return home. They are then given enough narcotics to sustain them until they reach home.

2. The aged or feeble who may require supportive treatment with particular attention to nutrition and adjustment of metabolic conditions before withdrawal is undertaken. This may be true, for instance, of diabetics. Several patients above eighty years of age have been successfully withdrawn at the Lexington hospital. Infirm patients should be kept on maintenance doses of narcotics while they are being built up for withdrawal, as if being prepared for major surgical operations.

3. A third group includes a controversial number of temperate addicts reported by some authorities to use small doses of narcotics for years without compulsion to increase their dose and with only beneficial effect upon the individual. Such benefits are alleged to be in the nature of the relaxation brought about by the social drinker who finds relief in an evening cocktail. Wolff[1] and Kolb[5] and others report occasional individuals, particularly physicians, who apparently have used drugs in moderation in such manner and continue to be quite capable of work and of fulfilling their duties for many years without constantly increasing the dose. If so, one would expect to find them principally among physicians or pharmacists, inasmuch as they may be in a position to obtain small doses by subterfuge from legal supplies without being detected. Such cases are so rare that, for all practical and statistical purposes, they do not occur, and no one should contemplate the possibility of using narcotic drugs in this manner, although in fact most addicts have believed at one time or another that they could use drugs moderately. The physician should not allow himself to be persuaded that he should prescribe drugs even in minimum

quantities for such an addict in whom the medical need is not very clear. Many addicts try to develop several physicians as sources of small supply, the combined total obtained being adequate for a large or increasing addiction; under the Federal narcotic laws, a physician may not prescribe drugs for the support of addiction.

In countries of the Orient and Far East, particularly China and India, it appears to be the case that some opium eaters and opium smokers do use opium as a more or less lifelong habit without increasing the dosage and without materially interfering with their effectiveness. Many others, of course, pursue the poppy more assiduously and waste an increasing amount of time and money in their addiction. There appears to be a considerable difference in the addiction liability of opium when smoked or eaten as compared with the hypodermic injection of it or its product as used in this country. However, a temperate or social use of opiates by needle is a fallacious conception which, when popularized as has been done in Wilson's *My Six Convicts*,[6] can, in the opinion of the authors, only serve to encourage addiction.

THE QUESTION OF GOVERNMENT CLINICS

Periodically, public proposals are made that clinics should be operated by the Government where "incurable" addicts could register and receive narcotics free or at a nominal price. Such clinics are conceived in the erroneous belief that the treatment of addicts is hopeless and that, as a group, addicts are better citizens with drugs than without. Proponents contend that many addicts who are now forced into a life of crime to support their habits would become law-abiding and useful citizens and that the illicit narcotics trade would be killed by automatic loss of customers.

Plans usually provide that only addicts existing at the date of registration receive narcotics from the clinic and that the amounts received be fixed at the dosage necessary to maintain the addicts without development of withdrawal illness. It is presumed that when the generation registered at the clinic dies out, there will be no more addiction, and the problem will be solved. Some years ago, such clinics were actually established in several states, and they have also been tried by several other countries. In each case in the United States, and in most instances in foreign countries, these clinics have been abandoned as unrealistic because a parallel contraband market in narcotics continued to exist and because conniving and frictions of various kinds developed within the clinics themselves. For the following reasons illegal trading in narcotics always continues.

1. Addicts, because of increasing tolerance, attempt to increase their dose constantly in an effort to recapture the original euphoria; consequently, registered addicts go to the contraband sellers for the increasing amounts of narcotics desired. Furthermore, addicts held on a permanent minimum dosage are in a perpetual state of mild withdrawal distress, since tolerance increases without a concomitant increase in drugs administered.

2. There is a well-recognized tendency for addicts to spread addiction among their friends and intimate associates. New addicts created in this way are presumably not eligible for registration at the clinic and inevitably patronize the illicit peddler.

3. Since there is always a coexisting black market, some registered addicts, by theft, deceit or connivance, attempt to obtain more narcotics from the clinic than they require and sell the surplus at high prices to nonregistered addicts. In order to eliminate the possibility of diverting drugs from the clinic for illegal sale, the drugs must be actually administered hypodermically in the clinic by trained attendants. This supervised administration is also required because most addicts, having lost the power of self-control with regard to drugs, cannot be trusted to allocate a given amount of drugs over a specified period of time. Since the addict requires his narcotics at intervals of four to five hours, the clinic must be open twenty-four hours a day; eventually it becomes a round-the-clock hangout for addicts.

4. A certain number of addiction-prone persons develop typical addiction through acquaintance with the effects of narcotics during the course of medical treatment. Unless the clinic constantly reopens its rolls to new registrants, which is completely unrealistic, such new addicts are forced to patronize the illicit peddler for narcotics.

5. Addicts are rarely effective people, whether they get drugs free or at a high price, pure or adulterated. For example, research

subjects on maintenance doses are not efficient, productive, ambitious or even happy and are always conniving to get more drugs.

Because the contraband traffic in narcotics flourishes concomitantly with the operation of clinics, the chief objective of the clinics is never established. Most recidivist addicts, of course, enthusiastically approve the proposals for such clinics, for they offer another source for the procurement of drugs. As one old-time addict who had had experience with a clinic said, "With what I got from the clinic, and what I got from the outside, I got along very well."

In addition to the hazards of furnishing narcotics knowingly to addicts, there is a risk that they may be given addicting drugs unwittingly, as in a publicized proposal to give a "dime's worth of methadone" daily to addicts on the street as a non-addicting substitute for heroin or morphine. It has been shown that methadone is an effective substitute for heroin or morphine only because it is also an addicting drug of the opiate series. Heroin was introduced the same way as a wonderful cure for morphine addiction.

It seems questionable to the authors that such a responsible body as the Medical Society of the County of New York should, in 1965, see any need to approve narcotics for ambulatory addict-patients in the community, even on a trial basis.[37] See Chapter 7 for notes on the "British System."

Where Should the Addict Be Treated?

The physician should insist that his patient enter a special institution where the nursing and medical staffs are experienced in the handling and treatment of addicts—one which is equipped with the recreational, occupational and rehabilitative facilities necessary for a long stay of four and one half to six months. Only the first few weeks of the first treatment period will need to be in an acute infirmary hospital situation; the rest of the time can probably be spent in a dormitory facility, where close attention may be given to any current medical and surgical needs as well as to any psychotherapy which may be indicated.

The entire treatment should be in a *closed* institution with maximum of supervision and a minimum of contact with the outside world in order to prevent the introduction of contraband narcotics, which so often interfere with successful treatment of addicts in an *open* type institution or general hospital not principally devoted to the treatment of addiction. Close inspection must be given incoming and outgoing mail as well as to visits with relatives and friends, which must be held to a minimum. Isolation from friends, relatives, home and business contacts is necessary if the patient is to make the sharp break with his previous life situation for the long treatment period necessary. The patient cannot continue to carry any of his usual family and business responsibilities while undergoing treatment. He must have made arrangements prior to entering the hospital for his responsibilities to be transferred to others in anticipation of the length of treatment required. Unless he is ready to make whatever sacrifices are necessary for such a period of treatment he is not yet prepared psychologically for treatment.

These recommendations remain as true today as when the first edition of this book was written. Exceptions of strong-willed individuals are too few to be significant.

State mental hospitals and general hospitals are often unsuited for treatment of addiction and are generally so crowded and inexperienced in treating addicts that the management avoids taking such cases if possible. Addict patients resent being domiciled and treated with mentally disturbed patients of the psychotic group and quite properly feel that they have no problems in common. Only about 2 per cent of the patients coming to the Federal narcotic hospitals for treatment are found to be psychotic.[7] Sometimes employees of hospitals are poorly paid and susceptible to bribes for bringing in narcotic drugs so that withdrawal may never actually be accomplished.

Some private sanitaria accept addict patients who are financially able to pay the cost of treatment. Most addicts do not seek treatment until they are unable financially to support their habits; others who have moderate funds may be able to pay only for several days or several weeks of treatment, after which they must leave. Experience at the Federal hospitals shows that patients leaving soon after beginning treatment almost without exception relapse to the use of narcotics. Furthermore, the paying patient at a private sanitarium—especially if he is a physician—sometimes tries to influence the management of his own withdrawal by threatening to leave. The tendency of private sanitaria is to prolong the period of withdrawal in order to minimize the dissatisfaction of its paying patients. In some cases, addicts with funds seek the extremely gradual withdrawal encountered in some private sanitaria for the purpose of obtaining drugs when their outside sources are temporarily unavailable. A prescription for narcotics for withdrawal must be definitely related to a program of actual withdrawal over a reasonable period of time in order to be considered legitimate. Even if clients of private sanitaria were able to pay the high cost of treatment over a period of four and one half to six months, most private sanitaria do not have the occupational facilities for such ambulant patients for that period of time. Consequently, most private sanitaria perform only denarcotization or withdrawal which, while essential in the rehabilitation of the addict, is perhaps less important that the subsequent convalescence and "deconditioning" to narcotics, which should be quite prolonged.

Withdrawal

The withdrawal of the addict patient at his home is even less likely to succeed than in the private sanitarium for obvious reasons. The family physician is not in a position to control the withdrawal regime, nor does he have the benefit of experienced nursing personnel. If withdrawal is actually accomplished, follow-up therapy is not available.

The gradual reduction method of withdrawal of physically dependent patients by office supervision of physicians is futile, and indicates either a lack of understanding on the part of the physician or a gullibility which is likely to make him very popular with addict patients. Federal narcotic agents look with great skepticism and suspicion on the physician who prescribes narcotics for a gradual reduction in withdrawal of patients on an office basis.

Addicts apprehended in violation of various laws are frequently forced to undergo withdrawal in a jail with little or no medical supervision. In jails, abrupt withdrawal or "cold turkey" is common. Sometimes, if funds are available, narcotics can be purchased, and withdrawal does not actually occur, or only incompletely so, in a jail or prison. If abrupt withdrawal in a jail cell does occur, it is a very traumatic experience, psychologically as well as physically, and even though death does not often result, the experience does lasting damage to the personality of the individual. For psychological reasons not well understood, it is apparent from talking to addicts that fear of withdrawal distress is no deterrent to relapse. Voluntary withdrawal by the reduction method or abruptly by the addict himself without medical supervision probably never occurs if drugs are obtainable and if addiction has been well established. It is possible that some patients who are taking heavily adulterated narcotics may be able to stop voluntarily because of weak physical dependence.

It was largely out of a realization that addicts should not be treated in the Federal penal system, particularly in association with other types of offenders, which led to the establishment of the Federal hospital for drug addicts in Lexington, Kentucky, in 1935 and a similar one subsequently at Fort Worth, Texas, in 1938. Federal prisoners who are believed by sentencing judges and the Attorney General to be more in need of medical and psychiatric treatment than penal discipline may be sent to these hospitals for treatment. Addicts who are convicted in Federal court may have their sentences suspended on the condition that they go to Lexington or Fort Worth for treatment. In these cases, the medical authorities set the discharge date whenever they believe that optimum results of treatment have been obtained; thereafter, these patients continue under the supervision of their parole officers at home for the remainder of their suspended sentences, an arrangement which seems to be helpful insofar as medical aims of rehabilitation are concerned. This arrangement provides for discharge at the best possible time after receiving treatment, and it gives continued supervision, which is also important in case of prisoner and voluntary patients. It may be that severe sentences requiring that patients be imprisoned long after completion of treatment tend to embitter them so that the danger of relapse is increased.

The laws establishing these hospitals provided that if beds remained after the treatment of prisoner and probationer patients, voluntary patients should be admitted. In the early years in these two hospitals, 80 per cent of the patients were prisoner and probationer patients and 20 per cent were voluntaries. Over the years, this ratio has gradually reversed itself, with 90 per cent of admissions being voluntary patients and only 10 per cent of admissions being Federal prisoners and probationers. The population at any one time is about two thirds Federal prisoners or probationers and one third voluntary patients. The discrepancy between the population at one time and the admissions is due to the fact that the voluntary patients demand their release against the medical advice and stay, on an average, a shorter time. This illustrates the futility of trying to treat addicts without the power to hold them. If they are able to do so, voluntary patients are asked to pay for care, but 95 per cent of voluntary patients do not pay. No distinction is made in the treatment of the voluntary patients and the prisoner patients, nor between free and paying voluntary patients. Both of these Federal hospitals are approved for psychiatric residency training programs, so the emphasis is on psychiatry. Competent medical and dental staffs, as well as a full corps of consultants in various specialities not represented on the regular staff, make complete medical treatment possible. Lexington has 1,042 beds and Fort Worth about 775 beds, with both hospitals frequently operating at more than capacity. There are also adequate occupational and rehabilitative facilities. Women patients are accepted only at the Lexington hospital, and application should be made to the Medical Officer in Charge, U. S. Public Health Service Hospital, Lexington, Kentucky, or Fort Worth, Texas. Patients should not come to Lexington or Fort Worth without prior notification, as it may develop that they are not legally eligible or that there is a waiting list. Applicants for first-time admission are given preference over repeaters. These hospitals are only for the treatment of those addicted to the drugs controlled by the Federal laws, that is, opium and all its derivatives and any synthetic equivalents, marihuana and cocaine. Those addicted to the use of alcohol or barbiturates are *not* eligible for treatment even though these drugs may be harmful and addicting.

Federal law establishes the confidentiality of clinical records concerning voluntary patients at the Lexington and Fort Worth hospitals. The institutions may not give information to law enforcement officers or anyone else who has not been specifically authorized in writing by the patient to receive such information. This provision is necessary, of course, since most voluntary applicants for treatment have been guilty of violating the narcotic laws and would not willingly place themselves in jeopardy on that account.

At this time no state having addicts in substantial numbers, with the exception of California, comes close to providing adequate facilities for the treatment of addicts. Although California has the third highest number of addicts, it was twenty-second in incidence of addiction based on admissions to the Federal hospitals. Thus, California takes care of most of its addicts at home.

In 1965, the Department of Mental Hygiene in New York state had 555 beds for the withdrawal and treatment of addicts, and New York City had an additional 300 beds for such treatment.

Compulsory Treatment

Is compulsory treatment necessary for narcotic addicts? A practical problem of great importance in treating narcotic addicts is to compel them to remain in the hospital long enough for completion of all phases of treatment. In the case of Federal prisoners and probationers, the authority to hold them for treatment is valid. In connection with voluntary patients, however, the compulsory detention of addicts may raise an important constitutional issue. When the Lexington hospital was first established in 1935, voluntary applicants were required to sign a statement giving the medical officer in charge the authority to determine the release date based on completion of treatment.

However, a few months after the hospital opened, a voluntary patient on petition of writ of *habeus corpus* obtained a decision in Federal court that, as a voluntary patient, he could change his mind regardless of what he might have signed. The judge reasoned that he had not been deprived of his liberty by due process of the law as a law violator, and neither had he been committed by due process of law as mentally incompetent. Such a ruling, however constitutional, seems to conflict with the acknowledged principle that an addict (having lost self-control with regard to the drug) must be confined to be treated successfully. As matters now stand, a voluntary patient, regardless of good intentions when applying for treatment, is not able irrevocably to sign authority for the medical officer in charge of a Federal hospital or the superintendent of any private institution to determine his release date. Accordingly, unless there are pressures which in effect remove him from the status of a voluntary patient, he may leave—and usually does—during the distressing withdrawal period when he has vivid memories of how quickly he will feel comfortable if he takes narcotics. Many who complete withdrawal become prematurely optimistic after two or three months of treatment and leave the hospital at a time when their chance for relapse is still relatively great. The minimum period for treatment recommended at Lexington is now five months.

It is axiomatic with most of those who work in the field of drug addiction that treatment usually cannot be successfully completed without an element of restraint.

Commitment of Addicts

Several states have provided for the commitment of narcotic addicts in the same quasi-criminal procedure by which alcoholics may be committed to state institutions for involuntary treatment. The procedure usually follows closely that provided for psychotic or insane patients. Federal Veterans' Hospitals can honor state commitments for mental patients. A bill has been introduced in the last several Congresses authorizing the Federal narcotic hospitals to accept cases committed by state courts, but it has failed of passage. If this were passed, it would give a desirable element of compulsion for an additional group of addict patients who otherwise are not likely to accept or complete treatment.

Presumably, if this Federal bill authorizing the Lexington and Fort Worth hospitals to honor state commitments of addicts became effective, many more states would promptly pass laws providing for such commitments. Usually an existing law providing for the commitment of inebriates can be broadened quite easily to include drug addicts.

Voluntary patients frequently have strong pressures to complete treatment. For instance, in the cases of doctors and nurses, their plight is usually known by the state medical and nursing licensing boards, and they are faced with loss of licenses if they fail to complete treatment. Or, when law enforcement agencies believe addicts to be victims of their addiction and not primarily criminals, they may be unofficially given the choice of seeking and completing voluntary treatment or of facing prosecution. These patients are asked to sign an authorization for the hospital to notify the referring agency if they should demand their release against advice, since otherwise the hospital would be powerless to give such notice. By and large, however, the treatment of addicts on a voluntary basis is futile; by the very nature of addiction, they do not hesitate to leave the hospital against medical advice in search of drugs to relieve withdrawal distress once it has begun. Several states, including New York and California now have laws providing for the civil commitment of addicts for treatment by noncriminal proceedings.

Voluntary patients under age twenty-one are not discharged prematurely against medical advice except on the authorization of parent or guardian. Consequently, most underage voluntary addicts stay for the full treatment, except where overindulgent parents are persuaded by the pleas of the juvenile addict to request discharge. Some juvenile addicts coming to the attention of the local police in the larger cities are given suspended police court sentences on condition that they go to Lexington for treatment as voluntary patients; non-cooperation in treatment then constitutes a violation of criminal court probation with consequent penalties when the youngster goes back home.

Motives for Seeking Treatment

In considering compulsory treatment of the addict, it is important to consider his attitude toward treatment. Prisoner patients, particularly of the recidivist type, may have no desire for treatment; they may admit freely that they are resigned to a life of addiction and only regret that society makes it difficult for them to maintain their addiction. Such recidivist types, of course, should not be sent to hospitals for complete treatment, since they serve as bad influences and lower the tone of institutional morale for the other patients who are sincere in seeking treatment. However, such cases are entitled to humane withdrawal, which could be accomplished even in prison or, if necessary, in special hospitals for addicts, after which they should be transferred to correctional institutions.

Many of the older recividist type prisoner addicts, as well as a great majority of the younger prisoner and probationer group and an even greater majority of the voluntary patients, sincerely wish to be cured. Even though they may believe that drugs would be a desirable means of adjustment for them, they also recognize the penalties imposed and the risks engendered by a continued life of addiction. Some voluntary patients have been forced by outside pressures of business associates, law enforcement officers, licensing boards or relatives to undergo treatment. Such patients are usually very critical of the hospitals where they go and soon magnify the inconveniences and discomforts of institutional life to the point where they can justify to themselves and to those who sent them, they hope, the absolute necessity for them to leave the hospital. These people, while classed as voluntary patients, have never accepted their own need for treatment.

At best, any institution which deprives a person of his liberty, even for his own good, is likely to be regarded quite critically both at the time and in retrospect. Since skeptical, cynical and sophisticated recidivist addicts in an institution are the most vociferous element of the population, they may give the impression that the majority of patients are not sincere about wishing to stay off drugs. The opposite is actually the case. At least 95 per cent of patients found in Federal hospitals wish that they could stay off drugs, even though many have serious doubts about their ability to do so. With the establishment of an active group, Addicts Anonymous, within the Lexington hospital, the addict sincerely in search of treatment may find associates who freely and emphatically proclaim to themselves and to others that they are determined to stay off drugs in the future. After release, some patients find great help from local chapters of Addicts Anonymous, or Narcotics Anonymous, as they are called in some cities.

A small percentage of addicts have no desire either to get off drugs or to remain off. They accept compulsory treatment resentfully and live for the day when they can go back to drugs. These people may be regarded at the present time as incurable. Often, though not always, they are underworld characters who can be kept away from drugs only by incarceration in a prison or hospital where drugs are not available at a price. There are also some addicts who view treatment as no more than an inconvenient means of reducing their consumption of narcotics; they are not able to withdraw themselves, but accept withdrawal under compulsion philosophically and use the treatment period to reduce their tolerance; they know that on release they can recapture part of the pleasure of their first experience with drugs at greatly reduced cost. They also know that, once they get out, they will build up their habits again to a point where they cannot maintain them under $40 or $50 per day and where pleasure will have largely given way to the need for warding off withdrawal distress. They will then again accept treatment, usually as a result of becoming involved with the law because of their constant need for large amounts of money.

As better rehabilitation programs become available, more recidivist-type addicts are motivated to try again to get off drugs permanently; this has happened in California.

The Time for Withdrawal of Opiate Drugs

Opiate drugs should be withdrawn at the earliest possible time after any medical need ceases to exist. Addicts frequently try to postpone the withdrawal as long as possible. The family physician must be prepared to use his strongest powers of persuasion to help his patient cooperate by allaying the frequently exaggerated reports of extreme suffering from withdrawal. Rather, the benefits of successful treatment should be emphasized, and the addict told that withdrawal supervised by experienced physicians is much less severe than that experienced by abrupt withdrawal or even gradual withdrawal managed by inexperienced physicians. The physician may agree to give small doses as necessary to sustain the addict until he reaches a qualified hospital, but he should explain that if he does more than that, he will be violating the law by supporting an addict. The patient and his relatives may be reassured that death is extremely rare during withdrawal; some patients may be no more than uncomfortable with the use of methadone.

While physicians and relatives should not exaggerate the severity of withdrawal illness, they should not deceive the patient who has yet to undergo complete withdrawal. There is no easy way to get off drugs, but the patient can be assured that, if he seeks treatment at a proper institution, the staff will prevent unbearable suffering, although in no case will the physician give the addict the amount of drugs which he would like to have. The judgment of the patient undergoing withdrawal is not valid with regard to his own treatment, which must be confidently placed with the physician. During this period, the addict is not in a position to appreciate that obtaining increased drugs also prolongs the withdrawal discomfort. It should also be explained that abstinence symptoms may not be as severe as expected because the drug which the patient was taking in relatively large quantities may have been grossly adulterated, sometimes containing as little as 2 to 5 per cent of the pure drug.

In considering the duration of withdrawal treatment, one considers *abrupt* withdrawal that in which all narcotics and sedative drugs are cut off instantly, *rapid* withdrawal that in which reduction is carried out from the accustomed dose to abstinence in a period of three to fourteen days and *prolonged* withdrawal in which the physician uses a system, sometimes very elaborate, of mathematical reduction of dosage over a period of several weeks or months.

In predetermining the duration of a withdrawal period, one must consider which of the three systems offers the quickest withdrawal within the reasonable capacity of the patient to endure it. If substantial doses of narcotics have been taken (say ten grains of morphine per day), and physical dependence is great, abrupt withdrawal is inhumane and sometimes dangerous. Prolonged withdrawal, on the other hand, extends the mental anxiety over an almost intolerable length of time, although the physical suffering may be minimal. Most physicians treating addicts today agree that rapid withdrawal within a few days, with substitute drugs, offers the best solution; however, withdrawal can be successfully managed by simply reducing the addicting drug rapidly according to objective signs of withdrawal observed.

The method used at the Lexington hospital from 1935 until 1948 was rapid reduction of the drug of addiction over a period of about ten days. In 1948, the usefulness of methadone, a synthetic drug closely related to the opiate drugs, was established by the research department. It has since been used routinely for withdrawal in the clinical service.[4, 8, 9] Methadone supports addiction to heroin, morphine or other drugs of the opiate series perfectly when the drug dosages are adjusted correctly. The distress following abrupt withdrawal of methadone is much less than that experienced after the withdrawal of morphine or other opiates. Figure 25 is a graph comparing the intensity of abstinence illness following withdrawal of methadone, morphine, Demerol and codeine.

Consequently, in clinical use there is a decided advantage in substituting methadone for the morphine or heroin and then carrying out the rapid withdrawal of methadone, usually over a period of about nine days. Narcotics given during withdrawal are

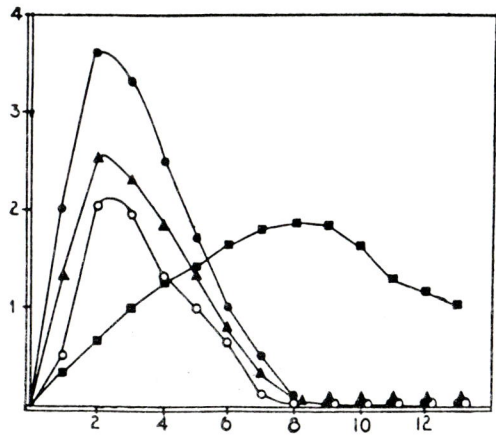

FIGURE 25.[4] Comparative intensity of abstinence from various drugs. The solid circles indicate abstinence from morphine, the open circles abstinence from codeine, the triangle abstinence from demerol and the squares abstinence from methadone. The vertical line of the figure shows the intensity of abstinence (clinical grades), and the horizontal row of figures shows the number of days of abstinence.

best administered by mouth in order to interrupt the "needle-habit" as soon as possible. A maximum of 20 to 60 mg of methadone daily for two to three days usually suffices for humane withdrawal.

Figure 26 shows how much withdrawal distress is alleviated by the substitution of methadone for morphine before rapid withdrawal. In each case, during a period of trial abstinence, the patient showed a "plus 4" habit as rated by the Himmelsbach scale. During morphine reduction, abstinence was held to grade 2 dis-

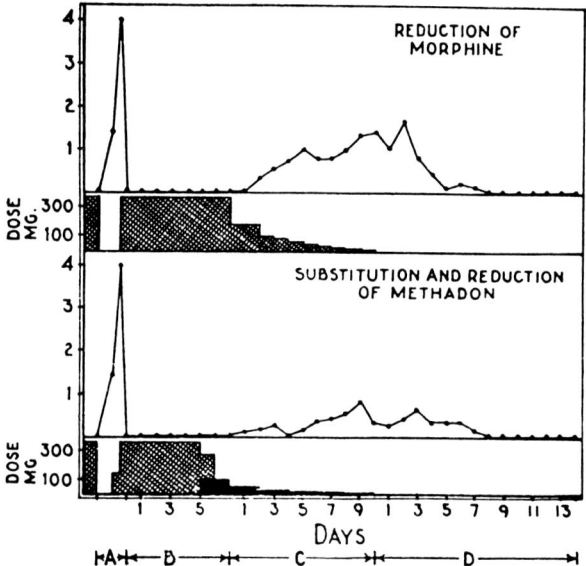

FIGURE 26.[4] Graph of treatment of physical dependence on morphine by substitution and reduction of methadone as compared to reduction of morphine. The points shown represent the average intensity of abstinence (grades 1, 2, 3 and 4 in vertical column at left) in ten patients who were addicted to 360 mg. (6 grains) of morphine daily. In the experiment, five patients were withdrawn by simple reduction of morphine and five patients were withdrawn by substitution of methadone for morphine, followed by reduction of methadone. Period A: preliminary 36 hour withdrawal of morphine for proof and assessment of intensity of physical dependence. Period B: restabilization on morphine. In the methadone graph, substitution of 90 mg. (1½ grains) of methadone for 360 mg. (6 grains) of morphine was effected on the sixth and seventh days. Period C: reduction of morphine or methadone. Period D: total abstinence from drugs.

FIGURE 27
INTENSITY OF ABSTINENCE SYMPTOMS

Mild (+)	Moderate (++)	Marked (+++)	Severe (++++)
(When only these signs are present)	(When these signs are added)	(When these signs are added)	(When these signs are added)
Yawning	Loss of appetite	Deep breathing	Vomiting
Eyes water	Dilated pupils	Fever	Diarrhea
Nose runs	Tremor	Restlessness	Weight loss
Sneezing	Goose-flesh	Insomnia	
Perspiration		Rise in blood pressure	

comfort, and after substitution of methadone and reduction, the abstinence illness was held to less than grade 1. In each case, the withdrawal illness by the objective point scale fell to zero in about nine days, which is the usual picture with the rapid reduction as practiced at the Lexington hospital.

Himmelsbach[10] first developed a system of objective rating of withdrawal signs (Fig. 27) and recommended that the management of withdrawal be adjusted according to such objective signs.

The withdrawal management at the Lexington hospital for patients who are taking opiates up to the time of their admission or who are in withdrawal distress at the time of admission is as follows: If there is no withdrawal distress evident, but the history is that opiate drugs were taken up to the time of admission, the patient is started on 5 mg of methadone three times a day; if he shows objective signs of withdrawal at the time of admission or if he develops such signs after being placed on the initial dose of 5 mg three times a day, methadone is administered according to the severity of withdrawal as rated according to Figure 27: 10 mg, three times a day for moderate (plus 2) withdrawal intensity; 15 mg methadone three times a day for marked (plus 3) withdrawal; or 20 mg three times a day for severe (plus 4) abstinence.

After about twenty-four hours on methadone as described above, the drug is reduced as rapidly as possible (usually not to exceed ten days) without allowing abstinence signs in excess of grade two severity to develop. It has been found that the dosage can be reduced quite rapidly at the beginning of the withdrawal and more slowly near the end of the withdrawal period. The methadone is best administered orally. Mild abstinence signs are still observed, but much less than during rapid reduction of morphine or heroin. Because addicts do not willingly bear even minimum discomfort, they may complain quite bitterly during methadone reduction, much as they do during rapid morphine reduction, but the objective signs of withdrawal distress are much milder.

It is not safe to believe the patient regarding the amount of drugs he has been taking and to adjust withdrawal doses accordingly. The addict may lie about his previous dosage in order to get more drugs, or he may be truly ignorant about his dosage, owing to the tendency of dealers to cut bootleg drugs heavily. Consequently, dosage based on the addict's statement might well be fatal. During withdrawal management, it is rarely necessary to give any substantial proportion of the known self-dosage in order to alleviate the symptoms. For example, in the straight reduction of morphine (without substitution of methadone) it is rarely necessary to give more than ½ grain (30 mg) of morphine every six hours to prevent entirely the appearance of abstinence during the first two days of withdrawal. Usually ¼ grain (15 mg) suffices.

Although death rarely occurs during withdrawal, the signs of impending collapse should be known—weak, rapid pulse and rapid, irregular breathing. If patients are seen every half hour during withdrawal, these signs should be observed by nursing personnel in time to summon medical aid.

The experienced nurse learns to be alert constantly and to distinguish between malingering and real withdrawal suffering. It is common for malingers to provoke emesis and to produce elevated temperature on a thermometer.

In addition to the measurable withdrawal signs, a distinct change in personality takes place during withdrawal. The patient becomes depressed, nervous, irritable and, of course, fearful. He is quite often antagonistic, becomes neglectful of his personal appearance and occasionally attempts suicide, or feigns suicide for the purpose of getting more drugs. Restlessness is often pronounced during withdrawal, so much so that the skin over bony prominences of the body may be worn off. Many patients, being uncomfortable in bed, will attempt to sleep on the hard floor. Because of the disturbances in taste and smell, addicts will greatly reduce the amount of tobacco which they smoke, although during later phases of the period of treatment after withdrawal they may smoke incessantly.

For extreme restlessness and insomnia during withdrawal, small doses of barbiturate drugs may be given. It is important not to use large doses of sedative drugs, since these seem to aggravate the development of emotional upsets during withdrawal. Furthermore, the use of non-opiate sedative drugs prolongs emotional dependence on drugs in general, and the relief of emotional dependence becomes increasingly important as physical dependence decreases. Continuous flow baths are often helpful in relieving excessive nervousness, and a special effort should be made to prepare attractive foods to minimize the loss of weight resulting from the lack of appetite and the abnormal loss of body fluids. For unusually debilitated patients, withdrawal may have to be extended over several weeks or even several months. This occurs in cases of chronic physical illness and in the aged. Although emotional upsets are common during withdrawal treatment, and psychoneurotic reactions frequently manifested, only one of 400 patients studied became actually psychotic during withdrawal.[7]

Many methods of withdrawing opiate drugs have been advocated in the past. Most of these have been illogical, and some have been more dangerous than abrupt withdrawal of the addicting drug.[12] Some of these withdrawal methods (largely obsolete today) include the Narcosan, the Rossium treatment, the blister treatment, heavy dosage of purgatives and such drugs as scopolamine and atropine. Insulin has recently been widely used in the withdrawal management of patients, but an objective evaluation of this therapy by Wieder[13] has shown it to be of no value; in fact, in some cases it seemed to intensify the abstinence illness. The administration of codeine in the management of the withdrawal from morphine and heroin has frequently been recommended, but this seems to be of no more value than the rapid reduction of the drug of primary addiction.

Mention has been made in Chapter 2 of various drugs of the opiate series which, when introduced, were highly recommended as non-addicting substitutes for morphine or opium, substitutes which could be used to bring about the withdrawal of other drugs of the opiate series without discomfort. Of course, in a sense, it is possible to treat addiction to one drug with another of the same series. The administration of heroin or Dilaudid or methadone in adequate doses will prevent all withdrawal suffering when morphine is removed, but when these drugs are in turn withdrawn, abstinence appears. It has been shown that any drug which will substitute smoothly for an addicting drug is equally as addicting as the primary drug. This substitution is one of the tests of addiction liability which researchers apply when studying new drugs proposed for sale as substitutes for morphine and other drugs of the opiate series.

The most common source of error in evaluating new drugs for the treatment of abstinence from opiates is that physical dependence is assumed on the basis of statements given by patients concerning the amount of drugs they have been taking. When the new drug or new withdrawal procedure is then tested and no great withdrawal distress is observed, the experimenters conclude that the new drug or the new regime has been effective in reducing or eliminating the withdrawal illness. Such conclusions, of course, should be made only when cases being treated have been allowed to experience briefly the withdrawal illness after abrupt withdrawal, with the degree of abstinence illness evaluated according to some objective scale similar to that developed by Himmelsbach. After this "control" period of observation has been completed to assure the existence of physical dependence, the patients are again made comfortable on the drug of their addiction and the substitute drug or procedure being tested is initiated. The degree of abstinence based on objective observation is then compared with that observed during the initial test period. This control period is, of course, uncomfortable and unpopular with the patient. Frequently, either for that reason or because the physician in charge of the experiment does not realize its importance, the control step is omitted and false conclusions are drawn regarding the efficacy of the new drug or procedure. Then too, any experimentation not carried on in a meticulously closed and isolated ward may be misleading, because contraband drugs may have been taken by the patients during the course of the experiment.

In the management of withdrawal, narcotics are never given intravenously but subcutaneously; in the rare cases of opium smokers, any opiate may be given in small quantities by mouth if objective abstinence intervenes. In the cases in which the various opiates, including opium itself, may have been taken by mouth, the severity of withdrawal illness may be controlled with small doses. Addicts who have not been taking narcotics by needle should not be introduced to that route. Narcotics given during the course of withdrawal should always be administered by a doctor or a nursing assistant and never allowed to be given by a patient, although addicts usually prefer self-administration. Drugs given during withdrawal should always be given at stated hours during the day, and the patient should learn that no deviation is made from this policy.

Severe habits with serious withdrawal illness are seen much less frequently than in years past. Because of the dilute nature of illicit drugs most addicts seen today require little or no gradual or substitute withdrawal if treated humanely otherwise. A California law requires that all narcotic withdrawals be under the supervision of a physician.

New Drugs Used in Opiate Withdrawal

At the Lexington hospital, ACTH and cortisone have been experimentally used in managing opiate withdrawals in human beings. However, neither cortisone nor ACTH alleviated the morphine withdrawal syndrome; indeed, they seemed to aggravate it.

Lomotil, an exempt narcotic related to Demerol, has been used experimentally for the relief of withdrawal symptoms. Favorable results await confirmation and it remains to be seen if this drug is attractive to addicts for continuing use.

Brain Surgery in the Treatment of Addiction

Frontal lobotomy has been used experimentally in the treatment of two phases of opiate addiction with some success, although it is not recommended as generally applicable at the present time. These two phases are the relief of a craving for narcotic drugs and the relief of the abstinence syndrome.

Neurosurgeons[14, 15, 16, 17, 18] have performed bilateral frontal lobotomy in narcotic addicts, usually those with intractable pain. They report that the operation abolishes the desire for narcotics and terminates drug addiction in these patients. One surgeon[19] reported similar results after unilateral frontal lobotomy.

In several reports,[14, 15, 19] it is stated that no physiological changes were observed after withdrawal of narcotics following bilateral or unilateral frontal lobotomy. Other observers[16, 17, 18] noted definite, even severe, withdrawal signs. These reports are difficult to evaluate because drugs were not withdrawn abruptly, observations were casual and irregular, and in no case was the degree of physical dependence measured prior to frontal lobotomy.

At the Lexington hospital, controlled studies have been made on one chronic morphine addict with pain in a phantom limb and on three schizophrenic patients who had not responded to treatment for addiction.[20] All four patients required lobotomy for therapeutic reasons. All were stabilized on known amounts of morphine, and on the three schizophrenic patients, "test withdrawals" were made to determine physical dependence prior to lobotomy. When morphine was withdrawn abruptly from these four subjects a week or more after bilateral frontal lobotomy, the physiological abstinence distress was the same in character and in intensity as before the operation. When abrupt withdrawal of morphine was accomplished concomitantly with lobotomy, the physiological withdrawal syndrome was reduced in intensity.

Therefore, in the light of present information (which, it should be noted, is not as extensive as might be desired) it may be concluded that bilateral frontal lobotomy does tend to reduce markedly the craving for opiate drugs in addicted patients; however, in patients whose addiction is related to serious personality defects, a relapse to addiction may be expected. It should be noted that frontal lobotomy *per se* does not prevent the abstinence syndrome in narcotic addicts. However, when abrupt withdrawal of narcotics is accomplished immediately after surgery, when the patient is generally lethargic and relatively unresponsive, the withdrawal distress may be attenuated, probably as a result of transient reflex autonomic paralysis (cerebral shock) which occurs after undercutting the frontal lobes.

It should be emphasized that frontal lobotomy is not recommended generally as a treatment for drug addiction since it is not yet certain that, from the patient's point of view, the personality defects consequent to lobotomy are to be preferred to the problems associated with narcotic addiction.

Post-Withdrawal Therapy

Following the withdrawal period, a week or two of further hospitalization, especially in the cases in which withdrawal has been severe, should be set aside for a convalescent period in a ward separate from the withdrawal service, where nutritious food is served in comfortable surroundings. During this period at the Lexington hospital, patients are given instructions concerning orientation and adjustment at the hospital and are prepared for the subsequent rehabilitation phase of treatment to extend for several more months. They are taught how to make their beds and clean their rooms and are prepared for subsequent occupational assignments, handled by an occupational assignment board, where consideration is given to results of psychological and psychiatric examinations and completed physical examinations which may have been made during the withdrawal and convalescent periods. A work assignment may be made in keeping with a patient's past experience or in terms of new vocational goals, or, for temporary periods, work assignments may simply fulfill necessities of the institution. It is important that a wide range of occupational assignments, both indoor and outdoor, including some which offer opportunities for education and training, be available.

There is a school for more or less formal education, and the patients' recreational and athletic interests are encouraged. During this period, any medical, surgical or dental treatment needed is given, and the staff psychiatrists assist the patients to understand whatever emotional or personality defects led them to be attracted by narcotics in the first place. Frequently, there is little or no insight into the need for psychiatric treatment, and, accordingly, patients often do not accept it. Nevertheless, it is important that the administration of the institution where addicts are treated should be psychiatric in tone. Psychiatric influence may be exercised through the rules and regulations prescribed for every day living, and in the management of behavior difficulties. The Addicts Anonymous group is active for those patients who wish to cooperate, and this organization is very helpful in sustaining the addict personally and psychologically.

The California Civil Addict Rehabilitation Program

With more than 10,000 addicts under correctional control, California has started a rehabilitation-oriented program with about 2,000 selected addicts who are residents in the California Rehabilitation Center at Corona and 1,000 more who have been transferred to outpatient status. The program at the Center is comparable to that previously described for the Federal hospitals except that intensive group psychotherapy participation is obligatory. This is carried on by a counselor for each sixty-bed dormitory for half-days, five days a week. The counselors are college graduates, including many with M.A. degrees in the social sciences.

When the staff believe that the residents have reached maximum improvement, including suitable community plans, they are interviewed by members of the Narcotic Addict Evaluation Authority, which authorizes release to outpatient status. Median time in the institution for men is fourteen months and for women eleven months.

In the community, they are assigned to a parole agent whose case load is limited to thirty. He assists with job and residence arrangements and continues the function of counselor, including group therapy sessions, arranged in order not to interfere with work. Family counseling is often carried on. Of great importance is regular and irregular anti-narcotic testing (see Chapter 5). This threat of quick exposure of relapse to narcotic use provides practical motivation which is valuable in any program of psychiatric treatment.

If relapse to drugs occurs, the diagnosis is usually promptly made by the parole agent, and the patient is returned to the Center for further treatment before he gets involved in serious criminal activities. This return is accomplished very simply by obtaining authorization by telephone from any member of the Authority. Of those returned, more than 90 per cent have not been convicted of further crimes. Under the revolving-door punitive system used elsewhere, addicts who commit crimes go to jail or prison, serve their sentences, go out until they are convicted of further crimes and then go back to jail. True, they have some parole supervision under this system, but as part of the large caseload of an agent who does not carry on the type of continued treatment desirable for addicts.

The addicts in the rehabilitation program are under supervision and treatment in or out of the institution for seven to ten years. Earlier discharge can be granted after three continuous drug-free years in the community following release from the institution.

Addicts enter the rehabilitation program after being convicted of either misdemeanors or felonies, if doctors testify that they are addicts (opiates) or in imminent danger of becoming addicted. If the judge sees the possibility of rehabilitation, he suspends sentence on the criminal charge and makes a civil commitment to the program. An addict who does not stand convicted of crime may apply to the court for admission to the program by his own petition or that of an interested person. It appears that this voluntary type of commitment will survive legal assaults on its constitutionality and provide compulsory treatment for a less sophisticated younger type of addict where treatment is likely to be more effective.

The California plan includes halfway houses where selected outpatients with inadequate plans are housed until permanent arrangements materialize. Several states have studied the California program, and it is likely to become a model for the civil commitment approach to the treatment of addicts. Meanwhile, California is looking ahead to improve the program.

Synanon Houses, not a part of the State Rehabilitation program, are operated by a private foundation in several California locations and in Connecticut. This controversial and unconventional organization for the treatment of addicts was founded and is headed by a non-addict who avoids professional guidance or staff, depending entirely on senior members for staffing. Members carry on an active public relations program, including books, magazine articles and movies, thereby obtaining considerable financial support from the public.

Synanon has undoubtedly helped some addicts to stay off drugs, but only a few are accepted and of these many cannot tolerate the unorthodox methods used. Great successes are claimed, but statistics offered to support these claims are not convincing to many of those who study them. Officers of Synanon have been critical of the State programs and the State's failure to approve Synanon or to allow State parolees to go there. The Director of the Department of Corrections in California has stated the conditions under which it might be possible to cooperate with organizations like Synanon:

1. Professional supervision of program activities;
2. Evaluation of the program by adequate statistics;
3. Compliance with laws;
4. Operation to be with high moral principles;
5. Financial records with complete information regarding income and expenditures. (The New Jersey Narcotic Drug Commission received persistent reports that addicts accepted at Synanon are expected to make financial donations of $500 to $1,000); and
6. Operation in keeping with policies of the Department of Corrections.

If California parolees are to be allowed to live in Synanon Houses, supervision by parole agents, including anti-narcotic testing, must be allowed, but Synanon representatives have said they would never allow a parole agent to come into a Synanon House for the purpose of supervising a State parolee or to give any Nalline or similar tests to check addiction status.

California law enforcement officers are unenthusiastic about the Synanon policy of importing addicts to California from the East for treatment in Synanon Houses.

The Withdrawal and Treatment of Non-Opiate Addicts

The treatment of cocaine and marihuana addicts poses no special medical problem, since no physical dependence is developed and no withdrawal illness ensues. The problem in treatment for users of these drugs is one of physical isolation from drugs, psychiatric management and emotional readjustment in an effort to enable the user to live without the abnormal mental stimulation obtained from cocaine and the sedative or intoxicating effect of marihuana. Individuals who use cocaine alone or marihuana alone do not seek hospital treatment as voluntary patients. Occasionally, if convicted of a violation of the Federal narcotic laws, they ask to be sent to special narcotic hospitals for treatment as addicts rather than to penal institutions for discipline.

The nature of barbiturate addiction is discussed in Chapter 3. The treatment of barbiturate addicts, like that of the opiate-addict group, consists of withdrawal management, convalescence and subsequent rehabilitation for a total period of several months. Abrupt withdrawal of barbiturates which have been taken in addicting doses is absolutely contraindicated because of the severity of the withdrawal illness. At least one death during barbiturate withdrawal has been observed: The patient was being treated for opiate withdrawal without the physician knowing that barbiturate addiction also was present. Treatment should always be carried out in a hospital. At Lexington[21] during withdrawal, patients are given 3 to 6 grains of pentobarbital or its equivalent by mouth about every six hours. This dosage should be adjusted to maintain a mild degree of intoxication during a period of study for a day or two. After this, reduction is slowly carried out by not more than 1½ grains daily. This withdrawal period should be extended over a minimum of two full weeks; frequently, three to four weeks is necessary. If a patient becomes weak, apprehensive and nervous, the reduction process should be temporarily stopped.

Another method for gradual withdrawal from barbiturates is to reduce the intake by one therapeutic dose each day. This cautious withdrawal is necessary in order to prevent the appearance of the severe convulsions and psychotic episodes which have been shown to occur rather consistently.[22]

The course of abrupt withdrawal of addicting doses of barbiturates is as follows. During the first twelve to sixteen hours of abstinence from barbiturates, patients improve deceptively, and the signs of intoxication disappear. They subsequently become apprehensive and weak; before the fifth day of withdrawal, usually about the thirtieth hour, many patients will have one or more convulsions which are indistinguishable from those of grand mal epilepsy. Whether or not convulsions occur, many patients develop a psychosis between the third and seventh day of abstinence which often follows a period of insomnia during which they experience visual and auditory hallucinations. These resemble those seen in delirium tremens from alcoholism. Convulsions and the psychotic behavior described can be prevented by the gradual reduction method described above.

If the diagnosis is made after convulsions or psychoses have appeared, the patient should immediately be given a large dose of some barbiturate intravenously. If such symptoms continue to interfere with the withdrawal management, the dose of barbiturate must be increased. Barbiturate cases should be kept under very close nursing observation; the beds should be provided with side boards, or patients should sleep on mattresses on the floor. In clinical practice, falls frequently occur, sometimes with serious results. Patients should not attempt to go to the bathroom or walk unattended during the acute state of withdrawal. It may be necessary to give intravenous fluids to maintain the necessary body fluids.

It is increasingly common to find addicts using addicting doses of both opiates and barbiturates. Therefore, it is important to elicit an accurate history so that the necessary barbiturates may be given during withdrawal from opiates. There is no contraindication to carrying out the simultaneous withdrawal of both types of drugs.

Effects of New Drugs on the Barbiturate Abstinence Syndrome

Results to date of the effects of cortisone and ACTH on the barbiturate abstinence syndrome are inconclusive. Certainly the electroencephalographic changes which characterize this syndrome are not altered by cortisone.

Recent work[36] has shown that there is a cross-tolerance between barbiturates and certain of the tranquilizers so that substitution of one group of drugs for the other with subsequent gradual withdrawal is possible.

Post-Withdrawal Treatment

The post-withdrawal treatment of the barbiturate user follows the same lines as those described for the continued treatment of the opiate addict over a period of four and one half to six months.

PROGNOSIS OR RESULTS OF TREATMENT OF ADDICTS

In evaluating results obtained from the treatment of addiction, it should be considered that drug addiction is a disease or, more accurately, the symptom of a disease, which is very likely to be chronic, with a tendency toward remission and relapse. That is, there are periods when the disease is active, with intervening periods when symptoms, i.e., addiction, are absent. In this respect, it may be compared to such diseases as high blood pressure, decompensating heart disease, tuberculosis, diabetes and cancer, all of which tend to be chronic and be marked by remissions and relapses, frequently requiring repeated treatments.

Persons interested in the treatment of addicts often ask, "How many are cured?" and when asked what they mean by "cured," they are not quite sure. Frequently, when pressed for an answer they say, "How many never go back to the use of drugs?" That question cannot be answered until all treated addicts have died, which is, of course, unrealistic. By comparison, treated cancer patients are considered cured if they have no recurrence for five years. The California rehabilitation law says, in effect, that addicts are considered cured and discharged from all supervision after three consecutive "clean" years following transfer to outpatient status. The program is not yet old enough for many cases to have come up for such final discharge, but of one group studied, 25 per cent were "clean" after being out one year; 23 per cent after 18 months; 21 per cent after 24 months; 20 per cent of the original group were still "clean" after 30 months.

Of those returned to the Center for more treatment, the average time out before return was seven months. Some patients will stay off drugs permanently. Also of great significance is the time that those who relapse stay in the community and the extent to which they become involved in criminality before returning for more treatment.

Many of the outpatients are expected to relapse, return to the center for further treatment and go out again as outpatients, all as part of the therapeutic process. This represents a long step forward in recognizing the stages through which rehabilitation is finally accomplished. Of those returned to the Center, only 3 per cent had been convicted of further felonies and 4 per cent of further misdemeanors.

The cost of maintaining a person in a rehabilitation setting is less costly to the economy than having him raise $40 or $50 a day to support his habit by crime. The element of protection of the public by a program of treatment and prompt return after relapse is considerable. California law specifies protection of the public as a legitimate goal when rehabilitation proves impossible.

Actually, no one can ever say that a recidivist is beyond hope, since there is an important maturation factor in the life history of addicts which results in many of them "cleaning up" and disappearing from the *scene* during the fourth and fifth decades of their lives. The reason for this is not fully understood, nor is the fate of older addicts known, although some become "winos."

The Duvall study indicates that addicts tend to use less drugs as they get older. In agreement with most other reports on follow-up after treatment which indicate a large prompt relapse rate, Duvall reported that 91 per cent of Lexington patients relapsed within six months, and 97 per cent became readdicted at some time during five years after discharge.

Vaillant, in another study of Lexington patients,[37] found that although 96 per cent relapsed within a year 48 per cent were abstinent ten years later. At some time or other within the ten-year study, 30 per cent had made a good abstinent community adjustment for at least thirty consecutive months. This author also showed that nine months or more of compulsory treatment followed by at least one year of parole supervision is 15:1 more effective than voluntary hospitalization. Also, he concluded that abstinence is not only connected with age but with compulsory supervision.

The fact that a patient does relapse after treatment does not mean that that case should be considered a complete failure. As in other chronic diseases, treatment may keep the patient free from symptoms for a considerable period of time, which is well worth the treatment. If an addict stays off drugs for one, two, three or ten years and then relapses, that case should not be counted as a failure, but as a worthwhile expenditure of effort and money. It is remarkable how recidivist addicts who have been treated several times may surprise the hospital staff—as well as themselves, perhaps—by staying off drugs for a long period of time or indefinitely. One recidivist patient had been addicted for more than thirty years, beginning with opium smoking and later using morphine and heroin intravenously. At the time of his last admission, he gained some inspiration from his association with the Addicts Anonymous group in the hospital, and since his last discharge has been off drugs for three years to the present time. He is actively associated with an Addicts Anonymous group outside and finds help for himself by continuing to help patients discharged from the hospital.

There is also the case of the professional writer who had been treated several times, with prompt relapse, but after the fourth treatment had been off drugs for several years until he died as a victim of an automobile accident in New York City. On his body there was found by police a card similar to that carried by diabetics, except that it read: "Notice. If found unconscious please do not give me narcotic drugs as I have been a narcotic addict." Both the authors know many addicts who have been off drugs for many years following one or more treatments, and some of these write regularly several times a year telling of their continued abstinence. Many of them have become successful people.

It has been determined that traces of certain physiological disturbances caused by drug addiction remain for as long as four or five months after the drug is stopped. This, together with certain statistical evidence for relapse of voluntary patients who terminate treatment earlier, determines at the Federal hospitals the minimum period of treatment which is recommended.

Regardless of the number of failures, we must accept narcotic addicts as sick people and treat addiction as we do other chronic diseases, even cases which have already progressed to an apparently hopeless stage. Compared to the results which can be expected under present methods for treating chronic tuberculosis, chronic cancer and chronic heart disease, the results achieved in the treatment of drug addiction are by no means discouraging. With improved techniques and more widely dispersed facilities, coupled with education in the dangers of addiction, strict law enforcement and pharmacological research, there is every reason to hope for a continued decrease in addiction as a chronic disease.

THE TREATMENT OF ACUTE DRUG POISONING

In the discussion of chronic narcotism, we inevitably come to the problem of how to handle acute poisoning from drugs commonly used by addicts. This is not to imply that all those who suffer from such poisoning are addicts or that addicts are commonly the victims of acute poisoning. Indeed, many persons who have never taken the drugs for addiction are poisoned, either accidentally or in attempted suicide; sometimes this is fatal, sometimes not. Among addicts, there is always the danger of accidental poisoning because the addict who is using bootleg drugs may not know the strength of the drug he has bought; also, among addicts, there is some suicide, or attempted suicide from deliberate overdosage. Overdoses of narcotic drugs or *hot shots* (poison) are sometimes given addicts, usually by substituting pure full strength drug for customary adulterated product, as underworld revenge or punishment for "double crossing" or informing.

The addict, however, has a great advantage over the non-addict in the matter of fatal poisoning from opiates in that when he is using drugs he develops a tolerance to quantities of drugs which would undoubtedly be fatal to a non-addict. For example, 1 or 2 grains of medical morphine taken by mouth may be fatal to the average non-addict; if the drug is injected hypodermically, less than that amount will probably have the same effect. Addicts often take from 2 to 10 grains of morphine every twenty-four hours, and many addicts take as much as 5 to 8 grains of morphine or heroin at a single injection. While the non-addict is not likely to have access to as much as 5 grains of morphine, he may well come into possession of large quantities of barbiturates because their sale is not so rigorously controlled. Consequently, barbiturates are often used in suicides or suicide attempts.

Addicts who use barbiturates alone, or in conjunction with

other drugs, may reach a state of intoxication in which memory and judgment fail, but the compulsion to take the drug continues, with the result that they continue to ingest large quantities until fatal coma envelops them. Tolerance to barbiturates develops much less slowly than to opiate drugs. In any event, many lives can be saved by prompt and intelligent action on the part of the police, physicians and other persons who may come into contact with deliberate or accidental poisoning from drugs.

It is the authors' opinion that many more addicts than is generally believed become non-users with passing time, some with treatment, some without. The decrease of the incidence of addiction in older age-groups is not entirely explained by early deaths. For instance, the Bureau of Narcotics, in a study of 16,725 addicts reported during 1953-54, found that only 5,921 were reported again during the following five years.

Opiate Poisoning

This includes poisoning from overdosage of opium or, more commonly, its derivatives, morphine, heroin, Dilaudid, codeine, etc. Two modern synthetics, Demerol and methadone, produce similar effects; poisoning is treated similarly. The drugs depress both the cerebral cortex and the respiration. Death from opiate poisoning cannot be identified by means of any specific anatomic changes; the pathologic findings resemble those of asphyxiation.

Three key symptoms suggest opiate poisoning: constriction of the pupils; some degree of coma; and marked depression of the respiration, with the victim sometimes breathing only several times per minute. In addition, it may be useful to know that opiate poisoning, if detected within half an hour after taking the drug, produces in the victim noticeable flushing of the face, neck and upper torso, nausea, dizziness and scratching to relieve itching of the skin. Drowsiness and sleep ensue, with marked decrease in the rate of breathing, often of the Cheyne-Stokes type. The pulse slows down, the systolic blood pressure is lowered, and postural hypotension is obvious. In very acute poisoning, there may be dilation of the pupils, cyanosis, severe drops in the blood pressure and rate of breathing, very rapid heartbeat and the accumulation of fluid in the lungs. With Demerol poisoning, convulsions may occur. The emergency treatment of acute opiate poisoning follows closely that developed by Isbell[24] for use at the Lexington hospital.

If an opiate drug has been taken by mouth, the stomach should be washed out with a solution of 1:5000 potassium permanganate. Fifty cubic centimeters of 50 per cent magnesium sulfate should be given through the tube before it is withdrawn. The patient should be placed in bed with the foot of the bed elevated. Patient should be lightly covered with no local application of heat which would increase the peripheral vasodilatation and aggravate the circulatory derangement. If necessary, an open airway should be inserted to keep nasopharynx passages clear from secretions. Continuous light reflex stimulation should be used, such as light slapping and pinching. The patient should be engaged in conversation if possible to keep him awake, but he should not be walked, as frequently recommended, because this contributes to low blood pressure which is already a problem. If the breathing is very slow, artificial respiration of the positive-pressure type should be started; oxygen should be administered, preferably with 5 per cent carbon dioxide mixed with the oxygen. Ten to 20 mg of Benzedrine should be given subcutaneously to counteract the peripheral vasodilatation and the cerebral depression. Nikethamide in doses of 5 cc of 25 per cent solution should be given as a respiratory stimulant. If this is not available, 0.5 gm of caffeine sodium should be administered. If neither of these stimulants is available, coffee may be given orally or rectally, if necessary. Respiratory stimulants should be repeated every fifteen minutes until recovery is assured.

The treatment of choice for opiate poisoning, however, is N-allylnormorphine (Nalline), which often gives spectacular results. It appears to be a specific antidote for opium, morphine, heroin, codeine, Demerol, and methadone.[32, 33] The antidotal action of this compound is of great interest, since the drug differs from morphine only in that an allyl group has been substituted for a methyl group on the nitrogen atom in the morphine molecule. This small change in structure produces dysphoria instead of euphoria, thus making the drug very unattractive to addicts; its effect might be described as the antithesis of morphine. It has already provided a valuable diagnosis for physical dependence on opiates.

N-allylnormorphine is very effective in counteracting the narcotic effects of large doses of morphine, heroin and methadone and has rapidly relieved the respiratory depression in experimental animals. The drug should be administered intramuscularly or intravenously. The action of the drug should become evident within five minutes after intramuscular injection and within one minute after intravenous injection. If the amount of opiate taken by the victim is known, one tenth of the amount of morphine taken or one fiftieth of the amount of Demerol taken constitutes proper dosage of N-allylnormorphine. If the amount of opiate taken by the patient is unknown, one should begin with 5 mg injections of N-allylnormorphine and repeat them every fifteen minutes until definite respiratory stimulation is evident. After that, doses should be repeated every three hours until the patient is out of danger. The other methods of treatment as outlined above should be employed concomitantly with the use of N-allylnormorphine.[25, 26, 27] Treatment is usually successful if the patient is not in coma or if he can be aroused from coma by the methods mentioned. If he is in coma but not in shock, prognosis is doubtful; if in the state of shock with dilated pupils and pulmonary edema, the prognosis is very serious.

There is a belief among addicts on the West Coast that instant coffee or milk injected intravenously is effective treatment for acute opiate poisoning. In the East, a teaspoon of salt dissolved in a little water is used as an antidote for an overdose of opiates. Theoretically, the caffeine in coffee might be an effective stimulant, but the hazards of injecting these foreign substances into the bloodstream must be great.

Acute Barbiturate Poisoning

Acute poisoning from barbiturates may occur either by itself or superimposed upon opium or alcohol. Dangerous doses may be taken either accidentally or intentionally in attempted suicide. Within the past few years, there has been a spectacular increase in the number of suicides by barbiturates. If the patient should be addicted (chronically intoxicated), the treatment for withdrawal outlined previously should be followed. Treatment for acute barbiturate poisoning as carried out at the Lexington hospital has been described by Isbell.[28]

The majority of patients with acute barbiturate intoxication can be readily aroused by persistently applied vigorous manual stimulation. In such cases, treatment with Metrazol or picrotoxin is contraindicated, and all the patient will require is protection and repeated application of manual stimulation whenever he attempts to go to sleep. Mild analeptics, such as hot coffee, 0.5 grain caffeine sodium benzoate or 20 mg of amphetamine sulfate orally or subcutaneously, may be used. If ingestion of barbiturates has been recent, gastric lavage may be performed, but the stomach should be emptied completely, and no wash water left in the stomach in order to avoid possible aspiration of stomach contents into the lungs.

Patients who cannot be awakened by vigorous manual stimulation may be in danger of death and require immediate institution of vigorous treatment, which can be divided into supportive therapy and analeptic therapy. Of these two phases of treatment, supportive therapy is actually the more important and is directed at maintaining adequate respiratory volume and at the prevention of circulatory collapse. The patient should be placed in bed, the foot of the bed elevated, the mouth and pharynx aspirated and, if necessary, an airway inserted. If respiratory depression is not great, oxygen may be administered by nasopharyngeal catheter. If respiration is markedly depressed, artificial respiration with an automatic intermittent positive-pressure respirator of an approved type is indicated. In emergency situations, manual methods of artificial respiration may have to be used. Mouth-to-mouth insufflation through gauze is more effective than the usual manual methods. If the patient's blood pressure is low and the pulse rapid and thready, plasma or whole blood should be administered at once; amphetamine or Neo-synephrin may be given in the infusion.

Since the patient may remain comatose for several days, he should be provided with at least 3,000 cc fluid daily in the form of two liters of 5 per cent glucose and one liter of physiological saline. Penicillin or other antibiotics should be administered daily to prevent pneumonia, the patient's position should be changed frequently, and careful attention should be given to the prevention of bed sores. Bronchoscopic aspiration may be necessary if collapse of the lung develops because of aspiration of vomitus.

Two analeptics which have been shown pharmacologically to be effective in treatment of barbiturate depression are available; metrazol and picrotoxin. Both of these drugs are powerful convulsive agents, but the action of Metrazol is prompt and brief, so the effects are readily controlled, while those of picrotoxin are sometimes delayed for as long as ten minutes, even after intravenous injection. Analeptic therapy should, therefore, be begun after supportive measures are underway by administering an "orientation" dose of Metrazol. Five cc Metrazol solution should be slowly injected intravenously. If twitching and grimacing occur, or if the corneal and deep tendon reflexes return, Metrazol is the analeptic of choice, and 5 cc of 10 per cent Metrazol should be administered every fifteen minutes until the patient is out of danger. If the patient does not respond to the orientation dose of Metrazol, a second dose of as much as 8 cc may be given fifteen minutes later. If this second dose of Metrazol is not effective, use of Metrazol should be discontinued and the administration of picrotoxin begun. Care should be exercised in the use of picrotoxin since, while addicts to barbiturates can assimilate the drug intravenously, non-addicts may show toxic reactions to an oral dose as small as 20 mg. We have seen several patients who failed to exhibit the convulsive stage with picrotoxin and were pushed into further depression and death from picrotoxin poisoning by injudicious use of picrotoxin. Fifteen minutes after the last orientation dose of Metrazol is given, 2 cc solution of picrotoxin containing 3 mg per cc should be injected intravenously at the rate of 1 cc per minute. The administration of picrotoxin should be discontinued as soon as muscular twitching or the corneal reflexes return. If the initial dose of picrotoxin does not produce the desired effects, the drug should be readministered, raising the dose 1 cc each time until 5 cc (15 mg) are given every fifteen minutes. As coma lessens, the dose of picrotoxin may be decreased and intramuscular administration begun. The aim of treatment with Metrazol or picrotoxin is to keep the patient constantly restless and active but to stop short of a convulsive dose. If convulsions are induced with either agent, sodium pentothal should be administered intravenously until the convulsions are controlled. For this purpose, minimal doses of 2 to 3 cc of 2.5 per cent sodium pentothal repeated as required should be employed.

Acute Cocaine Poisoning

Although cocaine may be taken in fatal doses (20 mg to 1.2 gm) it is not often used in suicide attempts. However, the fatal dosage differs considerably both with individuals and with the drug, which has a most variable toxicity. For this reason also, cocaine is now seldom used medically by injection, though it is still favored for local application to mucous membranes. Before applying cocaine in quantity for inducing local anesthesia, a safety measure is the administration of a dose of some barbiturate.

Poisoning with cocaine ranges from mild to fatal; even in mild states, anxiety and confusion are present, and with larger doses hallucinations and delusions may appear. Danger signs include tachycardia, elevation of the systolic blood pressure, dilation of the pupils and noticeable sweating along with dyspnea, Cheyne-Stokes respiration and tremors. In severe poisoning, convulsions and death result from apnea. Individuals with an idiosyncrasy to cocaine may suffer sudden cardiovascular collapse.

Isbell[24] recommends the administration of cortical depressants. For moderate intoxication, 0.25 gm of sodium amytal should be injected intramuscularly. In cases of severe poisoning, rapid treatment may be necessary, and 0.5 gm of sodium amytal or sodium pentobarbital should be injected intravenously at the rate of 0.1 gm per minute.

Treatment of acute poisoning due to idiosyncrasy to the drug is usually ineffective because of the rapidity with which symptoms develop. Patients should be placed in shock position and given intravenous injections of nikethamide.

Amphetamine Poisoning

Poisoning by amphetamine resembles cocaine poisoning, but the symptoms are milder and do not develop so rapidly. Amphetamines are powerful cortical stimulants and also potent sympathomimetic drugs. Chronic users of these drugs take as much as 250 mg at a dose by mouth or by needle. Patients who have been poisoned develop jerky, tremulous movements, tachycardia, hypertension and dilation of the pupils. A toxic psychosis, characterized by accompanying hallucinations and delusions of a paranoid type, may develop. Fatal poisoning by amphetamines has been known to occur.[31] Treatment for poisoning is simple: abrupt withdrawal of the drug, followed by judicious sedation.

Marihuana Poisoning

Although acute poisoning from cannabis is possible, it does not occur in a dangerous degree in the United States. Probably this is due to the fact that the marihuana consumed here does not contain a very highly concentrated form of hemp resin, cannabis indica, as do the charas and hashish preparations used abroad. Ingestion of dangerous amounts of cannabis by smoking as it is used in the United States is more difficult than by oral ingestion as it is taken in other parts of the world. Patients who have developed a toxic psychosis from smoking marihuana require observation and, possibly, restraint until the effects of the drug have become dissipated.

Tranquilizers

Essig[36] reported in 1966 the same type of severe withdrawal symptoms from tranquilizers, i.e., convulsions and acute psychiatric disturbances, as found following the withdrawal of barbiturates. He reported specifically on Valmid, Placidyl, Librium and Valium, in addition to the nonbarbiturates, Doriden and Noludar, observing that a cross-tolerance existed between these drugs and barbiturates. He described a procedure for the gradual withdrawal by substituting barbiturates.

LSD

The treatment of the acutely disturbed LSD user is an urgent psychiatric matter, inasmuch as suicide is frequently a danger and occasionally homicide. Intramuscular Thorazine is recommended in large doses for acute or chronic psychoses.

REFERENCES

1. WOLFF, P. O.: The treatment of drug addicts. A critical survey. *Bulletin of the Health Organization of the League of Nations,* 12(4):455, 1945-46.
2. VOGEL, V. H., WHITMAN, H., and WHITE, G. H.: How can we stop making drug addicts of our children? *Town Hall. Bulletin of America's Town Meeting of the Air.* Volume 17: No. 11, pp. 2-15.
3. *The Indispensable Use of Narcotics.* Chicago, American Medical Association, 1931.
4. VOGEL, V. H., ISBELL, H., and CHAPMAN, K. W.: Present status of narcotic addiction. *Journal of the American Medical Association,* 138:1019 (Dec. 4), 1948.
5. KOLB, L.: Pleasure and deterioration from narcotic addiction. *Mental Hygiene,* 9:699 (Oct.), 1925.
6. WILSON, D. P.: *My Six Convicts.* New York, Rinehart, 1951.
7. PFEFFER, A. Z.: Psychosis during withdrawal of morphine. *Archives of Neurology and Psychiatry,* 58:221 (Aug.), 1947.
8. ISBELL, H., and VOGEL, V. H.: The addiction liability of methadon (Amidone, Dolophine, "10820") and its use in the treatment of the morphine abstinence syndrome. *American Journal of Psychiatry,* 105:12 (June), 1949.
9. *The Merck Manual of Diagnosis and Therapy* (11th ed.), Rahway, N. J., Merck & Company, Inc., 1966. p. 1158.
10. HIMMELSBACH, C. K., and SMALL, L. F.: *Clinical Studies of Drug Addiction. II. "Rossium" Treatment of Drug Addiction.* With a *Report on the Chemistry of "Rossium."* Supplement No. 125 to the Public Health Reports. Washington, D. C., U. S. Government Printing Office, 1937.
11. HIMMELSBACH, C. K., and MERTES, O. T.: The nursing care of drug addicts. *The Trained Nurse and Hospital Review,* 99:495 (Nov.) 1937.
12. KOLB, L., and HIMMELSBACH, C. K.: *Clinical Studies of Drug Addiction. III. A Critical Review of the Withdrawal Treatments With Method of Evaluating Abstinence Symptoms.* Supplement No. 128 to the Public Health Reports. Washington, D. C., U. S. Government Printing Office, 1938.
13. WIEDER, H.: Objective evaluation of insulin therapy of the morphine abstinence syndrome. *Journal of Nervous and Mental Disease,* 110:1 (July), 1949.

14. KOSKOFF, Y. D., DENNIS, W., LAZOVIK, D., and WHEELER, E. T.: The psychologic effects of frontal lobotomy performed for the alleviation of pain. In *The Frontal Lobes*. Research Publications, Association for Research in Nervous and Mental Disease, Volume 27, Part 4, Chapter 33, pp. 723-754. Baltimore, Williams and Wilkins, 1948.
15. MASON, T. H., and HAMBY, W. B.: Relief of morphine addiction by prefrontal lobotomy. *Journal of the American Medical Association, 136*:1039 (April 17), 1948.
16. DYNES, J. B., and POPPEN, J. L.: Lobotomy for intractable pain. *Journal of the American Medical Association, 140*:15 (May 7), 1949.
17. HAMILTON, R. E., and HAYES, G. J.: Prefrontal lobotomy in the management of intractable pain. *Archives of Surgery, 58*:731 (June), 1949.
18. WATTS, J. W., and FREEMAN, W.: Frontal lobotomy in the treatment of unbearable pain. In *The Frontal Lobes*. Research Publications, Association for Research in Nervous and Mental Disease, Volume 27, Part 4, Chapter 32, pp. 715-722. Baltimore, Williams and Wilkins, 1948.
19. SCARFF, J. E.: Unilateral prefrontal lobotomy for the relief of intractable pain and termination of narcotic addiction. *Surgery, Gynecology and Obstetrics, 89*:385 (Oct.), 1949.
20. WIKLER, A., PESCOR, M. J., KALBAUGH, E. P., and ANGELUCCI, R. J.: Effects of frontal lobotomy on the morphine abstinence syndrome in man. An experimental study. *Archives of Neurology and Psychiatry, 67*:510 (April), 1952.
21. ISBELL, H.: Manifestations and treatment of addiction to narcotic drugs and barbiturates. *Medical Clinics of North America, 34*:2 (March), 1950.
22. ISBELL, H., ALTSCHUL, S., KORNETSKY, C. H., EISENMAN, A. J., FLANARY, H. G., and FRASER, H. F.: Chronic barbiturate intoxication. An experimental study. *Archives of Neurology and Psychiatry, 64*:1 (July), 1950.
23. LOS ANGELES COUNTY NARCOTICS AND DANGEROUS DRUG COMMISSION et al.: *Darkness on Your Doorstep*. Los Angeles, The Los Angeles County Board of Supervisors, 1964.
24. ISBELL, H.: Opium poisoning, cocaine poisoning, and chronic amphetamine poisoning. In CECIL, R. L., and LOEB, R. F.: *A Textbook of Medicine* (8th ed.). Philadelphia, Saunders, 1951, pp. 542-550.

25. UNNA, K.: Antagonistic effect of N-allylnormorphine upon morphine. *Journal of Pharmacology and Experimental Therapeutics, 79*:27 (Sept.), 1943.
26. HART, E. R., and McCAWLEY, E. L.: The pharmacology of N-allylnormorphine as compared with morphine. *Journal of Pharmacology and Experimental Therapeutics, 82*:339 (Dec.), 1944.
27. HUGGINS, R. A., GLASS, W. G., and BRYAN, A. R.: Protective action of N-allylnormorphine against respiratory depression produced by some compounds related to morphine. *Proceedings of the Society for Experimental Biology and Medicine, 75*:540 (Nov.), 1950.
28. ISBELL, H.: Acute and chronic barbiturate intoxication. *Veterans Administration Technical Bulletin*, TB, *10-76*:1 (Aug. 15), 1951.
31. SMITH, L. C.: Collapse with death following use of amphetamine sulfate. *Journal of the American Medical Association, 113*: 1022 (Sept. 9), 1939.
32. FRASER, H. F., WIKLER, A., EISENMAN, A. J., and ISBELL, H.: Use of N-allylnormorphine in the treatment of methadone poisoning in man. *Journal of the American Medical Association, 148*:1205 (Apr. 5), 1952.
33. SMITH, C. C., LEHMAN, E. G., and GILFILLAN, J. L.: Antagonistic action of N-allylnormorphine upon the analgetic and toxic effects of morphine, methadone derivatives and isonipecaine. *Federation Proceedings, 10*:335 (Mar.), 1951.
34. VOGEL, VICTOR H., and VOGEL, VIRGINIA E.: *Facts About Narcotics.* Chicago, Guidance Series Booklet, Science Research Associates, Inc., 1966.
35. THE MEDICAL SOCIETY OF THE COUNTY OF NEW YORK: Narcotics addiction. *New York Medicine, 21*:2 (Jan.), 1965.
36. ESSIG, C. F.: Newer sedative drugs that can cause intoxication and dependence of barbiturate type. *Journal of the American Medical Association, 196*:714 (May), 1966.
37. SMITH, W. G., ELLINWOOD, E. H., JR., and VAILLANT, G. E.: Narcotic addicts in the mid-1960's. *Public Health Reports, 81*:403 (May), 1966.

Chapter 7

LEGAL CONTROLS FOR DRUGS OF ADDICTION

INTERNATIONAL CONTROLS

THE close control of addicting drugs throughout the world is now rather generally recognized as desirable in the interest of the health and welfare of mankind. This is especially true of the opiates. Although in the elimination of most health hazards, education has been given at least equal status with legal suppressive measures, up to now at least, efforts to reduce or eliminate drug addiction have been almost entirely legislative.

In a way this emphasis on the law and law enforcement has had a favorable effect, since the more intensive the efforts at legislative control, the more the confirmed underworld addict is exposed to identification as a criminal. In the same way, the pressures of law enforcement have isolated and spotlighted the underworld traffic in drugs as one of our most vicious criminal rackets. The activities of criminal addicts resulting from their efforts to obtain money to purchase drugs have already been discussed. There remain to be considered the specific violations of the Federal narcotic laws themselves and the broader aspects of international efforts directed at the closer control of production and sale of narcotics for non-medical purposes.

On the international side, there were, between 1911 and 1936, six international agreements and conventions, followed by two international protocols agreed to by the United Nations in 1946 and 1948. The early anti-narcotic activities of the League of Nations were formally transferred to the United Nations, where a Commission on Narcotic Drugs holds frequent meetings and reports to the Economic and Social Council. In general, these international meetings and agreements have been for the exchange of information concerning the traffic in contraband opium and its derivatives; to a lesser extent, the same commission is interested in cocaine and marihuana. Although it is fairly generally agreed that the addicting use of the opiates should be suppressed, there are still some areas were governmental action is weak or nonexistent. Furthermore, there continues to be some disagreement among various countries as to the harmful effects of the use of cocaine as coca leaf chewing, and millions of people in various parts of the world regularly use hashish without governmental interference. There is, finally, official agreement by South American countries that the chewing of coca leaves is harmful, but it will be many years before this custom is stamped out.

In addition to assembling information concerning the production and use of opium and its derivatives, considerable success has attended international efforts to bring the world production of opium into line with the amount needed for medical purposes. It is true that large amounts of opium continue to be converted to addictive use, but for the past several decades the amount of opium diverted to this use has decreased.

In 1951, efforts were made in the United Nations to set up an international opium monopoly which would purchase all legitimate opium to be produced in accordance with quotas set up by that body. Opium and its products would, under this proposal, be sold by the official monopoly only to the various official agencies of the countries, which would be responsible for keeping the drug in legal channels for medical use. This proposal, to which most of the countries agreed in principle, failed primarily because no agreement could be reached as to the price to be paid the producing countries. Several countries depend heavily on the income from opium for economic equilibrium and thus asked for higher prices than the consuming countries felt they would have to pay in an open market. Furthermore, it was difficult if not impossible to guarantee the producing countries a stable quota year after year, in the face of increasing production of cheaper synthetic analgesic drugs, which potentially may largely supplant opiate drugs for medical use. All parties realized that opiate prices might have to be increased proportionately from year to year to maintain the total income desired by the producing countries, especially since the increased production of synthetics might not only threaten economic catastrophe for certain countries, but might force more of the opiate drugs into contraband channels unless international controls, which are now unforeseen, could

Legal Controls for Drugs of Addiction 241

be used to reduce the amount of opium grown in the world. Then, if the synthetic equivalents of opiate drugs are produced in clandestine laboratories more cheaply than opiates can be obtained in the contraband market, the natural opiates may become even cheaper and more readily available than they are now in many parts of the world. As desirable as international agreement on limitation of opiate production in the world is, it will probably be more difficult to achieve as time goes on, and can be accomplished only by serious economic sacrifices on the part of certain producing countries or by expensive subsidies raised by nonproducing countries.

At the 1951 session of the Commission on Narcotic Drugs, there was also some dissention over the possibility that certain opium producing countries would start manufacturing alkaloids of opium, which has up to now been carried on largely in the nonproducing countries. It is obvious that international control, while in the last analysis the basis for effective national control, is still a long-range project which is not yet operating on a functional level.

In addition, the United Nations World Health Organization in Geneva maintains an Addiction-Producing Drugs Section which has no authority to control or influence international agreements, or to limit production or traffic in narcotics. It is a purely scientific organization for the accumulation and dissemination of data on addiction and the drug traffic. Also, the International Criminal Police Commission, organized in 1923, includes a section on narcotics. This organization, nonpolitical in nature, includes thirty-nine nations and exists for the accumulation and exchange of information concerning persons engaged in international criminal activities. It also acts as an agency for the improvement and demonstration of police methods. Several references are given for the reader who wishes to obtain information concerning the international aspects of opium use and control.[1, 2, 3, 4, 5] The reader is also referred to current reports of Treasury Department hearings before the House of Representatives Appropriations Committee for interesting details of contraband narcotic traffic.

In 1961, the World Health Organization finally agreed on a Single Convention on Narcotic Drugs which brought the signatory nations into agreement on many aspects of addiction, including a list of drugs considered to be addicting.

NATIONAL CONTROLS

Federal laws regulating narcotic drugs in the United States include those commonly known as the "narcotic laws," the Harrison Narcotic Law and others, and the Federal Food, Drug and Cosmetic Act, often referred to as the Pure Food and Drug Law. Prior to the first decade of the twentieth century, there was no restriction of any kind on the importation or use of opium or its derivatives in the United States. Many patent medicines contained opium or derivatives of opium without carrying any warning label, and there were many people who were physically dependent, as addicts, upon medicines which were bought and sold without restriction. Women especially became unwitting addicts through taking patent medicines for "female disorders." Opium smoking, introduced by Orientals but spreading rapidly to all classes in the United States, went on unhindered. Physicians prescribed narcotics without supervision or limitation; pharmacists, general storekeepers and even grocers sold narcotics without prescription.

Today, the Federal narcotic laws are enforced by the Bureau of Narcotics established in 1930 in the Treasury Department.[6] The principal Federal laws regulating narcotics are these:

1. *Harrison Narcotic Law*, passed in 1914, now included, with amendments, in the Internal Revenue Code;
2. *Narcotic Drug Import and Export Act*, passed in 1922, now included in the Internal Revenue Code;
3. *Narcotic Hospital Law*, passed in 1929, providing treatment facilities for persons addicted to drugs controlled by the narcotic laws;
4. *Narcotic Information Act*, passed in 1930;
5. *Marihuana Tax Act*, passed in 1937, now incorporated in the Internal Revenue Code;
6. *Narcotic Transportation Act*, passed in 1939, amended in 1950;
7. *Opium Poppy Control Act*, passed in 1942;
8. *Narcotic Control Act*, passed in 1956; and
9. *Drug Abuse Control Amendments*, 1965.

Harrison Narcotic Law

In the form of a tax act, this law controls the importation, manufacture, processing, buying, selling, dispensing or giving away, of opium, coca leaves and all their compounds, derivatives and preparations. It requires registration and an occupational tax for all persons who deal in these drugs. Sales or transfers of the drugs under control are made only by the use of official order forms obtained by registrants from the Collector of Internal Revenue. Exceptions are made only for physicians, druggists, veterinarians and other practitioners to prescribe narcotics in accordance with medical needs other than to support addiction and to druggists and pharmacists selling such drugs pursuant to legal prescriptions.

Medicinal preparations which do not contain more than 1 grain codeine or ¼ grain morphine or 2 grains opium per ounce are so-called "exempt preparations." While they may be dispensed without prescription without violating Federal narcotic laws, the dispenser is responsible for selling them only for medical use and not for addictive purposes. Although the Federal law places no limit on the quantity which may be sold, many state narcotic laws do require them to be dispensed upon prescription only or limit the amount to one or two ounces which may be sold without prescription.

Persons licensed thus to deal in narcotics submit regular inventories and keep prescription records available for inspection by Federal narcotic agents. The Harrison Narcotic Law and the Marihuana Tax Act were frankly designed to suppress traffic in addicting drugs and are not intended to produce revenue, inasmuch as the appropriations to enforce the acts greatly exceed the taxes collected. However, both these laws as amended have been held by Federal courts to be legitimate exercises of taxing authority, despite their principal regulatory purpose and effect.[6] New drugs determined to have opium-like addicting liability may be brought under Federal control by Executive Order.

With the recent increase of juvenile addiction, numerous proposals have been made to increase the severity of penalties for selling narcotic drugs.

In 1951, mandatory sentences were provided for the first time for recidivists, and the Narcotic Control Act of 1956 requires minimum mandatory sentences even for first offenders selling either opiates or marihuana. These laws make no distinction between the professional peddler and the addict who may share his drugs or obtain drugs for other addicts largely as partial insurance for protecting his own future supply. Anyone familiar with addicts knows that every addict sooner or later technically becomes a seller, though he may never be a peddler in the true sense.

Many law enforcement officers believe that these severe mandatory penalties act as a deterrent to the drug traffic; others believe that severe mandatory sentences reduce the proportion of convictions by some juries, who wonder about the possibilities of rehabilitation of an addict faced with a minimum of five years in prison.

One of the authors was told by a narcotic agent that if he encountered an addict-peddler who was deserving of rehabilitation, he (the agent) would seek an indictment for possession of drugs which would allow a short suspended sentence for treatment, rather than an indictment for selling. In the authors' opinion, this power of discretion should rest with the court rather than with the police officer, who may be tempted to make a deal reducing the charge as a reward for informing on other addicts rather than on the basis of suitability for rehabilitation.

The authors hold no brief for leniency for the non-addict peddler who exploits the weakness of mankind for profit. They do feel that the court, if well informed, sometimes can, by the judicious use of probation or suspended sentences, further rehabilitation of law violators who may primarily be addicts and only drug traffickers in a secondary or technical sense. It is noteworthy that the Republic of China failed to eliminate addiction even though it established the death penalty for peddlers in 1955.

In 1951, a bill was introduced into the Federal Congress to bring the barbiturates under Federal narcotic laws. The Commissioner of the Bureau of Narcotics opposed the move on the grounds that enforcement would be all but impossible and that the estimated cost of five million dollars would far exceed the revenue. Finally, in 1965, effective legislation to control traffic in barbiturates and amphetamine stimulants was passed as the Drug Abuse Control Amendments.

Narcotic Drug Import and Export Act

This act as amended limits the importation of crude opium and coca leaves to the quantities necessary to supply medical and legitimate requirements only. Licenses are issued to three manufacturers only to import drugs for processing and resale to a larger number of pharmaceutical houses in the United States. The importation of opium for smoking is prohibited without exception. Under this act, the Surgeon General of the United States Public Health Service estimates annually for the Commissioner of the Bureau of Narcotics the amount of narcotics required for the following year for legitimate medical and research purposes.

Narcotic Information Act

This law is similar to the arrrangement whereby informants of Customs violations are rewarded; i.e., persons who give information concerning violation of the narcotic laws may be rewarded. In view of the numerous opportunities which exist for the smuggling of valuable but small volumes of drugs, this provision for rewards is important and is a valuable tool of the Federal enforcement agency.

Marihuana Tax Act

This law sets up taxes and regulations concerning the importation, manufacture and trafficking in marihuana which are similar to those specified for opium and cocaine under the Harrison Narcotic Law. Since marihuana and cannabis indica, its active principle, are not used medically, the enforcement of this act becomes one almost entirely of suppression rather than restriction and regulation of legal medical use.

Narcotic Transportation Act

This law, passed in 1939 and amended in 1950, makes it unlawful to use vehicles, vessels or aircraft to conceal or transport contraband drugs; the regulation provides for seizure of the means of transport if so used. Many vehicles and small boats have been seized. Under the law, which is intended as an obstacle to those wishing to transport illegal drugs, vessels and vehicles so seized are frequently used by narcotic agents in their investigations.

Opium Poppy Control Act

This law prohibits the growth in the United States of the opium poppy except under license. Inasmuch as there has been no need to produce it in the United States, no licenses have been issued under the law, and it is not anticipated by the Bureau of Narcotics that any will be issued. The law provides penalties, however, for any who might grow the opium poppy clandestinely.

Narcotic Hospital Law

Two Federal hospitals administered by the United States Public Health Service were authorized by this law: one at Lexington, Kentucky, which was opened in 1935; and one at Fort Worth, Texas, which was opened in 1938. When established, these hospitals were officially called "Narcotic Farms." This name was subsequently changed to "United States Public Health Service Hospitals" because of the obvious embarrassment to correspondents. Prior to the establishment of these hospitals, there had been no such public hospitals for treatment of addiction except one operated for a period by the State of California and another by the City of New York, both of which were discontinued before the Federal hospitals were opened.

In establishing these hospitals, it was recognized that addiction is not solely a perverse criminal action, but that it usually represents a symptom of underlying personality or emotional disorder which needs treatment, particularly of psychiatric nature, if rehabilitation is to be accomplished. These hospitals provide treatment for voluntary patients, in addition to patients sentenced by Federal courts. In the early years of operation, the Federal hospitals admitted about four prisoner patients for each voluntary patient. Through the years, the trend has been more to voluntary patients and the ratio is almost reversed, the admissions during 1964 favoring voluntary patients almost nine to one. However, during this time only about one third of the patient population at Lexington were voluntary patients, owing to the tendency to depart against medical advice. (Chapter 6 describes treatment at these hospitals.)

In the enforcement of the narcotic laws, the Bureau of Narcotics has operated quietly and efficiently with the result that the general trend in addiction has been downward in the United States since the Harrison Narcotic Law was passed in 1914—at least until the increase in juvenile addiction encountered from 1949 to 1952. Because of high profits involved, and the numerous opportunities for smuggling compact but valuable quantities of contraband narcotics into the country, it is extremely difficult to suppress the contraband traffic completely. The innumerable passengers and vehicles crossing our borders, and the large quantities of ocean freight being unloaded daily in our ports, cannot all be inspected thoroughly. Consequently, much reliance must be placed on information received from sources abroad and informers in this country. The rules of evidence which apply in Federal courts make it very difficult at times to obtain conviction in cases where guilt is quite obvious; the Federal courts are zealous, and rightly so, in protecting the constitutional rights of the individual. There have been many cases in which narcotic peddlers have been apprehended with large quantities of narcotics in their possession, but whose cases were dismissed because the rules pertaining to illegal search and arrest were violated. Narcotic agents commonly use informers, usually addicts themselves, in the investigation and apprehension of peddlers. It is sometimes claimed that informers and agents, in their zeal to achieve commendable records, use unfair methods of entrapment. However, the courts are usually alert for any abuses. In the authors' experience, Federal narcotic agents have in many cases withheld or delayed prosecution of addicts guilty of violating the narcotics laws, particularly professional people, in order to permit them to obtain treatment on a voluntary basis.

The annual reports made by the Commissioner of Narcotics, available each year from the United States Government Printing Office, show the trend in the narcotic traffic, give details of seizures of narcotics, including the many clever ways in which criminals seek to circumvent the narcotic laws, and the ingenious methods by which the narcotic agents seek to circumvent them. The Bureau of Narcotics has always been very inadequately staffed. With the great increase of juvenile addiction, the Federal agents have had to concentrate mainly on the apprehension of criminals who smuggle and sell narcotics on a large scale, leaving the apprehension of most of the small peddlers and addict peddlers to state and local enforcement offices, which frequently are more inadequately staffed than the Federal Bureau of Narcotics.

Federal Food, Drug and Cosmetic Act

The Federal Food, Drug and Cosmetic Act of 1906, as amended, is, as its title indicates, an act to prohibit the movement, in interstate commerce, of adulterated and misbranded food, drugs, devices, cosmetics, etc.

The act places all drugs in two classes: those to be dispensed on prescription only, bearing the label "Caution: to be dispensed only by or on the prescription of a physician (or dentist or veterinarian)"; and non-prescription drugs which may be sold by druggists over the counter without prescription. Certain drugs are designated as habit-forming drugs, and whenever packaged or dispensed they must bear the legend—"Warning—May be habit-forming." This warning may be omitted only when such drugs are prescribed by physicians with appropriate directions for taking. If prescriptions for these drugs are refillable, the warning legend must be attached.

There continues to be some misunderstanding as to whether any prescription, for a habit-forming drug or otherwise, which does not bear the instruction "not refillable" may be refilled. It is the opinion of the officials of the Food and Drug Administration that the law intends such prescriptions not to be refilled, but there has been no conclusive test case. The Food and Drug Administration has records of many instances where narcotic or sedative drugs not controlled by Federal narcotic laws, such as the barbiturates, have been sold in large quantities without prescription, or by irregularly refilling prescriptions. Such action may be stimulated by the profit motive or by ignorance of the addiction liability of the barbiturates or a combination of the two. In several instances, many thousands of barbiturate capsules were delivered on an original prescription calling for not more than one dozen. The Federal Food, Drug and Cosmetic Act is the legal basis for suppression of all sales of sedative drugs, particularly the barbiturates, except upon medical prescription, but flagrant violation continues because of the inadequate funds and personnel to enforce the law rigidly.

At the present time, the Food, Drug and Cosmetic Law allows the drug manufacturer to decide whether or not a given drug is restricted to a prescription sale only. Consequently, one company may market a harmful preparation on a "prescription-only" basis, while another company may distribute a similar preparation for over-the-counter sale without prescription. A bill to correct this defect by giving the administrator of the Federal Security Agency responsibility for designating "prescription-only" drugs was introduced into Congress in 1951 but failed of passage. At the present time, some addicting drugs, even though marked "May be habit-forming," may be sold over the counter without prescription—for example, patent and proprietary preparations containing bromides. Other factors which limit the usefulness of the Food, Drug and Cosmetic Law in the control of drug addiction are: that the law covers only drugs moving in interstate commerce; that control at the wholesale level is less complete that at the retail level; and that appropriations available for the enforcement of the law are grossly inadequate to meet the increasingly abusive use of addicting drugs.

Drug Abuse Control Amendments, 1965

This Federal law, passed in 1965 and effective February 1, 1966, gives the Food and Drug Administration strict inventory control, from manufacturer to consumer, over barbiturates, amphetamines and other drugs to be determined as dangerous. It limits the number of times a pharmacist may refill a prescription and makes it an offense to possess the drugs without a prescription. Other drugs to be included administratively are expected to be peyote, mescaline, LSD, DMT, Psilicybin and some tranquilizers. Special penalties are provided for the sale of drugs to be covered by this act to juveniles who for this purpose are designated under age twenty-one instead of age eighteen usually specified as the age for juveniles. A special Bureau, which may include 500 agents, is to be set up in the Food and Drug Administration for the enforcement of this law, which should do much to reduce the nefarious traffic in dangerous drugs other than those covered by the narcotic laws.

State Narcotic Laws

Under the leadership of the Federal Bureau of Narcotics, forty-two states, the District of Columbia and three territories of the United States have enacted a Uniform State Narcotic Law. Two other states, California and Pennsylvania, have adopted a different law which is considered to be equally effective. The states which lack an adequate narcotic law are Kansas, Massachusetts, New Hampshire, Washington, Hawaii and Alaska. The Uniform State Narcotic Law, when adequately enforced, supplements the Federal law by controlling the illicit small-time traffic, leaving the Federal agency to devote its major attention to the control of larger sources. The rules of evidence which are accepted in state courts are frequently less strict than those in effect in Federal court. Accordingly, many cases which are cooperatively investigated and prepared for prosecution through the joint action of Federal and state officials are prosecuted in state courts instead of Federal courts. In several states, including New Jersey, Kentucky and Louisiana, there is a habitual narcotic law which makes it an offense to be addicted to the opiates, cocaine or marihuana. In California such a law has been held unconstitutional. In this respect, they are unlike the Federal and Uniform State Law which provides penalties only for trafficking in narcotics.

Almost all states have passed special laws prohibiting the delivery of barbiturates to a consumer except upon prescription. However, personnel and funds for the enforcement of these state laws are frequently inadequate or completely lacking. The reader's attention is directed to Chapter 6 for a discussion of the California Civil Rehabilitation Program which minimizes the punitive approach to the addict problem although it provides for compulsory detention for treatment; this is a notable departure from previous trends toward more severe mandatory sentences without hope of probation or parole. In 1966, New York and New Jersey were starting new treatment and rehabilitation programs for addicts based on the civil commitment program in California.

Congress in that year also passed an act to create a similar treatment program.

Local Laws

With the recent increase in juvenile addiction, several cities most affected have set up special narcotic squads for the enforcement of local and state narcotic laws; Chicago has set up a special court which deals exclusively with addicts. To date, the chief weakness of these local laws appears to be their tendency to treat addiction *per se* as a crime, with a year in jail as the "therapy" recommended. Actually, drug addiction can best be combated on the local level—but adequate public facilities for hospitalization simply do not yet exist, with few exceptions—notably California—other than in Federal institutions. There is no magic legal formula for eliminating addiction and the illicit drug traffic.

Large scale traffic in addicting drugs really begins in the countries of production—and this means, by and large, those countries which produce opium, since the bulk of illicit drugs is derived from opium. Several times the amount of opium necessary for the world's medical needs is known to be produced in the Near East alone, under license; how much more is produced illicitly is anyone's guess, but we know that, at present, three fourths of the world's known supply must go into the contraband trade. Some cocaine passes into the world's contraband market, but not so much as formerly. Marihuana bulks large in the contraband trade in the Americas, while hashish is the major contraband drug of Africa and the Near East.

The contraband trade is worldwide and flourishes, despite international agreements to limit production and national efforts to intercept illicit drugs at ports of entry. The wholesalers and importers know and use every trick known to the smuggling trade, and the illicit retail traffic in drugs can never be suppressed until large-scale smuggling is so disrupted that the market cannot be supplied. While efforts are being made in this direction, the steady price of such drugs as heroin and marihuana on the bootleg market reflects a steady wholesale supply. Once illicit drugs are imported into the United States, for instance, the retail distribution is relatively easy for dealers and peddlers. There appear to be, at present, adequate laws to control this traffic, but the real problem lies in the labor of enforcement. Since drugs can come in at many ports of entry—as well as over unguarded frontiers—and since drugs can be smuggled in small, compact bundles concealed about the person, in or under motorcars or within shipments of legal imports, they are difficult to detect. Furthermore, the relatively small force of Federal narcotic agents in the United States, although assisted by customs agents, is hardly adequate to inspect all shipments at all ports of entry. Even close surveillance at the ports and through legitimate channels of commerce can be offset by one or two planes carrying compact but valuable loads of drugs across frontiers and dropping them at prearranged points.

The control of the wholesale drug market, then, depends on the effective control of smuggling in all of it ramifications—including the illicit importation of bootleg drugs under false narcotic or other pharmaceutical labels. Control means the discouragement of both large-scale smuggling and small-scale individual smuggling, of which there appears to be at present enough to sustain, in the aggregate, a considerable retail market.

While most addicts of the underworld variety purchase their drugs through bootleg channels, some prefer to use pure medical drugs and go to a good deal of expense and trouble to secure them through medical channels, but by illegal means. Urban addicts generally tend to patronize the underworld peddler, while rural addicts, especially in the South, show a tendency to procure a substantial percentage of drugs from medical sources; it is estimated that perhaps as many as half the rural and small-town addicts in the southern United States rely on medical drugs obtained in one way or another. Most addicts, it should be noted, prefer medical drugs because of their higher strength and greater reliability, but at the same time must run a greater risk in securing them, since most physicians and pharmacists are vigilant as well as law-abiding, and since the prescription records and purchase records of medical drugs are under constant check by the Narcotics Bureau; an addict caught using or selling medical drugs (even though legally prescribed and purchased) for the support of addiction is just as guilty of violating Federal law as if he were handling contraband medical drugs or bootleg drugs purchased in the underworld.

Medical drugs may be stolen during robberies or burglaries of either retail or wholesale drug dealers, in which case the price is rather high on the bootleg market, or they may be secured from physicians or druggists directly. If the physician or druggist is knowingly selling the narcotics to addicts (not an uncommon occurrence, especially in smaller communities), the price is likewise high. However, if the addict can, by a ruse, so simulate conditions which indicate the medical use of narcotics, he may deceive the physician and be able to secure medical drugs through the misuse of legitimate channels, and at a very nominal price. Furthermore, many addicts who are not underworld characters support their habits for long periods of time by the use of similar devices to deceive the physician, or by theft, forgery or misrepresentation involving violations of the narcotics laws.

Addicts who like medical drugs often become very adept at securing them. Professional thieves (who rank high among addicts, percentagewise) often steal drugs directly from pharmacists during business hours; a *heel thief* who makes a specialty of taking large amounts of cash from behind a teller's window during banking hours finds it relatively simple to take narcotics from a pharmacist, the only question being whether or not there are enough drugs to justify the trouble and the risk involved. Those who cannot steal drugs directly, or do not want to do so, can always find someone who will, for a price.

Sometimes narcotics are taken from druggists and even from physicians at the point of a gun during armed robbery. Although holdups by addicts out to secure drugs are not common, they are occurring with increasing frequency. More commonly, drugs are stolen from physicians' offices, cars, and from drugstores by breaking and entering. Also, because of the value of pure medical drugs on the bootleg market, stickup mobs who work drugstores seldom overlook a stock of marketable narcotics. There are cases in which members of these mobs are addicted and readily use violence to secure drugs.

By and large, however, it is the observation of the authors that addicts do not consistently use violence to secure drugs or even to get the money with which to buy drugs. They approach the physician directly, with a story of physical disability or a set of symptoms which, they hope, will persuade him that either a prescription for narcotics or an injection of narcotics in the office is necessary to relieve the symptoms. If a physician makes a bona fide diagnosis of a condition requiring drugs, he is well within his rights to prescribe, even to an addict; however, a physician who knowingly prescribes drugs for the support of addiction is liable to prosecution. There are exceptions even to this, since it is quite legal for a physician to treat an addict for withdrawal from narcotics on an office basis, with a carefully managed regimen of diminished dosage; however, physicians treating addiction on this basis must be prepared to have their inventories and prescriptions checked frequently by narcotics agents, since many addicts do not enter such treatment in good faith and use the treatment as a guise for obtaining narcotics; some even undergo the "reduction" treatment from several physicians simultaneously, thus securing a rather regular supply of medical drugs. Another exception (somewhat extra-legal, but well recognized) is that a physician may give an addict a small amount of drugs if he is convinced that the addict is en route to a hospital or other place of treatment for addiction. Although such administration is technically illegal, since it is at least temporarily for the support of addiction, it is usually ignored by narcotics agents—unless certain physicians seem to develop a large and obvious clientele of such transients. It should be added that many physicians give such treatment in good faith, but that the addicts often consult numerous physicians on the same basis and thus succeed in supporting their habits.

While every practicing physician has doubtless detected addicts in the act of simulating false symptoms in order to procure narcotics, it is surprising how many physicians have responded favorably to other individuals with other symptoms and an approach so disarming that the physician did not suspect that he was prescribing for an addict. Interestingly enough, the completely ethical practitioner is often victimized by certain types of addict more often than he suspects, since the physician who sees few if any known addicts is very susceptible to the ruses practiced by some addicts who operate on a very high level and sometimes use techniques comparable to those employed in some confidence games.

Characteristic Violations Involving "Medical" Narcotics

For the information of physicians and pharmacists who wish to protect themselves from inadvertently prescribing, administering or selling drugs to addicts, and for the information of law enforcement officers in the investigation of drug cases, several typical ruses used by addicts are presented.

1. An addict may read the death notices in the paper each day and visit any physician's widow immediately, representing himself as a narcotic agent or at least the representative of the Narcotics Bureau, and requesting permission to check the dead physician's inventory or, sometimes, claiming the right to take charge of it, giving a receipt on which payment will presumably be made later. Because physicians' wives usually know about Federal drug inventories, and because such an inspection does not seem unreasonable, many of them admit the addict to the office and even assist him in his work. Of course, such procedures are certainly not approved by the Narcotics Bureau, and anyone claiming connection with that bureau would in any case be able to show thoroughly reliable credentials.

2. An addict will appear at a physician's office simulating great pain. (Usually smart addicts do not ask directly for drugs, but manifest symptoms which they know are likely to call for narcotics.) The addict may give a set of symptoms strongly suggesting kidney stone; the physician then asks him to pass a urine sample, which, if it contains blood, may strongly substantiate the addict's story. However, the addict usually gets the blood into the urine from a small cut in the meatus (made just prior to passing the urine) or from a small cut or puncture in his finger. Many addicts are adept at getting blood into the urine even though the physician may watch the passage of the specimen. On the strength of this symptom, the physician may not only administer morphine immediately, but may prescribe narcotics for the addict to take with him.

3. An addict may reenforce the symptoms of kidney stone by sticking or taping to his body a small stone which will show in

x-rays as a kidney stone. The District Supervisor of the Bureau of Narcotics at Detroit, Michigan, reports a case in which an addict had a small pocket of scar tissue over the site of a kidney operation; he could easily insert a tiny piece of gravel in this pocket, and it would show up in any x-ray films taken. There are, of course, many variations of this technique.

4. An addict may enter a physician's office and expose a very pustulous and revolting abscess, often cultivated specifically for this purpose, pretend great distress and hope that the physician will give him an injection to quiet him and get him out of the office.

5. Some addicts are known as *wingding artists, twisters,* etc. They have learned to feign violent illness, sometimes in public places where they are likely to be physicians available and hope for the administration of an injection of morphine or other opiate. Many of these addicts are sufficiently convincing to be able to support small habits more or less regularly by this method.

6. An addict (sometimes accompanied by his girlfriend or wife to lend a family atmosphere) will often approach a physician describing the symptoms of a mythical member of the family who is ill and in great pain. He may reenforce his plea for help by showing letters, empty containers or other evidence that his regular physician has been prescribing narcotics for the patient. If the hour is late and the weather bad and the address far off, the doctor may succumb to the temptation to prescribe without seeing the patient, even though he knows it is an irregular practice. Some high-type addicts are very clever at documenting a story of prolonged or incurable illness, and at documenting it so thoroughly that very ethical physicians are persuaded to prescribe narcotics in considerable quantities at regular intervals for a patient whom they never see; sometimes the addict makes friends with the office nurse in order to facilitate orders for refilling prescriptions without even seeing the physician.

7. An addict may secure a legitimate prescription for narcotics through one of the ruses described above, and purchase, for instance, three dozen quarter-grain morphine tablets. Later he returns with the purchase, saying that his doctor wants him to cut down the dosage and wants the druggist to exchange the quarter-

grain tablets for eighth-grain tablets. However, the "quarter-grain tablets" he returns have been removed from the bottle and saccharin or other inert tablets substituted.

8. Addicts may break into a physician's office or otherwise secure temporary possession of it long enough to place calls for narcotics with one or more wholesale pharmacy supply houses. One of the addicts, wearing the doctor's coat and a stethoscope, signs for the purchases, presenting a forged narcotic order blank and either pays cash or asks the delivery boy to charge the purchase.

9. Addicts will often purchase pharmaceuticals which have a low narcotic content and are not sold on prescription or medicines like atropine-morphine combinations which are known to contain enough morphine to be addicting, but which are thought to be so unpalatable or adverse in their effects that no one could use them to support a habit. However, the addicts treat or alter these compounds so that they can reclaim the narcotic and eliminate all or most of the other unpalatable drugs. For instance, the morphine-atropine combination can be broken up by putting the tablet on a blotter and dropping a little water on it from a medicine dropper. The water dissolves most of the atropine, along with a little of the morphine, and carries the atropine into the blotter. The addict then injects the morphine residue without much ill effect from the slight amount of atropine remaining.

10. Nurses who are addicted or who supply drugs to friends or customers who are addicted use all sort of ruses to obtain narcotics illegally, ranging from downright theft from patients, physicians or hospital storerooms, to the forging of prescriptions.

11. Physician-addicts will often prescribe narcotics for a patient, but request that the pharmacist deliver them to the doctor's office, which is quite ethical, provided the patient gets the drugs.

12. Physicians sometimes prescribe narcotics for a patient, then ask him to bring his medicine to the office so that the doctor can examine it. The physician then substitutes non-narcotic tablets and keeps the narcotics for his own use. Also, occasional physicians who sell medical supplies of drugs to addicts may prescribe for mythical patients or for patients who do not require any narcotics, or who require only a little, and then divert the drugs into illicit channels, usually for a very good price. Since physicians are

allowed a reasonable amount of drugs for emergency use without keeping detailed records, small amounts may be diverted to illegal use, but sooner or later, the dishonest physician is forced by his addict customers to increase operations until they become apparent to narcotic agents.

13. Pharmacists who are addicted obtain narcotics for their own use by substituting non-narcotics for narcotics as they fill prescriptions, by adulterating prescription drugs, by forging prescriptions or by "raising" legitimate prescriptions so that they may keep the difference for their own use or for sale to addicts.

14. A very common practice among addicts seeking medical narcotics is to obtain, usually by stealing, prescription blanks and forge a prescription for narcotics, complete with signature which they then present to a pharmacist for filling.

15. Narcotic prescription drugs in home medicine cabinets are sometimes appropriated by other members of the family, especially juveniles. One teenage girl reportedly became mildly addicted and her mother inadvertently got pregnant because the girl, surreptitiously seeking contraceptives, interchanged the contents of prescription bottles containing narcotics, contraceptive pills, and vitamin tablets to cover her pilferage.

While similar instances could be related indefinitely, enough have been cited to illustrate the pattern of law violations of a certain type. If publicity sometimes focuses the public's attention upon the misuse of drugs by physicians, nurses and pharmacists, it must be remembered that these professions are constantly exposed to drugs and that their work is sometimes done under physical conditions which make the use of narcotics or stimulants very tempting; furthermore, not being criminals by nature, they are often not adept at concealing their illegal acts, and readily fall afoul of the law. A policy statement of the American Medical Association for the guidance of physicians in their use of narcotics has been published.[8]

Those in charge of stocks of narcotics in hospitals and pharmacies should critically reexamine at frequent intervals their precautions against thefts and misuse of narcotics. Narcotic thieves are clever and audacious.

Drug addicts and illicit drug dealers on all social and professional levels try to circumvent the laws which are intended to control traffic in addicting drugs. This evasion of the law is worldwide, with the ingenuity of the violators increasing with the severity and strictness of the law in any particular country. In the United States, where drugs are subject to stricter control than perhaps anywhere else in the world, the methods of evasion are legion, and the individuals who control the drug traffic at its source are big-time racketeers. The importers, dealers and peddlers are all motivated by the high profits in the contraband traffic. The addicts are mainly concerned with getting enough drugs to satisfy their own craving—although many of them like to secure enough so that they can sell a surplus, thus supporting, or helping to support, their individual habits. They are the addict-peddlers who are the retailers of the illicit drug business, and against whom much of the enforcement activities must necessarily be directed.

Citizens during the prohibition era became, if not complacent, inured to corrupt public officials and law enforcement officers linked with underworld traffic in liquor, but the same public is shocked to find that links exist between our legal representatives and traffic in narcotics. Revelations in Washington in 1952 concerning payments to police for protection of drug distributors came as a climax to a series of shocks with respect to corruption of public officials in the nation's capital. Testimony was given concerning the payment of money by drug distributors to the police for protection. The police also on occasion were said to have personally received shipments of drugs for their distributor friends and also to have used their official position to force drug buyers to patronize the distributors who were their friends. According to testimony given, local officials there even warned their underworld connections when they were in danger of apprehension by Federal narcotics officers. Testimony given indicated that narcotics seized from "unprotected peddlers" by the District of Columbia narcotics police were given to "protected peddlers" for resale. The truth is that the importation and distribution at wholesale levels, and frequently at retail levels, is likely to flourish only under some form of police protection, being similar in this respect to other rackets. If there are police who feel any revulsion toward giving protection for the sale of drugs, they may be unable to discriminate, since those buying protection for other underworld activities frequently combine drug traffic with their other enterprises.

To show how many agencies work more or less in cooperation in enforcing various aspects of the narcotic law, upwards of 200 agents work in this field in the Los Angeles area. These include Federal narcotic, customs, Food and Drug Administration agents, state narcotic and Food and Drug agents, city police and county sheriffs.

The so-called "British system" of narcotic control is often mentioned in the press as allowing physicians to prescribe drugs freely for addicts, thus preventing a criminal traffic in narcotics. In 1960, a team of medical men[7] from the New York Department of Health visited England to investigate these reports, and found, indeed, a very small narcotics problem very well controlled, with only about 350 known addicts in a population of 50,000,000 and only fourteen addicts among a prison population of 40,000. However, they found that *the controls there are effective because the problem is very much smaller, and not because of any unique "system."*

In 1964, however, the British reported a 100 per cent increase in the number of known addicts and a comparatively large increase in contraband traffic of narcotics and "dangerous" drugs. In 1965, a British Commission visited the United States to consider a more effective way of stemming the tide of addiction in England.

Actually, narcotics may be prescribed there, as in the United States, only for medical needs. The government instructions to doctors are that "The continued supply of dangerous (narcotic) drugs to a patient solely for the gratification of addiction is not regarded as a 'medical need.'" Medical need, however, may be interpreted a little more liberally than in the States, and government supervision of the dispensing of drugs may not be quite as rigid in England, but there is no loose or considerable furnishing of drugs to addicts. Violation of the law provides very severe penalties (£1,000 fine or ten years in prison, or both) for physicians or dentists convicted under the law. There are no "clinics" for the dissemination of drugs to addicts, who are hospitalized for treatment much as they are in the U. S. Public Health Service Hospitals here. This fact may come as a surprise to many Americans who have been reading favorable press accounts of the handling of the drug problem in Britain.

The chief difference between the States and England seems to be a marked difference in the susceptibility of the population to the use of drugs and to addiction. In other words, there is a strong and almost universal aversion in the British culture to the use of drugs, and this cultural difference (which deserves further study) seems to explain the small number of addicts as well as the virtual absence of a contraband drug traffic in England. By way of contrast, the port of Hong Kong, where the same British laws govern narcotics, supports a very large contraband traffic and probably has more addicts than there are in the entire United States.

REFERENCES

1. MAY, H. L.: The evolution of international control of narcotic drugs. *Bulletin on Narcotics,* 2(1):1 (Jan.), 1950.
2. UNITED NATIONS, DEPARTMENT OF SOCIAL AFFAIRS: Unification of conventions on narcotic drugs. Scope of the conventions: Definitions. *Bulletin on Narcotics,* 2(2):32 (Apr.), 1950.
3. LAUGIER, H.: International control of narcotic drugs. *Bulletin on Narcotics,* 1(1):4 (Oct.), 1949.
4. MARABUTO, P.: The International Criminal Police Commission and the Illicit Traffic of Narcotics. *Bulletin on Narcotics,* 3(3):3 (July), 1951.
5. LAVELLE, A. M.: Narcotic drugs and penal law. *Bulletin on Narcotics,* 3(3):16 (July), 1951.
6. ANSLINGER, H. J.: Control of the traffic in narcotic drugs. *The Merck Report,* 60:33 (Oct.), 1951.
7. LARIMORE, GRANVILLE W., and BRILL, HENRY: The British Narcotic System. *The New York State Journal of Medicine,* 60:107 (Jan.), 1960.
8. COUNCIL ON MENTAL HEALTH, NARCOTICS AND MEDICAL PRACTICE: A report of the American Medical Association's Council on Mental Health and the National Academy of Sciences—National Research Council's Committee on Drug Addiction and Narcotics. *Journal of the American Medical Association,* Vol. 185: No. 12, September 21, 1963.

Chapter 8

NARCOTIC ADDICTION AND CRIME

AT the beginning of this chapter it should be clearly understood that there are exceptions to almost every statement the authors make, and that anything said here can be modified by changing conditions and the collection of additional data. Generalizations in the area of drug addiction and its relationship to crime are not only difficult to make, but often unreliable after they are made. At the same time, generalizations offer a temptation, not only to sensational journalists, but to medical men, enforcement officers, the judiciary, criminologists, researchers and others who, the public assumes, may speak with authority. Once a sweeping statement is made and quoted or paraphrased in print, the public tends to accept it rather than to examine it critically; these generalizations accumulate in the form of public opinion, the result being that the public not only holds lurid beliefs about drug addiction as a causative factor in crime, but is prepared to believe reports that are even more lurid, at the same time rejecting or ignoring conservative statements based upon direct scientific observation and experience. Exaggerated statements on the one hand and too conservative disclaimings of causative relationships on the other are equally misleading.

This situation has been intensified by the release of figures during recent years showing a substantial increase of the number of narcotic addicts in various prison populations, especially in Federal prisons, without adequate explanation for this increase. As a matter of fact, if we accept figures from the Bureau of Narcotics, narcotic addiction has decreased steadily under strict enforcement of the Harrison Act, except for the relative increase between 1949 and 1964, an increase which is small when viewed in relation to the total picture. A similar but less sustained increase was observed following World War I. Furthermore, with the general increase in crime (or the publicity regarding crime) the public tends to associate narcotics with this general increase. This loose cause-and-effect association is the basis for what the authors believe to be some fallacious conclusions regarding drugs and crime.

In the light of modern sociological research, we are learning to recognize two large classes of criminals, the professional and the nonprofessional (see Fig. 28). The nonprofessional is usually a member of the dominant culture (that large segment of our culture which pays the taxes, makes the laws, establishes the schools and in general supports the institution of organized legitimate society), and when he seriously violates the code of the dominant culture he may be tried, convicted and sentenced, all of which gives him a criminal record. But he is not accepted by the professionals, nor does he have access to their *modus operandi*.

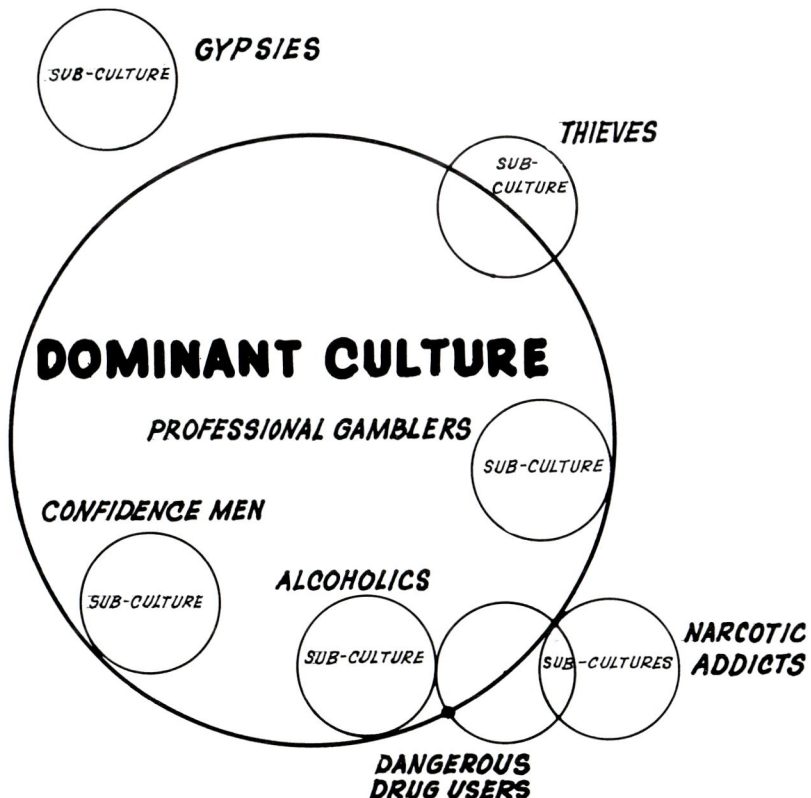

FIGURE 28. Culture structure.

On the other hand, the professional usually belongs to a subculture which is antithetical to the dominant culture. There are many of these criminal subcultures, some existing on the fringe of the dominant culture, some imbedded solidly within it and some definitely outside it. These subcultures have a set of values entirely or partially opposed to those held by the dominant culture. Most of these subcultures are very ancient, having migrated into Europe in the late Middle Ages and to North America from the seventeenth century on. There are close bonds connecting members of any given subculture, as, for example, pickpockets, and, in turn, looser but very real bonds connecting all professional pickpockets with all other thieves, of which there are dozens of varieties, all parasitic on the dominant culture.

Members of these subcultures may conform to some of the tenents of the dominant culture, but in the main they have their own mores, ethics and traditions. When they violate the code of their subculture, they must pay the penalty, often ostracism or death. When they violate the code of the dominant culture, they are processed by the courts and penalized the same as a nonprofessional from the dominant culture. Dr. Maurer has studied several of these subcultures in some depth and presents here only a superficial delineation of the relations of criminal subcultures to the dominant culture. For further details, the reader is referred to his recent study of one branch of professional thieves, their language and their culture pattern.[1]

Narcotic addicts form a very recent subculture, originating in America with the opium addicts of the late nineteenth century who congregated because of the social aspects of opium smoking. Since smoking was introduced by the Chinese, who not only had the supply of opium but the equipment and techniques for smoking as well, a small, essentially noncriminal subculture appeared wherein smokers from all walks of life gathered regularly. Although some criminals frequented these groups, largely concentrated in centers of Chinese life, they were mainly composed of people from the dominant culture and did not become predominantly criminal until after 1914, when the Harrison Act outlawed the drugs as well as the addict.

Today it is a very tightly organized subculture, supplied with drugs from the underworld and at the same time exploited by other criminal subcultures which prey on the addict. Also, the addict's subculture is infiltrated with criminals from many other subcultures, driven there in order to secure and use drugs. Members of the dominant culture who are addicted are also driven to the subculture of the addicts sooner or later and become a part of the so-called underworld.

The addict's subculture, while neither so ancient nor so hemogenous as, say, the subculture of thieves, is very large, highly organized from coast to coast and even on an international basis and has already developed a discernible behavior pattern as well as a highly specialized language. As soon as the addict finds the means—almost always illegal—of raising the large amounts of money necessary to support his increasing habit, he becomes a criminal, and often a professional or pseudo-professional, even though he may have originally been a solid member of the dominant culture. After a while, these addicts become indistinguishable from the other professional criminals who populate the criminal subculture.

This shift from the dominant culture to the criminal subculture is dramatically illustrated by the shift in the use of opiates by addicts. In 1914, all addicts used opiates or cocaine, with morphine and opium being the most popular. A few used heroin, only recently introduced from Europe, and, until the advent of the Harrison Act, as legitimate as opium, morphine or cocaine. In 1937, 50.7 per cent of the addicts received at the Lexington Federal Hospital used morphine, a legitimate drug. In 1964, only 9 per cent used morphine, the rest having adopted heroin, a drug long outlawed, and now the drug commonly used by most criminal addicts. Of course, this is only one of several variations in the use of drugs, not all of which show so clearly the development of the addict's subculture to one predominantly criminal.

Throughout this book, then, when we speak of the criminal narcotic addict, we mean one who has gravitated—either from the dominant culture or from some other criminal subculture—to the present subculture of the addict and who regularly employs some form of crime to support his habit. Most of his drugs now come from underworld sources. By the term "legitimate addict," we mean one who is still a member of the dominant culture, who has no connections through which to obtain drugs from the underworld and who does not support his habit by crime, even though he may technically violate the narcotic laws in the course of obtaining and using drugs. A nurse who diverts drugs from medical sources for her own use is a good example.

Among the folklore regarding drug addiction and crime, we frequently encounter the belief that holdup men, murderers, rapists and other violent criminals take drugs to give them courage or stamina to go through with acts which they might not commit when not drugged; some years ago cocaine was thought to be used for this purpose; today, when almost no addicts take cocaine by itself, there is a popular tendency to credit heroin (the accidental resemblance of *heroin* to *hero* has possibly had some influence) with this capacity to motivate and sustain a criminal during crimes of violence. It is believed that drugs stimulate sex crimes, that they make people vicious, that they cause moral degeneration, that they convert otherwise peaceable people into maddened, desperate criminals. Undoubtedly, one factor contributing to the perpetuation of these beliefs is the tendency of some criminals to claim, in court, that they are not responsible for their acts of violence because they were under the influence of drugs; this parallels the tendency, much more common, to claim consideration for a person committing a criminal act because he was under the influence of alcohol. However, in the case of alcohol, many people are familiar with its effects, often including members of the court, and because its use is widespread, there is a tendency to make allowances for criminal behavior by drunken persons, despite the well-established law to the contrary; on the other hand, because drugs are not so widely used, and because their effects are not familiar, the drug (whatever it may be) often is credited with effects on human behavior which cannot be scientifically substantiated.

As far back as 1925, Dr. Lawrence Kolb of the Public Health Service wrote a classic analysis of this problem,[2] and anyone seriously interested in drugs and crime should read Kolb's work as background material. Most of his conclusions are as valid today as they were then, although the general picture of drug addiction in our society has changed considerably, and there are new drugs to be reckoned with, not all of which fit Kolb's pattern for the opiates and cocaine.

There is a close and definite connection between drug addiction and crime—although that connection is not what it is generally supposed to be, and, with some exceptions, there seems to be little evidence to show that drugs, per se, motivate violent crime. While many nonviolent crimes—and occasional crimes of violence—are committed by underworld addicts, these crimes are committed in order to get money to buy drugs, and are not generally the direct result of any physiological action of drugs on the human organism or the human personality. It should also be noted that drugs are often taken by persons already suffering from various mental disturbances ranging from mild psychopathy to, in rare cases, advanced psychoses. There is a general tendency—especially among police officers—to conclude mistakenly that the erratic or criminal behavior of these persons is the direct result of some mysterious criminogenic narcotic, never identified, but firmly believed to account for their behavior.

Drugs and the Criminal Personality

Although not all abnormal people are criminals by any means, many professional or habitual criminals are demonstrably abnormal, with the preponderance of professional criminals showing strong psychopathic tendencies. However, it should be emphasized at the same time that a high percentage of psychopaths are not only noncriminal in behavior, but also that many of them achieve considerable success in contemporary society. In the Americas, the frontier was made to order for the psychopath; with the physical frontier gone, many of the attitudes of frontier days linger on, and there is still a place for the psychopath in industry, in the professions, in business, in politics and in some of our law enforcement agencies. As long as these psychopaths stay out of illegal activities (by however narrow a margin) and prosper, we often accept them as pillars of society; once they reach a certain level of wealth and position, it is no longer proper to recognize their psychopathy. And many personalities who would be classed as psychopathic by psychiatrists have indeed contributed much to the world of science, the arts, military achievement and industrial development, for almost always the psychopath has drive; at the same time, many of them, under the guise of constructive activity, have caused irreparable social harm.

Therefore, the authors wish to avoid the assumption, too often encountered these days, that all personality traits which can be classed as psychopathic are "bad," that all narcotic addicts are psychopaths and that all psychopaths are criminals or potential criminals. One finds all types and kinds of personalities using drugs, ranging from substantial and successful professional people to the very dregs of the underworld. All addicts are not criminals in the broad sense of that word, although technically and legally they are so classified, for they violate the narcotics laws whenever they possess drugs to support their habits; in fact, some state laws are so written that addiction itself may be a crime punishable by imprisonment. However, everyone who thinks about the nature of crime at all must rapidly go beyond the rather facile definition of crime as a violation of the law. Most of the people who read this book are law violators every day of their lives; few of them are criminals. And although it is difficult to define crime as such, it is important to remember that there must always be in everyone's mind—and this especially concerns those who must enforce or administer the law—a distinction between the law violator and the criminal. A criminal may be defined for the purposes of this chapter as one who preys on other people or social institutions habitually and consistently, without regard for the ethical, moral and legal code accepted by legitimate society.

Regardless of the legal implications, a drug addict who is otherwise a respectable member of the dominant culture cannot be regarded as a criminal simply because he uses drugs. For instance, a competent attorney who has been an alcoholic and who is enabled to carry on an ethical and successful practice only because he has shifted to small amounts of morphine daily is not a criminal. He has an unfortunate personality defect. There are a few such addicts in most communities (medical men, lawyers, businessmen and so on). They seldom become police problems. However, Smith, Ellinwood, and Vaillant[19] reported that 61 per cent of opiate addicts studied progressed from experimentation to daily use and physical dependence in less than a year with only 11 per cent using for more than three years without reaching full addiction. And if we drop morphine momentarily and consider alcohol, some readers will be able to recall successful surgeons who do not go into the operating room without taking a substantial amount of whiskey. These surgeons, too, have a personality defect, but their technical skill, their social position and their ability to keep their addiction to alcohol under control removes them from any criminal classification; in fact, many people would take the position that if they have to have whiskey to perform first-class surgery, they should have it. However, when the same surgeons have to take narcotic drugs, people are less tolerant, and the surgeon is technically a law violator; if he comes to the attention of the law, he may become a technical criminal with a prison record.

All this discussion leads us up to a single point: Both the professional criminal and the drug addict tend toward psychopathic personalities. Because both classes have a preponderance of psychopaths, there is an area of overlap in which both drug addicts and criminals are prevalent; this is probably the primary reason that most narcotic addicts, especially those with long records of recidivism, concentrate in the underworld. At the same time, there are addicts who are neither psychopaths nor criminals, just as there are many professional criminals who are not addicted. However, the numbers of psychopaths who are both addicts and have a life pattern of criminality are too large to be ignored.

There are several schools of thought regarding the influence which narcotics have on a life of criminality.

The authors believe, in the light of many years of observation of addicts, along with close contacts with many local, state and Federal enforcement officers, that an increasing percentage of addicts gravitate to the addicts' subculture from other criminal subcultures—thieves, *card* and *dice hustlers,* shoplifters, prostitutes, *short con men,* forgers, *grifters,* short-change artists, pimps and others.[3] It is notable that these largely comprise professionals from subcultures in which the tradition is one of nonviolent crime, or those lower-echelon criminals who live by their wits. Few professionals appear from the subcultures of the *big con,* the *heist* (holdup and bank robbery), the *heavy* (safecrackers and bank blowers), racketeering or extortion, to name only a few examples. It is remarkable that very few of those who control the traffic in drugs above the peddler level become addicted, and the number of those who do take to drugs dwindles rapidly as one goes upward through the powerful hierarchy which organizes and directs the traffic on a national and international basis.

On the other hand, several studies of large numbers of addicts have been made by researchers connected with the U. S. Public Health Service, notably Dr. Pescor,[4] who studied 1,000 cases, and Dr. Kolb,[2] who reported on 225 who were selected because they were basically criminal over and above any criminality necessitated by obtaining drugs, and by Dr. Vogel,[5] who reported on a large number of juvenile addicts admitted to the U. S. Public Health Service Hospital. Dr. Pescor shows that 75 per cent of the addicts studied had no criminal records prior to drug addiction, and Dr. Vogel's survey showed that 67 per cent of the juvenile addicts studied had no criminal records prior to addiction. Dr. Kolb's study is only partially relevant here for the reason that he deliberately selected 225 addicts whose criminal status was well established before addiction. Mr. Anslinger, formerly of the Federal Bureau of Narcotics, has suggested that this discrepancy may be partially explained thus: "It could be that there is a considerable degree of selectivity in each of our areas which differentiates the people coming to our attention from those seen at Lexington.

Smith, Ellinwood, and Vaillant[19] in 1966 reported, in a follow up study to Pescor's of addicts at Lexington, that the typical addict was first arrested at the age of 17 although the average age for beginning drug use was 20, indicating that the majority were involved with the law before they became addicted.

Perhaps addicts during the 1930's and 1940's represented a higher incidence of people who did not come from criminal subcultures and hence were not, in early life, involved in crime. Also, narcotics were much cheaper then, and it was quite possible for an addict to support his habit for a long time by legitimate employment. Today there is increasing evidence that addicts are involved in crime, usually of a minor variety, previous to addiction or coincidental to addiction.

Some idea of the complexity of this problem can be gained by examining one set of arrest records for 1963 from California, where the problems of addiction are being studied more closely, perhaps, than anywhere else. In 1963, a total of 7,932 persons (adults and juveniles) *who had no prior drug record* were arrested. Of these, 32.6 per cent had no previous police record, 43.4 per cent had a minor police record (probably a heavy percentage of misdemeanor charges), 18.2 per cent had a major police record (probably a heavy percentage of felony charges), and 5.8 per cent had been in prison.

In interpreting these figures, we must remember that, first of all, these persons were *arrested;* figures on convictions are not available, but the total number will be substantially lower. If we consider also that 32.6 per cent had *never been arrested,* and 43.4 per cent had been arrested (but not necessarily convicted) for minor offenses, we have a total 76 per cent who can hardly be said to have been established in a life of crime before their first drug arrest. This does not mean, however, that some of them had not been on drugs for some time without being arrested. The figures of 18.2 per cent (major arrest record) and 5.8 per cent (prison record) give us 24 per cent who may be said to have become closely associated with crime before their first drug arrest. However, again, we do not know how many of the 18.2 per cent were convicted, how many of both the 18.2 per cent and the 5.8 per cent had used drugs without being detected and how many of the total number arrested had committed various crimes without being detected before their first arrest.

We will return to these differences of opinion in detail later on. They are sketched at this point only to show that those who have spent many years in contact with drug addiction do not necessarily agree on the specific relationship between crime and narcotics, although all of them would readily concur in the belief that such a relationship exists and that it is very important in the overall picture of law enforcement and crime prevention. Furthermore, no one who has had experience with addicts will deny that profound personality changes occur *after* addiction when the addict is pressed for drugs; a person who was originally of the highest moral character will lie, steal or commit forgery to secure drugs; how far these criminal tendencies extend beyond the necessity for supporting his habit is, of course, open to question. At the same time, Kolb[2] has demonstrated that criminals of a vicious and violent type frequently shift to nonviolent criminality after addiction to opiates. Many addicts seem to be quite reliable in all matters where their supply of drugs is not concerned; many others appear to have lost all moral values and become unreliable in all areas of behavior. Meanwhile, the relationship of specific drugs to criminal behavior will be considered.

Drugs and Violent Crime

Different drugs have different effects upon the human being generally speaking; also, specifically, different drugs vary within limits in their effects on different individuals. Furthermore, the effects of the same drug are sometimes different upon normal and abnormal personalities. Therefore, when we generalize about drugs, we must keep these three levels of difference in mind; also, for every generalization, it is always possible to produce numerous exceptions, a fact which does not simplify the problem at hand.

First, all the opiates and their synthetic equivalents have a depressant effect, varying with the quantity taken, the length of time the addict has used them and the type of personality involved. Although the psychopathic personality (including the so-called addiction-prone type, whether or not the individual is a criminal) unquestionably experiences more intense euphoria from the opiates than does the so-called "normal" personality; this euphoria is of short duration and is so intense that it inhibits any type of physical activity, either criminal or noncriminal. The secondary effects of opiates are in the main so pleasant and so soothing that any violent psychopath will be deterred from following any impulses he may have to commit violent crime; he is robbed of ambition and the capacity for aggressive action to the point that he is eventually content with a life of idleness. This fact is well illustrated by the fact that so few men on the *heavy rackets* (holdup men, safecrackers, professional killers, etc.) are addicted to opiates. In theory, as Dr. Kolb has suggested, crimes of violence could be reduced if psychopaths could be supplied with enough opiates, on a regular schedule, to keep them thoroughly addicted. However, the authors emphasize that this is an entirely theoretical hypothesis; and that neither Dr. Kolb nor the authors would consider it ethically or morally suitable as therapy. While some addicts do commit crimes of violence, and while there are, with increasing incidence, cases of individuals on the *heavy rackets* who are in some degree addicted, these are exceptions to the general rule that opiates inhibit tendencies toward violence. Mental conflicts are resolved; lethargy ensues; the individual gets a sense of power and ease which he does not normally feel; again and again, psychopaths state that opiates make them feel "like a king." The contrast with his usual personality which the psychopath experiences is so great that he feels, by comparison, "happy" and wishes to continue this synthetic form of adjustment. The effects of opiates are, in general, exactly the opposite of the effects of alcohol, which tends to reduce normal inhibitions and to release aggressions. As Dr. J. D. Reichard says: "The alcoholic gets drunk, comes home, and beats his wife, but the opiate addict gets high, comes home and his wife beats him."

Opiates have been observed to have several other effects upon those who are criminally inclined. First, Vogel[6] has shown that they usually tend to increase suggestibility, although the reasons for this increase are not as yet fully understood. Theoretically, therefore, opiate addicts are open to suggestions from others to commit violent crimes and are more likely to act on these suggestions; actually, however, the sense of well-being and satisfaction with the world are so strong that, coupled with the depressant action of the drug, the individual is less likely to commit aggressive or violent crimes after he is addicted, even though he habitually or professionally did so previous to addiction. Second, there is a marked expansion of the personality, a feeling that the addict is "on top of the world," that he can accomplish anything, that success is his, that everyone likes him, that he likes everyone else and that he is an important person; this inflation of the ego, however, is offset by lack of will power and great reduction in the capacity for action. This ego expansion is notably present in psychopaths and notably absent in addicts who have stable personalities. In the words of Kolb:[2] "Both heroin and morphine in large doses change drunken, fighting psychopaths into sober, cowardly, non-aggressive idlers." Third, opiate addicts retreat even farther from reality and live inwardly; they gradually withdraw from all normal activity not associated with the support of their habit and eventually devote their entire lives to securing drugs; while often they perform criminal acts to secure drugs, these acts are usually nonviolent. However, within the past ten years the authors have noted an increase in the crimes of burglary (especially of drugstores) and robbery committed by opiate addicts, and although this increase is slight percentage-wise, it cannot be ignored. Fourth, the reduction or elimination of sexual desire tends to remove the opiate addict from the category of psychopathic sex offenders, even though he might have a tendency to commit sex crimes when not addicted. In fact it is well known that some homosexuals use opiates because drugs inhibit sex desire and remove them from conflict with society.

The effects of opiates on criminals or potential criminals, however, is not all beneficial. While these drugs may inhibit the more violent psychopaths, they put pressures on the personality which even well-adjusted persons cannot withstand. Because of the irresistible need for drugs, the bank robber who no longer has the courage to commit armed robbery usually becomes a conniver, a thief, a derelict who will turn to any trick not involving much effort or aggression to obtain money. However, with increasing frequency he may, when threatened with loss of his supply, commit armed robbery to obtain drugs. Furthermore, every addict, regardless of whether or not he is a psychopath, will turn to crime if necessary, and the volume of petty crime committed by addicts of all kinds is very large. However, there is no evidence to date which shows that opiates in themselves have the power to convert anyone into a criminal; the assumption is that, theoretically, if opiate addicts did not have to pay the very high prices for bootleg drugs, or violate the law in many ways to get them, they would not present a very great problem insofar as crime is concerned. Of course, this should not be interpreted as a recommendation that addicts be supplied with all the drugs they want at minimum cost (a proposal that is seriously advocated by some people as a solution to the problem of addiction), since there are many reasons that that procedure would increase rather than decrease addiction as well as the petty crime that goes with it.

While opiates or their synthetic equivalents are, at present, the drugs of choice among most of the criminal element, with heroin leading the list, other drugs are also used. The barbiturates and amphetamines are increasingly used by criminals in much the same way that they would use alcohol. This implies the heavy dosage demanded by this type of addict, often in combination with alcohol. While these drugs do not motivate specific criminal acts, they do induce irresponsible and even psychotic behavior. Addicts brought into mental institutions for observation are usually completely out of contact with reality. They suffer from delusions and hallucinations, frequently of a paranoid nature. They may have to be restrained because of their violent and assaultive behavior. Furthermore, most of these drugs are so readily available at low prices that addicts are not forced into crime to buy them. Those barbiturate addicts observed under controlled conditions became so thoroughly incapacitated that they could not stand and walk unaided; they became confused and disoriented; they lived in a stupor. However, there is one special type of crime that has increased spectacularly with the use of barbiturates; that is suicide, and the statistics now being collected in various cities where the problem has come to the attention of public health officers show that suicide from self-administered barbiturates has increased by several hundred per cent during the past few years. By way of interpretation, it should be added that many deaths from self-administered barbiturates are probably, in the last analysis, accidents caused by the impairment of judgment of the intoxicated addict, and that there is no way of knowing how many persons who committed suicide from barbiturates would have committed suicide by some other means had the drugs not been so easily available.

So far as the authors are able to determine, cocaine, marihuana and the amphetamines have a more significant relationship to violent crime than do the opiates and barbiturates. The use of stimulants by criminals has increased markedly in the years since the last edition of this book appeared.

At one time, cocaine was taken straight by many addicts, and was used frequently by criminal psychopaths. The effect of cocaine is exactly the opposite of the opiates. While of course it does not "addict" in the sense of producing physical dependence as do the opiates, it does produce a powerful emotional dependence and has all the other qualities of a dangerously addicting drug. Kolb[2] has summarized the relation of cocaine to crime very succinctly:

> Cocaine stimulates both mind and body and up to a certain point increases confidence and courage. Beyond the point of maximum stimulation, it produces uncertainty, fear, and anxiety. A criminal who takes cocaine is for the time being more efficient as a criminal unless he takes too much. The drug does not arouse criminal impulses in anyone, but it enhances the criminal's mental and physical energy so that he is more likely to convert his abnormal impulses into action. Beyond the point of maximum stimulation, the criminal and any other type of character becomes suspicious and fearful. They run away from imagined enemies, usually the police. They are in a paranoiac state, and in this state of fear might commit some act of violence if cornered. In the cases studied, addicts in this state have walked all night to escape imaginary policemen who peeped out from behind every tree; they have looked into bureau drawers, under beds, in match boxes, and through keyholes for police. One attacked with a hammer a laundry bag in his bathroom, under the delusion that it contained a policeman looking for him. Persons in this state are, of course, dangerous, but any crime they might commit would be due to the frenzy of fear. Such a person would be incapable of planning and committing a deliberate murder or of holding up and robbing a bank.

In this connection, it is interesting to note the rumors prevalent that the Communist Chinese were "hopped up" with opiates to prepare them for furious, reckless military attacks against the United Nations in Korea. As a matter of fact, we could wish nothing better than to have all enemy soldiers addicted to opiates, for nothing would so diminish or remove their fighting spirit. An excellent example of the effects of opiates on the will to fight and resist was seen in the deliberate application of opium and opiates by the Japanese to help subdue the Chinese population during the Japanese occupation in the years just before Pearl Harbor.

Today, addicts who take straight cocaine are rarely encountered. However, many opiate addicts mix cocaine with morphine or heroin in what are known as *speedballs*. They get some of the drive from the cocaine, but rely on the sedative effects of the opiates to cut down on the stimulant effect of the cocaine and to offset the delusional state described above. The amphetamines are now used more widely than cocaine as the stimulant to mix with opiates, and this mixture does not appear to incapacitate the criminal for aggressive, well-organized action as does cocaine or heroin alone.

It would be a mistake to conclude that no addict to the opiates or stimulants mixed with opiates will commit a crime of violence. There are too many instances to the contrary, and the number of narcotics agents who have been shot during the course of duty is very reliable evidence that some addicts will react violently. However, in order to maintain perspective, we should note that the number of Treasury Department agents shot in the course of arresting narcotic addicts is smaller than the number in a different branch of the same department who have been shot during the course of apprehending moonshiners. And, of course, most criminals commit acts of violence without contact with any drug. However, most opiate addicts are nonviolent, and the popular concept of a drug-crazed criminal running amok, or operating with superhuman cunning or cruelty, is more romantic than accurate.

One outstanding enforcement officer with a long record of effective service has commented that the only injury he ever suffered in the course of duty was being bitten on the finger by an addict whom he was trying to prevent from swallowing a supply of drugs. "Flight rather than fight" still seems to characterize the majority of addicts.

When we take up marihuana, we are handling a subject about which there is more controversy than there is about the opiates and cocaine, probably because there has been less opportunity to study objectively its relationship to crime, especially in this country, where its consumption is relatively recent compared to the use of opiates. However, any remarks concerning the relationship of marihuana to crime should be prefaced with the note that marihuana is a form of hashish, a most dangerous drug in its unadulterated form. We get the word *assassin* from the Italian *assassino,* which in turn is derived from the Arabic *hashshashin,* meaning one who uses hashish; this etymology reflects rather accurately the cultural pedigree of the drug, which has been known for centuries to release impulses toward violence. It is still used in the Middle East to prepare warriors for combat or massacre, since some individuals, intoxicated to the point of delirious crisis on hashish, are reported to become reckless, bloodthirsty and savage.

For a comprehensive and scientific description of the various forms and stages of intoxication from hashish and closely related forms of concentrated hemp products, the reader is referred to Dr. J. Bouquet, Cannabis Intoxication, *Bulletin on Narcotics,* Vol. *III,* No. 1, January, 1951; this is Part III of a longer treatise on the drug;[15] all of which makes a substantial contribution to our understanding of many of the aspects of hemp addiction and its various manifestations. There is also a useful bibliography. Dr. Bouquet's personal observations appear to have been made largely in the Mediterranean area, North Africa, Asia Minor and India; his study makes abundantly clear a condition suspected by most of the researchers who have, in recent years, attempted to study the effects of hemp-addiction; this is that the effects of consuming hemp in various forms differ widely with the culture, with different racial stocks, with various religious groups and with varying social status of the individuals who consume it. Furthermore, hemp raised in different parts of the world, while consistent in producing the essential *cannabinol* or intoxicating principle, varies widely in the content and strength of the drug produced; soil, climate, light intensity, latitude, etc. have a profound effect on the hemp plant. Also, the effects vary widely with the part of the plant consumed, and with the various methods of consumption. It can readily be seen that, with this number of variables, it is difficult to generalize regarding the effects of the drug in respect to crime. There is little doubt, however, that hashish as it is consumed in the Near East constitutes a dangerous drug leading to severe intoxication or mania, sometimes homicidal.

Unfortunately, Dr. Bouquet's study stops short of South America (which has been covered with considerable thoroughness by Dr. Pablo Wolff[7]) and does not include any firsthand work in the United States or in North America, of which Dr. Bouquet says:

> The problem is certainly not the same in North America. There cannabis addiction is a "new vice," which has a special attraction for young people, particularly in the large cities. It also appears that marihuana smokers are recruited from people who formerly did not indulge either in heroin, morphine, or cocaine. What is particularly alarming is the fact that investigations of the Governments of the United States and Canada show cannabis to have a marked influence on criminality among such addicts.
>
> The same cannot be said about North Africa or the Levant. There, at present at any rate, a large number of petty offenders (pilferers and thieves), some more serious offenders (assault and battery, minor acts of violence, and indecent assault), but very rarely persons guilty of more serious crimes, even attempted murder, are to be found among hemp consumers. It cannot therefore be said that cannabis addiction has an influence on criminality in the Moslem world at the present time; in North Africa nowadays there are perhaps more brawls, acts of violence, blows and wounds attributable to alcoholic liquor than to cannabis.
>
> In any case, it would be premature to draw conclusions, and further investigations must be pursued in the various countries where there are hashish addicts. There may be, moreover, no direct connection between drug addiction and criminality; each may arise from, and be explained by, a mental deficiency in the individual.

As a matter of fact, the status of marihuana in relation to crime in the United States is not very well established, although the position of the Bureau of Narcotics is that marihuana is a causative factor in many types of criminality including violent crime. Dr. Pablo Wolff, writing about marihuana addiction in Central and South America, is most emphatic in stating that, in that area, as well as in Cuba and other Caribbean islands, marihuana is used by mobs of violent criminals to stimulate them for deeds of violence. The La Guardia Report[8] minimizes the role of marihuana as used in New York and vicinity as a causative factor in violent crime. Dr. Reichard,[9] of the U. S. Public Health Service, in *Some Myths About Marihuana,* discounts greatly reports of marihuana as an incentive to criminal behavior. Allentuck and Bowman[10] indicate that, in their opinion, no permanent harmful effects follow the administration of cannabis and propose its use in tapering off morphine and opium addicts (a proposal not approved by the authors of this book). There are, of course, many intermediate views which cannot be reported here. R. P. Walton's[11] position is that marihuana smoking is a vice and that there are occasional instances in which an intoxicated person commits unpremeditated acts of violence in a homicidal frenzy. He also believes that criminals take marihuana in preparation for an act of crime.

Dr. Oswald Andrade, Director of the Botelhs Institute of the Ministry of Health in Brazil, has studied many aspects of the use of marihuana in that country.[12] His comment on the theory that marihuana is a criminogenic agent is: "On studying the dynamic action of the crime, we came to the conclusion that the crime was an expression of the morbid state of the patient, independent of his marijuana addiction."

It has been reported repeatedly by research workers[8, 13, 14] that temporary psychotic and delirious reactions occur in a fair percentage of persons taking marihuana. Unprovoked crimes of violence probably occur during such periods; the authors have observed experimental subjects in whom it was believed such behavior was possible.

Crimes committed by opiate addicts are likely to be nonviolent crimes against property committed by addicts in need of their drug; crimes committed by marihuana users are likely to be committed while under the intoxicating influence of the drug. Its effects are comparable to those of alcohol.

Marihuana, as has been indicated earlier, is a smoking compound made from a mixture of tobacco or other leaves with the pulverized ripe seedpods, stems and leaves of the hemp plant. It contains a very small percentage of the pure resinous form of cannabinol, and, as a result, cannot be compared directly to hashish in its effect; however, as a drug of addiction, it differs only in degree from hashish. We might say that it differs from hashish as beer differs from whiskey, except that most of the marihuana consumed in cigarettes in the United States appears to be relatively weaker in cannabinol content than beer is in alcohol. The concentrated hemp resin *(hashish, charas, chiras)* is not known to be smoked in any quantity in the United States at present, nor is there any market for the confections containing cannabis (of the *Manzul, Dawamesk, Garawish* type, etc.) or for the infusions, sometimes made with alcohol (*Assis Esrar* or *Bers* type). In Mexico, an alcoholic infusion is known as *potaguaya*. Probably the only reason there is no market for these concentrated forms in the United States is that marihuana addicts are largely youngsters who do not know about consumption of more concentrated forms of the hemp principle; also, the more concentrated forms require much skill to prepare, and the smuggling of the finished products would be difficult. At present there is every reason to believe that much of the crude marihuana for making cigarettes is grown in the United States; there are also smugglers who run it in from Mexico in bulk, to be mixed with tobacco and rolled into cigarettes later on by dealers. These cigarettes as a rule contain very little of the marihuana, which, in turn, contains relatively little of the resinous exudate in which cannabinol is found; some marihuana cigarettes are made simply from the ground, chopped or macerated leaves and stems of the hemp plant intermixed with tobacco; to a Near Eastern hashish addict, they would be so weak as to be useless.

The authors of this text, like everyone else who observes marihuana addicts, have also formulated some opinions based on many years of experience. The position of the present writers, with all due respect to other researchers, is, first, that while marihuana is a dangerous drug, its importance in the United States as a factor in violent criminality has been somewhat exaggerated by journalists. Second, we do not know of any objective study showing a direct or causative relationship between marihuana and violent crime in a significant number of cases. Third, although marihuana addicts manifest many undesirable and antisocial tendencies which will be discussed later, it has not been our impression from contact with many hundreds of marihuana users that these people are violent criminals; on the contrary, most of them appear to be rather indolent, ineffectual young men and women who are, on the whole, not very productive; a high proportion of them are devotees of various schools of swing music. While there may be occasional violent psychopaths who have used marihuana, have committed crimes of violence, and who have, in court, explained their actions as uncontrollable violence resulting from the use of the drug, these are exceptions to the general run of marihuana users, who, while they are almost universally petty thieves (unless they have an income or work for a living) become "criminals" chiefly in that they violate the narcotics laws. Most habitual users suffer from basic personality defects similar to those which characterize the alcoholic.

Marihuana is not possessed of any mysterious power to force people to commit acts which they would not otherwise perform. Like alcohol, marihuana is an intoxicating drug which releases inhibitions; the actions resulting from the release of inhibitions are as varied as the underlying personalities and impulses of the persons concerned. *In vino veritas* is a wise old proverb; the same thought applies to marihuana, which tends to release personality, not to change it; whatever you are before you smoke marihuana, the drug will only make you more so. By direct action, neither alcohol nor marihuana produces criminal activity, and criminal acts may result only insofar as the inhibitions operating on the personality are removed. Thus, well-balanced people under the influence of the small amount of cannabinol contained in one or two marihuana cigarettes would not be expected to commit violent crimes; psychopaths who smoke consistently or in quantities sufficient to intoxicate them might be expected sooner or later to become violent. We see this phenomenon regularly in connection with the consumption of alcohol; normal people who take wine with their meals or drink a highball before dinner, do not usually engage in brawls; such people, even though thoroughly intoxicated, usually remain affable, though their behavior may be silly or even disgusting. The psychopath, however—and we all have one or more among our acquaintances—often tends toward belligerence with the first few drinks and, with continued drinking, moves toward complete and uncontrolled violence; the dockets of police courts are crowded with these cases every morning and, of course, hundreds of others are kept out of court by good fortune or the handling of the drunk by friends, who excuse his fighting and brawling on the grounds that he has had too much to drink.

There is an important difference between alcohol and marihuana, however. Alcohol tends to impair motor coordination so that when an advanced state of intoxication is reached, the drinker cannot plan and execute any enterprise very effectively—whether it is criminal or not. Marihuana does not so rapidly produce motor incoordination, which means that the marihuana smoker may more frequently carry through criminal tendencies into action or perform impulsive acts more effectively than the alcoholic, whose motor incoordination prevents full and effective execution. This difference becomes very important when a marihuana user operates a car, for cannabinol distorts time and space concepts very radically; at the same time, the addict does not show the symptoms of intoxication as readily as a driver might show the effects of alcohol.

Furthermore, marihuana increases the suggestibility of those who use it, although we do not have any studies comparing it with the suggestibility induced by alcohol. Nevertheless, it is known that the marihuana smoker is, while intoxicated, notably more open to suggestion than he would otherwise be. If this influence is in the direction of criminal behavior, then marihuana smokers exposed to that type of influence are more likely to participate than when they are not intoxicated. This response to suggestibility is characteristic, in varying degrees, of all users of hemp products and may account in part for the widespread reputation which cannabinol has as an aphrodisiac, although it has been shown that none of the hemp products, including marihuana, have an aphrodisiac effect beyond that which may be communicated by suggestion. In fact, there are no known aphrodisiac drugs, not even the glandular hormones.

It has been the experience of Dr. Bouquet and others who have investigated the use of hemp that people begin to use it in the belief that it will preserve, improve or maintain their sexual powers; because there may be strong expectations in that direction and, because of the suggestibility induced by the drug, there may be some influence on the sex life of the individual; however, this is only temporary when it occurs at all, and the hemp addict soon becomes sexually inverted, losing all interest in sexual activity. In fact, in the East, mendicant monks and friars have used hemp from the earliest times, and still do, according to Bouquet,[15] who quotes Mohamet Shirazi Kalenderi's writing as follows:

> Their object in using this drug is, in addition to their pleasures in the visions it engenders, to dry up the seminal fluid; they thereby diminish the inclination to sexual pleasure and can the more easily avoid libertinage.

Said Theophile Gautier, one of the French intellectuals and artists who became hemp addicts during the late nineteenth century: "A hashish addict would not lift a finger for the most beautiful maiden in Verona."

Likewise, marihuana has achieved an undeserved reputation as an aphrodisiac in the United States, although it has been observed that it enjoys this reputation largely among people who do not use it and have not seen it used. In this country, it is largely used by young people from fourteen or fifteen to twenty-five, an age span during which no aphrodisiac is needed to stimulate sexual interest; however, its tendency to lower the inhibitions and increase suggestibility may lead to loose sexual behavior, especially if used in the atmosphere of a sex party. It is also sometimes "pushed" by prostitutes or peddlers to older men with the promise that it will increase virility, and these men may, to some extent, experience the suggested or expected effect. The authors have not encountered any marihuana addicts who admit deliberately using the drug to stimulate sexual interests, although some say that they have no objection to "balling" or engaging in sexual intercourse while they are "high." It would seem that, from the point of view of public health and safety, the effects of marihuana present a very minor problem compared with the abusive use of alcohol, and that the drug has received a disproportionate share of publicity as an inciter of violent crime. Unlike alcohol, however, marihuana forces its users to associate with criminal peddlers to secure it, and it is often used in an underworld atmosphere. Probably the most dangerous aspect of marihuana is the fact that it so often, especially among young people, leads to the use of heroin; the reason for this cycle of marihuana to heroin or heroin plus cocaine is not yet fully understood beyond the fact that environment and propinquity make for a desire to graduate from marihuana to opiates; it is possible that marihuana in some way conditions the user for heroin. This same cycle has been reported by Bouquet in the Near East and in Africa, although there heroin tends to replace hemp in many more mature addicts, and the use of hemp by teenagers is not epidemic as marihuana is in the United States.

Drugs and Nonviolent Crime

If drugs are not known to cause crime directly, there is a very close secondary relationship between drug addiction and crime, especially that of a petty and nonviolent nature.

There are undoubtedly some addicts who support small habits throughout their lives, who work regularly at their jobs, who never show any tendency to become criminals of any sort. There are others who have sufficient funds—or close contact with supplies of medical drugs—so that they can support larger habits without financial embarrassment and do not become involved in any sort of criminal activities except the violation of the narcotics laws. There are many thousands of medical addicts (persons suffering from very painful or incurable diseases) who are kept for months and even for years on opiates or opiate synthetics without showing any tendency to become criminals in any sense of the word; these people are supplied with medical drugs at very reasonable cost, and their habits are carefully managed by their physicians; many of them do not realize that they are drug addicts and will continue to be until they die. While many of these persons are quite ill and even bedfast, others are ambulant, and, as long as they get their proper dosage of drugs, feel little pain or discomfort; these addicts do not present any police problem.

However, the drug addicts considered in this chapter do not

fall into the categories listed above, and sooner or later they become very real police problems. The life of these addicts follows a pattern which might be schematized about as follows:

First, the potential addict begins to take very small doses of some addicting drug, let us say morphine, or heroin. He either does not realize what the drug will do to him, or he knows that others have become addicted but believes that it will never happen to him. It is not uncommon to interview physicians who should be thoroughly aware of the dangers of addiction, yet who have started taking small amounts of morphine in the firm and conscientious belief that they will never become addicted. On the other hand, it is even more common to encounter underworld characters who have been introduced to heroin by other addicts, who have seen the disintegration of the personality which goes with addiction and yet play around with the drug fully confident that they are immune. *It cannot be repeated too often that no one is immune to addiction.*

Second, the addict notices that the amount of drug he has been taking does not "hold" him, and, if he is addiction-prone, he no longer experiences the intense pleasure which he felt in the very early stages of the use of the drug. If he has been "pleasure-shooting" (taking small doses at intervals of several days or several weeks) he notices that he must increase these in size to continue to get any pleasure from the drug; eventually, of course, he will also increase the frequency until he is taking a shot four to six times daily. This inevitable increase in dosage (when opiates are used) is made necessary by the development of tolerance, a phenomenon which was discussed fully earlier.

Third, as the habit increases in size over a period of weeks or months, the addict who must buy his drugs from bootleg sources finds that more and more of his wages go for drugs and that he has less and less for the other necessities; in fact, other things come to mean less and less to him, and he becomes heavily preoccupied with simply supporting his habit. As he uses more and more drugs, he becomes increasingly incapable of performing his work steadily; any interruption in his supply causes immediate and disabling illness, and any accidental or intentional overdose puts him "on the nod" so that he is too drowsy and lackadaisical to work. He loses time, becomes inefficient and may lose his employment. With this, his income diminishes or is cut off completely, and he becomes desperate for drugs.

Fourth, it becomes obvious to him that he must have increasing amounts of money on a regular basis, and that legitimate employment is not likely to supply that kind of money. (It is not unusual to interview addicts who spend from $20 to $60 per day to support heroin habits.) Therefore, some form of crime is the only alternative. Sometimes the addict (if he knows something about medical or nursing procedure) forges some prescriptions. Sometimes he forges checks. More often, he starts to steal, from his home, from the relatives, from his employer, from strangers. If he lacks skill in thievery, forgery or embezzlement, he soon develops it under the pressures of addiction. During this period, he may or may not establish contact with underworld people or professional criminals. Some addicts, on the other hand, like nurses, pharmacists or physicians, build up very large habits without knowing anything about the underworld drug traffic and without going beyond the forging of prescriptions or the theft of narcotics which have very small value on the legitimate market; these addicts are not typical, however, and most addicts not only become acquainted with narcotics through the underworld, but depend on the underworld market to supply their needs and utilize underworld methods to support their habits.

While most addicts run afoul of the law sooner or later, those with an underworld background are usually in more or less constant conflict with it. If they are professional criminals, they usually have connections with the "fix" whereby they receive police protection for a fee or for acting as stoolpigeons; however, when this fails, or when they become involved with the Federal law, they may go to jail or to prison. While narcotics are available in many jails and prisons—for a price—the chances are that at this point the addict has his first experience with *kicking the habit*, usually "cold turkey." If he is a stable individual, regardless of whether or not he is a professional criminal, this first experience may be his last, for once he realizes the full implication of drug addiction as it applies to him, he may be sufficiently chastened to get away from drugs and stay away from them. If he is fortunate enough to *kick the habit* in one of the state or Federal hospitals, his chances for rehabilitation without relapse are better. On the whole, the trauma of withdrawal distress in jail, without any assistance, either medical or psychiatric, has a bad effect on both stable and unstable personalities and seems to increase the chances for relapse.

If the individual serves time among a jail or prison population, he is exposed (despite the best efforts of prison authorities) to all sorts of crime, degeneracy, graft and abnormal behavior. If he is not already engaged in the rackets himself, he has every opportunity to learn about them; if he already has a racket of his own, he has some status and is rapidly inducted into circles where he can learn much more than he already knows. Furthermore, narcotic addicts in prisons tend to congregate together, and the conversation inevitably centers about narcotics, so that the pleasures of their use are constantly in the minds of those who talk about them. Employment in jails is often inadequate, educational programs are frequently rudimentary at best, and there is little or no opportunity for rehabilitation, except in more advanced prisons. In fact, many prisons today do little except give legitimate society temporary protection from the psychopathic and the criminally inclined, meanwhile all too frequently turning out graduates and post-graduates in professional crime.

When the addict has served his sentence, he is at the crossroads. If he is a stable personality accidentally addicted, he may get a job, seek a new type of associates, stay away from narcotics and make good in the legitimate world. Everyone associated with prisons and institutional management has known such cases. They are to be admired. However, the odds are usually against such rehabilitation by the bootstraps, for a jail or prison record is hard to shake off; detectives and narcotic officers regard a man once convicted in a narcotics case as a "violator," and he may be picked up, arrested for questioning, his employment interfered with or pressure put on him to become an informer against persons he knew in prison or against other outside violators. The fact that a man has been a narcotic addict stigmatizes him socially to the point where he may find it hard to secure any type of legitimate employment; this stigma is in part justified, since narcotic addicts as a class have the reputation of being thieves, liars and petty criminals; in part it is not, for most employers fail to consider individual cases. Gradually, a better parole system, especially as sponsored by the Federal government and by California, is improving this situation. It would seem, in fact, that a carefully supervised and humane parole system following hospital treatment for addicts is one of the very important factors in rehabilitation. It is inevitable that, however sincere an addict's intentions are, if he cannot secure legitimate employment, he must live in some way, and he rapidly drifts to the underworld fringe.

If he already has a record as a professional criminal when he is released, he usually has no thought of legitimate employment (except as a token fulfillment of his parole, if any) and goes right back to the rackets. Professional criminals do not reform; they may "pack the racket in" temporarily for good reasons, but they do not change their whole way of working and living; they have become used to easy money and do not like to adjust to the scale of living which an ordinary legitimate income would give them. The professional regards arrest as inevitable, but depends on bribery and "the fix" to protect him in the long run from doing much actual time. He has come to regard the law as simply another form of racket which shakes down the criminal and preys on him, without ever putting him entirely out of business. To those professionals who are addicted, narcotics usually constitute only one of a number of vices. These people accept philosophically the fact that they will relapse, and they usually do. Strangely enough, the experience of withdrawal illness seems to have little effect in deterring the addiction-prone personality from going back on drugs. In fact, criminals who are addicts have usually relapsed many times; the established recidivist addict with a long criminal history presents one of the most discouraging problems in the treatment and rehabilitation of narcotic addicts; there is a saying amongst them that the only cured addict is a dead addict, and there may be much truth in that statement. However, observation of this class of addicts over a period of years shows that now and then an apparently hopeless case stays off drugs for a surprisingly long period; eventual reversion to drugs, however, is the pattern of the underworld addict, and exceptions are notable.

In the underworld, certain professions seem to show a much high percentage of addicts than others. The incidence of addiction is very high among shoplifters, pickpockets, the "pushers" of counterfeit money or forged checks and professional thieves of all types. There is also a high incidence among some types of gamblers and among prostitutes of certain types. This can be partially explained by the fact that prostitution or thievery is the easiest method of securing money when the addict is pressed, that aggressive or violent crime is not required to steal from a store or to prowl hotel rooms, that even poor thieves can steal some money or pawnable mechandise, that the work can be done at will, with the addict knocking off at will; also, the tensions developing among people who must commit many small separate acts of thievery, any one of which may land them in prison, tend to make the use of drugs a quieting, stabilizing factor. However, the high concentration of addiction among thieves in general may have deeper underlying psychological explanations and merits serious study by criminal psychologists. Prostitutes usually find the opiates agreeable because they deaden the physical and psychological stress of the profession and suppress or eliminate the menses.

On the other hand, some criminal professions are markedly free from addicts. Those criminals belonging the so-called "heavy" category (that is, those using violence or the threat of violence) show fewer addicts than those who live by their wits. While perhaps 60 to 70 per cent of thieves (including all types operating in the United States) are addicted, the percentage of addiction among holdup men, racketeers, safecrackers, bank robbers, etc. is much lower; until recently it was almost zero, but in the past few years addicts have been appearing among these groups. Also, until fifteen years ago, it was unusual to find drug addicts among big-time confidence men,[16] but addiction seems to be invading this group also to some extent; both con men and heavy men in the upper brackets of their professions are notably abstemious toward alcohol also, especially during working hours. The degeneration of addicts into thieves, pimps, prostitutes and other lower types of criminal characters is common the world over, since addiction generally precludes legitimate employment at least after it reaches a certain stage, and since an addict becomes eventually completely preoccupied with his habit and its support. Criminal activity is almost the only avenue open to people to whom drugs have become the most important thing in life. The cost of supporting a habit in the United States is, however, very high at the present time, and only criminals—or someone with a high legitimate income—can support a large one. A three-handed mob of pickpockets will, for instance, need about $600 to $900 per week for "junk-money," and must pay an average of $100 to $200 a day or even more for police protection when they are so operating; this is a very conservative estimate. That is, they must steal from $1,500 to $2,000 per week before they can even begin to make money for their own living expenses, which, with a road mob, will run quite high, since "class" mobs travel first class all the way. Therefore, they must have a very high gross income, "class cannons" averaging around $12,000 per year, over and above all expenses.

Eventually, most addicts with an underworld background—and some without it—become involved in the narcotics traffic. This is exclusive of the violation of the laws committed in the course of buying, possessing and taking the drug and usually involves trafficking with other addicts. Most addicts are very sympathetic toward others who need drugs; hence, they give away or sell, on occasion, some of their own supply. Other addicts, knowing that they may be out of drugs themselves, find it convenient to addict several other persons (preferably of some income or standing) who can be depended upon to help out in a "panic" or when funds are low. Addicts without "connections" purchase drugs through other addicts who are known to the peddler—sometimes for a share of the purchase. Addicts who depend on medical drugs use every known form of deception, including theft and forgery; if they are dealing with physicians who are also addicted, or who are engaged in the abortion racket, addicts who know this may use it as blackmail. See Figure 29, which shows the results of a raid on an abortionist physician. These include his obstetrical instruments, packaged supplies of heroin for wholesale distribution,

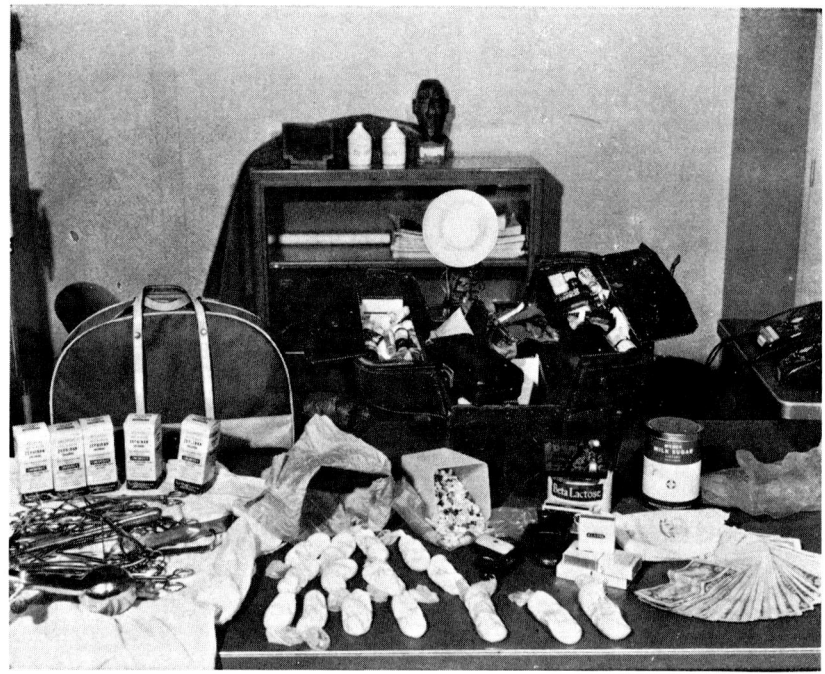

Figure 29. The equipment of a quack doctor who was arrested for narcotic sales. On the left are instruments for performing abortions. In the center are condoms ("balloons") filled with adulterated heroin and a large box of assorted stimulant and sedative pills. There are two cans of inert material for "cutting" the heroin, money received for a wholesale illicit sale and a gun for "protection."

sugar of milk used in cutting the drug before packaging, a considerable sum of cash which was involved in a purchase from him and a gun for "protection."

Although there are exceptions, drug addicts as a class have a reputation for being stoolpigeons and informers. In short, there is no limit to the conniving, scheming and petty crime which goes on among addicts themselves.

Eventually, however, every addict, and especially every underworld addict, is put into the position of being a peddler, if only momentarily when he sells or gives some of his supply to another addict. Some addicts carefully avoid being a peddler, even temporarily, because they believe—with some justice—that the law will be harder on a man who sells drugs than it will on one who only uses them. However, many addicts use their own addiction as a sort of security to both purchaser and wholesale dealer and support their habits either partly or wholly by peddling drugs to other addicts. This addict-peddler is the real link in the chain of supply from wholesale to retail levels, and he must protect himself from both sides as best he can. He always constitutes a risk to the dealer who supplies him and always runs the risk of being "fingered" or turned over to the law by addicts who make purchases for the law or by undercover agents who are sometimes addicts or pose as addicts. Furthermore, neither addicts nor peddlers are above using the law to settle personal grudges or to eliminate competition by turning informers. As a means of self-defense, many peddlers keep on hand a few "hot-shots" (capsules identical with heroin capsules, and perhaps containing enough heroin, or other drug to be injected, to pass a taste-test but loaded with lethal doses of cyanide of potassium). When a customer is known to have turned in a peddler or is even strongly suspected of having turned stoolpigeon, he may be given one of these capsules mixed in with his regular purchase. The fear of these "hot-shots" is well established among addicts, as could readily be seen from the testimony given (and often withheld) before the Kefauver-O'Connor Committee at Lexington and elsewhere.

While many peddlers are addicts themselves, and most of them are underworld characters, some peddlers are not addicts, and some make their living in other ways, merely supplementing their income by selling some narcotics on the side; this type of peddler is restricted largely to the medical and nursing professions and to pharmacists, drugstore employees or veterinarians who have access to addicting drugs. Usually these non-addicts are not underworld characters and often they continue their activities for long periods of time without coming to the attention of the law. An increasing number of these non-addict peddlers operate in the Los Angeles–San Diego area and in several East Coast cities.

As soon as we leave the level of the small retail peddler and go to the *dealer* or wholesaler (of which there are often several categories), we leave addiction behind, as a rule. The *dealers*, the *big men* behind them and the men running the highly organized smuggling activities which provide bootleg drugs from Mexico, the Near East and the Orient are not usually addiction-prone personalities, nor can they afford to be addicts. They are aggressive, resourceful, unscrupulous mobsters of which the notorious late Lucky Luciano is the archetype. These men have very large incomes from the so-called "syndicates" which dominate the illicit importation of drugs; they tie in with other large syndicates, such as those controlling gambling and, until recently, prostitution, and often purchase protection from the same political and police sources which protect other highly organized rackets. Basically, the so-called Mafia or Cosa Nostra is probably the most powerful of these syndicates. They are expert smugglers, with every facility for carrying on their work, including private planes. However, most drugs are smuggled in by passenger or freight ship or by air from the Mediterranean area and the Near East, while those from Mexico are often smuggled through by air or in cars, some of which have many ingenious secret compartments built in. The actual smuggling is seldom done by the ring leaders in person because of the risk involved; sometimes the people who carry the drugs in do not know what they are carrying, but more often the man who brings the drugs in is very well aware of the racket and makes his living at it. If a dozen or so of these racketeers in the higher brackets could be apprehended and convicted, the illicit drug traffic would be dealt a sound blow; on the other hand, enforcement against the small addict-peddler will always be expensive and inefficient as long as the major pipe-lines for smuggled drugs are open. The small-time peddler can always be replaced quickly by another addict greedy for the income and the guaranteed source for drugs; it is not easy, however, to replace a kingpin in the smuggling rackets. Steady enforcement, however, is paying off, and everyone who has observed the drug traffic operate knows well that, without the law enforcement work which has been done consistently in the past, and which is now being done, the present upsurge in drug addiction could spread to gigantic proportions; in fact, without constant enforcement, addiction could conceivably engulf a substantial proportion of our society.

Of course, the profit in illicit drugs comes from "cutting" or dilution. As an example of how this works, 3 oz of "pure" heroin sold in Riverside County, California, was traced through its various stages, its ultimate value upon resale to addicts being $60,480. This figure is based as follows: Suspects had in their possession 3 oz of heroin which is guaranteed by the pushers to be at least 70 per cent pure. Before the suspects sell this heroin, it would have been cut into 9 oz at 23½ per cent pure, which is the usual degree of purity, when sold by the ounce in this country. The purchasers of these 9 oz will, in turn, cut them into 27 oz at 8 per cent purity. Before resale, these 27 oz will be divided into grams, which amounts to 756 gm, still at 8 per cent pure. The purchasers of these 756 gm at 8 per cent pure will cut same to 1,512 gm at 4 per cent pure. These 1,512 gm will be divided into 15,120 capsules which will sell at a minimum of $4.00 each, and the total value of the original 3 oz is the figure listed above, $60,480.

The largest shipment of "pure" heroin ever taken by Federal agents was 209 lbs, confiscated in Columbus, Georgia, in December, 1965. This was a Mafia-backed operation, and the wholesale value of the drug was placed at $2,800,000, the retail value at $100,000,000. The size of this shipment not only gives some idea of the number of addicts necessary to support such a market, but also shows why drugs interest big-time criminals.

In addition to the large smuggling syndicates, there is, especially since World War II, a considerable amount of smuggling by individuals who are not in the rackets, but who travel back and forth from areas where drugs are produced. These people range from merchant seamen through migratory laborers (largely on the Mexican and to a lesser extent on the Canadian borders) to military personnel and persons who have official business for the government or for various import-export companies. These individuals discover that they can rather easily bring in packets of concentrated narcotics and sell them for a neat profit to a *drop* or agent for the wholesalers, often a *right* barkeeper on the waterfront. While these individuals account for considerable illicit narcotics, they would not be able to bring in enough to supply the illicit market if the big syndicates were put out of business; however, every such free-enterprise smuggler constitutes a potential big-time racketeer if and when the circumstances are propitious.

Some cooperative action through the United Nations (although not enough so far) plus rigid law enforcement at the ports of entry tend to curb this individual traffic somewhat, but not to stop it. The devices used by smugglers are as diverse and as ingenious as the human brain can make them and are too numerous to be described in detail here.

A variety of ingenious smuggling methods, including cannisters of narcotics carried in the stomachs of camels, have been encountered in the course of narcotic enforcement in the United Arab Republic by El Hadka.[20]

It should be noted also that some synthetic drugs are being manufactured in Europe (especially Germany) for the illicit market, and it has been reported by reliable sources that there are some illicit laboratories now operating in the United States for the refinement of opiates and the synthesis of opiate-equivalents. While this illicit synthesis of drugs in this country has not yet become widespread, it could become so if smuggling channels were cut off to a degree which caused the market to suffer.

There is an even larger problem posed by the legal synthesis of opiate-equivalents, which seem to have some medical advantages over the opiates refined from natural opium. If these are widely accepted and used by the medical profession both here and abroad, the market for the legitimate products of opium could be ruined. At that point, the entire legal opiate production of countries like Iran, Turkey, Yugoslavia, might be without a market; production there already far exceeds the world's medical needs. In these countries, the production and refinement of opium is a very important part of the national economy; any substitution of synthetics would probably force much more of their production into illicit channels, and might flood the world markets with illicit drugs on a scale never before experienced. Therefore, it is important that the United Nations work out a plan for the international control of opiates which will protect the medical supply of opiates and at the same time not ruin the national economy of any single country. Progress is already being made in this direction.

Counterfeiting also goes with the wholesale illicit drug traffic, where the duplication of tax stamps, labels, etc. may facilitate sale to dealers or transportation of narcotics through legitimate shipping channels. Within the past few years, parts of the mid-Atlantic and southern States have been flooded with large shipments of fake morphine (consisting largely of heroin hydrochloride and brucine, an alkaloid which had been added to give the characteristic morphine reaction in case anyone with a knowledge of pharmacology applied the nitric acid test) put up in tubes labeled as morphine tablets for hypodermic use. The labels, tax stamps and names of reputable pharmaceutical houses had been well counterfeited, and the containers were excellent imitations of those used by pharmaceutical houses. Many other such counterfeitings have been encountered by the Narcotics Bureau, some of them (apparently originating in the Philippines) being excellent imitations of the labels used by pharmaceutical houses who put up medical morphine for the armed forces, and appearing to be surplus stores or diversions from the Medical Corps.[17] These tablets contained no narcotic whatever. The strength and reliability of medical narcotics is, of course, well known to addicts, even though most of them depend on the bootleg market; therefore, medical drugs, apparently sealed in their original containers and stolen from legitimate sources, would be in great demand and would command premium prices in both wholesale and retail markets. Some of these counterfeit tablets traced through the markets by narcotic agents sold for from $1.00 to $2.50 per grain wholesale in lots of several hundred tubes at a purchase and reached the retail market at prices up to $7.00 per grain; as standard medical morphine, it would have been worth about 16 cents per grain on the legitimate pharmaceutical market.

To summarize, then, addicting drugs do not appear to be the direct cause of crime, with the possible exception of cocaine, the amphetamines and hemp, which is not as yet consumed in its concentrated form in the United States. In fact, the effects of the opiates are, in general, to make an individual less aggressive and more sedentary; they unfit people for the commission of acts of violence, even though those persons might be naturally so inclined. The stimulant drugs have a different action, and stimulants can cause delusions leading to murder. Marihuana is a potent disinhibitor which may, by breaking down inhibitions, release the psychopathic personality for criminal acts; its position as a direct cause of crime is not as yet fully evaluated, but it can be dangerous. Probably its most vicious effect is that it conditions the persons who use it for the switch to heroin.

The primary effects of drugs on crime may be small, but the secondary effects are undoubtedly very strong. Preoccupation with the drug habit removes an individual from his employment, breaks down his character, disrupts his family life and leaves him with but one motive for living—the satisfaction of his habit. The demands of this habit will, unless he has almost unlimited funds, force him to become a liar, a forger, a thief and, eventually, a total social parasite. In general, the deterioration of character and personality of the addict is inevitable, and when he is thrown into contact with the underworld—as most addicts are—he rapidly takes on the coloring of his environment and becomes a criminal, usually a thief or *grifter* of some type. Many criminal addicts were criminals before they became addicted; others have become criminals because of the debilitating effects of addiction on the one hand and the need for large amounts of money on the other. Most addicts sooner or later become police problems, and addiction is vicious especially in that it is the focal point for retail distribution of the drug through the addict-peddler. The major traffic in illicit drugs—usually not carried on by addicts—ranges through wholesale dealing to international smuggling and is a ruthless racket which should be suppressed with a great vigor.

In order to keep drug addiction and its relation to crime in perspective, we might compare it with the use of alcohol, which is sufficiently common to be familiar to everyone, and at the same time socially acceptable. If we accept conviction and imprisonment under the Federal laws as being indicative of serious infraction of the regulations governing both narcotics (including only those drugs at present Federally controlled, but not all those considered addicting in this book) and alcohol, we see that in 1950 there were 2,304 commitments to Federal prisons for violations of the liquor laws (including illicit manufacture, sale, transportation, violations of Federal laws in the legal whiskey business, etc.) and 2,029 commitments for violating the narcotic laws, including the Marihuana Tax Act.[18] No figures are available on the total state and local violations. Approximately four out of ten of the marihuana violators were users, and seven out of ten of those convicted in connection with other drugs were addicted. While no statistics are available on the percentage of alcoholics among liquor law violators, the authors are in a position to say that the incidence of alcoholism is very high among moonshiners, and, of course, the possession and consumption of illicit whiskey is a Federal crime comparable to the use and possession of narcotics.

If we accept the very conservative figures of the Bureau of Narcotics, we see that there are 57,199 known addicts in 1965 in the United States, but if we read any daily newspaper, ranging from small towns to large cities, we readily see that the police courts are busy with crimes connected with and resulting from the over-consumption of alcohol; reports of drunken driving, rape, murder, fighting, domestic trouble, etc. in which liquor plays a prominent role have become commonplace; the public accepts them with a shrug. However, if one defendant appears in court and pleads that his conduct was the result of the habitual or chronic use of drugs, there is a sensational and even hysterical interest in his case. On the whole, narcotics and narcotic addiction do not seem to present any greater hazard to public health, safety and established social institutions than do alcohol and alcoholics, yet it is characteristic of our culture that we accept a major problem in alcoholism casually, while we become very much aroused over a narcotics problem involving only a fraction of the number of people. Perhaps the explanation lies partly in the fact that everyone is familiar, either from observation or experience, with the effects of alcohol, which is taken socially and out in the open; narcotics, on the other hand, are almost always taken in secret, and the general public is totally unfamiliar with their use and with the effects they have on people. Because of the sensational stories written about drug-crazed addicts, most people feel an uncontrollable fear of any kind of addict under any circumstances. The average citizen who would brush off a drunk on the street, or perhaps even help him out of harm's way, would probably experience fear and shock if he were approached by someone whom he knew to be or even suspected of being a drug addict under the influence of drugs.

This retreat from reality characterizes much of our thinking about all social and criminal problems. We tend to ignore serious conditions until they get out of hand; then, when they are brought to public attention (usually very dramatically), drastic laws are passed (often in a hurry), and people relax with a sense of smug wellbeing because a law has been enacted which will take care of everything. Meanwhile, we have become not only the most thoroughly law-ridden but probably also the most crime-ridden of all Western nations.

The relationship between narcotics and crime is not an isolated phenomenon, but a part of the entire pattern in a culture where crime is accepted as one of the major industries. While some 295 Federal narcotic agents may do an heroic job of attempting to enforce the Federal law, and this may to some extent keep the drug traffic under temporary control, we cannot expect these men to eliminate either the tendencies toward addiction or the criminal enterprises which flourish along with addiction, often protected by the same political machines which sponsor other types of graft and corruption. As long as we support a mammoth underworld in which professional criminals can purchase police protection very much as anyone can buy fire insurance, as long as integrity tends to handicap persons seeking or holding public office, and as long as the legitimate citizen hides his head in the sand, the narcotic rackets will continue to flourish. Decent citizens must not be surprised when narcotic addiction invades their own homes through their own sons and daughters—for their own lack of participation in their own government at a local level and their own failure to assume moral and social responsibility will have been largely responsible. A society is no better than its people, and our society can be improved only by a concentrated movement to develop better individuals. This may take a long time. In the long run, however, it can and will produce results.

REFERENCES

1. MAURER, DAVID W.: *Whiz Mob: A Correlation of the Argot of Pickpockets with Their Behavior Pattern.* New Haven, College and University Press Services, 1964.
2. KOLB, L.: Drug addiction and its relation to crime. *Mental Hygiene,* 9:74 (Jan.), 1935.
3. ANSLINGER, H. J.: Relationship between addiction to narcotic drugs and crime. *Bulletin on Narcotics,* 3(2):1 (Apr.), 1951.
4. PESCOR, M. J.: *A Statistical Analysis of the Clinical Records of*

Hospitalized Drug Addicts. Supplement No. 143 to the Public Health Reports. Washington, D. C., U. S. Government Printing Office, 1943.
5. VOGEL, V. H.: Our youth and narcotics. *Today's Health,* 29:24 (Oct.), 1951.
6. VOGEL, V. H.: *Clinical Studies in Drug Addiction. IV. Suggestibility in Narcotic Addicts.* Supplement No. 132 to the Public Health Reports. Washington, D. C., U. S. Government Printing Office, 1937.
7. WOLFF, P. O.: *Marihuana in Latin America: The Threat It Constitutes.* Washington, D. C., The Linacre Press, 1948.
8. THE MAYOR'S COMMITTEE ON MARIHUANA: *The Marihuana Problem in the City of New York.* Lancaster, Pa., The Jacques Cattell Press, 1944.
9. REICHARD, J. D.: Some myths about marihuana. *Federal Probation,* 9:15 (Oct.-Dec.), 1946.
10. ALLENTUCK, S., and BOWMAN, K. M.: Psychiatric aspects of marihuana intoxication. *American Journal of Psychiatry,* 99:248 (Sept.), 1942.
11. WALTON, R. P.: *Marihuana, America's New Drug Problem.* Philadelphia, Lippincott, 1938.
12. ANDRADE, OSWALD MORAES: The criminogenic action of cannabis (marihuana) and narcotics. *Ban Narcotics,* XVI:4, p. 23.
13. BROMBERG, W.: Marihuana intoxication: A clinical study of cannabis sativa intoxication. *American Journal of Psychiatry, 91*: 303 (Sept.), 1934.
14. WILLIAMS, E. G., HIMMELSBACH, C. K., WIKLER, A., RUBLE, D. C., and LLOYD, B. J., JR.: Studies on marihuana and pyrahexyl compound. *Public Health Reports, 61*:1059 (July), 1946.
15. BOUQUET, R. J.: Cannabis. *Bulletin on Narcotics,* 2:(4)14 (Oct.), 1950.
16. MAURER, D. W.: *The Big Con.* Indianapolis, Bobbs-Merrill, 1940.
17. ANONYMOUS: Imitation morphine tablets in the illicit traffic. *Bulletin on Narcotics,* 3:(2)4 (Apr.), 1951.
18. UNITED STATES DEPARTMENT OF JUSTICE: *Federal Prisons, 1950.* Leavenworth, Kansas, U. S. Penitentiary, 1951.
19. SMITH, W. G., ELLINWOOD, E. H., JR., and VAILLANT, G. E.: Narcotic addicts in the mid-1960's. *Public Health Reports, 81*:403 (May), 1966.
20. EL HADKA, A. A.: Forty years of the campaign against narcotic drugs in the United Arab Republic. *Bulletin on Narcotics, 17*:1 (December), 1965.

Chapter 9

DRUG ADDICTION AND YOUTH

THERE is no doubt that during 1949, 1950, 1951 and 1952, there was a considerable increase in drug addiction among persons under twenty-one. The press and the popular magazines sensationalized it and colored it with a view toward catching the reader's eye, rather than toward giving him some knowledge of the problem and how to deal with it. At one extreme it was reported in the press, for instance, that there are 30,000 narcotic addicts in New York City alone, with 15,000 of these under twenty-one years of age. At the other, the Superintendent of Schools in New York could report only 154 addicts as of June 4, 1951, though in later interviews he conceded that he might have overlooked a few.

As of 1965 in California, the incidence of juvenile (under age 18) narcotic addiction seems to be much smaller than commonly believed. The Attorney General of California reported in 1965 that there were only sixty juvenile arrests for hard narcotics violations. This compares with ninety-eight arrests for 1964 and 157 arrests in 1960. Juvenile arrests for all types of drug offenses, however, increased in 1965 by 33.5 per cent to 2,677 over 1964, but the bulk of these arrests (95%) were for marihuana or "dangerous drug" violations. "Dangerous drugs" refer principally, of course, to amphetamine stimulants and barbiturate sedative drugs. Juvenile arrests for all drug violations were only 11 per cent of the arrests of all ages for drug violations. Juvenile arrests for hard narcotic offenses were only 1.7 per cent of similar arrests of all ages in California.

Smith, Ellinwood, and Vaillant[5] in 1966 studied the addict population at the Lexington Hospital and reported that the typical patient left school, after frequent truancy, before finishing high school, was first arrested at age 17, and first used "hard" drugs at age 20. The mean age of first arrest was ten years younger than a similar group studied in 1938.

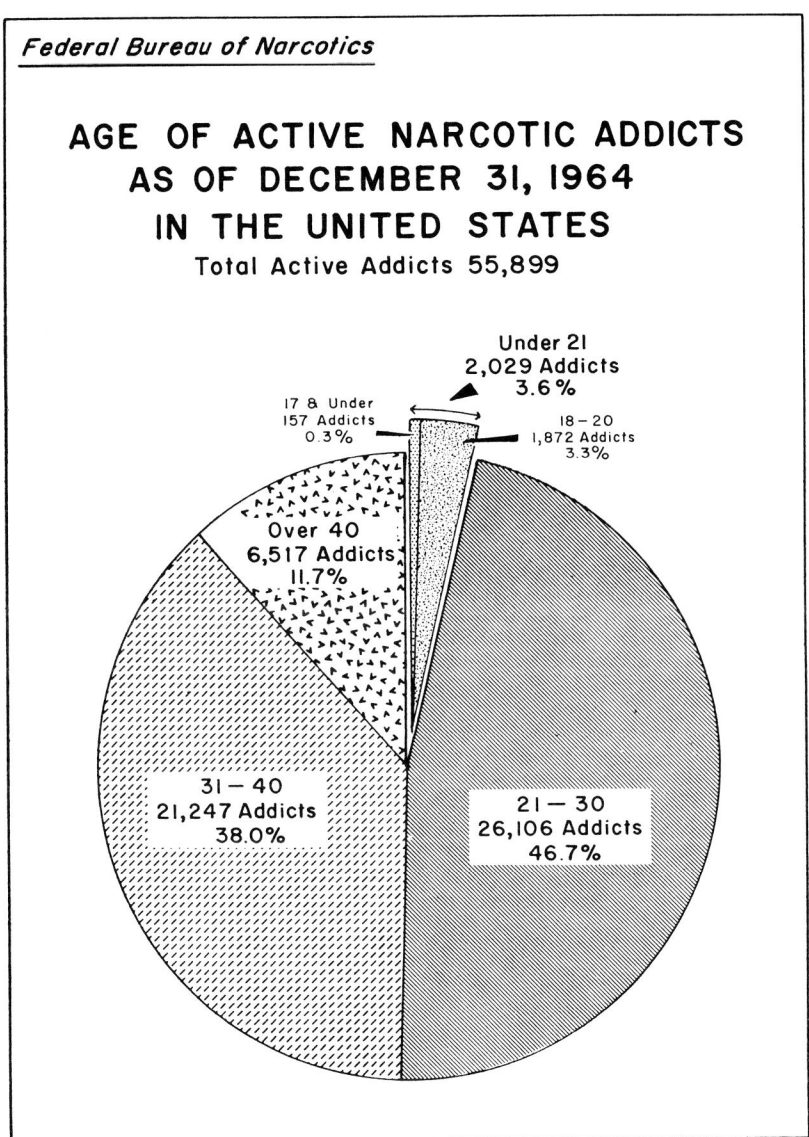

Figure 30. Addicts by ages.

On the other hand, there were 1,011 juvenile marihuana arrests in 1964, compared with 503 for the previous year, an increase of 101 per cent, compared with 677 for 1960, an increase of 50 per cent. Marihuana juvenile arrests for 1964 were 17 per cent as numerous as the adult arrests. Referring to dangerous drugs (Benzedrine, other stimulants and barbiturates), there were 584 arrests in 1964, compared with 657 in 1963 and 503 in 1960. There were 14 per cent as many juvenile arrests for dangerous drugs as there were adult arrests for the same drug involvement.

From these figures, it appears that narcotic use, referring to the opiate drugs, is a minor problem under age eighteen, compared to use by older age groups, but that marihuana use by juveniles is rapidly increasing and constitutes a serious proportion of the users of this drug by all age groups. The incidence of dangerous drug use by juveniles statistically comes in between narcotic use and marihuana use, and the consumption of these drugs, in California at least, does not seem to be increasing. Case histories of narcotic addicts seen at the California Rehabilitation Center program, however, confirm that many of those using marihuana in their youth change to heroin soon after passing age eighteen into the adult age group. So with the increasing juvenile use of marihuana, it may well be that we may encounter a rapidly increasing number of heroin addicts of older age during the next few years. The Federal Drug Abuse Control Amendments of 1965 are expected to show a decline in "dangerous drug" use by both juveniles and adults.

Although the Federal statistics for narcotic addiction are probably somewhat lower than the actual figures, they should indicate a valid trend from year to year. For 1964, the Federal figures show that 3.6 per cent of the addicts were under age twenty-one (Fig. 30), compared to 4 per cent for 1960.

The Bureau of Narcotics[2] believes that ". . . This increase in addiction, particularly amongst teen-agers, is worldwide. It is also present in Europe, the Near East, and Asia. Former Commissioner Anslinger, our representative on the United States Narcotic Commission, has urged all nations to examine this situation closely, as this is a world social danger." ". . . Now we are faced with a great social emergency, 'teen-age' delinquency, of which

Drug Addiction and Youth

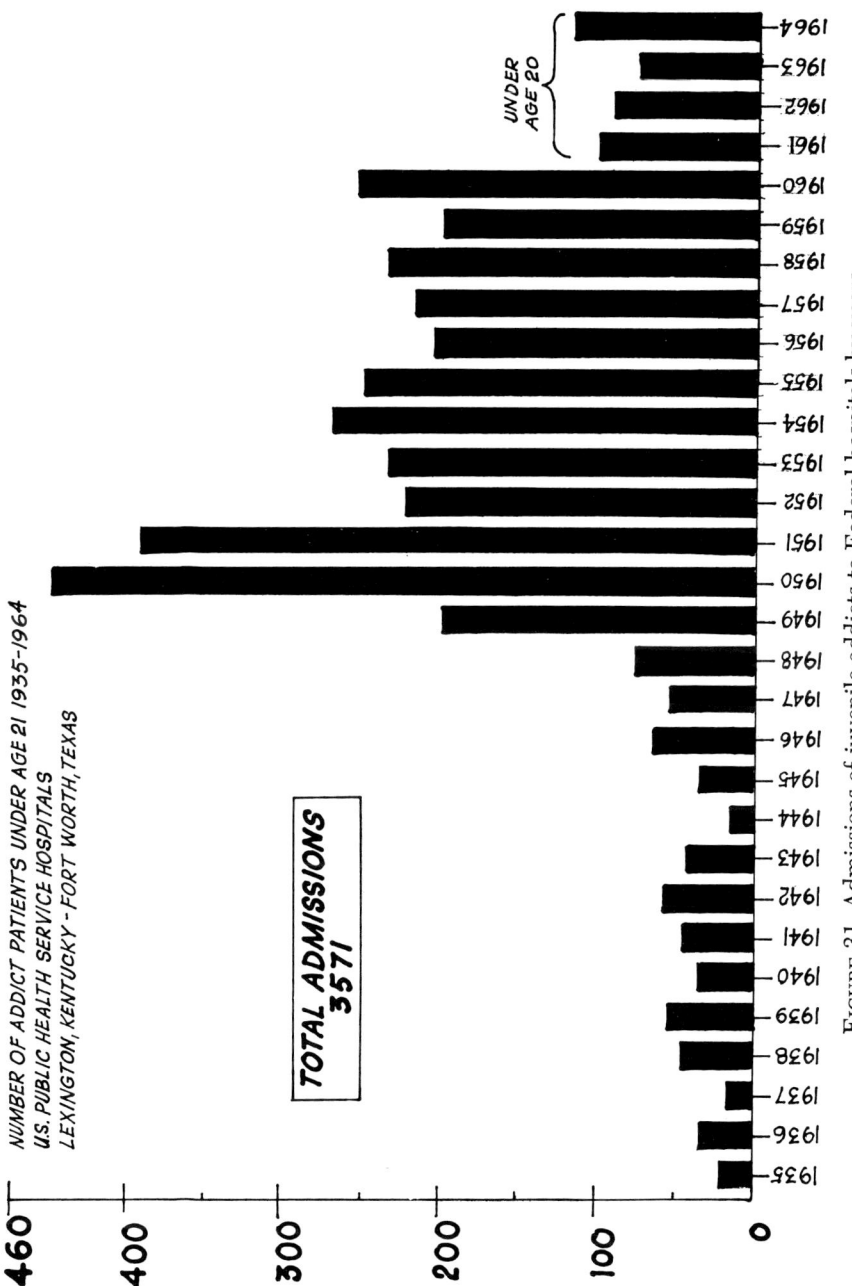

Figure 31. Admissions of juvenile addicts to Federal hospitals by years.

addiction is a dramatic and shocking phase." "... A ruthless quarantine is imposed when facing an epidemic of smallpox. The 'epidemic' of addiction, a secret vice, is equally dangerous."

However, no one knew exactly how many addicts there were during this period, nor what percentage of these were youngsters. But one thing is certain: Although there had been a downward trend in narcotic addiction over the past two or three decades, there was a sudden reversal of that trend, and the use of drugs increased perceptibly. Furthermore, it is obvious to those who work with the problem that, while some adults were involved, this increase was largely accounted for by the spread of the narcotic habit into the teenage and young adult groups.

Figure 31 shows the numerical increase in youthful addicts, as reflected by the population of the Federal narcotic hospitals at Lexington and Fort Worth. While the number of admissions (especially of young people) between 1947 and 1951 rose perceptibly, the numbers were much smaller than the very high figures reported in the press. Only toward the end of 1950 were Federal facilities overtaxed with an influx of addicts; as a matter of fact, since March, 1951, there have been some 200 beds unused at the Federal institutions, although there is usually a waiting list for women applicants at Lexington. Juvenile admissions during 1952 continued at about the same rate as in 1951. The decrease in admissions to the Federal hospitals during 1951-52 does not necessarily indicate a decrease in addiction; it may only indicate that increased vigilance on the part of law enforcement officers in the centers of addiction is apprehending larger numbers of youthful addicts who are being sentenced to city and state penal institutions and thus are unable to come to the Federal hospitals for treatment.

Figure 31 shows a downward trend after the big increase in 1949, 1950 and 1951. Just why this discrepancy between popularly believed incidence of juvenile addiction and cases known to be under control or treatment existed is not entirely clear, but factors influencing the situation probably were: a. lack of knowledge of what constitutes addiction in the minds of the press, the police and many public officials, especially in the schools; b. a fear on the part of youthful addicts or their families that entering a Federal institution would stigmatize the young people and perhaps throw them into contact with hardened criminals; c. the desire on the part of both youngsters and parents to keep addiction secret as long as possible; d. a lack of knowledge of Federal facilities, despite widespread publicity given them. (There were even reports that the Federal hospitals were refusing to admit patients because of overcrowding); e. exaggerated reports on incidence of addiction. News sources reflected uncritical estimates of the number of juvenile addicts. However, the statistical effect of increased admissions of young addicts to the Lexington hospital was to lower the median age of patients from thirty-seven to twenty-six from 1946 to 1950. At any rate, the thousands of youthful addicts reported by the press did not show up for treatment at Federal institutions. By the end of 1960, the Federal Bureau of Narcotics estimate that less than 4 per cent of active addicts were under age twenty-one.

If we accept narcotic addiction as a kind of disease, it may be regarded during the period of 1949-52 as being in an epidemic stage and, like other dangerous diseases, especially unfamiliar ones, it was probably accompanied by greatly exaggerated reports, not only of the seriousness and the extent, but of the harmful effects themselves. Lack of experience in dealing with it caused uncertainty and fear. The population tended to become alarmed and reacted in ways which would spread rather than control the disease. Thus we find that some people attributed the epidemic to a Communist effort to undermine our youth. The death penalty was seriously proposed for anyone peddling narcotics to teenagers, and life sentences were authorized in Illinois. It was suspected—and in several instances verified—that youngsters deliberately addicted themselves to avoid Selective Service. Others probably merely reported themselves to be addicts.

Some communities recommended and sponsored the erection of large hospitals in which to house the addicts of tomorrow; other communities planned, somewhat fallaciously, for their present general hospitals to treat addicts together with other types of patients. In some cities, special courts were established to handle teenage narcotic addicts who were treated by a simple formula—they were sentenced to jail usually for a year, and often without the benefit of the pre-sentence and follow-up services which they would receive had they been processed through juvenile court.

It is easy to understand why the public reacts as it does. Everyone fears the unknown, and the nature of narcotic addiction and its effects on teenagers is still somewhat obscure, even to specialists. When anyone acquires this strange "disease," often considered repulsive, the respectable members of any group to which he belongs reject him as if he had smallpox, and he is forced to associate with other addicts. As these addict groups grow in size, an antagonism develops between them and those who are not contaminated; the addict groups have a tendency to go underground and to live on the underworld fringe, since they get their narcotics from underworld sources. They are acceptable in the underworld, but not in legitimate society. Sensational publicity arouses the fear which uninformed people have of the addict and inflames the public; hasty, unwise legislation which does not discriminate between the naive beginner and the hardened, confirmed addict, may drive the addict group much farther underground, making both them and their underworld sources of supply much more difficult to handle.

It is obvious from medical history that no disease has ever been checked by driving it underground or by cloaking it in secrecy.

Venereal disease was not checked by ignoring or concealing venereal infections; it was brought under control only after a vigorous campaign—often bitterly criticized by conservative groups —to enlighten the public. The discovery of penicillin and the sulfa drugs made treatment much easier once people felt free to consult reputable physicians. No disease can be treated if it is regarded primarily as a moral instead of a health problem; nor can it be understood if free discussion of it is taboo. However, we must remember that narcotic addiction does not behave exactly like a communicable disease. It is spread deliberately by the underworld, where narcotic dealers are willing to capitalize on adolescent curiosity. They must have an ever-increasing market in order to sustain their profits. It is a most lucerative racket which can penetrate any area or any neighborhood without regard for class or color. Each new addict that is made is compelled to spend from $5 to $40 or more a day for drugs and is almost always forced into thievery or prostitution in order to obtain the money necessary to purchase a steady supply of drugs.

There is no limit to the number of addicts which can be made, for no one is immune to the power of opiate drugs; on the other hand, the number of new addicts can be minimized if people are taught the dangers inherent in drugs; at the same time, vigorous action must be taken to stamp out the illicit sale of addicting drugs. The public must realize that frequently the underworld drug dealer gets protection from the same political forces which protect the large-scale gambling interests and other rackets.

What are the important factors in dealing with youthful drug addicts in any community?

First of all, there is one important "don't." *Don't* try to handle juvenile addiction entirely as a problem in crime. While the cooperation of the police is absolutely essential, police methods alone are not sufficient to cope with the problem City or county jails are not the place to rehabilitate young addicts.

Second, the authors are convinced that people should be told in frank and simple terms how to deal with youthful drug addiction if it infects their community. They should also understand something of the nature of addiction, as well as the psychological factors which make it spread so rapidly in teenage groups.

By way of gaining perspective, adults should remember that fads are very common among teenagers; in fact, behavior which is meaningless to adults often occurs *en masse* among young people, who are under very strong social pressure to conform to the behavior-pattern of the group. Historically, we know that these fads, often regarded as very serious at the time, tend to pass without damaging human society perceptibly.

Admissions to the Federal hospitals indicate that the recent increase of youthful addiction was limited (at the time of publication) to large cities, particularly New York City, Chicago, Detroit and Los Angeles. Most patients at these hospitals were Negroes from deteriorated slum sections, but doctors in private practice report that white youths from homes of moderate or better circumstances are also under private treatment. Juvenile fads and fashions, including peculiarities of dress and tastes in music, have also started in Negro groups.

There is every reason to believe that the present craze for smoking marihuana and using heroin will eventually pass like the others—with one very important and sobering qualification. Both marihuana and heroin are dangerously addicting drugs. Heroin is one of the most dangerous drugs known to mankind; once its use is begun, the youngster finds that he must repeat his dosage every few hours in order to avoid extreme physical suffering as well as acute mental distress. Marihuana usually prepares the way for heroin. No one is immune to addiction. After several weeks of regularly sniffing the drug or injecting it hypodermically, he is addicted. Without the help of others, it is then difficult if not impossible for him to stop, and as he develops physical tolerance to the drug, his needs increase rapidly until he requires very large amounts of heroin to give him the same satisfaction that single capsules gave him at first. While marihuana is not so dramatic in its effect, it is also addicting; it breaks down the personality and degrades the user.

Glue sniffing by juveniles in the larger cities has become a major problem and is an addiction of importance in that substantial harm is caused to the user and to society, but particularly to the user, who may suffer very serious organic damage, and manifest delinquent behavior related to the intoxicating effect. The solvents in the various types of plastic cements are the harmful agents. Used similarly and with similar harmful effects are solvents which may be found outside of glues including xylene, acetone, isopropyl alcohol, trichloroethylene, lighter fluids, cleaning fluids and gasoline.

Although these substances are central nervous system depressants, the intoxicating effect may result in hyperactivity from released inhibitions. Doctors Sokol and Robinson have reported more than 750 cases admitted to Juvenile Hall in Los Angeles.[3] A high incidence of serious damage to the liver, kidneys and blood-forming organs of the body was reported, along with some fatalities.

The usual technique for glue sniffing is to saturate a rag with a half to a whole tube of a plastic cement, the fumes from which are inhaled deeply through the open mouth. The saturated rag may be held in a paper or plastic bag in order to concentrate the fumes.

The following are notes from the record of one glue sniffer in Los Angeles Juvenile Hall treated by the doctors mentioned.

> J. S., age seventeen, admitted on charge of glue sniffing. Charge stated eight tubes of glue sniffed a week for past five months.
>
> 4:00 A.M. Admitted to Juvenile Hall. Appears nervous and confused. Pupils dilated greatly. Disoriented.
>
> 5:00 A.M. Hyperactive and irritation. Walking around looking at the floor, and picking up "no things."
>
> 7:30 A.M. When asked to make his bed said it was already made. Said "Say, where is that flywheel?"
>
> 10:00 A.M. Talks to wall and acting bizarre. Admits being in Camarillo State Hospital for "glue sniffing." Feels he is in jail. Claims he hears his brother's voice. Feels that staff has ammo and are trying to kill him.
>
> 11:45 A.M. Threw tray against window, rubbed food into screen and on door window—apparently hallucinating, disturbing other patients.
>
> 4:30 P.M. States "there's a baby" in the peaches.
>
> 6:30 P.M. Pounding on door. Sees coins on floor; complains of the mess money is making.
>
> 6:45 P.M. Reaching and picking things out of the air. Room all torn up. Has all clothes off. Advised to put clothes back on and make bed, which he did after some urging. Quiet if someone talks to him, but becomes noisy, pounding and shaking door when alone.
>
> 9:10 P.M. Boy drinking out of toilet. Very noisy and disruptive.

Another boy is reported as hearing barking dogs late at night and screaming with fear of hallucinations that "the devil is coming in the window to take me away. Help me!" Another fifteen-year-old boy was arrested for attempting to steal an auto while intoxicated after sniffing six tubes of cement in rapid succession.

So far as the dangerous toxic effects on the body are concerned, it may be seen that glue sniffing is a more dangerous habit than heroin use, in which there is no constant specific damage known to the organs of the body.

Glue and other solvents are not addicting in the sense that they cause physical dependence followed by withdrawal illness, but they are drugs of intoxication which may cause serious damage to body and as well as dangerous aberrant behavior.

In each local community or neighborhood, the people who can deal most effectively with the teenage addiction problem are the parents, the schoolteachers and the police. They can be assisted by such organizations as the Parent-Teachers Association, local service groups, church groups, Boy and Girl Scout troops, neighborhood houses, social service centers and mental hygiene centers. Local physicians, psychologists and psychiatrists can also help as individuals; however, the most effective work can be done by the parents at home and the teachers in the school—provided they know what to do. Both parents and teachers should be supplied with reliable information about narcotic addiction; so far as we know, little information is available in a nontechnical form, although several communities, notably New York, are preparing a digest of the things which parents, teachers and other interested persons should know. We disagree with those who believe that education will tend rather to excite youthful curiosity than to warn youngsters away from drugs. One of the authors[1] has prepared a booklet for use by students in high schools. It is accompanied by an instructors' guide for teachers' use.

These brochures on youthful addiction should include clear statements on the nature of addiction, a description of the common drugs of addiction, a distinction between addiction and habituation, a specific discussion of the symptoms of drug-addiction including the withdrawal syndrome, a listing of the equipment used by addicts, an honest and sound discussion of the relationship between drugs and sex, a description of the best methods now used in the treatment of addiction and a discussion of the phenomenon of recovery and relapse, with special reference to control of addicts during withdrawal, and the addiction-prone personality. In addition, there should be suggested courses of action through which youthful addiction can be attacked. If the truth about drug addiction will not discourage potential youthful addicts, then neither untruths nor ignorance will do so. The California State Department of Education has prepared a comprehensive manual for teachers' use in complying with a law which requires public school instruction regarding narcotic addiction.

In attempting to reduce or eliminate addiction in juvenile groups, all those concerned should remember that it is not a hopeless problem. In fact, there is every reason to believe that by intelligent cooperation it can be solved. Compared to the older criminal underworld addict, the teenager has many advantages. His addiction begins in a community setting and not in a joint or criminal hangout. When the first edition of this book was published in 1954, most juvenile addicts were of the accidental variety and not the product of a delinquent subculture. Now, at least in California, the reverse seems to be true.

Martin Ortiz, Area Director, Welfare Planning Council–East Central Area, Los Angeles, California, and a member of the Narcotic Addict Evaluation Authority in California has studied the Spanish-American juvenile subculture in Los Angeles. Large numbers of youths of both sexes in slum areas of East Los Angeles find peer acceptance in a strong subculture in which children progress from group to group, beginning at age five, six or seven, to the late teenage gangs which are finally attenuated as the members are graduated into the penal institutions of the State[2] (see Fig. 28). The steps of progression leading to full membership to the Varrio Nuevo gang in Los Angeles are shown graphically in Figure 4. A search for peer acceptance by older groups in a different atmosphere is found in Greenwich Village, New York, and North Beach section of San Francisco where narcotic addiction, especially marihuana, is fashionable. Here also are the dilettantes experimentally using the hallucinatory drugs including peyote, mescaline and LSD.

While most criminal addicts have a long-standing record of the use of morphine, Dilaudid and other full-strength medical preparations, the youngsters seldom use these drugs and depend upon heroin from bootleg sources; most of them have not been exposed to full-strength opiates, since heroin is heavily cut with sugar of milk before it is sold to youngsters. Furthermore, the young addict is usually a legal minor, which means that he is frequently processed by juvenile courts and not by criminal courts. He can be confined in a hospital or sanitarium from which he cannot leave without the consent of his parents; this makes treatment easier and his prognosis better. Prospects for successful treatment are better for a young addict with a short history of addiction than for a confirmed adult addict with a history of several relapses. However, the teenage group can easily become a generation of adult fully conditioned addicts unless the situation is handled carefully.

As an approach to the problem, we suggest the following steps. First, the teenage addict should be given adequate medical treatment, both for humanitarian reasons, and to remove him as a focus of "infection." In November, 1951, a separate ward was opened in the Lexington hospital for the treatment of youthful male addicts, improving the treatment for this group by eliminating undesirable close contact with older sophisticated recidivist addicts. At about the same time, the National Institute of Mental Health of the U. S. Public Health Service made financial grants to agencies in New York and Chicago to make careful studies of the community factors involved in juvenile addiction. Another project was started to provide accurate follow-up information regarding patients being discharged from the hospital to the New York City area.

Second, peddlers should be located and removed from contact with youthful groups. Teenage addict-peddlers should be given severe commitments or probated sentences to rehabilitative institutions.

Third, an extensive educational program should be developed for use in the public schools, as well as in neighborhood houses and other organizations where young people congregate. This should be based upon a very straightforward and frank discussion of addiction and its effects upon the human being and human society. It should be well balanced and directed toward youth at all levels.

If narcotic addiction is to be eliminated, the potential addicts must be reached before they are exposed. They should understand that drugs are dangerous playthings and that addiction can ruin their lives. They should know that the pleasure derived from narcotics has been considerably exaggerated, that the use of drugs indicates a weakness of character rather than a proof of manliness, that once an individual starts using drugs he has no choice about continuing. He must go on taking drugs in ever-increasing quantities until he is forced by others to give up the habit. He should be shown what his life will be like if he is foolish enough to put his future in the hands of a narcotics peddler. All this information should be presented to high school students as an integral part of courses in hygiene, physiology or physical education.[1]

The Bureau of Narcotics, meanwhile, has apparently modified an earlier stand against public education, and has now issued a four-page pamphlet entitled *Living Death*. The Interdepartmental Committee on Narcotics reported to the President in January, 1961: ". . . Since the date of the last report, the Committee has given further consideration to the advisability of the use of special information concerning narcotic drugs in educational media, especially in schools . . . and the Committee believes that educational authorities . . . should consider the careful development of a program for use in schools in the sensitive area."

In connection with this education program, every new medium in education should be utilized, including the motion picture. At present such movies have been produced by the New York Department of Education and the Juvenile Protective Association with the Crime Prevention Bureau of Chicago. Movies should be scrutinized closely before being shown for educational purposes. At the time this book is written, there is no educational motion picture recommended by the authors for use in schools. However, the education program comes down, in the last analysis, to personal contact between youngsters, their homes, their schools and their churches. Ultimately, the youth is shaped and molded by contacts with adults, teachers, parents and friends. These people should be prepared to discuss narcotic addiction with the same frankness that they would discuss any other health or safety problem; in other words, the vice should not be made to appear attractive by treating it as a taboo.[2]

Fourth, psychiatrists, public health workers and private physicians must study the addiction-prone personality type with a view to ultimately reducing the incidence of this type to a minimum. This implies a long-range mental hygiene program which goes beyond the scope of this study, but nevertheless will constitute in the long run perhaps the most effective attack on the problem. Last, we need a vigorous law enforcement program beginning with international treaties designed to limit the production of addicting drugs to the quantity needed for medical purposes and ending with careful, rigorous and honest law enforcement on a local level. Such law enforcement is always improved by the intelligent interest of enlightened citizens.

In California, there is an active program to discourage unescorted juveniles from crossing the border to Tijuana. During the first six and one half years of this program, 48,810 of 61,693 youths interviewed were turned back, and therefore this is believed to be an extremely effective deterrent to juvenile addiction and delinquency because of the availability of narcotics and dangerous drugs in Mexico. Although this program costs $44,500 a year, it is considered to be a bargain in public protection.

The County of Los Angeles, California, has published an interesting booklet, "Laws For Youth,"[4] for the information and guidance of parents. This summarizes the laws having particular reference to juvenile behavior with the aim of minimizing juvenile law violations. There is a special section on narcotics.

Considering that the recent outbreak of teenage addiction is so far localized in certain large cities, there appears to be little reason to doubt that it will yield to the application of the principles which have been enumerated in this chapter. The development of a sensible educational program, a vigorous enforcement of existing laws and treatment of individual cases will result in ultimate control of the situation to the extent that, eventually, the recent increase in teenage addiction may appear as only a slight bulge in the downward curve in addiction since the Harrison Narcotic Act was passed in 1914.

REFERENCES

1. VOGEL, V. H., and VOGEL, V. E.: *Facts About Narcotics and Other Dangerous Drugs.* Chicago, Illinois, Science Research Associates, 1966.

2. Los Angeles County Department of Community Services: *Darkness On Your Doorstep.* Los Angeles, California, Los Angeles County Board of Supervisors (published in English and Spanish).
3. Sokol, J., and Robinson, J. L.: Glue sniffing. *Western Medicine,* 4:192, June, 1963.
4. Los Angeles County Department of Community Services: *Laws For Youth.* Los Angeles, California, Los Angeles County Board of Supervisors.
5. Smith, W. G., Ellinwood, E. H., Jr., and Vaillant, G. E.: Narcotic addicts in the mid-1960's. *Public Health Reports,* 81:403 (May), 1966.

Chapter 10

THE ARGOT OF NARCOTIC ADDICTS

THE SOCIAL ASPECTS OF ARGOT FORMATION

IT is basic to human social organization that whenever people are closely associated, they develop certain special aspects of language, often on several different levels. Most trades and occupations, for instance, carry with them a specialized vocabulary which not only is useful in the performance and perpetuation of the work pattern, but gives status to the worker. Thus printers, sailors, railroaders, physicians, etc., develop a sort of occupational language which is functional as well as social in its nature.

Sometimes these specialized linguistic phenomena are associated with religion or sacred ritual, and, among primitive peoples, we may find the language used by warriors on the warpath, or the language used by priests or medicine men, considered as sacred and often kept completely secret from the outgroup. The presence of these sacred languages among Stone Age people shows us that this tendency in language is very very old, and perhaps fundamental to human society.

When we go into the underworld we find that the forces which motivate the formation and use of secret or semi-secret languages are intensified. First, legitimate society is organized against the professional criminal, who may experience both social and economic ostracism during his entire lifetime. Professional criminals, on the other hand, have formed a counter-organization in order to protect themselves as best they can from the pressures of legitimate society expressed through the law.

Second, because the criminal organization is much tighter than the organization of the legitimate world, it is extremely powerful, and part of its power emanates from the close-knit structure made possible by the fact that all criminals share certain habits, certain stigmata and certain security problems in common. Within some occupational groups, this group-solidarity is greater than in others, but in all groups it is observable to some degree, and finds expression not only in mannerisms, beliefs and customs, but most characteristically in the use of language. Speech patterns reflect the behavior patterns of the group, as well as the traditions and group subculture, insofar as this rudimentary culture differentiates the criminal group from legitimate society on the one hand, and from other criminal groups on the other. To a greater or lesser degree the language of the group is semi-secret; it is, in effect, a union card, for it is difficult for an outsider to know and use the argot like a professional. These argots are keys to the behavior patterns as well as the techniques used by various specialized crminal groups.

Third, the modern underworld is composed of four or five major social and occupational divisions, within which there are literally hundreds of specific criminal activities. A professional criminal is usually identified loosely with one of the social divisions and speaks the idiom common to that division, in addition, of course, to standard English, on whatever level he would normally use it. Furthermore, he knows and uses the specialized vocabulary of the specific racket or rackets with which he makes his living. These aspects of language in the underworld are called argots, and a confidence man, for instance, would speak the general argot of the *grift*, with special reference to the *big-con* or the *short-con;* he might further specialize his vocabulary according to the individual con games which he consistently practices. Some widely experienced operators will know and use several argots, and have a peripheral knowledge of several more, but these individuals are increasingly rare.

We now know that each of the many subdivisions of professional criminals constitutes what we might call a subculture or microsystem, which is a cultural entity differing both in behavior pattern and language from the dominant culture. Some of these subcultures are almost outside the dominant culture and have little in common with it—as, for instance, the gypsies. Others, like the confidence rackets, share many cultural indices with the dominant culture, and simulate the behavior of successful business men so well that good big-con men are usually accepted in very respectable financial circles; they have to be to operate. While we do not know exactly how subcultures begin, we suspect that both criminal and noncriminal subcultures are language-generated, and much of the socio-linguistic evidence collected by Dr. Maurer during many years of socio-linguistic field work among criminals tends to strengthen this suspicion.

When a professional criminal learns his occupation, as, for instance, thievery, with specialization as a pickpocket, he starts with the very specialized techniques of pocket-picking in terms of a specific language. More than that, he constantly thinks of his occupation in terms of that language and discusses his work with other pickpockets in terms of their common language. In other words, his entire occupational frame of reference is both technical and linguistic, and the language is fundamental not only to the perpetuation of the craft of thievery but to its practice.

Last, a professional criminal usually takes great pride in his craft. He identifies himself with it very closely and rationalizes its importance in the underworld and his importance within the group in a way which is satisfying to his own sense of self-importance. To each individual, a knowledge of the language of his own craft, as well as perhaps that of several others, is a mark of status in the underworld. Also, it furnishes identification and provides him with recognition. Among people who live and work constantly under a legal, social and perhaps moral stigma, this element of recognition is very important.

Thus we see that the formation of specialized argots within the underworld is a natural phenomenon, and we know from having explored many of the highly specialized rackets, together with their appropriate argots, that a vast body of secret and semi-secret language is used by people in the underworld. As yet it is imperfectly explored, and its relationship to the legitimate language has not been fully charted. However, we have observed that professional criminals operating in a certain technical and social area developed a specialized argot, while nonprofessional or occasional criminals performing similar criminal acts as individuals do not know or develop a specialized language pattern. For instance, a professional killer or *torpedo* for a racket mob will know and use the argot of his profession fluently; a psychopathic murderer who might well have committed more murders in a lifetime than the professional killer will not develop any standardized language pattern in connection with murder. A bank teller might indeed embezzle more money over a period of years than a competent professional *heel-thief* would steal (and both would take it from behind the cashier's window), yet the embezzler would have no knowledge of the argot spoken by the thief, nor would he form an argot to be used in speaking or thinking about his own criminal activities. An individual forger will never develop an argot on his own, but professional passers of forged checks have a well-defined argot, though they almost always work alone. While legitimate gamblers have some slang (largely borrowed from professionals), those who gamble professionally in the underworld have a large and highly developed argot.

We now know that the so-called "underworld" is nothing more than an aggregate of criminal subcultures, all parasitic on the dominant culture and each distinct from the others to a variable degree. Each of these subcultures has its own characteristic behavior pattern, including mores, technology, modes of defense against the dominant culture, attitudes toward professional bisexuality, etc. Language is one of the most significant of these subcultural indices.

Argots, then, are a reflection of social structure. They are learned and transmitted and used within organized groups in the practice of a criminal profession. They are indeed the earmark of the professional. They are used almost entirely within the in-group and are spoken almost exclusively in the presence of other members of that group. Contrary to popular belief, argots are seldom used to deceive victims, to mystify noncriminals or to fool the police. In fact, they are seldom used at all in the presence of outsiders.

Because argots reflect the way of life within the group, and the way of life within many professional criminal groups is insecure and sometimes dramatic, the language pattern of those groups is often vivid and salty. For thousands of years the argots of professional criminals in many languages have constituted a fresh source of vivid phraseology which is used to enrich the standard languages spoken and written by noncriminals. As far back as the *Satyricon* of Petronius, for instance, we find that much of the author's freshness stems from his lively use of the argots of the

Roman underworld. In the Golden Age of Spanish literature, it was fashionable for writers, some of them great, to affect the usage of thieves, vagabonds and swindlers; this custom was carried so far that today much of the writing of an author like Francisco de Quevedo defies exact translation; in fact, during the seventeenth century, a whole literary genre, the picaresque novel, concerned itself with the adventures of thieves, written in what passed for a reasonable facsimile of their own language. This school of writing was popular not only in Spain, but all over Europe. Shakespeare borrowed freely from the underworld argots of his day, and other Elizabethans, like Thomas Dekker, acquired a very accurate first-hand knowledge of criminal argots. Such masters as Defoe, Fielding, Smollett and Sterne flavored their literary vocabularies not only with older underworld terms, but with contemporary eighteenth century argot phrases which were strong and colorful. Today, most popular slang is borrowed or discarded from the underworld, but the closed corporation of modern big-time crime makes current argots less accessible to modern writers than were the argots of the Renaissance, when it was fashionable for gentlemen and writers to rub shoulders with rogues.

However, it is only within recent years that linguists have realized the importance and the extent of the contribution which criminal groups make to standard usage in all civilized languages. Naturally, when words and phrases from criminal groups become widely used by outsiders, those words are usually replaced by others known only within the profession, so that criminal argots are often less stable than standard language, with a high birth rate of words balanced by a high death rate within the ingroups, and a relatively low survival rate compared to standard language. These birth, death and survival rates are also influenced by the fact that most criminal argots are not generally written, and almost never printed. Argots live principally in the minds and on the tongues of individual speakers, and the turnover in terminology is frequently very great, especially among those argots which, through contact with legitimate people, become known outside the ingroup. Some criminal argots, however, remain surprisingly stable, with a portion of the vocabulary becoming almost traditional. While in this study we are mainly concerned with words, or lexical elements, it should be noted that argots differ from the standard language in some aspects of structure, and especially in intonation, pitch and juncture. These are now being investigated in the argots used by professionals.

The importance of a study of argots has been recognized only recently, with the realization among psychologists, anthropologists and linguists that the language of any group is one of the most reliable keys to the culture pattern; and, since this culture pattern is not so obvious or so easily observed as the life pattern of the groups which do not operate outside the law, a knowledge of the argot is not only useful in penetrating the ingroups, but is essential to understanding the motives, the techniques and the attitudes of the professional criminal.

A study of these linguistic phenomena implies a simultaneous anthropological study of the subcultures in the same depth with which some primitive cultures have been studied. At present, we can only make some generalizations about them with some degree of validity.

First, subcultures and specialized linguistic phenomena seem to arise spontaneously and simultaneously; language seems to lie at the heart of their cultural genesis. They develop against the background of a dominant culture already highly sophisticated in handling symbols, and this tends to shape the subcultures into entities of special symbolism, all of which tends to nurture a heightened sense of group identity.

Second, subcultures really begin to expand and intensify and differentiate when pressures from the dominant culture are generated. In fact, it appears that, without some of these pressures, subcultures become abortive or tend to atrophy. There must be a threat from the dominant culture—or from other subcultures— and this threat intensifies the internal pressures already at work. The language indigenous to the subculture tends to intensify the attitudes, values and technology which characterize the group. The development of techniques, especially those which may be a threat to the dominant culture, may be disapproved or suppressed, which excites increased linguistic activity, usually accompanied by an intensification of internal cohesive forces and an increased emphasis on secrecy.

This special language or argot is a strong influence toward homogeneity; through it, group identity is further developed, and, as the subculture becomes stronger, it tends to pull away from the dominant culture, becoming more aware of itself as its communication system becomes more versatile. It comes to believe what it hears, and is more positive in what it says. The behavior pattern shapes itself ever closer to what the group says it is and what its acts prove it to be.

Third, when the dominant culture senses the presence of a criminal subculture, it tends to draw away, and this dichotomy increases the differentiation, which process is speeded up as social distance becomes more and more obvious.

It is not accidental that the dominant culture usually first becomes aware of an emerging criminal subculture through the leakage of terms and idioms from this group. At first these new expressions provoke humor, derision and some curiosity in the dominant culture. As soon as it becomes apparent that they have linked with them a hostile and even sinister behavior pattern, the dominant culture manifests first fear, then hostility. The dominant culture may counterattack with suppressive measures—usually enacting a new law or the shoring up of an old one—for society has a firm belief that a new law, and preferably a very stiff one, will take care of everything. Increased pressure provokes stronger resistance, and there is now a minor power struggle in the making. By this time, the subculture has structured a set of laws of its own—often more severe and more rigorously enforced than those of the dominant culture—and has no intention of accepting the laws of the dominant culture. However, we of the dominant culture still cling to the myth that we can convert professional criminals into law-abiding citizens if we only apply enough law, enough psychiatry, or both.

Last, we might note that this hostility between the dominant culture and various criminal subcultures has characterized the growth of American civilization. Indeed, there have been times in our history—and this by no means excludes the present—when highly organized criminal subcultures have taken over entire communities and even large cities. When these subcultures maintain an exclusive membership, a tight code of enforcement and the utilization of pressures from the dominant culture to strengthen their own sub-system, they become formidable indeed. Such a group is the modern Mafia, which is well-nigh untouchable. Sometimes these subcultures have been battled, in the past often in bloody fashion, by vigilante-type splinter groups from the dominant culture, with very little real law involved in the struggle. Sometimes, also, the dominant culture has been dismayed when the very people who subdued the criminal subcultures (which are usually only driven out, not exterminated or effectively subdued) turned out to be mere exploiters of these groups for their own profit after the furor died down. This is the cycle of so-called "reform" governments on the local level in the United States.

ARGOTS AND THE NARCOTIC ADDICT

Narcotic addicts fall into two main groups. First, there are those legitimate people who become addicted but who do not resort to organized crime to support their habits. They do not secure their drugs from underworld sources or habitually associate with underworld characters. These people have no knowledge of the argot of the underworld narcotic addict, and modify or utilize colloquial or medical terminology when they think of or discuss the use of drugs. A second larger group of addicts inhabits the underworld, lives by a criminal profession, secures its drugs from underworld dealers or peddlers and associates with other addicts. These addicts know and use the argot of the underworld addict. It is with this group that we are particularly concerned.

It is important to note that addiction is very common in some underworld professions and rare in others, that it is acceptable in some professions, even highly respectable ones (from the underworld point of view) and not acceptable in others. For example, among professional thieves the incidence of narcotic addiction is very high, and addiction is socially acceptable among most thieves, especially pickpockets and shoplifters. The authors estimate addiction among thieves at between 60 and 70 per cent, depending upon the type of thievery. On the other hand, among stick-up mobs, bank robbers, payroll bandits, etc., the incidence of narcotic addiction is very low, and addiction is looked upon as a sign of weakness and unreliability.

We should also note that different groups of professional criminals have differing attitudes toward the use of various drugs. Old-time safecrackers, for example, accepted the smoking of opium as a gentleman's vice, and this toleration of the use of opium is still found in some of the higher brackets among the underworld, noticeably among big-time professional gamblers and big-time confidence men. These same groups, and especially the old-timers in these groups, tended to reject the use of the needle along with morphine, heroin, etc., although some of them accepted the needle as a substitute for the pipe only because the smoking of opium while traveling was too cumbersome and too dangerous. There is also a tendency at the present time for those criminal groups who accept the use of narcotics by needle to look down upon those who use narcotics by other methods, or those who use other types of drug. A mob of professional thieves who use morphine, for instance, would not accept a marihuana user on a level of equality; in fact, they would distrust him completely and would probably refuse to recognize marihuana as a drug of addiction. Among modern heroin users, however, this pattern is changing, since so many of them started with marihuana and consequently carry over into heroin addiction their earlier argot usage connected with marihuana. In a sense, they have "corrupted" the argot of the users of hard drugs by needle in something of the same manner that needle addicts "corrupted" the argot of the old-time opium smoker.

Among underworld addicts, the use of various drugs, then, carries with it varying status in different groups, with opium smoking still remaining the almost inaccessible preference of the aristocrats of the underworld. Furthermore, among some underworld groups, the size of the habit is an important index to status, with those who support large habits feeling more important and receiving more recognition than those who have small habits, this recognition being more common among professionals in the lower brackets. This differentiation is in part influenced by economic considerations, since, with drugs at the present high prices, a professional who can support a large habit must *ipso facto* be sufficiently successful at his profession. However, among opium smokers, the support of a small regular habit is considered a gentleman's privilege, but at the same time, successful big-time criminals do not as a rule regard overindulgence in opium as a mark of distinction; in fact, quite the reverse. The opium addict who can hold his habit down to a reasonable level is considered "smart." The same thing is true of alcohol, for it implies a high degree of self-control. *Big-con* men, for example, almost never drink while they are working.

Also in the underworld a distinction is made between the individual who supports a narcotic habit as a luxury which interferes to a small extent or not at all with the practice of his profession, and the one who works at a criminal profession for the sole purpose of supporting a habit. Usually, the latter type tends to degenerate in his profession, to lose status among his associates and to go downhill rapidly.

Professional criminals who use narcotics have a tendency to work together; thus, a non-addict may work temporarily with a mob whose members are addicted, but he will probably not enjoy this association, nor will a non-addict mob accept without reservations a member who is addicted, despite his skill or special abilities. Temporary or fill-in work would be an exception. This acceptance or rejection, while partly based on moral and social reasons, is primarily a result of the physical limitations which addiction places upon an individual. An addict must maintain regular contact with sources of supply; he must withdraw from his work at very regular time intervals in order to take drugs, which may appear to others to be an unsavory and time-consuming process; the transportation of drugs and equipment may be difficult among traveling mobs; and the possession of these articles constitutes a safety hazard for the rest of the mob, since drugs and equipment for using them might cause the arrest of a mob or involve the entire mob in difficulties not connected with the usual hazards of their work. Furthermore, among non-addict criminals, the taking of narcotics is often looked upon as distasteful, and non-addicted professionals have a tendency to distrust addicts; however, addicts work rather well together in mobs since their problems are the same, and since they have all accepted the phenomenon of addiction. Thus a pickpocket mob will stop work at certain intervals to take narcotics, one member of the mob may do the purchasing of narcotics for the entire mob, and needles and accessories sometimes are shared, though a certain class of addicts prefer not to share this equipment.

In addition to associations on the road or in the course of a criminal occupation, narcotic addicts have a tendency to gather in taverns, restaurants, saloons and other places where it is convenient to meet. Sometimes these establishments supply drugs, or someone living near them can be contacted in order to secure drugs. Also, addicts sometimes congregate in the places where drugs are supplied to users. Some addicts cannot use the needle themselves or prefer not to, and require the services of an attendant to make the injection.

Where opium is smoked, a chef (either professional or amateur) is always available to cook the pills for the smokers. In these establishments (usually referred to in literature as "opium dens" but known to the addicts as *hop joints* or *lay down joints*), conversation is lively, and addicts enjoy associating with their friends. Among opium smokers, especially where the smoking is done in groups, conversation is a notable concomitant to smoking; the general sense of well-being and mental relaxation tends to stimulate conversation. This tendency to converse, often on a high intellectual level, has been noted by noncriminal opium smokers—such as the artists and writers of Paris and other bohemian centers—but seems to be notably absent among needle addicts, who like to "coast" and enjoy the drug subjectively.

At these meeting places, addicts confer and gossip freely, and here the argot is coined and transmitted. Since many of these addicts are in trouble with the law rather frequently, they carry the argot into the jails and eventually into the prisons.

In both these institutions, addicts have a tendency to congregate and to connive in order to secure drugs, a procedure which is not too difficult in most correctional institutions if the addict or his friends outside have any money. In prisons, the argot of the narcotic addict is recognized as different from the argot of the other professional groups, and the association of addicts in prisons tends to stimulate the production and use of argot.

Within the past few years, the close fraternity of addiction (which was previously tightly closed to outsiders) has been invaded by literally thousands of newcomers, many of them youngsters under twenty-one who, twenty years ago, could never have penetrated the underworld circles where they now circulate freely. While underworld opiate addicts formerly excluded the "weedheads" or marihuana addicts from their company, the marihuana traffic has now become vast and immensely profitable; furthermore, marihuana paves the way for heroin, and youngsters now become opiate addicts almost overnight. Twenty years ago, most drug addicts were over thirty, and a juvenile addict had yet to be encountered. All this activity has not only introduced a vast new class of addicts, but has also disturbed the argot. Phraseology which, thirty years ago, was standard and well stabilized to opium smokers or needle addicts, is now used in all sorts of new and unorthodox ways by the younger generation of addicts; furthermore, the drastic changes in the bootleg market and in the drugs available, as well as in the rackets adopted by addicts to support their habits, have forced the incorporation of many new terms and the corruption of many older ones. The conservative, sometimes dignified and intelligent opium smoker has given way to an increasing number of cool needle-pushers and marihuana smokers who are not only playing havoc with the drugs of addiction, but with the argot as well. Consequently, one hears some surprising adaptations and applications of what was formerly a fairly stable argot.

Also, among addicts there is a very close relationship between argot usage and the psychic and physical effect of drugs. As addicts verbalize their reactions to drugs, they also reinforce the effect which these drugs have on them, and the association of certain terms with specific experiences tends to create an associative pattern which undoubtedly plays a part in the satisfaction which the addict gets from the use of the argot. Many terms in the argot describe vividly and graphically not only the effects which drugs or abstinence from drugs produce, but also, by use of metaphor and suggestion, relate the sensations derived from drugs to other physical and emotional sensations, notably those connected with sex.

Although many underworld people are strongly inclined to be gregarious, addicts are especially so; as soon as two or more gather, the conversation turns to drugs, which may be consumed simultaneously with the visiting and gossiping that goes on among the users.

This tendency to give drugs a prominent place in the conversation increases noticeably when addicts gather in places where drugs are not readily available, such as a prison, a narcotic hospital or jail, where the talk of narcotics is continuous and intense.

Historically, the argot of the narcotic addict is interesting for several reasons. First of all, it seems to spring from the language used by opium smokers; some old-time smokers have retained the basic argot, much of it Chinese or Oriental in origin, which they learned thirty or forty years ago; however, as pipe smokers were forced by circumstances to take up the needle and substitute morphine or heroin for opium, a good deal of the pipe smokers' argot was adapted to the use of narcotics injected hypodermically. Now many younger addicts are quite unaware that much of their argot is derived from the opium traffic. Also, marihuana smoking on a large scale is relatively new in the United States; marihuana apparently entered through New Orleans about 1910. It became obvious as a problem about 1935, and its use has since expanded tremendously, so that there are now more marihuana smokers than all other types of narcotic addicts combined. For a time the users of opiate drugs refused to accept marihuana smokers into the fraternity, and the argot of marihuana smokers was looked upon with contempt by opiate addicts. Now, however, with many young marihuana smokers turning to heroin and with marihuana recognized as the link between the use of heroin or heroin and cocaine mixed, the argot of the marihuana smoker is no longer so distinct a phenomenon, and some of it is being accepted into the general argot of the narcotic addict.

It is probable that the smoking of marihuana has been carried on in the United States from Colonial days to the present, though on a very small scale and in isolated communities. The impetus which brought about the present popularity of marihuana in the last few years seems to have come from Mexico, Central America and Cuba. Because of the close association between swing music and the consumption of marihuana, the marihuana smoker has not only adopted much of the slang and argot characteristic of swing music, but has contributed heavily to it. Some of it also comes from the black-and-tan joints, the tea pads and the brothels of such large metropolitan centers as Los Angeles, San Francisco, San Antonio, New Orleans, Memphis, Louisville, St. Louis, Chicago, Cleveland, Pittsburgh and New York. The important centers in the evolution of the slang of swing music, however, have been New Orleans, Chicago and New York. Furthermore, many youngsters are quite familiar with the language of swing, including some of the argot of the marihuana smoker, and use it freely even though they are not addicted.

The argot of the marihuana smoker, then, is somewhat different from the argot of opiate users in character, imagery, connotation and in the life pattern reflected. Compared to the argot of opiate users it appears to the authors to be thin, obscure and affected. It reflects the very different type of person who uses marihuana, the marihuana addict usually being young, naive, unseasoned and parasitic, while the opiate addicts, especially the old-timers, are cynical, sharp-witted, mature and rich in life experience. Especially among the ranks of the opium smokers there are some brilliant minds to whom the carefully turned phrase and the meaningful metaphor are very important.

To some extent, the argot of the addict is affected by the kind of drug he consumes and the method by which he takes it. For instance, addicts who sniff cocaine or heroin may have very little knowledge of the argot of the needle addict—until their increased tolerance forces them to substitute injection for sniffing; if they continue to take cocaine or heroin by inhalation indefinitely (a very unusual circumstance), they might never become aware of the argot of the needle addict; however, most needle addicts are familiar with the phraseology of those who sniff drugs, since large numbers of needle addicts were formerly inhalers. Users of drugs like Benzedrine and the barbiturates may never become familiar with the argot of the opiate addicts unless they are thrown with these addicts in intimate association. Even so, users of Benzedrine are looked upon by opiate addicts in much the same light as are marihuana smokers. Perhaps they are even less acceptable to the fraternity than users of marihuana. Also, it is noticeable that the users of barbiturates and Benzedrine have contributed very little to the argot of narcotic addiction. Neither have the addicts who take drugs by mouth been very active in developing the argot, with the possible exception of opium addicts, who eat opium or drink it in solution; these addicts usually know the argot of opiate addiction and use it, largely because sooner or later they go to the needle themselves.

The argot used by narcotic addicts, then, reflects rather vividly the way of life of the addict—the ecstasy of narcotics, the necessity for escape from the world of reality, the compensatory effect of drugs upon the inadequate personality, the constant preoccupation with the needle as a symbol, the eventual exclusion of all other motives for living and the complete preoccupation with the necessity for securing drugs. There is also the ever-present evidence of the substitution of drugs for sexual activity. A study of this argot has already proved of value to psychoanalysts, psychiatrists and sociologists, since through the argot the addict unwittingly reveals a considerable portion of the unconscious which is preoccupied with addiction.

On the whole, relatively little of the argot of the underworld addict passes into general usage while it is currently popular in criminal circles, although, as time goes by, a rather large body of archaic or obsolescent argot finds its way into the language of the dominant culture. As new terms appear, the ones which they replace often are discarded, sometimes because they are already beginning to be used by "squares." A great number of terms, however, seem to remain in the argot for a long time and do not seep out into the dominant culture. Much of the argot which does get out develops meanings somewhat different from those used within the addict subculture. However, the argot used by underworld addicts is definitely expanding in size, and it is still obscure to the outsider. Therefore, a rather comprehensive glossary of words and phrases associated with addiction is appended.

Several points should be made regarding this material, which has been collected from practically all regions of the United States where addiction is at all common. It represents the usage of literally hundreds of addicts, although it is unlikely that any one addict would know all the terms included, since no single addict is familiar either with all geographical regions or all the social classes from which the usage has been collected. Certain subcultures are open to some addicts, closed to others; from these subcultures, only the terms used by these criminals *as addicts* have been included, since otherwise the whole of these specialized languages would have to be treated. However, with the proliferation of addicts into some subcultures from which they were largely excluded fifteen or twenty years ago, even in the marginal status which they now have, some of the words from these specialized subcultures are beginning to appear in the general usage of addicts. Also, only a small portion of the data collected on each word can be included here because of the need for condensation.

Readers with a linguistic background who use this material will note immediately that there is an apparent inconsistency in the forms used in each main entry. This is deliberate, since many terms have incomplete paradigms, with the form listed usually being the most common, or in some cases, the only form used. For example, some terms occur only in the plural, others only or mostly in a participial form. Verbs defined as infinitives usually have a complete, or hypothetically complete, set of paradigms. Many idioms have a variable usage, and only one or two illustrations are given from the many recorded.

Cross-referencing is somewhat irregular, since many items which are near-synonyms but have slight differences in meaning need to be linked together for the general reader. There has been a rather close cross-referencing of terms intimately connected with drugs and addiction, since that is the main concern of this book, while terms less closely associated with addiction are not cross-referenced or rather loosely treated in this respect. The spelling is somewhat arbitrary, since most of the words are taken from verbal usage and must be rendered in graphics according to the best judgment of the writers. There simply is no authority to consult in this connection, for the great bulk of this linguistic material was first put into print by Dr. Maurer, who always reserves the privilege of altering spelling in the light of new information, usually of an etymological nature. For example, one term for marihuana was first recorded as *greefo* or *griffo*, until its probable relationship to Mexican Spanish *potación de guaya* (drink of grief) was noted, after which the variant *griefo* was added. *Potación de guaya* (marihuana pods soaked in wine or brandy) is an old Mexican term, incidentally also probably the source of the very modern *pot* for marihuana to be smoked. Addicts are seldom if ever aware of these etymological connections.

It will be noted that the qualification *obsolescent* appears after a number of terms. This means only that a number of informants have expressed the idea that a given term is out of date, or not so much used as more popular ones, or the informant indicated that he knows the word but does not use it himself. However, the situation with regard to obsolescence varies dramatically from area to area, with a word which is already old-fashioned in one area being at the height of popularity in another. Sometimes these popular words are new contributions; more often they are simply older terms rediscovered and used in original senses, or given new meanings. Often these words are modifications or corruptions of older terms which the current generation regard as new only because they have never heard the older form. And so, while obsolescence is a kind of cyclical phenomenon, it is rare that a word can be labeled truly obsolete, for about the time that label is applied, it is almost certain to pop up in another area or among a different class of addicts; it has merely been kept alive in some obscure circles which have not been currently studied. It is notable that, thirty or thirty-five years ago, younger addicts learned the argot from their elders and imitated it rather carefully; today, because of the preponderance of younger addicts, the older ones seem to go along with the language currently in use in order to maintain status and identity within the subculture. In general, a movement of terms from East to West has been observed, although there are many exceptions to this, and new words tend to generate and reach popularity in any center where a number of addicts congregate. However, it is a common experience to find that a new term on the East Coast is unknown on the West Coast, and by the time it reaches the West Coast—if it does—it may well be obsolescent in the East. At the same time, one can observe terms used on the West Coast, or from the Chicago or Detroit areas, which are unknown in the East, though eventually they may appear there.

Phonologically, there is little to say about the argot of addicts at the present time, largely because this phase is difficult to study, and because the evidence is far from complete. However, we might oversimplify a bit and say that the phonology of addicts tends to follow that of the geographical regional dialect as well as the social level to which they are indigenous. At the same time, there are some para-linguistic and kinesic factors which, though very subtle, seem to be almost universal among American underworld addicts, who readily recognize one another by these means, even though they may be hard put to it to explain exactly and specifically how they do this. A trained observer, however, can, after sufficient experience with addicts, readily isolate and identify some of these.

While this glossary is by no means complete, pains have been taken to see that it is representative. Consequently, there is a sprinkling of terms from the institutional argot of narcotics hospitals, jails and prisons which, several years ago, would not have been characteristic. Also there are some terms for the "hustle" or small-time racket by which the addict supports his habit; often these are modifications, corruptions or improper applications of terms already established in other rackets, for they have been hastily adapted by young addicts who have had no real experience in the rackets proper before drugs forced them into some form of criminal activity. There are also a number of terms which originated or were adapted by Negro addicts, reflecting not only the preponderance of addiction among Negroes, but the spreading psychology of the so-called white Negro as well.

REFERENCES

Note: There are no references to previously published material in Chapter 10 because the authors felt that it was desirable to include a fresh study of the argot, based on field-work done during 1965-66. However, the following titles are relevant to any consideration of the argot, at least in an historical sense, because of the obscure nature of addicts' usage and in the light of the widespread changes which have taken place in that usage within the past decade.

1. BERREY, LESTER V., and VAN DEN BARK, MELVIN: *The American Thesaurus of Slang.* New York, Thomas Y. Crowell, 1942. (Contains some data on the argot of addicts, very loosely edited,

based on the work of D. W. Maurer, with acknowledgments in the fifth and subsequent printings.)
2. COWDRY, E. V. JR., and GOTTSCHALK, L. A.: *The Language of the Narcotic Addict.* The United States Public Health Service Hospital, Fort Worth, Texas, 1948.
3. GOLDIN, HYMAN E., O'LEARY, FRANK, and LIPSIUS, MORRIS: *Dictionary of American Underworld Lingo.* New York, Twayne Publishers, 1950. (Contains some sound data on the usage of addicts, especially in prisons.)
4. MAURER, DAVID W.: Junker lingo: A by-product of underworld argot. *American Speech,* 8:2 (Apr.), 1933.
5. MAURER, DAVID W.: The argot of the underworld narcotic addict, Part I. *American Speech,* 11:2 (Apr.), 1936. Reprinted by the United States Public Health Service, 1936.
6. MAURER, DAVID W.: Addenda to addicts' argot. *American Speech,* 11:3 (Oct.), 1936.
7. MAURER, DAVID W.: The argot of the underworld narcotic addict, Part II. *American Speech,* 13:3 (Oct.), 1938. Reprinted by The United States Public Health Service, 1938.
8. MAURER, DAVID W.: *The Big Con: The Story of the Confidence Man and the Confidence Game.* New York, Bobbs-Merrill, 1940. (Contains notes on the use of narcotics among confidence men and consequent reflection in their argot.)
9. MAURER, DAVID W.: The argot of forgery. *American Speech,* 16:4 (Dec.), 1941. (Contains notes on addiction among forgers and passers of forged checks.)
10. MAURER, DAVID W.: Speech of the narcotic underworld. *The American Mercury,* 62:266 (Feb.), 1946.
11. MAURER, DAVID W.: Marijuana addicts and their lingo. *The American Mercury,* 63:275 (Nov.), 1946.
12. MAURER, DAVID W.: *The Technical Argot of the Pickpocket and Its Relation to the Culture-Pattern.* A paper presented before the Modern Language Association, Detroit, Michigan, December, 1947. (Contains notes on the use of drugs among thieves and pickpockets, with consequent reflection in the argot. Also, *Whiz Mob: A Correlation of the Technical Argot of Pickpockets With Their Behavior-Pattern.* Publication No. 24 (Book) of the American Dialect Society, 1955. Publication No. 31, 1959 contains a word-finder list for the above book. Trade edition, New Haven, College and University Press Services, Inc., 1964, 216 pp.

13. MAURER, DAVID W.: *The Argot of the Criminal Narcotic Addict.* A paper presented before the Foreign Language Conference, The University of Kentucky, April 25, 1952.
14. MAURER, DAVID W.: *Reflections of the Behavior-Pattern in the Argot of Underworld Narcotic Addicts.* A paper presented before The American Dialect Society at the convention of The Modern Language Association, Boston, December 29, 1952.
15. PARTRIDGE, ERIC: *A Dictionary of the Underworld, British and American.* New York, Macmillan, 1950. (Contains data on the usage of addicts, rather loosely edited, based on the work of D. W. Maurer, with acknowledgments in the second American edition.)
16. PROVOST MARSHAL GENERAL'S SCHOOL: *Glossary of Colloquial Terms Used by Narcotic Addicts, and Commercial Preparations Containing Narcotic Drugs.* (Vol. II of *Narcotics and Other Drugs.*) Camp Gordon, Ga., 1952. (Argot materials contributed by D. W. Maurer.)

GLOSSARY

A.B.C. An adverse behavior report (Lexington). Elsewhere, often called a *gunsel*, a kind of obscure pun on adverse (perverse) behavior, since a *gunsel* is a kind of "pervert." See *shoot (him) down*.

ab or **abb.** An abscess which forms at the site of injection on needle addicts, largely as a result of impure drugs or unsterile needles. For details see text and photographs. Addicts are sometimes literally covered with draining sores. Barbiturates also produce abscesses. Also, *Raspberry, cave*. See Fig. 4. "The worst abs I ever saw were caused by yen shee, cooked and shot in the line or in the skin." "Yen shee will not cause an ab if shot in a vein or deep in muscle. Worst abs are caused by Nembutal when the vein is missed."

Abe. A five dollar bill. Also *Lincoln, nickel, fin*, etc.

ace. 1. A one-year sentence. Also *bullet*. "He laid an ace on me for that score." 2. One of anything. 3. Or *ace note*. A one dollar bill. Also *Abe*.

acid. Lysergic acid diethylamide (LSD-25), a powerful psychomimetic drug, produced synthetically, which duplicates in a highly concentrated form the same hallucinogenic agent found in peyote, mescaline and psilocybin. It appears on the contraband market in the form of powder, liquid in ampules and sugar lumps on which a drop of the concentrated drug has been deposited. Much used by amateur experimenters, but of little or no interest to opiate addicts. See text for a detailed discussion.

acid dropper. One who uses LSD. Also *acid head*.

acid head. A user of LSD. Also *acid dropper*.

acid test. The experience involved in taking LSD. A common phrase among users is, "Can you pass the acid test?" (meaning, Can you take the psychological consequences of using this drug? Have you been initiated to it?)

action. 1. The selling of narcotics. 2. Anything pertaining to criminal activities. "All the action is going on at Pete's pad" (meaning *planning*). See also *happenings, skams*.

all lit up or **lit up.** To be under the influence of narcotics; to be obviously experiencing the euphoria immediately following an intravenous injection. Usually restricted to needle addicts, especially *speed ball* shooters. Also *coasting, floating, hitting the gow, hitting the stuff, in high, on stuff, on the gow, picked up*, some with specialized meanings.

"He was racing his motor and all lit up too." "Their eyes shine and stay lit up. . . ." Commonly used by squares to refer to anybody under influence of anything. Not commonly used by West Coast addicts. See *geed up, ripped, smashed, wired up, charged, zonked, stoned, loaded, knocked out*.

amp. A 1 cc Methedrine ampule, legitimate.

around the turn. For an addict who is *kicking the habit* to have passed through the worst of the withdrawal syndrome, which reaches its maximum intensity in from thirty-six to seventy-two hours from the last regular injection. Also *over the hump, reach the pitch.* Present-day addicts without habits so severe as in former years often use it to refer to the last day of withdrawal. "Doc, give me a pick up and it'll put me around the turn."

artillery. The outfit used to inject drugs hypodermically, that is, usually, a medicine dropper fitted with a hollow needle. Specialized to needle addicts. Also *Bay State, emergency gun, gun, hype, joint, Luer, nail, needle, works,* some with specialized meaning. ". . . it (a needle) is referred to as a spike usually, and a dropper is a dripper. Put them together and you have artillery."

ask for the cotton. 1. To ask for another addict's filtering cotton in order to squeeze out the residue for a very small shot. An indication that the addict is broke and out of drugs. "He was around T.O. asking for the cotton a few weeks ago." 2. By extension, to dislike a person. "I wouldn't ask that bum for the cotton."

attitude, show an attitude, have an attitude, etc. Hostile or aloof and uncooperative. "I pegged him for a lame with an attitude. . . ."

away. Incarcerated.

away from the habit. To be *off drugs.* Also *to break the habit, to be off, to catch up, to fold up, on the up and up, washed up, cleaned up.*

back up. 1. To allow the blood to come back into the glass (dropper or glass syringe) during a vein shot. See *register, jack off, booting.* "He always liked to back up a shot three or four times." 2. To refuse to make a connection because of suspicion that the addict (or the peddler) may be a stool pigeon. Also to *blow the meet.* 3. To fold up or back away from something.

bag. 1. A quantity of drugs packaged in small paper or cellophane parcels, e.g., five dollar bags. Also *balloon,* though a *balloon* is usually a condom or small rubber balloon. See *bindle.* 2. To put in a classification as convict, thief, con man, etc.

balloon. A quantity of drugs packaged in small paper, cellophane or rubber parcels. See *bindle.*

bambalache. Marihuana (New York). See *muggles.*

bamboo. An opium pipe. Specialized to opium smokers. Obsolescent. Also *gong, gonger, dream stick, hop stick, joy stick, saxophone, stem, stick, yen cheung, crock, gongola, log.* "Seems like I can't get my habit off this morning. Let's have another crack at that bamboo. . . ."

bang. 1. An injection of narcotics, usually taken intravenously, but may refer also to subcutaneous injections. Restricted to needle addicts, and usually means morphine, heroin or cocaine or a combination. Also *bang in the arm, fix up, geezer, jolt, pop, shot, bird's eye, skin shot, vein shot, speed ball, jab,* with specialized meanings. All these terms indicate a ration of drug prepared for injection, as contrasted to a *bindle, check, deck,* etc., which indicate units of drug as they are sold retail. "I'll loan you a bang till you score. . . ." 2. The thrill or drive experienced immediately after a vein shot; euphoria. Restricted to needle addicts. Also *bing, boot, drive, jab off, kick* or *kicks, belt, buzz, flash, charge.* "I took four shots of that flea powder and couldn't get no bang out of it." "Yeah, I noticed I didn't get the right bang out of that last shot myself." 3. The lift or exhilaration experienced from taking drugs in any manner. "Now I'm on horse, I can't get no bang out of muggles any more." 4. To inject narcotics, especially in the vein, but may refer to *skin shooting* also. Also to *shoot*, to *get with it*. See *bang in the arm*.

bang in the arm. Usually shortened to *bang*. An injection of narcotics. Obsolescent. See *bang 1*. "A bang in the arm and we'll be dead ready for that tip tonight."

Bay State. A standard medical hypodermic syringe, usually of glass with metal reenforcement, using a plunger and screw type needle. Derived from the trade name of the syringe. Seldom used by underworld addicts. Also *Luer* (for a standard syringe). "She wouldn't use anything but a Bay State to fix, but I liked a dripper. . . ."

bean. A Benzedrine tablet or capsule. See *benny*.

bean trip. Intoxication from ingesting Benzedrine; a *benny jag*.

bear down on (one). For a habit to come on, especially the early withdrawal symptoms. See *habit*.

beat. 1. To cheat. 2. Sick for lack of drugs. 3. Down and out. 4. To rob. See *knock off 4*.

beat a till. To steal from a cash register. See *till tapping*.

beat the gong. To smoke opium. See *hit the gong, kick the gong*.

beat the rap or **beat the beef.** To be acquitted of a charge.

bee that stings. A drug habit, especially one coming on; *a monkey on my back*. See *habit*.

bees and honey. Money. From "Australian" rhyming argot, in which the meaning rhymes with the second element in the phrase and is filled in by the one who hears it. *E.g.*, "twist and twirl" means "girl."

beetlebrow. An aggressive female homosexual.

behind stuff. Using heroin.

belly habit. A drug habit satisfied by taking drugs orally. See *mouth habit*.

belt. 1. The euphoria following an injection of narcotics. See *bang 2*. 2. A shot, or a quantity of drugs to be injected. "Gimme a belt of stuff."

bending and bowing. To be under the influence of narcotics. Obsolescent. See *high, all lit up*.

benny. Benzedrine (amphetamine) in tablets, capsules or inhalers. Also *whites, crosses, beans, blancas* (Mexican), referring to capsules.

benny jag. Intoxication from ingesting Benzedrine. Also *wired on whites, bean trip, white scene*. See *benny*.

Bernice, Burnese, Bernies. Crystallized cocaine used either for inhaling or for mixing with morphine or heroin in the form of hypodermic injections. Sold in papers or capsules. Also, *C, Corine, Carrie, coke, Cecil, Cholly, happy dust, heaven dust, dust, snow, star dust,* and other similar terms beginning with ℭ.

". . . soon as I get Bernice we'll go for a ride."

big man. The brains behind a dope ring; the one who seldom takes the rap. Most traffic in narcotics is controlled by gangsters of a vicious type, often with sound political connections. The *big man* wholesales drugs to dealers and for peddlers, and may racketeer them for protection and the privilege of selling. *Big men* are usually not addicted.

bindle. A quantity of narcotics (usually restricted to morphine, heroin and cocaine) prepared for sale, as contrasted to a *ration*, which is prepared for injection. Both *bindles* and *rations* vary widely in size and strength. Also *cap, card, check, cigarette paper, cube, deck, O., O.Z., piece, balloon, half load, load, bundle, bag,* with specialized meanings. ". . . and this connection had bindles for five dollars, ten dollars and twenty dollars, good H, too."

bing. An injection of drugs. Also *bingo, bird's eye, fix, gee, go, jab, pop, load, penitentiary shot, pick up, pin shot, geez* or *geezer, point shot, prod, prop,* with specialized meanings. See *bang.*

bird cage hype. A down and out underworld addict, probably so called because he often lives in a *bird cage joint* or flophouse where the cots are separated by chicken wire. There is also a saying that a down and out addict "has a bird cage on one foot and a boxing glove on the other." "He's just a bird cage hype stemming his score dough." Obsolescent. Current popular term, *gutter hype.*

bird's eye. 1. A half size or small ration or narcotics. "A bird's eye is generally what a junker takes in his first bang after being on vacation for a while. . . ." 2. A small pill of opium, especially opium prepared for smoking. This is the smallest size. The next in sequence are *buttons* and *high hats.* 3. A very small quantity of drugs. "When Whitey bought the cap I took just a tiny bit—a bird's eye—and gave the rest to him." 4. A small quantity of narcotic solution held in the *joint* for another addict to take; equivalent to "butt's" on a cigarette. "Save me two or three points of that for a bird's eye." Also *taste, lightweight taste.*

bit. A prison sentence. Also *jolt, stuff.* "I started in San Quentin and finished my stuff in Chino."

bitch or **the bitch.** The death penalty or life imprisonment. Also used for a long sentence given to a habitual criminal. Clipped back from *habitch,* in turn clipped from habitual.

biz or **business.** 1. An outfit (*joint* and *spoon*) for taking drugs hypodermically. Also *factory, joint, layout, machinery, works,* etc. See artillery. "Have you got the business? I'm sick." 2. The hypodermic needle as separate from the syringe. Also *harpoon, point, tom cat,* with specialized meanings. "Let me use the business." 3. Narcotics in general. See junk. "What I want is the business." 4. The "third degree" administered by the police. "Everyone gets the business from those dicks in Cincy." 5. Death or a beating given a stool pigeon. "They finally gave that rat from Chi the business." 6. As *B.I.Z.* To emphasize the action, with each letter pronounced separately. "That dude is really taking care of the B.I.Z." (He is being successful in criminal activity.) 7. The end of anything. 8. Bad or fake dope. See *blank.*

black and white. A policeman.

black shit. Smoking opium. See *black stuff.*

black stuff. 1. Opium prepared for smoking, as contrasted to crude gum. Also *gee yen, hop, gum, mud, pen yen, san lo, tar, black shit, yen shee, ah pen yen, dai yen, fi doo nie, hok for, sook nie, li yuen, gee, gonger 3, lem kee,* with specialized meanings. 2. Laudanum is now being called *black stuff* by extension. 3. Concentrated paregoric cooked down for injection. 4. Dark brown heroin that comes from Mexico.

blackjack. Paregoric which has been cooked down to be injected in a concentrated form. See *P.G.*

blancas. Benzedrine tablets (Mexican).

blank. 1. A quantity of bad or fake dope. Also *turkey, sugar, flea powder, talcum powder, queer 5, business* 8. 2. An individual who is nothing, especially as far as the rackets are concerned.

block. 1. A *cube* of morphine as sold by the can (or ounce). "It comes 120 to 130 blocks to the ounce." 2. Crude bootleg morphine. 3. A kilo (2½ lb.) of bulk marihuana.

block buster. See *yen shee baby*.

bloomer girls or **bloomer broads.** Shoplifters who wear specially constructed underwear in which stolen articles are concealed. See *hustling drawers*.

blow. To inhale narcotics in powder form, usually heroin, though cocaine was formerly popular taken by sniffing it up the nose, usually from the back of the hand. Narcotics in tablet form are crushed between two coins before inhaling. ". . . when I could get a dozen heroin tablets for fifty cents, I'd blow one just before I went on (the stage) and one as soon as my act was over. . . ." "You know Slim. Well, he first started blowing C around a layout." Also *horn, snort*. 2. To smoke marihuana, as to *blow weed*.

blow a pill. To smoke opium.

blow a shot. To waste drugs by missing a vein, or because of a break or malfunction of the equipment. Restricted to needle addicts. ". . . never seen it fail. On short stuff I'll always blow a shot." Also *skin* or *skin the punk*. 2. To spill the solution.

blow the meet. To fail to keep an appointment, usually because of suspicion on the part of either addict or peddler. ". . . considered high treason for a peddler to blow a meet, he will lose his customers quick . . . it's bad for the addict, too." "It takes a pinch or its equal to make me blow a meet." Also *hang him up, blow the scene*.

blow the scene. 1. To fail to keep an appointment, especially for the sale or purchase of narcotics. Also *hang (someone) up, blow the meet*. 2. To flee; to leave precipitously.

blow weed. To smoke marihuana.

blue grass. To obtain a commitment to the Lexington Hospital under certain conditions. If an addict breaks those conditions, he usually serves a year in jail. This term is now loosely applied to similar situations elsewhere, although the practice is not much used now in Kentucky. Used as adjective, noun, or verb. "If you leave Lexington, the Kentucky authorities will place a charge against you for drug addiction unless you recommit yourself and stay until you're pronounced cured. This is called a blue grass commitment."

blue heaven. Sodium Amytal in capsules. Also *blue birds, blues, blue heaven, jack up*.

blue velvet. 1. Sodium Amytal. See *blue birds, blue heaven*. 2. Pyribenzamine.

blue birds or **blues.** Sodium Amytal in capsules. Also *blue heaven, blues, jack up*.

boat sailed or **boat's in.** Said when narcotics are successfully smuggled into prison. See *drive* 4.

bo bo bush. Marihuana. See *muggles*.

bogart. To take more than one's share, usually by violence.

bogus beef. See *meat ball rap*.

bogus smack. See *blank*.

bogus trip. False information regarding drugs or peddlers.

bombita. An amphetamine capsule; from Mexican Spanish for "little bomb."

bonaroo. 1. Good narcotics, uncut or cut only a little; the best. 2. Wearing starched, pressed clothing in a prison or a narcotics hospital. "That dude was looking bonaroo when he flashed at the board (parole board)."

bonche. A group of marihuana smokers using the drug. Also *cofradia* (Cuba and New York City).

bonita. Mexican Spanish, slang term for milk sugar, which is used to adulterate heroin.

boo gee. The *gee rag* used to make a tight connection between syringe and needle. Probably a variant or corruption of the medical term *boogie*. Rare. Also *geep, boat, collar*. See *gee rag* 2.

book. The maximum penalty, usually in the phrase, "He threw the book at me," "He gave me the book." Also *stuck it to me* (West Coast).

boomer. An addict who moves frequently. Borrowed from the lingo of the old-time railroaders, meaning a railroader who drifted from job to job, working a while at each, or riding freights when he had no work. Cf. German *bummeler, bummel-zug*, etc. Also *globe trotter, drifter, floater, boot and shoe*.

boost. To shoplift. Probably the most common way of supporting a habit, excepting prostitution. The noun form is often recorded in such idioms as *rooting on the boost, on the boost, working the boost*.

booster. A professional shoplifter, male or female.

booster stick. 1. A cigarette of treated marihuana, reputedly potent. Also *gold leaf special*. 2. An ordinary cigarette, the tip of which is dipped in a concentrated essence of marihuana preserved in alcohol. It is lit, blown out when it flames, and inhaled.

boosting drawers. See *hustling drawers*.

boot. 1. Euphoria following injection. See *bang, belt, flash, gassed, stoned*. 2. The *gee rag* used to make a tight connection between needle and dropper. 3. To back blood into the dropper, allow it to mix with the drug, then shoot it back. Also *verification shot*.

boot and shoe. 1. Down and out, as applied to an underworld addict. Probably derived from the bizarre garb worn by some addicts, especially those who make a living by begging or panhandling. "The boot and shoe junkies made that joint a hangout, so it was really hot." The plural is sometimes used with adverbial function. "All hypes eventually go boots and shoes." Also *bird cage hype, broker*.

booter. One who uses *boot shots*. See *boot* 3.

boots on. In on the know, informed. Recorded as *have (one's) boots on, keep (one's) boots on*, etc. "Tell Joe to put his boots on, to wise up."

boss. Wonderful or choice. Also *righteous, groovy, solid, out of sight, something else, too much, (the) end*.

boss habit. A very heavy habit.

bottoms. A male homosexual who is the passive receptor in pederasty. Also *sissy, stuff, sex punk, rap and bag it, queen pussy, boy girl*.

bow sow. Narcotics. West Coast, obsolescent.

box. 1. A record player. 2. The vagina. 3. A carton of cigarettes. 4. Radio. 5. Television. 6. A safe.

box of L. 100 ampules of Methedrine in a pharmacist's box.

boy. Heroin. See *Racehorse Charlie*.

boy girl. 1. See *bottoms*. 2. A person who adopts the mannerisms of the opposite sex.

brace and bits. The breasts. From "Australian" rhyming argot.

bread. Money.

break the habit or **break.** 1. To go *off drugs*. See *kick the habit*. "I have to break the habit for I have a State case coming up." 2. To suffer severe localized withdrawal distress. An opium smoker may say, "I always break the habit in my stomach."

brick gum or **brick.** 1. Crude opium after it is cooked into smoking opium or prepared opium. "Sometimes it comes in bricks weighing a pound, and sometimes in odd-shaped lumps." "Used to get brick gum for $40.00 to $60.00 a pound;

now it's $300.00 to $450.00." 2. *Brick* (only). A kilo of marihuana (2¼ lb.).

bring up. To distend the vein into which the *shot* will be injected by holding up the circulation with a cord or tourniquet, simultaneously massaging the skin over the vein toward the tourniquet. Also *tie off*, which is more popular on the West Coast.

britch. A pocket, especially a side pants pocket. Borrowed from pickpockets, who seldom use *britch* alone, but rather *right britch* or *left britch*, and then only for side pants pockets.

Brody. 1. A feigned "fit" or spasm staged by an addict to elicit sympathy and perhaps a ration of narcotics from a physician. Obsolescent. Also *cartwheel, circus, wingding, figure eight, twister, toss out, meter, Duffy, bitch,* as in *pitch a bitch.* "He threw a Brody for the croaker and scored for some stuff." 2. A long chance, derived from the dive of Steve Brody from Brooklyn Bridge. ". . . an awful Brody he took, but he made a clean get."

broker. A down and out addict. See *boot and shoe*.

brown eye. Coitus *per anum*.

buffalo. A five-year sentence. Obsolescent. Also *nickel, fin*.

bug. 1. To inject an irritant such as kerosene or the creosote disinfectant often used in jails into the muscles or beneath the skin to produce a swelling or abscess; used to solicit narcotics from a doctor. "That time seven guys bugged themselves and got junk for a while, also a rest. . . ." 2. To annoy someone, especially a guard in a prison or jail. "Steve had two speeds, slow and slower. He'd slip into slower to bug the hack." 3. To tap a telephone line. 4. An abscess or sore, self-inflicted and used to solicit narcotics from physicians. Probably derived from the *bugs* or sores cultivated by old-time beggars.

build up the habit or **a habit.** To increase one's tolerance to narcotics by gradually increasing the dosage, usually inevitable with opiates. "A guy can build up one hell of a habit using Dilaudid before he realizes it." Also *strung out, hooked, got a thing going*.

bull. 1. A policeman. Also *the man, the heat, screw, black and white, hudda* (Mexican). 2. An aggressive female homosexual, clipped from *bulldyker,* sometimes rendered as *bulldagger, q.v.*

bull horrors. The delusions often experienced by cocaine addicts; part of the anxiety complex produced by the drug and sometimes reinforced by paranoid tendencies in the user. Policemen *(bulls)* and detectives often figure prominently in these delusions, hence the term, "Monty had the bull horrors bad. . . ."

bulldagger. Varient of *bulldyker*. See *bull 2*. Also *butch*.

bullet. A currently popular expression for one year sentence, supplanting *ace* on the West Coast.

bum beef or **bum steer.** False complaint or information, which is usually given deliberately to the police.

bum kick. Boring, unpleasant.

bum rap. An arrest or conviction for a crime the man actually did not commit, as distinguished from denying it. See *rap 2, rap partner, rap sheet*.

bum steer. False or unreliable information about drugs or peddlers. "You gave me a bum steer, Jack, about that joint. . . ." Also *bogus trip, bum wire, jive*.

bum wire. False information regarding peddlers or drugs.

bummer. Anything boring or unpleasant.

bundle. 1 A quantity of narcotics for

sale. Variant of *bindle.* 2. A sum of cash, especially a roll.

bunk habit. 1. The desire to hang about where opium is being smoked; actually, a mild opium habit can be contracted from continually breathing smoke-filled air. See *bunk yen, lamp habit* 3. "His girl don't smoke but she has a bunk habit." 2. An opium habit (smoking). 3. A tendency to sleep a great deal; used to refer to addicts of any kind by extension. "They ought to call her The Pajama Kid; she has an awful bunk habit."

bunk yen. 1. A small opium habit requiring only two or three pills to satisfy. Also *bunk habit* 2, *lamp habit* 3. ". . . well, he only had a bunk yen, but he would get so sick. . . ." 2. The slight addiction acquired from breathing the smoke-filled air in a *lay down joint* or in a room where opium is regularly smoked. Also *bunk habit* 1. "I used to let the pup lay down with us, and he finally got a bunk yen. . . ." (Many West Coast prostitutes formerly had Pekingese or other lap dogs who were obviously addicted.) "Some Chinese broads did not smoke, but had a bunk yen just from cheffing. . . ."

burn. 1. To cheat. 2. To cheat or steal from someone. 3. To sell bad or fake drugs. "I burnt that poop butt. I sold his some Ajax." 4. The initial exhilaration following the injection of opiates. See *jaboff.*

burned out. A sclerotic condition of the veins resulting from abscesses and continued puncturing. Also *up and down the lines.* ". . . had to go to the skin, all his lines are burned out." See *soul searching, up and down the lines.*

Burnese. Variant of Bernice, *q.v.*

bush. Marihuana.

business. See *biz.*

bust. 1. To arrest or be arrested. See *put away, down, nailed, clouted, snatched, rousted, knocked off, knocked out.* 2. To catch someone redhanded. "I knew I'd bust Jimmy dipping if I left the smack on the table."

bust the main line. To inject narcotics intravenously. Also *to shoot, to take it in the vein, to take it main, hit the sewer, send it home, geeze* or *geez.*

From my dropper I'll shake the dust
From my spike I'll scrape the rust,
And my old main line I'll bust. . . .

busted on a buzzer. See *meat ball rap.*

butch. See *bull.* A *butch* is not necessarily a *bull,* however. She may simply be the active lesbian partner.

butch game. 1. An ultimatum to cooperate or suffer heavy penalty. Also *murder game.* 2. The technique used by a lesbian prostitute beating her trick for money without going through with the sexual act.

button. A pill of smoking opium, in size between a *bird's eye* and a *high hat.* See *bird's eye.* 2. A nodule of peyote, not addicting but used experimentally by some "far-out" beatniks.

buy. 1. A narcotic peddler. 2. A purchase of narcotics.

buy money. The money used to purchase drugs. See *connection dough, score dough.*

buzzer. 1. A homosexual. 2 A prison guard. 3. An enforcement officer's badge. "We got his leather that had his buzzer in it."

C. Cocaine. See *Bernice.*

C. Vol. An addict who has been committed to the USPHS Hospital by a county court in Kentucky. He usually volunteers for such commitment.

call. The initial exhilaration following the injection of opiates. See *jaboff.*

canary. A nembutal capsule. See *yellow jacket*.

candy. 1. Barbiturates. 2. An obsolete term for opiate drugs. 3. Cocaine or Benzedrine.

canned stuff. Commercial smoking opium, usually put up in tins, as *li yuen* (No. 1 quality), *low foo kee* 2, *lem kee* 3, and *san lo* 4.

cannon. An expert pickpocket; one with "class."

cap. A capsule containing a drug, usually heroin or cocaine. The contents vary widely in both quantity and strength according to the source. Today, addicts measure both their purchases and their habits by the number of *caps* bought or taken per day. Seldom applied to morphine. Often used also to indicate barbiturates. See *paper*. 2. A person's head or mind. "That nic nac's cap is wide open, like he's howling at the moon." 3. Or *cap up*. To transfer drugs (usually heroin) from a loose bulk form to individual capsules for retail sale. "I like to cap it on a big mirror as that way you don't lose a bit."

card. A *bindle* of opium sold (usually in a *hop joint*) ready for smoking. About four to six *fun* of prepared opium is weighed out on a card—often a playing card—and the chef or the smoker rolls the *pills* from this supply. "We laid down in the joint together, then she ordered four cards of hop. . . ." "Playing cards are used, except the ace of spades." Street peddlers (now rare) use blue or red cellophane envelopes about two inches square.

carpet. See *Murphy*.

carry. 1. For a given amount of narcotics to support an addict, or prevent withdrawal signs, for a specified length of time. "It takes at least a grain and a half to carry me four hours." "Six pills don't carry me all day." 2. A *plant* of drugs, secreted on the person to be used only in case of arrest, sometimes called *Miss Carrie*.

cartwheel. A feigned illness or "fit." Restricted to needle addicts and notably used by circus and carnival grifters who use drugs. Obsolescent. See *Brody*. "All you had to do in those little burgs was turn a couple of cartwheels and some croaker would fix you."

cat. 1. A person, especially a young Negro who has a *hustle* to support his habit. 2. A cat nap. 3. A destitute person who sleeps in a different place each night. 4. Generalized to refer to anyone.

cat nap. To get small (and very welcome) snatches of sleep during the withdrawal period.

catch up or **be caught up.** To be *off drugs*. Rare. Obsolescent. "Yeah, he's all caught up now."

cave. An abscess at the site of injection. The reference seems to be not to the cavity, but to the fact that the vein "caves in" at this spot. See *cave digging*.

cave digging. searching among caved-in veins for one which can be used for injection.

Cecil. Cocaine. See *Bernice*.

cement. Wholesale illicit narcotics as they pass into contraband channels. Restricted to *big men* or wholesalers of the New York area. Not used by addicts.

cement arm. Heavy deposits of sclerotic tissue over the veins. Obsolescent, giving way to *dirty arm, needle tracks, tracks, service stripes*.

change. A short jail or prison sentence.

changes. Adjustments, especially as *being put through the changes* in prison or hospital prison life.

channel. A vein or *main line* into which drugs are injected. Also *sewer*, *home;* when referring specifically to the cubital area, *ditch* or *pit*.

charged or **overcharged.** 1. Stupefied or drowsy as a result of taking too much of a drug. This state may range from mild drowsiness to complete unconsciousness, or sometimes fatal narcosis. See *play the nod, O.D., overjolt, zipped, out of sight, gowed.* 2. Charged only. Under the influence of narcotics.

Charley. Cocaine.

Charley Coke. A cocaine addict (restricted to New York and New England). Obsolescent. "That boy you met last night, he never smoked, he is just a Charley Coke, and there aren't many left."

Charley Cotton. One of the mythical Cotton Brothers, C., H. and M. Cotton. See *cotton, Cotton Brothers, rinsings.* "He's strictly a Charley Cotton man. . . ."

che chees. The breasts.

cheater. An attendant in a *joint* who is skillful at mulcting the addict of his *shot* as it is administered. He does this by putting a bit of cotton inside the medicine dropper bulb so that he can draw most of the shot up into the bulb and keep it there, injecting only a small portion into the customer. Some *cheaters* steal much of the shot for themselves by pinching up a bit of skin, then running the needle through it and into their own thumbs or fingers. The customer feels the needle enter, but does not get much of the drug (Chicago, Detroit and vicinity). Also *burn artist.* "Georgie the Rat could palm a cotton and cheat more gow than eight guys could steal the money to buy. He was a cheater and no mistake." 2. Any dice or card *hustler.*

check. A *bindle* of narcotics, usually heroin or cocaine. See *bindle.* ". . . and she said, 'Hon, get two toys of grease and three checks of C on you way home.'"

chef. 1. The attendant in a *hop joint.* He warms the pipe and rolls the pills for the smokers. He may be a professional supplied by the house, or, on private parties, a smoker who has the necessary skill to officiate. Also *cook* or *cooker.* "A chef can't always cook opium from gum to prepared." 2. The act of rolling and cooking pills. "In my time I've been called on to chef for some fairly important people."

Chicago green. A good grade of marihuana. See *muggles.*

Chicago leprosy. Multiple abscesses.

chicharra. The communal cigar or cigarette (sometimes wrapped in a cornhusk) made of tobacco and marihuana combined, used by Latin American addicts (New York City).

chicken shit beef. See *meat ball rap.*

chicken shit habit. A relatively small drug habit; one which is satisfied with a small quantity of drugs. Distinguished from a *chippy habit,* which is irregular. Also *light-weight nothing.*

chill. 1. To make someone fearful. 2. To give someone the cold shoulder. Also *shine him on, freeze, play the shoulder.*

Chinaman on my back or **monkey on my back.** 1. Suffering abstinence symptoms. 2. Supporting a drug habit.

Chinese needle work. An euphemistic expression for using or dealing in narcotics, especially opium. "He has a store in Frisco, now, sells jewelry and novelties and Chinese needle work. . . ."

chingadera. The outfit or *kit* used for injecting drugs (Mexican-American usage). See *artillery.*

Chino. A Chinese. While some (mainly li yuen) of the opium traffic in North America is still in control of

Glossary 349

the Chinese, and especially the *Tongs*, *q.v.*, they seldom deal in other forms of narcotics, and the older generation refuse to take drugs by needle. Most Chinese who deal in opium are also addicts. The bulk of smoking opium in the United States today is controlled by Mexicans, and is sold in cans or *tins*. "You can never tell about a Chino, what he is thinking. . . ."

chipping. Using drugs irregularly, as a *chippy*. See *chippy habit, pleasure user.*

chippy habit. A small irregular habit which precedes almost inevitable addiction. Also *coffee-and habit, ice cream habit, cotton habit, three-day habit, hit and miss habit, weekend habit, pleasure user, Saturday night habit, chicken shit habit,* with specialized meanings.

Christmas roll. An assortment of barbiturates, so called because of the variety of colored capsules. Also *rainbow roll.*

Christmas trees. Tuinal capsules.

chuck habit, chuck horrors or **chuckers.** The ravenous appetite for food which an addict develops after he goes through the withdrawal illness. "I don't get the chuck habit like I use to. But still, I do feel it for a few days. . . ." See *grease* 6, *root.*

cigarette paper. A *bindle* of heroin, today mostly in prisons or jails, put up in a folded cigarette paper. On the street heroin is not sold anymore in cigarette papers, but in capsules, cellophane or a *balloon.* ". . . so you could ask for a cigarette paper anywhere and no fear of being fingered for stuff. . . ."

circus. A feigned spasm or "fit." Obsolescent. See *Brody.*

clean. Away from the habit. Also *straight, squared up, hang it up, put it down.*

clip. 1. To steal. 2. To arrest.

clip joint. 1. Any place where *hustlers* and prostitutes hang out. 2. A known crooked gambling house.

cloud nine. See *in high.*

clout. To steal, especially as a shoplifter. Many, if not most, underworld addicts support their habits by thievery of one kind or another. "Right then they went out to clout a new front for Alabam." Also *boost, gaffel, sneeze.*

coasting. 1. The sensation of euphoria following the use of a drug. Used of all drugs except cocaine. See *in high, floating.* "That day, when the phone rang, I was just laying there coasting and getting my kicks." Also *grooving, tripping, T.V. action.* 2. Serving an easy prison sentence.

coffee-and habit. A form of *chippy habit, q.v.* The inference is that it is no habit at all. Probably taken from the phrase *coffee-and pimp,* one who gets only enough from his girl to buy doughnuts and coffee (pronounced coffeeann).

cofradia. A group of users smoking marihuana. Also *bonche* (Cuba and New York City).

coke. Cocaine. See *C.* "Just a little coke is the thing to use with tincture of opium, then it requires no cooking or burning the alky off, just drop the coke in and shoot it."

coke and crystal. Parties at which addicts drink beer or gin and sniff cocaine.

cokie or **coke head.** A cocaine addict. Rare; addicts who take cocaine straight are uncommon today, but once were prevalent. Obsolescent.

cokomo or **Kokomo.** A cocaine user. Obsolescent.

cold turkey. Treatment for addiction (withdrawal) in jails, hospitals, etc. where addicts are taken off drugs suddenly without the tapering-off process always desired by the addict. "It's something to kick the habit cold turkey. . . ." "I'll never forget the first cold turkey kick I went through. . . ." See *kick cold.*

collar. 1. The small piece of paper, thread or rubber used to make an airtight connection between dropper and needle. Also *gaff, shoulder, jacket, jeep* or *geep.* See *gee rag.* 2. To arrest.

con. 1. To make contact with a *peddler.* 2. With *for* indicates that someone else is buying narcotics for an addict. "I just got there and he was conning for me."

connect. 1. To make contact with a peddler. Also score. 2. With *for* indicates that someone else is buying narcotics for an addict. "When I was so hot, he was connecting for me. . . ." Also *score for, con for.*

connection. 1. A generalized underworld term for getting anything—usually with the implication of illicit traffic; the person who controls, sells or obtains certain items. "To cop the short you gotta see that heavy set kayducer (conductor). He's the connection." 2. In the narcotics rackets, specialized to mean a fairly important figure near the top; a big dealer or wholesaler. "Jeez, I never see five ounces of stuff. You'll have to see the connection." 3. Used by some addicts to mean a peddler, physician, or anyone through whom or from whom narcotics are obtained. "Sometimes Bill used to jump 500 miles across country to see the connection and get junk for the mob." Also *the man,* in all three senses.

connection dough. The price of a *bindle* of narcotics. Also *buy money, score dough.* "He's nuts, planted his connection dough and can't find the plant."

conned. 1. To be the victim of a small-time confidence game. 2. To be persuaded.

contact high. 1. The emotional contagion of jazz musicians who are *on* may be picked up by a musician who has not used drugs. 2. One who has not smoked marihuana but is nevertheless *high* from the smoke in the room is said to be *contact high.* See *bunk habit.*

cook. 1. An individual who knows how to cook up raw gum opium for prepared smoking opium. Sometimes a *chef* can do this, but by no means always. "A cook is most always a chef, but a chef isn't always a cook." 2. Sometimes used interchangeably with *chef, q.v.* (West Coast).

cook a pill. To prepare a small quantity of opium for smoking; usually done by the *chef,* but may be done by the smoker. The sticky opium is manipulated on the *yen hok* over the flame and worked on the top of the bowl or some other flat, hard surface. For full description, see text. Usually the *pills* are smoked immediately, but may be prepared in advance. "He used to cook a few extra pills so I could take some yen poks along on the road."

cook it up. To prepare heroin (or other opiates) for injection by heating it in a *cooking spoon* or other *cooker* held over a small flame, such as a match or a cigarette lighter. The drug is dissolved in a very small quantity of water.

cooker. 1. The receptacle, usually a spoon with a handle bent back, a small bottle cap with a wire handle or a little glass vial, used to boil the narcotic solution before it is injected. "Never leave your cooker dirty and in sight. People are so nosey." 2. Or **cook.** The *chef* in a *hop joint* who prepares the *pills* and *cooks* them for the smoker.

cookie. A *chef, q.v.* Restricted to Chinese or Chinese-Americans of the older generation.

cooking spoon. Variant of *cooker, q.v.*

cool. 1. A vague term of approval, now being supplanted by *groovie* or *groovy*, with the same meaning. 2. Reserved.

cool it. 1. To remain reserved or quiet under pressure. 2. To take it easy, relax, stop any activity. 3. To take drugs, but conceal the effects from others. 4. To go silent and aloof, usually in anger. Also *freeze, dummy up, lighten up, hang tough.*

coozie stash. Drugs hidden in the vagina, usually in a condom or balloon. See *stash.*

cop. 1. To obtain. "Do you dig spending all your time trying to cop?" 2. To steal or rob.

cop a fix. To obtain a ration of narcotics.

cop a peek. To get the *lay* of the *joint* to be *knocked off;* to *case* the *outfit.* (Used by addicts who have progressed to robbery or burglary.)

cop a pill. To smoke opium; the act of inhaling one's smoke. "Let's cop a few more pills before we go. . . ."

cop a sneak. To sneak away, to escape by running or walking away.

cop man. 1. A narcotics dealer. 2. A middle man in the narcotics sale. 3. A *fence* who will buy stolen goods.

cop out. To plead guilty. Generally used by all underworld people and many enforcement officers.

copper. 1. A policeman. 2. *Good time* in prison.

cotics. Drugs in general, especially those of the opiate series and cocaine; *white stuff,* including principally morphine, heroin and cocaine. Also *junk, Miss Emma, gow, M., G.O.M., God's medicine, horse, courage pills, C., skamas,* some with specialized meanings. Any kind of narcotics used by confirmed addicts, excluding marihuana smokers and barbiturate users. "They got three grand and a kiester full of cotics."

cotton. The small wisp of cotton placed in the cooking spoon and used as a filter when the solution is drawn up into the needle. See *cotton shooter.* "Save your cottons, boy. We may be in for a panic."

Cotton brothers. 1. Narcotics. (H., M. and C. Cotton.) "Are the Cotton brothers in town?" might mean "How is the drug situation here?" 2. The cottons used by addicts to filter drugs before injecting, and often reused by addicts who are broke. See *cotton shooter.*

cotton habit. A small irregular habit which an addict may support by begging or retrieving *cottons, q.v.* See *chippy habit.*

cotton shooter. A down and out addict who hangs around other addicts and begs or picks up the *cottons* used to filter drugs. The *cottons* are soaked for the narcotic residue they contain. Some addicts use them over and over. ". . . one cotton would knock out the average junker today." "Did you ever see so many characters around T.O. (Toledo, Ohio) on the pling (begging) for cottons?" "Cotton Bob took a geezer of cottons that had soured and bumped himself off. The pistols thought he had an O.D."

cotton tail route. Suicide.

Toes turned up, ass full of cotton,

Long gone, but not forgotten.

See *Dutch route.*

count a man out. 1. To short-change a person. 2. To fail to *cut someone in* on the score. 3. To leave someone out of a *caper* because he's not safe.

courage pills. Heroin in tablet form, usually ⅛ to ½ grain. Obsolescent as argot, but used by *squares.*

cracking shorts. Breaking into cars to support a habit.

crank handle. A voluntary patient in a

prison or narcotics hospital. Also *self-starter, stem winder, winder, hitchhiker, Mr. Fish.*

crazy. Very good. Also *groovie, righteous, boss, too much, George, way out, cool, out of sight, something else, insane.*

creep. A disgusting person. Also *lame, jerk, rumdum, low rider, poop butt, nic nac, punk, gunsel, rumkin.*

creep on the cash register. See *heel, till tipping.*

crib. 1. One's home or apartment. 2. A house of prostitution. Also *flat, pad, notch house.* 3. A hypochondriac with many persistent symptoms.

croaker. An addict's term for physician; also in general underworld usage, especially for a prison or jail doctor. "All that croaker will give you is salts or cc. pills." Also *horse doctor, vet.* See *ice tong doctor.*

croaker on the make. See *ice tong doctor.*

crock. 1. An opium pipe. See *bamboo.* 2. The bowl of an opium pipe. Obsolescent. 3. A person who talks foolishly or senselessly. Also *loose, cap's loose, talking trash.*

crocked out. An addict who has committed suicide.

cross-country hype. See *R.F.D. junker.*

crosses. *Benny pills,* Benzedrine tablets.

crutch. A split match or twig used to hold a short marihuana cigarette butt.

crystallized. Having taken too much Methedrine. Also *over-amped.*

crystals. Methedrine.

cube. 1. Crude bootleg morphine in the wholesale trade. 2. A small cube (3 or 4 grains) sold in ounce cans which contain 120 to 140 such morphine cubes. Currently, 1-grain cubes are more common. The large ones are sometimes called sugar lump cubes. "Pushers shaved these cubes to a uniform size and wrapped them in tinfoil and sold them for $.50 to $1.00 each when a can of M was $25.00."

cure. 1. The length of time volunteers are required to stay in the USPHS Hospital, to be released as hospital treatment is completed. 2. To treat bulk marihuana with sugar and/or alcohol to produce a milder smoke.

curtains. 1. The end of anything. 2. An arrest. Also *end gate, the business, snatched, nailed,* etc. 3. A life sentence or the death penalty.

cut. To adulterate drugs, usually with sugar of milk. Modern bootleg heroin for instance may be cut from five to ten times before it reaches the consumer. "This flea powder passed through fifty hands, and everybody must have cut it."

cut (someone) in. A specialized form of general underworld usage. Addicts use the term to mean sharing a purchase made by someone else with the purchaser. See *connect, score.* "He is getting cut in by four different people that I know of, so he must have stuff. . . ."

cut (someone) loose. 1. To release. 2. To exclude someone from the *action;* to refuse to associate with him. Also *freeze on, shine on.* 3. Among established professional thieves, working on an "in and in" and "out and out" basis, to agree to exclude one member of the mob from any given theft, at the same time removing his *fall dough* from jeopardy should an arrest be made and excluding him from any share in the proceeds.

cut out. To leave a certain place.

cutered pill. A strong, unpalatable smoke obtained when the bowl of the pipe is too hot or when too much *yen shee* has accumulated. Sometimes caused by too much poorly reworked *yen shee* in the opium or by an inexperienced cook who does not take it off right. Also *green pill.* "Nothing has the foul taste of a cutered pill or the heavenly taste of a good one."

cutting up. Cutting the wrists in the hope of getting drugs. One phase of a *Brody*, q.v.

dabble. To indulge irregularly in narcotics. Now widely used by *squares*. See *chippy habit, chipping.*

daisy. A male homosexual. Also *sissy, queen, sex punk,* etc.

D.C. commitment. A person committed to the Lexington Hospital from Washington, D.C., usually required to do a *cure*.

deadwood. Arrested with narcotics on the person, or in the automobile or room of the addict (or peddler) (West and Southwest). "Glommed, eh?" "Yeah, deadwood, too. Obsolescent, except among old-timers. Current popular terms, *dead bang, dead bust.*

dealer. 1. Anyone who buys or sells stolen goods or contraband. 2. A wholesale dealer in narcotics. 3. A peddler. Also *the man*.

dealer's hand. A method of *holding* a paper of heroin, used by peddlers. A rubber band around the wrist or the finger is used to flip the paper away if arrest is imminent.

deck. 1. A *bindle* of morphine, cocaine or heroin. Now more commonly *paper* or *balloon*. 2. Rarely used to refer to smoking opium. See *bindle*.

deuce. 1. A two-year sentence. 2. Two of anything.

diambista. Marihuana (Cuba, Central America, New York City).

dig. To understand or appreciate; to be *hip* or *hep*. "You dig working day and night trying to cop?"

digits. The *numbers racket*.

dime. 1. A ten-year sentence. 2. Ten dollars. 3. Ten of anything. 4. Or *dime paper*. A ten dollar packet of drugs. Also *sawbuck, sawsky*.

ding. Marihuana. See *muggles*.

dingus, deazingus, dinghizen. The medicine dropper, the bulb, the needle or any part of the works, or the entire assembly. A loose, general term, synonymous with *phystaris*. See *artillery*. *Deazingus* taken from a carnival grifter's usage and an example of *cezearney*, an argot based on phonetic distortion.

dip or **dip artist.** A pickpocket who works with a mob; to professional pickpockets, a *tool, wire* or *hook*. *Dip* is not much used any more by pickpockets, but has been adopted by some addicts not very familiar with *the whiz*.

dirty. 1. Possessing or transporting drugs. 2. Having sclerotic or scarred veins from injecting drugs. See *cement arm*.

dirty jacket. A bad police record. Also *bad rap sheet, snitch sheet*.

ditch. The cubital area of the arm, a favored spot for injections. Also *pit* (West Coast).

do popper. A needle addict. Obsolescent. See *needle fiend* 2.

dog it. 1. To malinger or loaf on the job. 2. To run from a fight.

domino. 1. To complete any action, as, "Did you domino?" (meaning, did you *score?* were you able to purchase drugs? etc.). 2. To achieve sexual gratification in prison or out. "What kind of machinery is she? Did you domino?"

dope. 1. Narcotics. 2. Information. 3. To drug. This term, like *dope fiend*, tends to be taboo among addicts, though they use both perjoratively.

dope hop. A prison term for drug addicts, mostly used by guards, turn keys and police. "Where is the dope hop tier? On the flats like it used to be?"

do-right people. Non-addicts, or legitimate people as contrasted to underworld characters. Also *square apple, Joe lunch pail, lame*. Sometimes heard as *do-right John*, but rare among underworld addicts. Obsolescent. "Should get this kite out Sunday through one of the do-right people." "Don't crack now, that character is a do-right John."

doubleheader. Two marihuana cigarettes smoked simultaneously in the belief that euphoria is increased.

down. Incarcerated, *put away, busted.*

dozens. 1. Gossip, especially about one's parents or close relatives. Also, *to play the dozens,* to gossip or run someone down. 2. Low-rating or cursing someone violently, especially about his mother.

Dr. White. A code word for narcotics, especially *white stuff.* Obsolescent. "Dr. White is a grand old man. . . ."

drag. Anything which is boring or unpleasant. Also *bummer, bum kick, hum bug, rank.*

dream stick. An opium pipe. See *bamboo.* Also *stick* or *stem.*

drifter. An addict who has no permanent base of operations.

dripper. See *dropper.*

drive. 1. Euphoria. See *bang* 2. "I like the drive I get from H; suits me better." Also *buzz, flash, charge.* 2. To force a person to *pull a caper* against his will. 3. To put a woman out to work as a prostitute. "I have to drive that bitch to get her on the track." 4. To smuggle drugs into prison. Also *drive in.* "The man is going to drive in tonight so be on the point."

drive in. See *drive* 4. ". . . expect Mr. B to drive in this week and I'm anxious."

drop. 1. To arrest with the merchandise, usually as to *get the drop on.* 2. To sell or deliver, as a *lightweight pusher* or delivery man. "I'm dropping smack for Sam." 3. Widely used for *fence.* "Joe was a good drop until the heat was put on him." 4. Place of concealment. "Do you know of a good drop for this trash?"

dropped. Arrested. Also *busted, nailed, snatched.*

dropper or **dripper.** The inevitable medicine dropper used by needle addicts to make a *joint, q.v.* "The dropper is the thing for a mainliner. It's easier to manipulate."

dropping or **dropping rainbows.** Taking drugs by mouth. This may include all forms of addicting drugs in capsules, tablets or solution in water or alcohol. Also *scarfing,* or *scoffing, pill dropping.*

dropping rainbows. See *dropping.*

drugstore stuff. 1. Barbiturates or amphetamines as distinct from heroin. 2. Legitimate drugs (usually opiates) as distinct from bootleg drugs.

drum. A dormitory, usually in a prison or hospital.

duck. See *gopher, Hoosier fiend.*

ducking and dodging. Wanted by the law.

Duffy. 1. A feigned fit staged to obtain narcotics. See *Brody* 1. 2. Sometimes recorded as *Arthur Duffy.* Escape by running away. Also recorded as *on the Duffy, on the A.D., on the Arthur,* to *take a Duffy,* etc.

dugout. 1. An addict (or non-addict) who eats all the time; especially applicable to one whose appetite increases strongly following withdrawal. See *chuck horrors.* 2. An addict who has reached the bottom, especially one of the *boot and shoe* class. One who is, as the saying goes, "lame, lazy and crazy," or "sick, lazy and lame." 3. A playful expression, as "Why, you old dugout." Also *dug, Douglas, garbage freak,* in all three senses.

duke. 1. The hand. 2. To hand. 3. With *in.* To include someone in a *caper* or a deal. 4. With *out.* To exclude someone from a *caper* or a deal. May include fighting with him. "I had to duke that lame out the other day."

dummy. Bad or fake dope, passed as genuine in the traffic. "Caught selling dummies. . . ." Also *turkey, blank, the business, jaloney, flea powder, dust, bogus smack, sugar.*

dummy up. 1. To refuse to give information. Also *freeze, play the clam, play the exhaust, put it down, play the iggie* (for ignore or ignorant). 2. To take it easy, quiet down.

Dutch route. Suicide. Also *Gillette way out, crack out, cotton tail route.*

dyke. A woman taking the masculine role in a lesbian act; clipped from *bulldyker,* sometimes recorded as *bulldagger.*

dynamite. 1. Bootleg drugs which are strong or not very highly *cut.* "That stuff he pushes is dynamite. . . ." 2. A knockout dose concealed in narcotics, often a *hot shot.* 3. Someone who is *wrong* or who may be a stool pigeon.

easy time or **doing easy time.** A prison sentence that is served smoothly and without difficulty; one in which the time does not drag too heavily. Also *having a ball, laying back and doing it, coasting, jailing it.*

eater. An addict who takes drugs by mouth. See *belly habit, scoff.*

eighth or **eighth piece.** About one gram or approximately 60 grains of *white stuff,* usually morphine. May also apply to commercial heroin, as ⅛ oz. containing about 2 per cent pure heroin. "I had about an eighth left when I came in off the road."

embroidery. 1. A term like *Chinese needle work* for opium or smoker's supplies. 2. Black scars, or *tracks* from injections, also known as *service stripes.*

emergency gun. An improvised *joint* or *works* made from a medicine dropper and a safety pin, nail, sewing machine needle, etc. The skin is punctured with the sharp point and the solution injected into the flesh or under the skin. It is makeshift, usually used in jails or prisons, and is not to be confused with a conventional *joint, q.v.* Also *fake, gaffus, the thing, makeshift gun.*

emsel. Morphine. Obsolescent. See *M.*

end. 1. The best, as "That's the end." 2. On the West Coast, *end* in various combinations means just the opposite of *end* 1, *i.e.,* the worst, the finish, etc.

end gate. 1. The end of anything. 2. A maximum penalty such as life imprisonment.

ends. Money.

engine. 1. The opium smokers *layout, q.v.* 2. The *works* for other narcotics. "I've got the engine but no smack or cotics."

eye opener. The first *shot* of the day, taken on awakening. Also *morning shot, wake up* or *wakeup shot, get up.* "To wake up without an eye opener has only happened to me twice in all the time I've been on junk."

factory. 1. A needle addict's *layout* for injecting narcotics. "Get out the factory, the doctor is here." 2. A wholesale distributing depot for peddlers where *caps* are filled. "I wouldn't go around that factory for all the gow in China." 3. A homosexual. "That factory is tops and bottoms" (two-way).

fag. A pimp. Not to be confused with the general slang *fag* (a homosexual), clipped from *faggot.*

fake, fakus, or **fake a loo.** 1. The medicine dropper for a needle addict's *layout.* ". . . just get the fake out and let's fix. . . ." 2. See *ice tong doctor.*

fall. 1. To be arrested. See *bust* 2. 2. To receive a prison sentence.

fed. A federal agent, usually a narcotics agent. Also *the man, narco.*

feel the (my, his, etc.) **habit coming on.** To experience the early symptoms of withdrawal; to need drugs.

Also *hurting, it's bearing down on me, to feel a thing coming on, get a righteous thing going.*

fence. A person or establishment dealing in stolen goods. Also *drop* 3.

fiend. A disparaging term used by addicts for an addict who has lost control to the point where he cannot plan his dose schedule. He uses all of the drugs he can get and has no other interests besides drugs. Also *hog, pig, junk freak. Fiend* is used only in anger. This is basically a *square* term clipped from *dope fiend.*

figure eight. See *Brody.*

fin. 1. A five-year sentence. Also *buffalo, nickel.* 2. A five dollar bill.

finger or **finger of stuff.** 1. A rubber finger stall or condom filled with narcotics and swallowed or concealed in the rectum. Also *keyster (or kiester) plant, stall.* 2. *Finger* only. The act of pointing an addict out to the police for an arrest. "I know the finger came right out of that joint. . . ."

finif or **finski.** A five dollar bill. (Variants of *fin.*)

fink. A stool pigeon; an untrustworthy person. Also *wrong, no good, rat, snitch.*

fire or **fire up.** To inject narcotics hypodermically. Also to *geez, bang, fix, get with it.* See *bang.*

fire plug. A large opium pill. Also *high hat.* Also applied to a large *yen pok* taken away to eat later. "He took off about eight pills, but four of them were fire plugs."

fish. 1. A voluntary patient or prisoner addict. See *Mr. Fish.* 2. A new arrival in jail. 3. Greenhorn, sucker. 4. A pimp. Cut back from *fish and shrimp.* "Steve is a righteous fish. He has four ponies (prostitutes) on the track."

fistaris or **fisstaris.** Also *phystaris.* A currently popular word meaning about anything, especially anything connected with narcotics. "Hand me the fisstaris" might mean the needle, the dropper, the cord—or even a cigarette or matches. "Button up before you show your fisstaris" might mean shut your mouth before you show your ignorance, or close your fly before you expose yourself.

fit. A hypodermic *outfit.*

fix and flash. See *jolt.*

fix up or **fix.** 1. A ration of narcotics; specifically, the amount it requires to *fix* a particular habit. "He just couldn't spare me a fix up." 2. To inject drugs. "We can fix in the can."

fixed up. The state of balance achieved by an addict after he takes a *fix up.*

fixer. A lawyer or politician who can intervene to get charges reduced or dropped.

flash. 1. Euphoria following injection of narcotics. See *belt.* One addict of long experience describes the sensations immediately following injection as follows: "Codeine gives a severe burn, turning the skin ruby red, and is painful. Morphine is a tingle or flash. Heroin gives a flush but no burn. Gum opium (in solution) gives a slight flash without the tingle, and more of a thumping or pounding sensation. With Nembutal one gets a black out, the vision going from yellow to blackish green, to black all in a matter of seconds. Paregoric gives a dull flush, not a flash and no tingle." 3. To vomit, as a phase of withdrawal.

flea powder. Highly diluted narcotics, especially heroin.

flip. 1. To inform. 2. To change one's routine. "I've got to flip; my habit's out of sight."

flip over. 1. To go off narcotics (usually

temporarily). 2. To go homosexual. Also to *turn around*.

flipped. Knocked out by chloral hydrate or some other drug, usually given an addict or user in order to render him unconscious. Sometimes used in connection with *rolling* or robbing addicts.

floater. 1. A vagrant. 2. A particle of blood in the butt of the needle which, when dried, is difficult to remove.

floating. Under the influence of narcotics. See *coasting*.

fluke. An unjust conviction, a *bum rap*.

fly. Sophisticated yet carefree; wise in the ways of the underworld.

fold up. 1. To stop taking narcotics. See *to be away from the habit*. 2. To stop selling narcotics. "When George was guzzled, all the pushers had to fold up. . . ."

frame or **frame for.** 1. To prepare or lay the groundwork for obtaining narcotics by deceiving a physician. 2. To pretend illness in order to get narcotics. "He would frame for a croaker and score for a bang." See *Brody*. 3. **Frame** (alone). A very slender or "skinny" prostitute.

freak. 1. An addict who enjoys playing with the needle, same as *needle fiend*. 2. A sexual deviate. 3. See *nic nac, weird, buzzer* 1.

free loader. A down and out addict. Also *gutter hype, 24 karat poop butt, low rider*. See *boot and shoe*.

freeze or **freeze on.** 1. To ignore, disregard, or refuse to acknowledge a person. "You'd better freeze on that snitch—he'll get you busted." 2. To refuse to give information.

fruit merchant. A homosexual. Also *fairy, sissy, punk, gunzel, stuff, works, queen, factory, nic nac*.

fu. Marihuana. See *muggles*.

fun. (Pronounced *foon* in the Midwest and West, *foong* or *fong* in New York and the East.) Singular and plural forms identical. A unit of measure applied to opium; 5.79 grains. Most prepared opium is sold and used by the *fun* rather than by the grain. "The toys usually contained 10 to 12 fun."

fuzz or **fuzzy.** A detective. Cut back from *fuzzy tail*.

gaffel. 1. To shoplift or steal. 2. To arrest.

gaffus. See *emergency gun*.

gap. 1. To yawn and salivate, the first signs of withdrawal distress. "About then she was feeling rough and starting to gap." 2. The female genitalia.

gapper. An addict in need of drugs. "The joint was full of gappers, a hot spot to stop at. . . ."

garbage. Inferior heroin. See *flea powder*.

garbage freak. See *dugout*.

gassed. Experiencing euphoria following injection.

gay. Homosexual.

gazer. A Federal narcotic agent. Also *whiskers, uncle* (New York and vicinity). "Watch that gazer at the corner table." 2. A pervert who likes to window-shop sexually; often specialized to *doodle gazers, kiester gazers,* etc. May or may not be homosexual. A man who shops in a crowd by touching women intimately is a *muzzler*.

gear. A sexually perverted person, usually a male.

gee (pronounced to rhyme with Mc-Gee). 1. Prepared smoking opium, probably from Hindustani *ghee*, though derivation from the *g* used as an abbreviation for *gow*, etc. is also possible. 2. A person, as, "he's a right gee." Probably from guy.

gee chee. 1. A Negro from the Sea Islands. 2. Any bright skinned Negro, as contrasted to "high yellow."

gee fat. The *yen shee* which forms inside the pipe stem after opium is smoked. Probably a variant of *gee yen.* "There was at least 50 fun of gee fat in that old pipe."

gee rag or **gee.** 1. The small square of cloth with a hole in the center, used to make a tight connection between the shank of the bowl and the stem of an opium pipe. "The gee rag is about half the size of a woman's small wipe—about three inches." 2. Sometimes loosely used for the paper, thread or rubber used to make a tight connection between needle and dropper, properly known as a *collar, gaff, boot* or *geep.*

gee stick. An opium pipe. Obsolescent.

gee yen. Opium which precipitates in small quantities of thin or nearly liquid gum in the stem of the pipe. It is sometimes retrieved with a hot wire and reworked for selling or smoking. "They had about a half a pound of yen shee and gee yen to go in that batch."

geed up. 1. A down and out addict. See *boot and shoe.* 2. More generally, by extension, any person or thing or place which is undesirable, broken or out of order. "That was a geed-up joint. . . ."

geep or **jeep.** The gee rag, *q.v.* Also *boot, collar, boo gee.*

geetis or **geetus.** Money. Also *bread, scratch, green, lettuce, bees and honey,* etc.

geez. 1. An injection of drugs. 2. To inject drugs.

geezer. A *shot* of narcotics injected hypodermically, especially a small shot. Also *geez.* See *vein shot, bang.*

George. Very good.

George Smack. See *McCoy.*

get a finger wave. The process of having the rectum searched for drugs.

get a thing going or **have a thing going.** To build up a big habit. "I saw Jake the other day and he's got a thing going."

get in the wind. 1. To leave a place, sometimes in haste. 2. To become emotionally detached; to be at loose ends.

get next to. 1. To upset someone's defenses. 2. To become emotionally involved. 3. To get in with police by acting as a stool pigeon. 4. To establish a good *connection*, especially with a physician or druggist.

get off on. To take drugs regularly; probably an extension of *to get the yen* or *habit off.* "At that time I was getting off on H and speed balls."

get or **be on the point.** See *play the point.*

get straight. See *get the habit off.*

get the bitch. To be convicted under an habitual criminal act.

get (the) habit off. To satisfy the desire for drugs at the regular time when abstinence symptoms are about to be felt or are felt slightly. "Seems like I can't get my habit off this morning." Also *get straight, get (the) yen off.*

get the works. 1. To receive punishment, especially in prison or jail. 2. To be killed or beaten up.

get up. 1. The first shot of the day. 2. The last day of a prison sentence. "I've got four days and a get up."

get up steam. To drink whiskey, followed by an intravenous shot of morphine, heroin or mixed cocaine and heroin. ". . . they would get up steam, take a drink and then fire up. . . ." Addicts disagree on this, as on many other aspects of drug use. "You *must* fix first. There is no quicker way to commit suicide than to take a big drink of whiskey, then take a shot of morphine or opium."

get (one's) yen off. 1. To satisfy a need for drugs; to take drugs. "I'll be seeing you when I get my yen off— and it will take several fixes to get *my* yen off" (note from an addict doing a two-year sentence). 2. Indulging in any pastime (or vice). "Charley is down at the corner getting his yen off" (meaning Charley is down there betting on the horses). 3. Sometimes used to apply to the substitution of any drug one can get for the drug of choice; often shortened to *get off on, q.v.*

get with it. To inject narcotics intravenously. See *bang*.

getting a righteous thing going. Experiencing early withdrawal symptoms. See *feel the habit coming on*.

gig. 1. A job or method of making money. 2. A *high* to pill droppers. "Get a gig on."

giggle weed. 1. Marihuana. 2. Marihuana combined with wine.

Gillette way out. Suicide.

girl. Cocaine.

give (someone) some skin. To shake hands. Also *give (someone) five*. Largely restricted to Negroes.

give the chatter. To talk or answer questions of the authorities. Also transitive, as *give (someone) the chatter*. Also to give them a *grade B movie script*.

giving birth. Expelling the hard fecal matter inevitably resulting from the use of opiates. Also known as *giving birth to a duster* or *to a block buster*. This usage seems to be used largely by old-timers who have used opium. See *yen shee baby*.

giving up backs. Being initiated into homosexual practices, usually specifically anal intercourse.

glass. Methedrine in ampules.

globe trotter. One who moves frequently.

glom. 1. To steal. 2. To take drugs. 3. To take more than one's share, to be *on the muscle*. Also to *bogart*.

go. 1. A *bindle* or quantity of narcotics, often indicated by the price—a two dollar *go* is less than a five dollar *go*. A *bindle, cap, package balloon,* or *deck*. "I was giving him quite a play at five bucks a go." 2. A connection. "I had a good go with Joe."

go by. 1. A refusal to recognize an acquaintance. ". . . if not wanted or disliked, they get the go by." 2. Refusal by a peddler to recognize an addict or to deal with one whose reputation he does not trust. "He didn't think anybody was hep to that business in St. Louis, but that's why he got the go by." See to *chill*.

go in the sewer. To inject narcotics intravenously. See *bang*.

go in the skin. To inject drugs subcutaneously. "I'm in a hurry, Jack. Go in the skin with that one. . . ."

go on a sleigh ride. To inhale cocaine, with the consequent exhilaration. Related to *snow* for cocaine. Also *snow ride,* both obsolescent.

go over the hill. To escape by running away. Also *pull a rabbit,* take a *rabbit parole*.

God's medicine. Morphine. The phrase is credited to Sir William Osler. "Yes, it's God's medicine, for if there were any better, it would be kept in heaven for the angels to use."

going downhill. Past the halfway point in a prison sentence. Also *over the hump*.

going up the dirt road. Coitus *per anum*. Also *bust your brown, round eye,* etc.

gold leaf special. A marihuana cigarette which is (theoretically) more potent and sold at a premium. Usually a *booster stick* or cigarette of treated marihuana. See *stick* 2.

G.O.M. Literally, God's own medicine, a phrase borrowed from medicine.

gone. See *in high*.

gong or **gonger.** 1. An opium pipe. See *bamboo*. "You bring the gong, the rest of the layout is here. . . ." 2. *Gonger* (only). An opium smoker. ". . . used to be a gonger, but squared up. . . ." 3. Opium or opium derivatives. "Any gonger around L.A.?" See *kick the gong*.

good time. The time allotted on a sentence for working in an industry and/or obeying the rules. Also *copper, stuff.*

goods. Narcotics, especially as they are bought and sold. Used by addicts or dealers in letters, phone calls or telegrams. Also *merchandise.* "Ship goods to Dayton, Ohio, same address."

goof artist or **goofer.** One who uses *goof balls,* inhales glue or gasoline, drinks cough syrup, such as Cosanyl, terpin hydrate, Cheracol.

goof ball. 1. A barbiturate capsule. 2. An addict who uses barbiturates. "He's a goof ball." "Them goof ball artists are really pitiful." 3. One of any kind of drug capsule, not restricted to barbiturates.

goofed up. 1. Intoxicated on marihuana; also used by heroin addicts (youngsters) who carry the usage over from marihuana. 2. Somewhat stupefied from taking too much drugs. See *gowed.*

goofer. 1. A barbiturate addict. 2. Sometimes used by youngsters to indicate an addict to heroin and cocaine in combination with barbiturates. 3. Generalized to mean any addict who takes drugs (especially barbiturates or amphetamines) by mouth; may include glue sniffers, gasoline inhalers and drinkers of cough syrup containing drugs. The implication is that he really doesn't have a *habit* of any size.

goofing. 1. Enjoying euphoria; used especially by youngsters who combine heroin with barbiturates or cocaine. "I was in a movie house goofing when they picked me up." 2. Applied to youngsters who mix barbiturates with wine, and hence are *goofing off* or *fouling up.*

gopher. One who accepts unpleasant circumstances apathetically. "Yes, I'd call a gopher a 'lame,' a 'trick,' a 'chump' or a 'duck.'"

got it beat. 1. To have passed through the most severe abstinence symptoms. 2. To have served half or more of a prison sentence. "I've got it beat" or "I'm going downhill."

gow. 1. Narcotics in general, especially those used hypodermically. Probably of Chinese origin and originally used for opium, but no longer so restricted. Obsolescent, being supplanted by *smack, schmeck, stuff,* although modern heroin users do not include morphine or opium. 2. To ream out the bowl of the opium pipe with the *yen shee gow.* ". . . gow the bowl, trim the lamp and fill it, too. . . ."

gow head. Originally an opium addict, but now generalized to include all types of addict except marihuana and barbiturate users. However, oldtimers still use it to refer to opium users. "Doc, you put it your way and I'll put it mine. A gow head goes for the gow shee. Eats at the Y. Peeps in the heater. Goes for furburgers. Correct me if I'm wrong."

gowed. Having taken more narcotics than needed to satisfy a habit, and consequently being in a state of stupor or intoxication. (Past participle form only generally used.) "One pop in the main line and he's gowed." Also *dosed, out of sight, zipped, overamped, O.D'd,* though the last term may mean seriously knocked out or killed by an overdose.

gowster. 1. A needle addict. 2. An opium smoker. Old-timers still like to restrict this term to opium users. "He's a gowster and won't go for the spike."

Grade B movie script. See *give the chatter.*

grapevine. The system by which messages and other items circulate in prisons; the person-to-person contacts which lead an addict to a peddler. Usage of this term in the underworld is mostly whimsical: "Where did you get that lump?" "Why, Officer, I picked it off the grapevine." Also *trolley* in some prisons. *Grapevine* is also applied to the very effective communication system used by criminals outside prisons.

grass. Marihuana. Also *pot, weed, gage* and many others. See *muggles*.

grasshopper. A marihuana addict. See *reefer man*.

grease. 1. Prepared smoking opium. See *black stuff*. 2. To flatter. 3. Flattery. 4. To bribe. 5. A lawyer or politician who can intervene to get charges dropped or reduced; in effect, a *fixer* with political influence. See *juice*. 6. To eat ravenously after withdrawal. Also *root*. See *chuck habit*.

grease ball. 1. On the East Coast, an Italian. 2. On the West Coast, a Mexican, often *greaser*. Both are fighting words.

green ashes. Improperly or incompletely combusted opium; opium ash or *yen shee* from which some smoking opium may be retrieved by reworking. Obsolescent.

green hype. See *J.C.L.*

green mud. Smoking opium not cooked long enough or improperly prepared. Better for *shooting* than for smoking.

green pill. An improperly cooked pill of opium. See *cutered pill*.

green score. Profit made by passing counterfeit money.

griefo or greefo. Marihuana. "Smoking griefo is my idea of nothing to do." Much used in Texas and the Midwest. Sometimes recorded as *griffa*.

grift. The nonviolent rackets, as contrasted with the *heavy rackets*. Usually refers to a confidence mob working the *short-con games*. Also pickpockets, some types of gamblers. "He played the grift at the 12th Street shed."

grocery boy. 1. An addict who has drugs but wants food. 2. An addict who has developed the *chuck habit, q.v.*

groove with junk. To be *high*.

groovie. Very good.

grooving. Experiencing euphoria following the use of drugs. Also *coasting, tripping*.

guage or gage. Marihuana.

guinea. 1. An Italian. 2. A Creole. 3. A bright-skinned Negro.

gum. 1. Gum opium swallowed in small pieces broken off a larger brick or ball. A solution is sometimes used intravenously by needle addicts. 2. The raw *mud* from which smoking pills or *yen poks* (for swallowing) are made. Today it is sold in *papers* of 7 to 10 *fun* at $10.00, or 25 *fun* at $20.00 or $25.00.

gun. 1. An addict's hypodermic outfit. See *artillery*. 2. A pickpocket. 3. To look at closely.

gunk. Morphine. See *M*.

gunzel, guntzel, gunsel, gonsil. 1. A disgusting person. 2. A male homosexual. 3. See *A.B.C*.

gutter or gutter hype. A depreciative term used of and by *boot and shoe* addicts to indicate a down and out user; also applied to alcoholics who take *pleasure shots*. ". . . you know he's a gutter and can't hit a line. . . ."

guzzled. Arrested. Also *busted, batted out, glommed, glued, sneezed, snatched in the neck, paid off in gold, gaffeled, clouted, rousted, nailed*, etc.

H. Heroin. Also indicated by any words in which H is initial or conspicuous. Also *courage pills, horse, witch hazel, stuff, shit, junk, q.v.* Obsolescent.

habit. The need for a drug (especially opiates) as indicated by physical and emotional dependence. This term used with a great variety of shades of meaning: "My habit's coming on"; "I've got one hell of a habit"; "I traveled all day with a habit"; "That's a chicken shit habit"; etc. Also *run*, as "I've got a six-month run," and *strung out* as "I've been all strung out for a year."

hacks and croakers. The staff at the Lexington Hospital (guards, doctors, attendants, etc.). Names for guards in other places are *legion—hooligan, screw, the man, the buzzer, nix crackin-Jimmy Bracken*, etc.

half or **half piece.** Half an ounce of *white stuff*, q.v. See *piece, O.Z.* "Junkers usually say 'half' these days and the 'piece' in 'half piece' is understood."

hancty. Conceited.

hang it up. 1. To be away from the habit. 2. See *lay it down*.

hang (someone) up. To fail to keep an appointment for the exchange of narcotics. Also *blow the meet, blow the scene*.

hang tough. 1. Take it easy, quiet down, stop. 2. To *chill*, q.v.

hang up. 1. To abstain from using or selling drugs. Also to be *clean*, to straighten out, etc. 2. To be preoccupied with something.

hanging paper. Passing worthless checks, usually on a mass production basis.

happenings. Action, planning of activities, criminal and narcotic. Also *skam*.

happy dust. Cocaine, especially cocaine used for inhaling. The trend is to regard this term as *square*, with addicts holding to *Cecil, coke, snow, crystals* or just plain *C*.

hard time. To be unhappy under confinement, as to *do hard time*. This includes convicts who have lost their *copper* through disciplinary problems. Also *tough time*.

harpoon. The hollow needle used with a *joint*. "I can get you cut in if you can dig up a harpoon." Also *spike,*

silver serpent, pin, machine, tom cat, fisstaris, etc., with specialized meanings.

Harry or **hairy.** Heroin (West Coast). See *H*.

have a ball. To serve a smooth and easy prison sentence.

have a Chinaman (*or* **a monkey**) **on** (**one's**) **back.** To feel the need of drugs strongly; to experience the early stages of withdrawal distress. See *sick*. "When I woke up I sure had a Chinaman on my back. . . ." Chinese addicts sometimes say, "Your grandma die?" when they see the running eyes and nose in early withdrawal. Other phrases are, "*I'm hurting,*" "*I'm up tight,*" "*I'm sick,*" which are recognized by any addict or peddler.

have a habit. To need drugs; to be addicted. See *sick*. This term now losing favor with addicts who prefer *strung out, long run* and other euphemisms.

have a yen. 1. To feel the first symptoms of needing a *shot* or a smoke of opium. 2. To desire anything. Obsolescent, giving way to *coming down, hurting*, etc. See *have a Chinaman on (one's) back*.

have something going. To be engaged in some illegal enterprise.

hawk. A guard in a Federal prison. Obsolescent. "Hawk was very seldom used in my time, except by guys chopping up old scores."

heat. 1. Police pressure. 2. A police officer or narcotic agent.

heater. The female genitals.

heaven dust. Cocaine, especially as inhaled. Whimsical or "square" phrase.

heaves. 1. The vomiting and gastric discomfort accompanying withdrawal. See *twister* 3. 2. The vomiting usually following the first shot of heroin taken by a beginner.

heaves and squirts. Vomiting and diarrhea accompanying withdrawal.

heavy. 1. Intelligent or educated. 2. One who uses firearms or force in his *racket*. 3. A safecracker. 4. A violent person.

heeb. A Jew. Also *mocky, rabbi, skinless, popcorn,* etc.

heel. 1. To steal in a sneak thief manner. 2. A specialized type of highly skilled thief, especially a *bank heel*.

heist. 1. To rob. 2. To lift someone's *plant, q.v.*

hemp. *Cannabis sativa* or Cannabis indica. The plant, the flowering tops or pods used in marihuana. See *muggles*.

he's in. Said of anyone regularly using narcotics.

high. Variant of *in high, q.v.* Also *gassed, stoned, zonked, tripping, loaded,* etc. 2. The maximum euphoria experienced by *pill droppers* or those who take drugs by mouth. "I get my high in about thirty minutes." "I seldom get my highs anymore."

high hat. 1. A large drug habit. 2. A large pill of smoking opium. See *bird's eye* 2. 3. A tall opium lamp, or the shade thereof. Obsolescent. "High hat lamps were used around some old-time lay down joints."

highsiding. See *stepping high* 3.

hip or **hep.** To be aware of; to know. To be wise in the ways of the underworld. This is an old argot term which has enjoyed several cycles of popularity. It was originally recorded as *Joe Hep* in 1938 among grifters who remembered using it in the 1890's. Some old-timers still use *Joe* as a verb. "Let me Joe you to that, Doc."

hippies. Those who like to associate with jazzmen, many of whom are drug users.

hipster. 1. A *finger man* who cases a joint to be *knocked over*. 2. Among *squares* or part-time users of drugs, one who is much preoccupied with jazz and jazz musicians.

hit. 1. To succeed at anything. "Did you hit?" 2. To purchase narcotics. "Right after that he went on downtown and H. and R." (He *hit and run, i.e.,* bought drugs from the peddler and left town.) 3. For narcotics to register; for the user to feel euphoria. "Did that shot hit yet?" 4. To get a hypodermic needle into a vein. "You know he's a gutter and can't hit a line." 5. To borrow or attempt to borrow (especially narcotics). "Just now, did he hit you for stuff?" See *score*.

hit and miss habit. A small, irregular drug habit. "A guy with a hit and miss habit don't have half the trouble kicking."

hit on. 1. To make a proposition, especially to proposition for sexual activities, either homo or hetero. 2. To ask for something, to "put the bum on" someone. Also *put the lug on, put the bee on,* etc.

hit the gong. 1. To smoke opium in a group or party. Not used to refer to smoking alone. Also *hit the pipe, kick the gong, roll the log, beat the gong.* "We would phone the Chino then and see if it was OK to kick the gong at Charlie's place." 2. Recently adapted by marihuana smokers in the same sense. "Weed smokers say 'kick the gong,' too, but not the bebops. . . ."

hit the gow. 1. To be addicted. "I hear Annie is hitting the gow again after all these years. . . ." 2. The act of taking narcotics. (Used largely by police officers and others who come into contact with addicts.) See *hooked*. 3. To an old-timer, to smoke opium.

hit the sewer. To inject narcotics intravenously. Also *go in the sewer*. See *main line*.

hit the stuff. Meanings and usage the same as to *hit the gow* except that currently this phrase is much used by police officers. See *hooked*.

hitch. A prison sentence. Also *bit, jolt, fall, skam,* etc.

hitchhiker. A voluntary patient in a narcotics hospital. See *C. Vol.*

hocus. Morphine prescribed in solution by physicians who believed it could not be resold for addict use in this form. Obsolescent. "In T.O. (Toledo, Ohio), the croakers all wrote for hocus for a while and stuff sold for so much a dripper."

hog. See *fiend*.

hold. 1. (Transitive only.) To support a habit. See *carry*. "That stuff won't hold me at all." 2. (Intransitive only.) To have drugs for sale, especially on one's person. "Yeah, I'm holding, but I can't let him have much."

(the) hole. Solitary confinement. Also *(the) slab*.

home. The vein into which drugs are injected. See *main line*.

homey. A person from the same home town.

hook. See *yen hok*.

hook shop. A house of prostitution. Also *shop, house, crib, joint, notch joint, pad, scatter, spread,* etc. Because of the widespread tendency for addicts to become pimps, many terms from the *broad rackets* are infiltrating addict usage. These include words for various kinds of brothels, types of prostitute, the genitalia and various kinds of sex acts.

hooked. Addicted to narcotics. Also *on the gow, hitting the gow, on stuff, hitting the stuff, on junk, got a run going, hitting, strung out,* etc.

hooker. 1. Notice that one is wanted by the law. 2. A prostitute.

Hooligan. A prison guard. See *hacks*.

Hoosier fiend. 1. An inexperienced addict; a yokel who doesn't realize he is *hooked*. 2. Any addict who is not of the underworld; a business or professional man. "She filled in with that Hoosier fiend; they say he has plently of scratch." Also *square hype, trick hype, trick, duck,* in both senses.

hop. 1. Opium for smoking. 2. Narcotics for injection or inhalation. Non-smokers use the term to mean any kind of drugs which will satisfy their habit, or any drug they are using at the time.

hop head. A narcotic addict. See *hype*. Restricted to opiate users in addict usage, but encountered increasingly among *squares* to mean any drug user.

hop joint. A place where opium (or other drugs) are sold and/or consumed. An "opium den" to *squares*. If opium is smoked there it is also a *lay down joint, q.v.*

hop layout. An opium smoker's outfit, including pipes, stems, bowls, lamp, suey pow, etc. "Blowed a fine hop layout in 1927."

hop stick. 1. An opium pipe. See *bamboo*. 2. Sometimes the *stem* only as contrasted to the *bowl*.

hop toy or **toy.** A small container (metal salve box, English walnut shell, etc.) for smoking opium. (Sometimes needle addicts buy opium and use it in place of *white stuff* in a panic.) See *toy*. A toy usually contains about 25 *fun* of opium. "I had to score for hop toy since the heat's been on."

horn. To sniff cocaine or heroin. Also *snort, blow*. See *joy powder*.

horse. Heroin. A term much used by the younger generation of addicts. See *Racehorse Charlie, snort*.

horse doctor. Prison or jail doctor. Also *vet, croaker*.

hot. The condition of being wanted by the law. Also *smoking, dead, in the freezer, on ice, no action* and many others.

hot money. 1. Stolen or counterfeit

money. 2. Money (with serial numbers recorded) which is given to informers by narcotics agents for purposes of proof of sale.

hot shot. Cyanide or other poison concealed in narcotics to kill a troublesome addict, or to remove a stool pigeon. Sometimes very strong, uncut heroin is used. The *hot shot* kills the addict in contrast to *flipping him* or *taking him* with knockout drugs. "I hear that Mike got a hot shot in New Orleans." Also called a *ten cent pistol*.

hot spot. 1. The place to which a victim is brought for the purpose of defrauding him. 2. The state of being uncomfortable or anxious, such as a *sick* user experiences when he is without a *connection*. 3. A place with the police staked out.

hot stuff. 1. Stolen *merchandise*. 2. Bad narcotics. See *turkey*.

hots. 1. Meals. 2. Among pickpockets and short-con men, a place or person which may involve *heat* if they work. For example, a bus or train depot today; a plainclothesman picked as a victim, etc.

hudda. A policeman (Mexican-American usage).

hummer. A fake arrest on any pretense which will permit a search, such as a traffic violation. "I was busted on a hummer."

humming gee bowl. The bowl of an opium pipe made, according to legend, from a piece of the human skull. Obsolescent. "Humming gee bowls were made in China by a certain clan or family. . . ."

hung up. Dependent on narcotics; addicted.

hurting. Experiencing early symptoms of withdrawal. Also *in trouble*.

hustle. 1. To obtain money by illegal means such as shoplifting, pickpocketing, pimping, con games, prostitution or other *rackets* commonly worked by addicts. 2. The *racket* or *hustle* by which an addict supports his habit. Also *stick*.

hustling drawers. Specially made underwear, worn by women shoplifters, in which stolen goods can be concealed. The incidence of addiction is high among shoplifters. Also *boosting drawers*.

hype. 1. An addict, especially a needle addict. Also *junker, gowster, hop head, joy popper*, etc. "The fuzz didn't know Al was a hype. . . ." 2. The entire *works* used to inject narcotics. See *artillery*. 3. The hypodermic needle considered separately from the syringe. 4. Or **hypo.** A placebo or nonnarcotic injection sometimes given addicts during withdrawal for its psychological effect. Largely institutional usage. "A hypo will take those butterflies out of your stomach."

(the) hype. 1. A *short-change racket* much used by addicts. Also called *laying the note*. "Papa Cole was a real specialist on the hype." 2. To swindle someone with this racket. "Sometimes we'd let our bankroll run down, and then we'd turn ourselves over and come up with a couple of ones. Two bumblebees will get you a deuce, and with that we'd hype till we had a five or two. Then we could hype for a saw. With a saw, we'd hype for a twenty, and be right back in business again."

hypo smecker, smacker or **smecker.** A needle addict. The short form usually used nowadays. Formerly, this term differentiated smokers from needle addicts and probably dates from the 1920s when many smokers were taking to *white stuff*. *Smeck*, probably from German or Yiddish *schmecken*, is an old term for opium. "Many a hypo smecker would be a smoker today if he had his choice."

ice cream habit. A small, irregular habit. See *chippy habit*. "Hit him with an aspirin tablet and a wet towel; he only had an ice cream habit to begin with."

ice tong doctor or **ice tong croaker.** A physician with a shady reputation; one who will perform abortions or sell narcotics. Obsolescent. Also *ice water croaker, fake, fakaloo, taker, right croaker, croaker on the make, solid M.D.*

ice water cure. See *iron cure.*

ice water John. A cold-hearted doctor at Lexington or Ft. Worth; one who will not give additional drugs during withdrawal.

idiot juice. Nutmeg and water mixed for intoxication, largely used in prisons.

in action. Actively selling narcotics. Also *doing business, turning, operating.*

in flight. Very high on Methedrine. See *in orbit.*

in front of the gun. To peddle narcotics, usually with the understanding that the peddler "takes the rap" if caught and protects the dealers or *big men* for whom he works; a specialization of the general underworld phrase meaning the same thing. Ex-addicts just out of prison (not a hospital) are actively recruited by big *dealers,* who use this type of *pusher* ruthlessly for two or three months. Many of them are content if they can get drugs and make good money for as much as six months before going up again. "Just out of stir, and there he is in front of the gun."

in high or **high.** At the peak of euphoria from morphine, heroin or cocaine injected intravenously or in the skin. Giving way to the more popular *stoned, loaded, gone, (on) cloud 9.* See *coasting.* "She was sure in high when I saw her."

in on the know. See *hip, in the know.*

in orbit. Having taken exactly the right amount of a drug, especially heroin, amphetamine, Methedrine. See *in flight.*

in paper. Said of narcotics smuggled into a penal institution. The powdered drug *(white stuff)* is, for instance, folded into very thin tin foil, placed inside a split postcard, and pressed flat with a hot iron. There are various other methods, such as concealing Dilaudid (crushed) under postage stamps or the flaps of sealed envelopes.

in the sack. 1. In bed. 2. The situation when a peddler has made a sale to a government agent and is sure to be arrested. Also *in hock, dead.*

in trouble. Short of drugs; experiencing early withdrawal distress. "I'm in trouble. Bring over a gram." Also *hurting.*

Indian hay. Marihuana. See *muggles.*

insane. Very good.

iron cure. The cold turkey treatment used in many jails and prisons where the addict *kicks the habit* out on the floor of his cell. Also *steel and concrete cure, iron bound cure, ice water cure.* See *quarry cure.*

iron house. A city jail. Most other underworld terms (*can, joint, band house,* etc.) are also used by addicts. "I can't recall hearing *iron house* in England or Canada, but I have talked to a few fellows who have."

jab. 1. An injection of drugs, with consequent euphoria. The problem here is to hit a vein, especially when shooting in the buttocks, since the vein is not *brought up,* and since the addict must guess at its exact location. For this reason addicts who *jab* and miss are called *jabbers* or *jab artists.* Those few who can hit a vein regularly are called *whizzes, sharp shooters, the greatest.* See *bang, jaboff.* "I like to take a jab under my left shirt tail. . . ." 2. To inject drugs.

jab artist. See *jab*.

jabber. 1. A Needle addict.

> *A jabber he was*
> *And a jabber he'll be*
> *Till the day he's planted*
> *'Neath the old apple tree. . . .*

2. An addict who has trouble hitting the vein. See *jab*.

jaboff. The extreme exhilaration or euphoria immediately following intravenous injection; often described as resembling a prolonged sexual orgasm. Also *flash, burn, rush, call*. "You know, he wanted a jaboff every time he fixed, and finally took one that killed him."

jab pop or **jab poppo.** Drugs injected hypodermically. "I used to know a flat jointer (carnival) who would say,

> *J.P., that's not a justice of the peace,*
> *Who will marry you or worse,*
> *It's not jab poppo with its bitter curse,*
> *It's Jack pot, with all the money in my purse. . . ."*

jack a fix. A deliberately prolonged *verification shot*. Also, *jack off shot*. Also called *jacking off a fix*.

jack off. To allow the blood to come back into the glass during a vein shot. Also *booting*. See *verification shot*.

jack roller. One who robs drunks. Formerly, restricted to getting lumberjacks just out of the timber drunk and rolling them; now generalized.

jack up. Sodium Amytal.

jacket. 1. See *collar*. 2. A police record, from the folder or filing envelope in which it is kept. A *dirty jacket* is a bad police record.

jacking off a fix. See *jack a fix*.

jailhouse pimp. See *playboy*.

jailhouse romance. A romantic attachment between inmates, either heterosexual or homosexual. See *playboy*.

jailing it. Serving an easy prison sentence. Also *coasting, have a ball*.

jaloney. Bad or fake dope. See *turkey, hot shot*.

jam. 1. Trouble with the law; a case in court. ". . . finally squared that jam with five C notes." 2. To leave the *scene*.

jammed up. Overdosed with drugs.

jap. A hair straightener made of lye, potato peelings, and oil or grease. Much used by Negroes in prison. Also *strap, strap Johnson* or *konk*.

Jasper. An aggressive female homosexual. Also *butch, bull, sergeant, beetle brow*.

J.C.L. or **Johnny come lately.** A beginning addict, or one who has not yet established a regular habit; one who has not been on drugs long. Also *1962 model* or *1963 model* (using the current year to indicate recency). Also *shirt tail hype, green hype, lame hype* or *lame*. See *student*.

jeep. See *collar*.

jeff. To be obsequious, especially Negroes in relation to whites.

jenny barn or **ginny barn.** The dormitories for females at the USPHS hospital.

jerk simple. Mentally disturbed as a result of masturbation; a mythical condition probably originating in popular folklore.

jerker. See *leapers*.

jive. To be insincere or fickle.

jive talk. Insincere, fickle or "double talk."

jobbed. Framed or arrested by entrapment techniques.

John. 1. Any male, usually not of the underworld, or not addicted. 2. A customer for a prostitute addict. Also *trick*.

joint. 1. The *needle, dropper* and *connection*; the complete outfit with which to take drugs hypodermically, in contrast to a regulation hypodermic syringe. See *artillery*. 2. A prison. 3. A place of questionable reputation. 4. The penis. 5. Marihuana, or a marihuana cigarette. 6. A place to be robbed or burglarized.

jolt. 1. A *shot* of narcotics taken either in the vein or in the skin, but usually the former. "Let me try a jolt of that H." 2. A strong feeling of euphoria, or *drive*. *Fix and flash* is a popular synonym. "I get an awful jolt out of powdered Dilaudid that I don't get out of tablets. 3. A prison sentence or term. Also *stuff* 2.

Jones. 1. A drug habit, especially a large one. 2. A variable term used widely by Negroes as a greeting.

joy pop. See *joy popper*. A common rationalization is often heard: "I don't use; I just joy pop."

joy popper. A person, not a confirmed addict, who takes an occasional injection of narcotics; however, joy popping is usually the beginning of permanent addiction. See *hype*. "They all think they can take just one joy pop, but it's the first one that hooks you...."

joy powder. Heroin inhaled from a hollow quill or straw. Originally a quill toothpick was used; today a soda straw is used, or even a small paper tube. Any such device is called a *horn*.

joy smoke. Marihuana. See *muggles*.

joy stick. 1. An opium pipe. See *bamboo*. 2. A marihuana cigarette.

jug. 1. To tease. 2. A city jail or a holdover. 3. A 10 cc. multidose vial of Methedrine.

juice. 1. Political pull, connections with the *fixer*. Also *grease* 5. "If we get busted in Frisco, I have plenty juice there to fix the caper." 2. Bribe money. See *grease* 2, 3.

jumpy Stevie. See *leapers*.

junk. 1. Narcotics in general—any habit forming derivative of opium, including all new pain-killers (some synthetic) that are habit forming such as Dolophine, Demerol, Dilaudid, Pantopon. 2. Any specific kind of drugs except barbiturates and marihuana; the opiate series, with some exceptions. To very old-timers, this meant anything but opium. See *cotics*.

Even C is junk.
Gum opium is junk.
Grease is junk.
Yen shee is junk.

junk freak. See *fiend*.

junk hog. 1. An addict who takes more drugs than he needs to *hold* him, or who takes his *shots* oftener than necessary. A term of contempt. If applied to a female, the term is usually *pig*. 2. Sometimes used in a friendly or kidding way toward someone taking an extra *shot*.

junker or **junkie.** A narcotic addict, especially a user of *white stuff*. This term seems to have been originally applied to addicts who sniffed drugs—cocaine especially. See *hype*.

keek or **kook.** See *needle fiend*.

keen cat. See *slick*.

keep the meet. For addict and peddler to meet so the addict can buy drugs. Addicts are traditionally punctual, peddlers traditionally late; the reason—self-preservation on the part of the peddler. See *blow the meet*.

key. A volunteer addict patient. This term is probably related to *crank handle, stem winder, self-starter*, etc., with similar meanings in various narcotics hospitals.

keyster or **kiester plant.** A finger stall or condom used to conceal drugs in the rectum. "In Canadian prisons they are cylinders made of metal or wood . . . you must always keep your valuables in this keyster plant, for that is the only hiding place that is not searched—ever. . . ."

kick. 1. Euphoria. See *bang.* 2. To suffer abstinence symptoms. 3. A pocket. 4. Any form of preoccupation, as movie *kick,* etc.

kick back. 1. The addict's almost inevitable return to narcotics after having *kicked the habit.* "You know he'll kick back. . . ." 2. Return of stolen goods. 3. A portion or percentage of the take paid for cooperation or protection.

kick cold. Treatment in which the addict is taken off drugs suddenly. See *cold turkey.*

kick freak. See *joy popper.*

kick the gong or **gonger.** 1. To smoke opium, especially in a group. See *hit the gong, beat the gong, roll the log.* Obsolescent, except among old-timers. 2. To smoke marihuana in groups.

kick the habit or **kick.** To undergo the withdrawal syndrome, either with the aid of drugs (tapering off) or suddenly and without drugs (cold turkey). Also to *break the habit.*

kiester. The rectum, a common hiding place for drugs, especially in prison where such a stash is called a *kiester plant* or *keyster plant.*

kiester stab. Coitus *per anum.*

kiester stash. See *keyster plant.*

king kong. Home-made gin, especially in prisons.

kipping. 1. Sleeping after having passed the crisis of withdrawal. "I've got around the turn but still not *kipping.*" 2. Sleeping normally. An old underworld term.

kite. An unauthorized letter, smuggled in or out of prison.

knock off. 1. To stop. Also *freeze, hang it up, cool it, lighten it up.* 2. To arrest. Also *busted, rousted, sneezed,* etc. 3. To kill someone. Also *snuff, give (someone) a hot shot.* 4. To rob a person or place; *knock off a score.* Also *pull a job, beat a joint.*

knocked out. Under the influence of narcotics. Also *gassed, stoned, out of sight, loaded, zonked, smashed, tore up, ripped* and many others. See *all lit up.*

knocker. Anyone who actively criticizes addicts; usually an underworld character who works with addicts or is around them. "There is a saying among junkers: 'a knocker will eventually get hooked.'" "He went the way of all knockers, he's hooked."

knockers. 1. The testicles. 2. A woman's breasts.

konk. 1. A mixture of lye, grease and potato peelings used by Negroes to straighten hair. Also *Jap.* 2. Or **konk out.** To go unconscious, as from an overdose of narcotics.

kook. See *needle fiend.*

kooked. See *build up the habit.*

K.Y. or **Ky.** The Lexington Hospital.

LSD. Lysergic acid diethylamide. A few years ago this term was known only to a limited number of researchers and psychiatrists; now it is a common argot term widely used among those who deal in contraband drugs.

lamb. The passive receptor in a homosexual relationship (usually pederasty). Also *gunzel, guntzel, gonsil, punk, brat, daisy.*

lame. 1. A dull person. Cut back from *lame brain.* 2. A disgusting person; an inexperienced addict.

lamp habit. 1. An excessive desire for opium; a large habit. "He has to produce, with his broad, the horses and a lamp habit. . . ." 2. By extension, any large habit. "Does he have a habit? I'll say, a lamp habit." 3. A slight opium habit acquired from inhaling the fumes where opium is smoked. See *bunk habit.* "He won't have a tough time kicking, he only had a lamp habit."

later for that. A laconic phrase meaning "Never mind."

laugh and scratch. 1. To take drugs (*white stuff*), especially intravenously. There is a prickling or itching reaction, especially if the addict has been off drugs for a time. "He had a laughing and scratching good time last night. . . ." 2. Extended to the use of marihuana, which often produces uncontrollable laughter, but no itching.

laughing grass. Marihuana. See *muggles*.

lay. 1. A place to be robbed. 2. The plan of a robbery or crime. 3. A place to smoke opium; a *hop joint*. See *lay down*. 4. The act of smoking opium. "How's chances for a lay?" 5. The privilege of smoking in a *hop joint*. "They didn't charge much for a lay at Ty Lane's place." 6. A *shot* of narcotics, not restricted to opium users.

And there's that lay of M.
My good old pipe and stem,
Good God how I love them. . . .

"We'll have to pack in for a lay before long."

lay down. 1. The act of smoking opium. 2. The price of smoking opium, but only in such a phrase as, "What's the lay down here?," which is really elliptical, with "price of a" understood. "What do you get for a lay down?"

lay down joint. A place where opium is sold and smoked. See *hop joint*.

lay it down. To avoid something or let it alone. Also *hang it up*. "He thought he could take a couple of fixes and lay it down."

lay the note. To *short-change* a person by means of *the hype*, which is a kind of *short-con* game.

laying back and doing it. Serving an easy prison sentence. Also *coasting* 2, *having a ball*, etc.

laying paper. Passing checks.

laying queer. See *pushing queer*.

layout. 1. The outfit of an opium smoker, varying in quality from cheap to very elaborate and expensive. Basic elements are *stems, bowls, yen hok, yen shee gow, suey pow, lamp, lamp trimmer, yen shee can,* peanut or vegetable oil for the lamp, etc.

Ten thousand hop layouts, all
inlaid with pearl,
Every hop head fiend will bring
along his girl. . . .

2. The hypodermic needle, spoon, cotton, etc.

leaf gum, leaf or **leaf hop.** Crude opium before it is prepared for smoking. So called because it is often wrapped in dried poppy leaves. See *black stuff*.

leak. 1. To disclose information. 2. A person with a slack jaw; one who talks too much.

leapers. Users of cocaine who reach an advanced stage where jerky movements resemble St. Vitus dance.

leaping and stinking. Under the influence of drugs. See *high*. Obsolescent. "An old-timer once told me leaping and stinking comes from a junkie being high on coke and stinking from want of M. . . ." "A sick addict throws off the most offensive odor imaginable. As you probably know, many addicts are caught at the border because of this. I have heard of dogs being used to locate them."

leaps. A state of extreme anxiety with delusions, sometimes paranoid, resulting from continued use of cocaine. This state may vary from the ludicrous to homicidal mania. "After three or four days with Cecil he had a mild case of the leaps. . . ." "This is the stage where one sees bugs on (his) body and will draw blood getting them off."

lem kee. Chinese "brand" name for prepared smoking opium. Probably, like *li yuen*, etc., based on the family name of Chinese opium merchants. These terms have now generalized, losing their former family associations. See *black stuff*. Also *rooster brand, li yuen*.

lemon. Bad or fake dope. See *turkey*.

lemon bowl or **orange bowl**. A hollowed-out half orange or lemon fitted to the bowl of an opium pipe like a cover; used when the bowl gets hot, or to avoid changing bowls. "Make a lemon bowl and we can cop a few more."

lemonade. Very poor narcotics, usually very highly diluted heroin.

lent or **lint**. Japanese morphine in fibrous form; introduced into contraband trade about 1936, but never available in great supply. Many American addicts never knew about it. "It's true most lent was used on the West Coast; junkies who used it say it was powerful."

lie on your hip or **lay on the hip**. To smoke opium, which is done lying on the side with the head resting on another smoker's hip or, more exactly, in the hollow just about the hip bone. "Want to lay on the hip tonight?"

(the) life. The world of the *hustlers*. Also *(the) swinging life, (the) groovie life, (the) living end*.

light green. A grade of marihuana.

light-weight chipper. An occasional user with a very small habit. See *chippy habit*.

light-weight nothing. A small drug habit. "That lame's got a light-weight nothing going and thinks he's righteous strung out."

lighten up. Take it easy, quiet down, stop.

Lincoln, A five dollar bill. Also an *Abe, fin, finik, finski, nickel*.

line. See *main line*.

line shot. An injection into the vein. See *mainline, bang 2*.

lip the dripper. To suck the air out of the medicine dropper before taking a shot; the common test is to make it stick by vacuum to the lip or tongue tip. "Needle pushers always lip the dripper, and smokers lip the pipsky too, bowl and stem, then both together."

Lipton tea. 1. Poor quality drugs, especially heroin heavily cut. The implication is that it is as mild as tea. 2. See *Mickey Finn* 1, where it is a euphemism.

lit. Variant *of all lit up*.
After I do this bit
In my old Morris chair I'll sit
Oh, Gee! how I'll get lit. . . .

li yuen. High quality smoking opium; originally a trade name for a brand of prepared smoking opium imported from China. See *lem kee*.

load. 1. Among needle addicts, the usual ration of drugs. "Got a load for this gun?" 2. Among opium smokers, more than the usual number of pills. "Boy, what a load he had on."

loaded. Under the influence of drugs. See *in high*.

lobby girl or **lobby shopper**. A prostitute who solicits in hotels.

lobby gow or **lob**. A hanger-on around a hop joint; usually an addict who runs errands or acts as a *connector*. "That old man was a lobby gow for the combination." "He's harmless, just a lob."

loco weed. Marihuana.

log. An opium pipe. See *bamboo*.

long run. An acute need of drugs. "On that Saturday morning, she had a long run I remember."

long-tailed rat. A stool pigeon of the lowest order. Also *ring tail* or *ring tail skunk*. "That long-tailed rat has lived much too long. . . ."

looking dap or **looking boss**. Well dressed, sharp.

louse. A stool pigeon. Also *rat, long-tailed rat, finger, finger gee, mouse,* etc. "Yeah, that louse works for the city and the feds."

love weed. Marihuana. Set *muggles*.

low rider. Down and out addict. Also *free loader, 24 karat poop butt, gutter hype*.

Luer. A glass syringe (standard medical equipment) for giving hypodermic injection. Differs from a *Bay State*, *q.v.* in that the needle slips on a *Luer*, but screws on a *Bay State*; the plunger on the *Luer* is solid. Most "square" addicts use a standard hypodermic syringe. See *Yale*, *spike*.

lug. 1. A Person. 2. The ear (obsolescent), which survives in the phrase to *put the lug on (someone)* (meaning to "bend his ear" or beg narcotics from him).

M. Morphine. Also *junk, cube, lent, white stuff, white angel, God's medicine, Miss Emma, emsel, gunk, uffi, unkie, sweet Jesus, Miss Morph*, etc., with specialized meanings.

machinery. The equipment for taking drugs by needle. See *artillery*.

mack man. One who *hustles*, especially a pimp. Also *fish* 4.

mahoska or **hoska.** Any kind of narcotics, especially heroin (East Coast, particularly New York City).

main. In the vein, as applied to intravenous injection, and distinguishing this from *skin shooting*. "Man, I take it main. . . ."

main line or **line.** 1. The vein, usually in the crook of the elbow or instep, into which the needle addict injects narcotics. When these large veins become sclerotic, addicts, may use others in any part of the body where they are accessible. "A main line bang gives me action right now." 2. **Main line** (only). To inject drugs into the vein. "I can main line that 10-8-20 and not tell it from H." 3. An addict who *vein shoots*. "She was strictly a main line broad and it took her an hour to fix."

main liner or **main line shooter.** A vein shooter. See *bang, bang in the arm*. "I don't think a main liner has the aches and pains kicking a habit that a skin shooter does."

make. 1. To obtain something. "He went out to make a croaker" (obtain drugs from a physician). "That Texas mob was trying to make old Sam" (obtain his drugs by theft). 2. To detect. "The captain would gun hell out of (look hard at) the line trying to make (detect) the cons (prisoners) who were fixed (who had taken a shot)." 3. To be fingerprinted and photographed after an arrest. 4. To arrive, as in the phrase *make the scene*.

make a hype pitch. To work a *short-change racket*. See *(the) hype*.

make a spread. 1. To set out the equipment for taking drugs; hence to prepare for a period of indulgence; often refers to addicts who gather together for a spree or to take their regular *shots*. Also *spread the joint*. "Make a spread, Mike's all right." 2. To cohabit with a girl, or set up such a proposal.

make bush. To escape from prison.

make the drive. To smuggle narcotics into prison. See *boat sailed*.

mamma die? A set phrase probably originating among West Coast Chinese, euphemistically recognizing early withdrawal distress, especially the tears. The next step is probably a purchase of drugs. See *monkey on my back*.

(the) man. A policeman.

manicure. To trim the top leaves and flowering tops from the hemp plant to make marihuana cigarettes. Also *sift*, especially where screens are used to separate the seeds, which, if smoked, produce a violent headache.

manita. Milk sugar used to adulterate heroin. (Largely Harlem usage).

marcia. A water pipe used to smoke

marihuana (South America). May be encountered in New York City; reported by Wolff in Brazil, and described as resembling the nargile or African water pipe used for smoking hashish; a hookah. In the Americas, the smoke may be drawn through wine or soda water.

margin man. A drug runner or smuggler who transports drugs in wholesale quantities between the *big men* and the dealers. "Margin men are usually non-addicts, so the term is rarely used among addicts." Also *straight man, runner, mule.*

mark. The victim of any *racket* or *hustle;* a sucker. An old term, but getting competition from *trick, q.v.* among addicts.

Mary Warner. A variant of marihuana. Obsolescent. See *muggles.*

McCoy. 1. Medicinal drugs in contrast to bootleg drugs. Obsolescent. 2. Any drug with a high narcotic content; usually refers to bootleg drugs today. Also *righteous stuff, George, smack.*

meat ball rap. An adverse behavior report of a mild offense, or any relatively insignificant charge. Also *chicken shit beef, busted on a buzzer.* See *gunzel.*

medicine. 1. To the opiate user, any drugs of the opiate series; cocaine is usually excluded, also often codeine. 2. Cod liver oil with prepared opium, *yen shee,* morphine or heroin added. The cod liver oil disguises the drug and prevents its recognition by casual inspection. This preparation is carried on the road by opium smokers instead of a *layout* and, taken by mouth, *holds* the addict until he can smoke again. Other liquids are also used. 3. Any drug taken temporarily to sustain a habit while the drug of choice is unavailable.

meet. An appointment arranged between addict and peddler; a specialized sense of the general underworld usage. ". . . had a meet at the PO (post office) at 10, but he didn't show."

merchandise. Narcotics, especially in wholesale quantities. See *goods.*

meter. See *Brody, throw a meter.*

mezz. Marihuana. See *muggles.*

Mick. To give a victim a Mickey Finn, *q.v.*

Mickey Finn or **Mickey.** 1. Chloral hydrate in a drink to knock out a victim. Also, euphemistically, *Lipton tea.* 2. A powerful physic such as croton oil, slipped into a whiskey to make the victim sick or to drive him away from a hangout. ". . . slip him a Mickey and slough the donicker on him" (lock him out of the toilet room). "Just Mickey Finn got lost."

Miss Carrie. A *plant* of drugs, secreted on the person in case of arrest. So called because it "carries" the addict if his supply is interrupted. See *stash.*

Miss Emma. Morphine. A variant of *M.* See *cotics.*

Miss Morph. Morphine. Obsolescent.

mitt me, Slim, the ship is in. A kind of set phrase indicating that the *connection* has arrived.

mockey or **mockie.** A Jew. Also *popcorn.*

mojo. 1. Narcotics of any kind in contraband trade, but usually signifies morphine, heroin or cocaine. Largely used by Negroes. "Bud, you got any mojo?" 2. Among Negroes, a good luck charm; *Toby.*

moll. A girl on the petty rackets. A very old term, *e.g.* Moll Flanders, Moll Cutpurse, etc.

moll buzzer. One who specializes in robbing women by snatching handbags. Not a true pickpocket. Also *prowl rat.*

monkey on my back. 1. Early abstinence symptoms. Also *hurting,*

Chinaman on my back, mama die?, etc. 2. A drug habit.

monkeyman. An obsequious person, especially a Negro in relation to whites. Also *weasel, sucker, brown nose, Jeff,* etc.

mooter. Marihuana. Also recorded as *mota* or *moota.*

morning shot. The first shot of the day. See *wake up.*

mouse. 1. A stool pigeon. See *louse.* "The difference between a rat (long-tailed) and a mouse is, the mouse will not finger his own mother. . . ." 2. A young prostitute, just starting out, or a girl ripe to be recruited into the *racket.*

mouth habit. A drug habit which is satisfied by taking drugs orally. Also *belly habit, scarfing, scoffing, pill dropping.* "Most all pipe smokers who went to the needle went by way of the mouth habit first—after the pipe, that is."

Mr. Broadshoulders. A social worker. Also occurs as **Miss Broadshoulders** for a female social worker.

Mr. Fish or **fish.** 1. A newcomer in any penal institution, including jails. 2. A voluntary patient in a Federal hospital for narcotic addicts. Obsolescent. Now called *winders, self-starters,* or *crank handles, keys,* though *fish* is still used in some places.

Mr. Twenty-six. A needle. See *spike, Yale, artillery.*

mud. Prepared opium before it is rolled to be cooked for smoking. In emergencies opium in solution is sometimes used by morphine or heroin addicts for intravenous injections instead of the *white stuff* preferred by needle addicts. This is a cumbersome process, resorted to only in great necessity.

mug. 1. The face. 2. To be photographed. 3. To rob by strong arm techniques.

mugger. A small-time strong arm operator; one who *puts the arm on* anyone on the street. May be loosely extended to include *moll buzzers.*

muggled or **muggled up.** Under the influence of marihuana. ". . . we were muggled up. . . ."

muggles. 1. Crude dried marihuana before it is rolled into cigarettes. See *griefo, hemp, Indian hay, Mary Warner, mess, mez, mutah, tea, Texas tea, viper's weed, weed, bambalache, marihuana, fu, bo bo bush, ding, joy smoke, laughing grass, love weed, sweet Lucy, root, rope, Chicago green, good giggles.* Some of these terms also indicate rolled cigarettes. 2. Marihuana cigarettes. "What is the tag on muggles?" "Bale or stick?" (by the pound or by the cigarette).

mule. See *margin man.*

murder game. An ultimatum to cooperate or suffer a heavy penalty; pressure used either by the authorities or the underworld.

Murphy. One type of short-con game, worked on a *mark* who is looking for a prostitute. In the West, sometimes called *(the) carpet* or *(the) post.*

mutah or **mooter.** Marihuana. See *muggles.*

nail. 1. The hollow needle, considered separately; especially the needle exclusive of the shank. 2. Anything sharp enough to take a *pin shot* with; a nail, safety pin, sewing machine needle, etc.

nailed. Arrested.

narcos. Narcotics detectives, especially Federal agents. Also recorded in the singular *(narco* and *nark).* See *fuzz, (the) man.*

narcotic bulls or **narcotic coppers.** Federal narcotic officers.

needle. 1. The entire outfit for injecting narcotics (East Coast and West Coast). See *artillery.* 2. The hollow needle alone (South, Southwest, and Midwest). 3. *White stuff* taken intravenously, as contrasted to opium. "He used to smoke, but went to the needle."

needle fiend. 1. A drug addict who uses the needle. Also *needle pusher*. Obsolescent. 2. An addict who gets pleasure from dallying with the needle, often pricking his flesh or inserting an empty needle for the psychological effect. "Needle fiends are addicts off the drug who like to jab themselves with needles or give themselves injections of water."

needle habit. 1. A habit which is satisfied by hypodermic injections. 2. The habit described under *needle fiend* 2.

Needle Park. To New York addicts, upper Broadway and Sherman Square.

needle pusher. An addict who takes drugs hypodermically, usually *white stuff*. See *needle fiend* 1.

needle shy. A state of phobia against the use of the hypodermic needle; often encountered among beginners, and sometimes among confirmed addicts. "Go ahead and shoot her, she's needle shy. . . ."

needle trouble. Mechanical difficulties in making an injection; usually caused by clogging, breakage, leakage of air, etc. "You never have needle trouble when you have plenty of time." See *floater*.

needle yen. 1. A desire for narcotics taken hypodermically. Obsolescent. "Two drinks of whiskey and she had a needle yen." 2. A masochistic desire to dally with the needle, as described under *needle fiend* 2. Rare. "There is a word used to describe people with a needle yen."

nic nac or **nick nack, knick knack.** 1. A homosexual "He'll nic nac for monkeys" (he'll participate in any perversion in any way). See *freak*. 2. A disgusting person. See *creep*.

nickel. 1. A five-year sentence. See *buffalo*. 2. A five dollar paper of heroin. 3. A five dollar bill. Also *Abe, fin, Lincoln*, etc.

nickel bag. A five dollar bag of heroin.

nimby or **nimbie.** A Nembutal capsule. Also *yellow jacket, canary, goofer*.

nodding. Dozing as a result of drug use. Also *coasting, sailing, floating*, with slight differences in connotation.

nose burner or **nose warmer.** The butt end of a marihuana cigarette.

notch joint. A house of prostitution. See *crib*.

nut. 1. To ignore or disregard. 2. Nutmeg; occasionally inhaled or drunk in solution by someone attempting to become euphoric; a prison substitute for drugs. More often drunk in solution. See *idiot juice*. 3. A psychotic. 4. The cost of maintaining a habit. "My nut ran me about a double sawski ($20) a day." 5. The expenses involved in any *racket*, such as living expenses, *fix money*, transportation, etc. "We can always clear $200 a week apiece, over and above the nut."

nut city. A mythical place in which anyone feigning insanity is said to live.

O.D. 1. An overdose of narcotics. This may simply put the addict into a stupor temporarily, or it may be fatal. There are several folk remedies for the severely *O.D.'d* addict —among them instant coffee or a stiff salt solution injected intravenously for heroin overdose. See text for the medical antidotes for various drugs of addiction. 2. Officer of the day in prisons or hospitals.

off or **off drugs.** 1. To be temporarily free from the *habit*. Also *clean, straightened up, squared up, turned over*. "It can be done. I know quite a few who have been off for years." "Every addict has a desire to be off drugs, sooner or later." 2. **Off**

(only). To steal something. "Why didn't you off that ring?"

off the wall. An abrupt change of subject in conversation. "Why do you come off the wall when we're getting down to business?"

oil burning habit. A large habit; perhaps related to *oil burner*, from race track argot, perhaps a variant of *lamp habit* 1, 2, *q.v.* The lamp used in opium smoking burns peanut oil. Now extended to include all "hard" drugs. "Not too many junkies are capable of supporting an oil burning habit. . . ."

old Steve. Morphine, heroin or cocaine. Obsolescent.

on. 1. To be using drugs regularly, as contrasted to *chipping*. "They can't make up their minds to be on or be off, so the feds step in and make the decision." Probably related to *turn on, turn (someone) on.* Formerly, *on drugs* was often encountered, but this phrase is disappearing. 2. To be honest, dependable, trustworthy. Probably derived from the gambling phrase, "you're on" and unrelated to sense 1, although identical in form, and used mostly in regard to transactions in drugs. "That deal don't sound on to me." "It don't have to be on." "I'm on with Pete. You can't touch him."

on ice. 1. In jail. 2. To lie low or go off a *racket* temporarily, usually due to police surveillance, or a police stakeout in the neighborhood. 3. Wanted by the law. Also *dead, no action, in the freezer, ducking and dodging,* etc.

on the bricks. Free on bond or released from custody. Also *to hit the street, in biz, in circulation, out of the cooler* and many others.

on the gow, or **on gow.** 1. Addicted to narcotics. "We were three handed, all on the gow." 2. May be used to indicate an addict under the immediate influence of opiates. Rare. Originally an opium smoker's term and now seldom encountered, though *gowed up (overcharged)* is still in use.

on the ground. Not incarcerated, out of prison. See *on the bricks.*

on the mojo or **on mojo.** Addicted, largely refers to *white stuff* users (Negro usage, mainly).

on the nod. A state of near stupor achieved by an addict who has just taken a stiff shot or a little too much.

on the point. To stare fixedly into space for a long interval as a result of taking Methedrine. Not to be confused with *play the point, q.v.*

on the send or **to have someone on the send.** 1. To obtain drugs through a runner or intermediary who makes the *connection* for a fee or a share of the drugs. Also *on the tracks.* "We had three different people on the send at the same time." 2. To send a confederate for bond money. 3. To send a *mark* home for more money with which to play a confidence game.

on the shorts. 1. Low on drugs. 2. Low on cash to buy drugs. See *short.*

on the streets. Out of prison. Also *on the ground, on the bricks.*

on the stuff or **on stuff.** Addicted to narcotics, usually indicating *white stuff.* "The whole mob was on stuff."

on the track. See *on the send.*

on the up and up. 1. To be *away from the habit.* "He packed it in and he's on the up and up." 2. To be trustworthy or *right.* "You can deal, he's on the up and up."

operating. Actively selling narcotics.

orange bowl. 1. See *lemon bowl.* 2. A half orange scraped out and used for a shade for an emergency opium lamp shade. "Use a small condensed milk can for the oil and half an orange scraped out for a shade, punch a few air holes, and you have a fine little lamp.

out in the cold again. Out of prison. See *on the ground, on the bricks.*

out of sight. 1. Beyond comprehension. 2. Impossible. 3. Stupified as a result of having taken too much of a drug. See *gowed.* 4. An extreme in any direction, expressing all reactions from high approval to total rejection.

outfit. 1. Equipment used for administering drugs. 2. The vagina, especially as it is involved in the concealment and transport of drugs.

over the hump. 1. See *around the turn.* "You'll soon be over the hump." 2. To build up a state of euphoria until a maximum of pleasure is reached. "I'm over the hump now; I'll have a good bang of that M." 3. To have passed the halfway point in serving a prison sentence. Also *going downhill.*

overamped. Having taken too much Methedrine.

overcharged. Having taken more narcotics than necessary to *get the habit off.* "That day I went to work (thieving) overcharged, so anything could happen." See *gowed, charged.*

overjolt. Too much of a drug taken at one time. See *O.D., overcharged, gowed.*

O.Z. An ounce of narcotics, especially morphine, but may be applied to heroin, cocaine, opium and even marihuana, when it is handled in wholesale or large-scale transactions. Rare. Individual addicts of thirty years ago frequently bought an ounce of hard drugs at a time, but this is now a thing of the past, except on a wholesale level. See *piece, half piece.*

P.G. Paregoric. Also *P.O.,* rarely. Contains nearly two grains of opium per fluid ounce. Addicts drink it or refine it for injection by vaporizing the camphor, alcohol, etc. by cooking it down *(blackjack)* or by chilling it to separate the camphor and then boiling off the alcohol. Recently, on the East Coast, many addicts have begun to inject straight paregoric into the vein in large doses—as much as 20 cc. "I think pipe smokers were the first to drink P.G. to hold them." "The camphor in P.G. will become solid if you place it on ice."

P.O. 1. A parole or probation officer. 2. Paregoric. Rare. See *P.G.*

pack your keyster. To place a condom filled with drugs in the rectum or vagina. See *coozie stash.*

pad. 1. Home or apartment. 2. A bed. 3. House of prostitution or, more commonly, a room used for prostitution purposes. Sometimes this also means the place of sale or use of drugs, especially marihuana.

paddie. A white person, especially used by Negroes.

paid off in gold. Arrested by a Federal officer who flashes his gold badge. Sometimes used as an ironical way of describing a purchase by an agent who "pays" for it by showing his badge. Obsolescent. "Shorty was paid off in gold that night. . . ."

panic. 1. A shortage of drugs in a certain locality. "There was a real panic in Memphis after that. . . ." 2. Failure of an addict to secure drugs, either because he cannot make a *connection* or because he has no money. "The panic is on with me right now, Jack."

panic man. An addict who is short of drugs or unable to secure them. Obsolescent.

paper. 1. A *bindle* of narcotics put up by folding the powder in paper or cellophane so that all ends are folded in. "There are five dollar papers, ten dollar papers and so on." 2. A small package of prepared opium put up in oiled paper. "A paper of hop." "A paper of grease." See *nickel paper, dime paper*.

paper fiend. One who uses the paper *strips (q.v.)* inside inhalers as a source of amphetamine.

paper hanging. Passing forged checks systematically as a *racket* or *hustle*.

party. A group of LSD users taking the drug together. These sessions last many hours and stereophonic music, exotic lighting and even bizarre costumes are sometimes used in conjunction with taking the drug.

passing queer. See *pushing queer*.

past Monday. Extreme. Obsolescent.

pat down. To search a person. Also *skam* 3.

peddler. A retail dealer in narcotics; sometimes not addicted, but usually supporting his own habit by selling. "Shorty is a peddler and a square." See *pusher, in big, the man, connection*.

peg. 1. The police. 2. To recognize. See *make*. 3. To stare steadily at someone. "When you peg a lame, you're playing the hinge."

pen and death. An indeterminate sentence.

pen yen. Opium. A term used mostly around *hop joints* and in conversation with Chinese in pidgin English. "You catchem pen yen, me yen shee quay...."

penitentiary shot or **pen shot.** 1. Variant of *pin shot, point shot, q.v.* "A few more pen shots and he's through." 2. A small shot due to scarcity or cost. Epsom salts is often added to *boost the kick*, or so some addicts believe.

period hitter. An occasional user. See *chippy habit*.

peter. 1. Knockout drops, especially chloral hydrate. Probably by extension from the *peter man's* term for nitroglycerine used to crack safes, which is *pete* or *peter*. 2. The racket of robbing people (addicts, drunks, customers of a prostitute, etc.) by the use of chloral hydrate. "They take off a lot of cash on the peter."

phystaris. See *fisstaris*.

pick up. 1. A shot of narcotics, usually given another addict as a gift or favor. See *bang*. Also *taste*, meaning a shot to hold an addict until he can *score*. "He sure was sick when I saw him, so hell, I gave him a pick up." 2. An arrest on a charge which is usually dropped, the idea being to get the addict into custody for questioning. See *hummer*.

pick (someone) up. To provide narcotics, clothes, money, etc. for an addict who is broke. "I know Ernie picked him up three different times coming out of stir."

picked up. Under the immediate influence of narcotics; feeling euphoria. "He said, 'You are picked up right now with a line shot.'" See *bang*.

piddle or **pital.** A hospital or sanatorium where a drug addict may be treated. See *pogie*. "There are piddles that are pogies, too. Then there are pogies that are not piddles, and there are piddles that are not pogies—do I make myself clear?"

piece. 1. An ounce of narcotics, especially morphine, heroin or cocaine. Formerly, addicts or groups of addicts often bought a *piece* and divided it up or rationed it over several weeks. Within the past three to ten years, purchases of this size by individuals are rare, but are still made in the wholesale trade. Today, an "ounce" must be suspected of dilution or reduction by one means or another. Medical or pharmaceutical morphine may be sold pure; heroin never. "You know, Shorty was guzzled (arrested) with forty

pieces (ounces) in a kiester (suitcase)." See *O.Z.* 2. A pistol (largely teenage gangsters).
pig. 1. See *fiend.* 2. A female addict who takes more drugs than she needs to *hold* her. See *junk hog.*
pill. 1. A *ration* of opium, prepared for smoking. 2. (Plural). Used to distinguish prescription drugs from bootleg drugs. "Let me have a few pills" means that the addict wants to borrow or buy morphine, Dilaudid or Pantopon, *not* heroin. 3. By extension, also usually plural, the amphetamines or barbiturates, even though some of them are in capsules.
pimp. One who lives from the earnings of a prostitute. Among addicts, both are usually using drugs, though not always. Often one *pimp* has several girls working for him. Many addicts without much criminal experience drift into the *broad racket* because it is one of the most obvious ways to support a *habit.* When the pimp is also the *connection,* he has a high degree of control over the girl. Also *tail towel checker, fish, fish and shrimp,* etc.
pin. 1. To act as a lookout. 2. The hollow needle used with a *joint.* 3. The safety pin, nail or other sharp object used to take a *pin shot, q.v.*
pin man. A lookout.
pin shot. An injection of drugs made with a safety pin or other sharp instrument, and a medicine dropper. The pin is put into the flesh and left for a while to assure an opening, then the dropper is placed over the opening and the shot slowly forced in. Sometimes the dropper is actually pushed into the opening. Also *penitentiary shot.* "Pin shots are the accepted way of taking stuff in most stirs."
pinned. Said of an opiate addict's eyes when the pupils constrict noticeably after a shot. From "pin pointed." This condition has recently assumed great significance among addicts with the introduction of the Nalline test, which reverses the constriction in the eyes of opiate users, causing measurable dilation.
pipe. An opium smoker. Obsolescent.
pipe fiend. An opium smoker. Obsolescent. The word "fiend," while it survives in such phrases as *needle fiend, pipe fiend,* etc., is not much used by addicts, and the term *dope fiend* is almost taboo.
pipe smoker. An opium addict who uses a pipe. "That guy you saw me with last night was a pipe smoker for years, but he finally went to the needle."
pit. See *ditch.*
to pitch. 1. To retail narcotics in small quantities. Also *to push, to shove, to shove shorts, to push shorts,* with somewhat specialized meanings. "He's pitching now for Louie on 14th Street." 2. To manifest, as *to pitch a toss out, to pitch a wing ding,* etc. (meaning to put on an act or feign sickness for drugs). 3. The role of the male partner in the homosexual relation. "The butch pitches, (the) queen pussy catches."
plant. 1. Narcotics hidden away, either on the person or secreted in a hiding place. "At that time I had a plant of about 50 Dilaudid tablets in my fly (trousers)." "My plant was in the toilet room." 2. To smuggle narcotics into jail by concealing them on an individual and causing him to be arrested. "We could always count on Sam to plant a few bindles on some crumb bum. . . ." 3. A hiding place for narcotics, on or off the person, in jail or outside. "They had a plant in the radio that would hold a piece of stuff." See *stash.*
play around. 1. To begin to take *plea-*

sure shots now and then and cultivate a *chippy habit.* Also *dabble.*

play the clam. To refuse to give information. Also *play the exhaust, play the iggie, put it down* 2.

play the exhaust. See *play the clam.*

play the iggie. To pretend ignorance in order not to give information. See *play the clam.*

play the nod, on the nod or **to get the scratch and the nod.** See *charged.* "We sat around punching gun (chewing the rag, shooting the breeze) till he started playing the nod."

play the point. To act as a lookout. Also *get* (or *be*) *on the point.*

play the shoulder. See *chill.*

playboy. A prisoner who forms a romantic attachment for another inmate. Also *jailhouse pimp, romancer, player.*

pleasure jolt. An occasional *shot* taken by someone who is not a confirmed addict. Usually taken subcutaneously, but may be intravenous. See *chipping.*

pleasure shooter or **pleasure user.** An individual who takes an occasional *shot;* one who *dabbles* or develops a *chippy habit.*

pleasure smoker. One who smokes irregularly and does not become thoroughly addicted. A genuine *pleasure smoker* is not merely *playing around;* he smokes at will over a period of years without developing a full-fledged habit. Restricted to old time opium smokers. "I'd give anything to be a pleasure smoker."

pogie. A workhouse, or poor farm or a certain type of free hospital where minor offenders are sometimes sent and where down and out addicts can spend the winter, either as voluntary residents or prisoners. See *piddle.* "I told him, 'If you feel so bad, why don't you get into some pogie?'"

point. 1. The hollow needle used with a *joint.* "Haven't you got a point stashed (hidden) around here somewhere?" 2. Any substitute for this needle, especially a sewing machine needle. See *tom cat.*

point shot. 1. A type of injection taken when a hypodermic needle has been broken and cannot be replaced. The point of the needle is inserted into the vein or under the skin and the glass shank of a medicine dropper slipped over it so that the solution can pass into the blood when the bulb is pressed. Distinguished from *pin shot.* 2. An injection taken with a substitute for the hollow needle, especially a sewing machine needle from power sewing machines used in prisons. See *tom cat, pin shot.*

poison. 1. A *wrong gee;* a stool pigeon. "Watch out for that little guy, he's poison." 2. A *knocker, q.v.* "Don't let his wife hear you, she's poison." 3. The opiate drugs and cocaine; *white stuff.* 4. A physician who will not sell drugs or prescriptions to addicts. Obsolescent.

poison act. The Harrison Narcotic Act, including its various amendments and revisions.

policy. The numbers *racket.*

polluted. See *high, in high.* Obsolescent.

pop. 1. A shot of narcotics. See *bang.* 2. To arrest. 3. To inject drugs, especially in the skin.

pop stick. A homemade opium pipe.

popcorn. See *mockey.*

post. See *Murphy.*

pot head. A marihuana addict. See *reefer man.*

potaguaya or **pot.** Crude marihuana, especially the flowering tops; the seed pods of the hemp after the leaves have been stripped, sometimes soaked in wine or liquor (New York City). See *muggles.*

pound. 1. A five-year sentence. 2. Marihuana in bulk, theoretically a pound by weight. Sales (wholesale) are commonly made in units of a pound, half pound, kilo, half kilo and can (about 8 oz). Sales practices vary in different areas.

powder. 1. To leave or run out. 2. Bad narcotics. Also *turkey, blank.*

powdered bread. Money which has been dusted with luminous powder so that it can be traced under fluorescent light.

pratt or **prat.** A hip pocket. From the pickpocket argot *prat kick.*

Procter and Gamble. Euphemism for paregoric *(P.G.).* One of several terms which coincidentally match the older abbreviation in initial letters. See *P.G.*

prod or **prop.** 1. A shot or bang of narcotics; the use of the needle. Obsolescent. "She was always on the prod." 2. **Prod** (only). Activity. "Harry is always on the prod. I mean on the hustle." "The narcos are really on the prod around here, rousting, making life miserable when they can't catch you dead bang." 3. The penis.

prowl rat. A thief or mugger who robs women on the street, especially prostitutes. Also *moll buzzer,* though these terms are not exactly synonymous.

puff. To smoke opium. Much used in Canada. Also *to roll the log, q.v.*

pull a job. To commit a crime. Also *knock off a score, beat a joint,* etc.

pull a rabbit. To escape by running away.

pull one's coat or **sleeve.** 1. To enlighten someone. 2. To stop one from doing something foolish.

punk. A male homosexual who practices pederasty. "Punks are different from queens or fags. They're penitentiary made."

purring or **purring like a cat.** Said of an addict who has taken just the right amount of drug to make him *high* (East Coast and South to Florida). See *floating, coasting, in high.*

push or **push shorts.** To peddle narcotics; to retail them in small quantities as a sub-agent or small-time peddler. Usually restricted to *white stuff,* but has been encountered rarely to include small retailers of opium (Detroit and vicinity). "When did you start to push?" Also *hold, stick, deal, swing.*

pusher. A narcotics seller, one who works the streets.

pushing queer. Passing counterfeit money. Also *laying queer, passing queer, passing green.*

put in a shot against him. To write an adverse behavior report on a prisoner. See *A.B.C., gunzel.*

put (it) in writing or **in paper.** The act of concealing narcotics between the split halves of post cards or other paper, or saturating a letter with drugs in solution. "Morphine can't be satched. Heroin is O.K. in paper, then ironed." "Chinese in Frisco used to wear large work shoes with the strings and the tongue satched with hop. Some types of leather belts were used too."

put it down. 1. To go off drugs. 2. See *play the clam.*

put the arm on. To strong-arm a person. Also occurs as *arm,* as, "They tried to arm that punk." Also *roust, mug* 3.

put the bee on. The act of begging narcotics. See *hit on* 2.

put the croaker on the send. See *Brody, frame* 2.

put the finger on. 1. To arrest. 2. To inform on. 3. To signal a friend for anything needed at the moment— a gun, knife, car, etc.

put the heat on. 1. To interrogate. 2. To inform on someone. 3. For the police to stake a place out.

put the lug on. See *hit on* 2.

put the shiv on. To threaten with a knife.

quarry cure. One form of *cold turkey* treatment in which addicts are worked in the stone quarry while they are *kicking the habit*. Restricted to the Chicago Bridewell and to addicts who have done time there. Obsolescent. "Iron Jaw of the quarry cure was the reincarnation of all the masters of cruelty since the Spanish Inquisition." "Obsolescent my ass! Ever hear of Big O'Rourke and his quarry cure built around the rock crusher in K.C.?"

quarter piece. A quarter of an ounce of morphine, heroin or cocaine. A very common unit of sales for heroin, though of course the strength varies. See *piece, O.Z.*

queen pussy. Passive receptor in the male homosexual act.

queer. 1. A sex pervert. 2. Counterfeit money. 3. To disillusion or inform. 4. To sell (someone) highly diluted or fake narcotics. 5. Or **queer stuff.** Diluted or fake narcotics. "Queer stuff is flea powder, crap." See *turkey, blank.*

quit. To leave, especially a *joint* or *pad* when it gets "hot."

rabbi. A Jew, See *mockey.*

rabbit parole. Escape by running away.

Racehorse Charlie. Heroin and, rarely, cocaine. Possibly influenced by an old brand name for heroin, "White Horse," no longer in existence. Also suggested association with the racetrack and drugged horses—though cocaine and strychnine, not heroin, are usually used at the track. Note the very popular term used by younger addicts for heroin—horse. "Doc, I've known many hypes with Racehorse Charlie as a monicker, but never knew why. Thanks."

rainbow roll. An assortment of vari-colored barbiturates, popular among addicts on the West Coast.

rap. 1. To converse with or speak to. 2. An arrest or conviction, usually the latter. See *bum rap.* 3. (With **to**). To recognize someone. "I was there but he didn't rap to me." "He won't rap to you here unless you raise for him."

rap partner. 1. A close friend in whom one confides. 2. The partner in crime who serves the sentence or takes the responsibility when arrested. This happens when one man has a minor record (implying a lighter sentence), when one has an easier case to "beat" than the other or when one is forced to take the rap for the other.

rap sheet. One's prison record or *jacket*, *q.v.*

raspberry. An abscess at the site of injection. Also *ab, cave.*

rat. 1. A stool pigeon. See *long-tailed rat.* "A rat used to have two chances of survival—a bum chance and no chance at all. Nowadays it's different. . . ." See *ring tail, wrong, fink,* etc. 2. To act as an informer or stool pigeon; to *stool.* See *rat row.*

rat row. The cells or section of a prison where informers are segregated for their own safety. Also *snitch joint.*

rayfield. 1. Unusual jeopardy for quick gain; a crime involving considerable risk. 2. To take more than one's share, usually by violence or a threat of violence. 3. Any crime involving violence.

reach the pitch. To pass the crisis in withdrawal. See *around the turn.*

reader. 1. A prescription for drugs; *to make a croaker for a reader* is to persuade a physician to write a prescription for narcotics. Also *script.* 2. A warrant for arrest.

reader with a tail. A prescription for

narcotics, often an illicit one, which is being traced by narcotics agents. ". . . been scoring in that burg for over a year, same croaker, but that last reader had a tail. . . ." Also *script with a tail.*

red bird. A Seconal capsule. Also *red devil.*

red devil. See *red bird.*

reefer. A marihuana cigarette.

reefer man. A marihuana smoker. Also *tea man, viper, grasshopper, stick man, pot head,* etc.

register. 1. For an addict to assure himself that he has hit the vein by applying a slight suction to the *dropper* and watching for the blood to show in the glass before injecting the *shot.* See to *back up* 1, *verification shot.* "He was very careful, and registered that shot as if it was his last one, and it was—a hot one." 2. For a shot to *register* by showing blood in the *dropper,* indicating that the vein is punctured.

rehash. 1. To try something again. "Do you want to rehash the croaker?" (that is, Do you want to see if he will give you another *shot?*). 2. The act of repeating something. "Will Charlie go for a rehash, do you think?" 3. To reuse the *cottons.* See *cotton, cotton shooter.*

R.F.D. junker, R.F.D. gowster, dopey, dope head, floater, cross-country hype. An itinerant addict who depends for his drugs upon small town or country doctors. Obsolescent. "I believe the R.F.D. dope heads have the best go. . . ."

rifle range or **shooting gallery.** The withdrawal ward of a narcotics hospital.

right croaker. A physician or dentist who will, out of sympathy or for financial gain, sell drugs or prescriptions to addicts. Reputable physicians often supply drugs because of the trickery of the addict, which is described in the text. "I'd say that the croakers who really deal—the right croakers—are very much in the minority." "There is only one right croaker in town." Also *swinging croaker.*

right guy. A narcotic addict who will not inform when arrested. Also *solid, stone righteous.*

righteous. 1. Wonderful or choice. 2. Very, or the equivalent, as an intensive.

righteous scoffer. One who eats ravenously after withdrawal. Also a *dug out, Douglas.*

righteous stuff. See *McCoy.*

ring tail. A stool pigeon. See *rat.*

rinsings. The residue of solution remaining in the cotton after an addict fills the *joint.* A little water is usually drawn into the glass to rinse the *joint,* and this may be shot into a little ball of cotton and saved, especially by *skin shooters; vein shooters* cannot save it long because it usually contains some blood. "They shoot the rinsings into a ball of cotton, and over a period of a year can save quite a bit of stuff." See *cotton, cotton shooter.*

ripped. 1. See *geed up* 3. 2. Or **ripped off.** Stolen.

roach. The end of a marihuana cigarette. Also *nose burner, butt, nose warmer,* etc.

rod. 1. A gun. 2. The penis.

roll a pill. 1. To prepare opium for smoking; usually done by *tchi-ing* the pill on the pipe bowl with the *yen hok,* and sometimes smoothing the pill afterward on the heel of the hand. 2. By extension, to roll a marihuana cigarette. Also *roll a stick.*

roll a stick. See *roll a pill 2.*

roll of reds. Ten Seconal capsules sold in a roll.

roll stuff. 1. To transport narcotics in wholesale quantities. 2. To deal in or sell narcotics wholesale, as distinguished from peddling or dealing in small quantities.

roll the log. To smoke opium. See *hit the gong.* Rare, obsolescent.

romancer. See *playboy.*

rooster brand. A cheap brand of commercial smoking opium.

root or **root on the derrick.** 1. To steal from stores, or shoplift, especially to support a habit. See *clout.* "We went down the valley three handed, rooting on the derrick. 2. Or **root** (only). Marihuana. 3. Or **root** (only). To eat ravenously. See *chuck habit.*

rope. Marihuana. So called because when smoked it smells of burning hemp. Obsolescent.

Roscoe. A pistol.

rosenbloom or **rosebud.** A swollen rectum, the result of expelling the hard fecal matter which follows opiate use.

round eye. 1. The anus. 2. Pederasty.

roust. 1. See *sneezed.* 2. See *put the arm on.*

rub. To search a person, as by an officer. See *pat down.*

rumble. 1. Sexual intercourse. 2. An encounter with the law. 3. A fight, especially among teenage gangs.

rumdum. 1. A disgusting person. Also *rumkin.* 2. An alcoholic in the later stages.

rumpsty dumpsty. Anal intercourse. Also *giving up backs, q.v.*

run. See *habit.* "I've got a six-months' run."

run it down. To explain.

run (it) through the greaser. To subject something to change.

runner. See *margin man.*

rush. The first exciting euphoria from injecting opiates. See *flash 1, jaboff.*

sack. Bed. Also *kip.*

saddle and bridle. An opium smoker's *layout, q.v.* Obsolescent.

sail. For a physician to give or sell drugs to an addict. See *turn.* "He went sailing for twenty tabs."

Sam. 1. Uncle Sam, *i.e.,* the Federal Government. 2. A widely used greeting in a sort of formula, with variations. "What's doing, Sam, what's the flimflam?"

san lo. A cheap grade of smoking opium made from *dog* with *yen shee* added and the whole mixture reworked. Sometimes recorded as *sam lo.* "If the original gum was good, the san lo would be almost as good as the first cooking." "Been smoking san lo down at Ty Ling's and I could hardly tell the difference." "The first smoking is hop. The second is yen shee. The third is san lo."

sand. 1. Sugar, especially in prisons. 2. A jail term.

satch. A method of concealing narcotics or smuggling them into jails. Part of the garment (usually the shirttail) is soaked in a saturated solution of drugs (white stuff), dried and the drug later dissolved for injection. See *put (it) in writing.*

satchel. A girl.

satchel habit. A weakness for a girl; "carrying the torch."

Saturday night habit. See *chippy habit.*

sawbuck. A ten dollar bill. Also *saw, sawski, dime.*

sawski. See *sawbuck.*

saxophone. An opium pipe or opium *layout*, sometimes carried in a case. Obsolescent. "Did you check the saxophone at the shed?" (*Layouts* were often checked at railway stations, check rooms, etc.)

scene. Any place, event or happening. Usually in such combinations as *on the scene, make the scene, blow the scene,* etc.

schmeck, smeck or **smack.** Narcotics. From Yiddish or German *schmecken.*

schmecker or **smecker.** An addict.

scoff. To eat a drug or take it by mouth.

Glossary

Usually used when there is some compulsion which prevents taking the drug in the usual way. Formerly used in referring to a regular *mouth habit*. Now generalized to taking drugs by mouth for any reason. "We scoffed the forty tabs between us just before we got snatched. . . ." When arrest is imminent, addicts often swallow all they have with them. See *scarf, drop pills, scoff stuff.*

scoff stuff. To think or daydream about *dropping pills.* When addicts are *away from the habit,* they spend much time thinking and talking about taking drugs. This is especially true in prisons.

scorch. To abuse someone verbally and very severely; to *play the dozens,* q.v.

score or **score a connection.** 1. To purchase drugs from a peddler. Also *cop.* 1. Also used as a noun, meaning the purchase. 2. To secure drugs by any means—theft, prescription, etc. *Score* common in the Midwest, South, Southwest and West. *Score a connection* more common on the East Coast. 3. To hit the vein with a needle. 4. Or *score* (only). To take money on any *racket* or *hustle.*

score for a connection. 1. To secure drugs in quantity from a *connection* or *T-man.* 2. May also be used to mean arranging a purchase for one's connection, on a wholesale level. Rare.

scratch. Paper money.

scratcher. 1. A forger. From *scratch,* a pen, originally a quill pen. 2. A low-class addict, or one who is down and out. "That cotton scratcher is always on my back."

screw. 1. A prison guard. 2. To run out on the police. 3. A policeman or detective. "Nix cracken, Jimmy Bracken, the screw is on the Erie."

script. A prescription for narcotics. See *reader.*

script with a tail. See *reader with a tail.*

seccy or **seggy.** Seconal. See *red devil.*

self-starter. A voluntary patient. See *crank handle.*

send. 1. The pleasurable effects of smoking marihuana. "I take a half a cap of horse and two red birds and drink a glass of milk and it really sends me" (teenager speaking). 2. To smoke marihuana. A technique is used whereby air is drawn in at both corners of the mouth when the smoker puffs on the cigarette. This provides extra oxygen in the lungs when the smoke is inhaled. "You don't smoke it like a regular cigarette—you send it."

send it home. To inject narcotics intravenously.

sergeant. An especially masculine-mannered lesbian. See *Jasper.*

service stripes. Black or blue scars from injections. Also *tracks.*

set or **set of works.** Instruments for administering narcotics hypodermically.

set up. 1. The arrest of a *pusher* or *dealer* by the police, usually brought about by an informer making a purchase. 2. To inform on. "Tracy set me up to the narcos to protect himself."

sewer. The vein into which drugs are injected. "If I miss the sewer, then the geezer is wasted."

sex punk. The passive or "feminine" partner in a male homosexual act.

shades. Tinted glasses. Also *fades, cheaters* (not necessarily tinted), *fakes,* etc.

shadow. An undercover agent formerly working in the Leavenworth Annex. Widely known and feared by addicts. "Another character was called The Shadow; his name was Hobson, and he was a thorn in old dopey's side in the Annex. . . ." "I knew Hobbie well. The shakedown was about his only duty."

shakedown. 1. To search. 2. A search of the cell or the person. 3. Blackmail. 4. A form of pressure sometimes exerted by addicts on peddlers, mostly *squares*. The addict tells the peddler that he has hidden some heroin in the peddler's *pad*, and threatens to *finger* him to the narcotics officers if the addict's supply is not regularly available. The *connection* never knows for sure whether the addict has done this or not, but does not dare take a chance. "Texas and Oklahoma were notorious for the shakedown. It works."

shakedown bust. See *sneezed*.

shank. A knife. Also *shiv, blade,* etc. Mexican-Americans often use *fila*, from the fact that in prison knives are ground out from a file.

sharp. Dapper in appearance, as in *sharp threads*. Also extended as a general term of approbation.

sharp shooter. See *jab*.

shave. To reduce the size of morphine cubes by shaving the flat sides with a razor blade. This is done when drugs pass from dealer to dealer or to addicts buying by the can or the cube. Restricted to morphine; other drugs are *cut, q.v.* ". . . out of a can, he would shave at least a dram of stuff."

sheep. A passive pederast. Also *lamb*, if he is a young boy. Both these are very old hobo terms.

sheet writer or **sheet artist.** An agent for the *numbers racket* (policy).

shine (him) on. 1. To ignore someone. See *chill*. 2. To threaten or intimidate someone.

shirt tail hype. See *J.C.L.*

shiv. A knife. See *shank*.

shoes (or boots) laced up tight. To be well informed. Also occurs as to have your *boots on*. "Tell Joe to put his boots on" ("Tell Joe to 'wise' up").

shoot. Take narcotics by needle, either subcutaneously or intravenously. See *bang* 4. ". . . Oh shoot no more the main lines, Oh shoot no more today. . . ." "If I ever shoot again, I belong in jail."

shoot an angle. See *shoot the curve*. Also occurs as *shoot the angles*.

shoot (him) down. To write an adverse behavior report on a prisoner. See *A.B.C.*

shoot gravy. To reheat a *boot shot* after a vein is missed and reinject the mixture of blood, water and drug. An addict who is very short on heroin may do this if his needle clogs or breaks and the shot cools before he can make repairs.

shoot the curve. To connive in prison to secure certain privileges, sometimes including the use of drugs. "One of those curves he shoots is going to hit him right in the schnozzola. . . ." Also recorded as *shoot a curve, shoot the curves*.

shoot yen shee. To inject a solution of any form of opium, but especially that made from *yen shee, gee yen* or the residue accumulated in a *gee rag*. Injected intravenously, it satisfies an opium or morphine habit temporarily; injected under the skin, it usually causes an abscess. Most addicts resort to it only when there is a panic. "In the old days, you could compare hypes who shot *yen shee* with the lushes who drank derail or canned heat; however, if *yen shee* were obtainable today, a lot more junkies would shoot it."

"Old Chinese smokers saved their yen shee to give the working class Chinos. Now it sells for five or six bills a tael, if you can get it at all."

shooting gallery. 1. The withdrawal ward of a prison or hospital. 2. A place where an addict can go and use a needle to inject his drugs either free or for a fee. "All his friends . . . stream in, and the place turns into a shooting gallery."

shooting up. Injecting drugs, usually heroin. See *bang* 4.

shop. A house of prostitution, or a room used for this purpose. Probably cut back from *hook shop*, an old word in the *broad rackets*.

short. 1. A small quantity of drugs sold by a peddler. See *push shorts*. 2. A quantity of drugs (including the *short can* or *short toy* of opium) which has been shaved, cut or tampered with. 3. Having only a short period of confinement left on a sentence. See *on the shorts*, which is related.

short can, short toy, or **shorty.** A can of opium which has been tampered with so as to contain less than represented. See *short piece*.

short-change racket, or **(the) hype.** 1. A small-time swindle worked by one or two operators on clerks or cashiers; a small purchase is made, a large bill is offered in payment, and the clerk confused into giving more change than his customer has coming. Mostly the *hype* takes $5.00 out of a $10 bill or $10 out of a $20 bill. 2. To short-change someone by this racket. Anyone working this racket professionally is *on the hype*. Also *make a hype pitch*. This racket has several other names, including *(the) sting, (the) note, laying the note, (the) flue,* with slight variations in meaning. All these terms are old-time *grifters'* argot.

short-con. Any of numerous confidence games which are played for the amount of money the victim has on his person, as contrasted to the *big-con* games, which involve more sophisticated methods, *the send* and much larger amounts of money. Many addicts try their hands at various of the simpler *short-con* games; few addicts are found among the *big-con* operators, though *big-con* men use *short-con* games to carry them between *touches*.

short go. A small or weak *shot;* the implication is that the peddler has not given the addict his money's worth. This is a universal complaint among modern addicts. See *bird's eye, go*. "He is pushing an awful short go for a fin."

short piece. A quantity of narcotics, usually an O.Z., which has been shaved or otherwise reduced. See *short can*. "He specialized in short pieces and taking the first count on everybody. . . ."

shot. 1. An adverse behavior report. See *shoot (him) down*. 2. A Negro pickpocket. A variant of *cannon*, a first-class white pickpocket. 3. A big operator in illicit business, especially narcotics. Probably cut back from *big shot*. 4. An injection of narcotics. See *shot in the arm*.

shot or **shot in the arm.** An injection of narcotics, either subcutaneous or intravenous. Nowadays usually shortened to *shot*. See *bang, vein shot, skin shot*.

shot up. 1. Under the influence of drugs. See *high, in high*. 2. Said of an addict with multiple abscesses.

shoulder. 1. See *collar*. 2. To refuse to have anything to do with someone. See *play the shoulder*.

shove. To peddle or retail drugs. See *pitch*. "He used to shove for me. . . ."

shove shorts. See *pitch, push shorts*.

shuck. 1. To feign or pretend. 2. To loaf. 3. To converse. 4. To throw a *wing ding, q.v.*

shy. To prepare a pill of opium for smoking. See *tchi*.

sick. 1. To manifest withdrawal distress, for a description of which see *panic man*. Many addicts are *sick* even when they are not actually deprived of drugs or *kicking the* *habit;* as each injection wears off, they have a mild attack of withdrawal symptoms, which disappears as soon as they take narcotics. The term sick is often specialized to the early morning craving which conditioned addicts like to satisfy before they arise. Also *to feel the habit coming on, to have a habit, to have a yen, to have a monkey (or a Chinaman) on one's back, to gap.* "He took that extra bang even though he knew he'd be sick in the morning." 2. Mentally ill.

sift. See *manicure.*

silver serpent. See *harpoon.*

sissy. Passive receptor in the male homosexual act. Also *stuff, sex punk, queen pussy, bottoms.*

sixty-nine. Mutual oral-genital contact, either homosexual or heterosexual.

sizzling. Wanted very badly by the police.

skam. 1. Action, happenings, planning of narcotic or criminal activities. 2. A prison sentence. 3. To search someone. Also *pat down.*

skamas. 1. Smoking opium. See *brick, cotics.* 2. Drugs in general. "Skamas is an old time word; seems like the Hebes (Hebrews) use it the most, along with smack or smeck. . . ."

Skid Row. Convalescent ward at the USPHS Hospital, Lexington.

skin or **skin the punk.** To miss the vein and *blow a shot.*

skin shot. An injection of narcotics beneath the skin. Some addicts prefer subcutaneous injection, and stay on it for years; for others it is only a prelude to *vein shooting.* Some *vein shooters* use it to *hold* them during a *panic.* "A skin shot will last you longer."

skinless. A Jew, or Jewish.

skinner. 1. A *skin shot, q.v.* 2. One who uses *skin shots* regularly.

sky rocket. A pocket. One of numerous examples of so-called Australian rhyming argot which are beginning to infiltrate addict usage.

(the) slab. See *(the) hole.*

slam. A city jail. To be *slammed* is to be in jail.

sleepers. Barbiturates. Used by *squares* or young addicts just initiated.

slick. 1. Opportunistic. Also *swift.* 2. Sophisticated. Also *swift.*

smashed. Under the influence of narcotics. Also *geed up, ripped, wired up, charged, zonked, stoned, loaded.*

smeck or **smack.** 1. A *bindle of drugs,* especially a card of opium. "He's O.K., a C-note in the seams and smeck in the plant." 2. Generalized to include all drugs. From Yiddish or German *schmecken.*

smecker. A narcotic addict; sometimes still means an opium user. Now giving way to the variant *smacker* and generalized in meaning.

smoke that off. 1. To examine something; to be interested in someone or something; to check it out. "Smoke that broad off. She looks good." 2. To do something easily or deftly. See *smoke the habit off* 4.

smoke the habit off. 1. For an opium smoker who has been on the road (thieves, confidence men, etc.) and subsisting on *yen she suey* or *yen poks,* to return to the pipe for a time. "When we get to Boston we can smoke our habits off." 2. Applied also to regular morning or night smoke. 3. By extension to needle addicts, to return to customary injections of drugs after a period of shortage or using drugs by mouth. 4. Currently, a trend is noted to apply this phrase to a very weak or mild habit, as "I could smoke this one off," or "I could sleep that habit off."

snatch. 1. A woman. 2. The female genitals. 3. To grab a woman's purse and run away. See *moll buzzer.* 4. To arrest.

snatched or **snatched in the neck.** Arrested. See *bust*.

sneeze. 1. To steal or shoplift. 2. See *sneezed*.

sneeze it out. To kick the habit; cold turkey. So-called because withdrawal may be accompanied by or followed by violent sneezing. A guard may say to an addict who begs for drugs in prison, "You shot it in, now sneeze it out." Sometimes the sneezing follows withdrawal and continues into the convalescent period.

sneezed or **sneezed down.** For an addict to be arrested or held without charges (and without drugs) in order to persuade him to supply information to the law. Obsolescent. **Sneezed** (alone) still used commonly for "arrested." This usage stems from the fact that as soon as an addict is deprived of drugs, he begins to sneeze. "Well, he was sneezed down for seven days, but he didn't sing...."

sniff. To inhale narcotics, specifically cocaine. Also *to snort, to horn*, now largely applied to heroin. "Pipe smokers sniffed quite a bit of C in the old days." See *joy powder*.

sniffer or **snifter.** An addict who takes drugs by inhalation. Restricted to cocaine or heroin. "Yeah, those boys are both sniffers. They're needle shy."

snitch joint. A dorm or wing for informers in prison. Also *rat row*.

snort. To take cocaine or heroin by inhalation, usually from the back of the hand, sometimes through a paper tube. See *sniff*. Also *horn, sniff*.

snow. Cocaine. Obsolete among underworld addicts, but still used by police officers and the public. "C was always something else besides snow. We'd call it Corine or Cecil, as all the fuzz referred to junk as snow...."

snowbird. 1. A cocaine user. Now obsolete among addicts, but still used journalistically. "You could tell he was a snowbird." 2. Current usage on the West Coast, an "Anglo" or Caucasian who associates with Mexican-Americans.

sol. Solitary confinement. This usually implies that the prisoner is "on a diet"—bread and water—with one slice in the morning, two slices at noon, and three slices in the evening. "Guys in sol could always get a little cough syrup (codeine terpin-hydrate) from the croaker in a cup and would put it on bread. This was when it was piss and punk for seven days at a stretch."

solid. Okay, fine, all right.

solid M.D. A physician who will write *script*. See *ice tong doctor*.

solitary cure. See *iron cure*.

soul searching. The vein shooter's constant search for veins he can use.

speedball. 1. An injection of morphine or heroin mixed with cocaine. "I'd like two speedballs for a wake up. . . ." See *whiz bang*. 2. An injection of heroin combined with amphetamine for a smoother effect. 3. Seconal and wine taken by mouth. "These J.C.L.'s speak of two reds and a glass of wine as a speedball. What's this world coming to, Doc?"

spike. 1. The hollow needle used with a *dropper* to make a regulation *joint*. Also often *ikespay* or *speezike*, standardized in a sort of pig-Latin. Also *Mr. 26, fuete, Yale*. 2. The nail, pin or other substitute used to make an *emergency gun*.

split. To leave a place, sometimes in haste.

splivvy or **spivvy.** To be well dressed or sharp.

spoon or **cooking spoon.** 1. See *cooker*. "Some wag once called junkies the 'knights of the bended spoon' and it stuck." 2. A small quantity of heroin, usually about 1/32 oz of retail heroin.

sporting life. The life of the *hustlers.* Also *the life, q.v.*

spot for (someone). To act as a lookout for an addict while he takes a *shot* in a public place or in a prison where a guard may see him. "I want this chair to spot for Jim while he fixes. . . ." Also *play the point* or *get on the point.*

spread the joint. See *make a spread.* "Give him room to spread the joint so we can fix."

square. 1. A member of the dominant culture. 2. Anybody who is disliked or stupid. 3. Any nonuser of drugs. Probably cut back from *square apple* or *square John,* which is the older term.

square apple. A non-addict. See *do right people.* "Watch your chatter, the gee with Joe is a square apple."

square business. The truth.

square John or **square.** A non-addict. See *do right people.* "How did he get in Narco? I thought he was a square John."

squared up. See *away from the habit.*

squawk. To inform or complain.

squeal. To inform.

S.S. 1. A *skin shot, q.v.* 2. A suspended sentence.

stable. The community of girls who prostitute for one pimp. Sometimes these girls know each other, sometimes not. Also *stake bag.* The pimp may also use *crib, flat, joint, pad* as an equivalent, even though the girls may not all live there.

stall. See *finger.*

star dust. Cocaine. Journalistic usage. See *white stuff, Bernice.*

stasch or **stash.** Variant of *satch.* Probably a hybrid word resulting from a combination of *sach* or *satch* (from *saturate*) with *cache.* A concealed plant of narcotics, usually one which an addict keeps as a last resort in case of arrest. The variety of these plants is limited only by the ingenuity of the addict. The most popular one in jails is a blotter or a piece of cloth—often one of the garments—soaked in a saturated solution and dried. But there are many others. See *finger of stuff, keyster.* "You can put your stuff in my stasch."

steel and concrete cure. See *iron cure, quarry cure* 1.

*We must slap them in the hole,
On the concrete let them roll.
That will fix them, Dr. H——,
You've said it, Dr. K——.*

"The steel and concrete cure is the only cure I recommend for stool pigeons."

stem. 1. An opium pipe. 2. The bamboo stem of a pipe. There is a Chinese belief that if the pipe is broken in and smoked by a man, the stem (bamboo) will split if it is smoked by a menstruating woman. See *bamboo.*

stem winder or **winder.** A voluntary patient. See *Mr. Fish.*

stepping high. 1. See *high, in high.* "He was stepping high every time I saw him." 2. Operating a profitable *racket* or *hustle.* 3. Pretending to be a big-time operator. Also *highsiding.*

stevie. Hallucinations experienced by marihuana users. "A real seal named Cleo, with a shark's head, once ate my arm and leg off, a bite at a time, smiling all the while."

stick. 1. A homemade or makeshift opium pipe made of a bottle and rubber hose. Obsolescent. See *bamboo.* 2. A marihuana cigarette. 3. A one-year prison sentence. 4. Occupation or way of making money, as, "His stick is boosting." The equivalent of *racket* or *hustle.*

stick it to (someone). For a court to give the maximum penalty.

stick man. A marihuana smoker. See *reefer man*.

stir. Prison. Also *joint, trap, pen, hatch, frame*, etc.

stir bugs. See *stir simple*.

stir simple. Mentally disturbed as a result of confinement. Also *stir bugs* (most common), *psycho, flipped his lid, blew his top, jerk simple, stir happy*, etc., with various shades of meaning.

stomach habit. The habit of eating opium or drinking it in solution, an obsolescent form of *mouth habit*, and used only by old-time pipe smokers. Also *belly habit*. See *scoff, scoffer*. "The old hop heads used to refer to a mouth habit as a stomach habit."

stone. A prefix element meaning confirmed or totally given over to something, as "he's stone police," he's stone crazy."

stoned. 1. Under the influence of narcotics. 2. Drunk on alcohol, or a combination of alcohol with barbiturates or amphetamines.

stool. 1. A stool pigeon, used by officers to catch addicts or peddlers. *Stoolie* is often used by the law. Also *rat, fink*, etc. "It's supposed to be right guys who are stools that cause all the grief." 2. To act as a stool pigeon. See *rat* in various combinations. "He has been ready to stool on someone for years, never had enough pressure put on him before."

stool pigeon. A government informer; an addict or peddler used to trap others. "A good dick is one who knows how to handle stool pigeons." "In the old days you could make book that a stool pigeon wouldn't live six months." See *rat* in various combinations.

store. The female genitals.

straight. Said of an addict who has had the proper *ration* to make him feel normal. See *bang, fix, gowed*.

straight man. See *margin man*.

straighten out. See *hang up* 1.

strap or **strap Johnson.** See *Jap*.

strip. 1. A letter. 2. The impregnated paper or fiber from inside an amphetamine inhaler, used as a stimulant.

strung. Addicted. See *strung out*.

strung out. To be severely addicted. "I've been all strung out for a year now."

stud. 1. A male, especially a male Negro. 2. An aggressive female homosexual. Also called a *stud broad, boss broad*, etc.

stud broad. The masculine partner in a lesbian combination. Also occasionally recorded as meaning any girl or woman.

student. A beginning addict who has not yet established a regular habit, or who has difficulty establishing one. See *J.C.L*. "He's a student now, but he'll get squared away. . . ." This term appeared long before the use of drugs spread to actual students in high school or college and is now very popular.

stuff. 1. A generalized term for narcotics, especially *white stuff*. "That word 'stuff' is in use again everywhere. A few years ago you seldom heard it." "To the new generation, only heroin is stuff." See *junk*. 2. A prison term. "I started in San Quentin and finished my stuff in Chino." 3. A passive homosexual. See *sissy*.

suede. A Negro. Also *stud, spook, blood*, etc.

suey pow. A small sponge, cloth, or powder puff dampened and used to clean and cool the bowl of an opium pipe. Part of the *layout*. "She threw him on the suey pow and stabbed him with the yen shee gow. . . ."

sugar. 1. Narcotics. 2. Inferior or fake dope. "He sold me sugar." *Sugar* seems to have been used for drugs well before cutting with sugar of milk became common. See *sugar lump cubes,* which were and are pure medical morphine, though they are no longer so common in the contraband traffic.

sugar cube or **sugar lump.** A *ration* of LSD as it is sold on the illicit market in the form of a lump of sugar containing a drop of the drug.

sugar habit. A light narcotic habit, so called from the heavy sugar of milk content in much of the heroin sold today.

sugar lump cubes. Large cubes of bulk morphine. See *cube.*

Sunday popper. An occasional user of narcotics. See *hype, chippy.*

Sweet Jesus. Morphine. See *M.*

Sweet Lucy. The resinous gum of marihuana (hemp) dissolved in wine. See *muggles, potaguaya.* 2. Muscatel wine, often used by alcoholics (wine heads) or for consumption with barbiturates.

sweet lumps of lead. See *sugar lump cubes.*

sweet stuff. 1. Narcotics, especially *white stuff.* Obsolescent. Used somewhat around jails and prisons, but there was a conflict with the several other and unrelated meanings of the term. 2. A homosexual.

swift. See *slick.*

swing. To peddle narcotics. See *push.*

swinging croaker. See *swing, right croaker, sail, turn.*

sympathizer. A social worker. Also *rabbi, preacher, chaplain, Mr.* (or *Miss*) *Broadshoulders.*

syrup. Dark brown heroin of Mexican origin. Heroin ranges from almost white through tan to dark brown...

T or **T man.** 1. A *big man, q.v.* Now more widely used than *big man.* It indicates *the top.* 2. A Federal agent, especially a treasury agent or *narco,* as contrasted to an FBI man.

tabs. 5 mg methedrine tablets.

tail towel checker. A pimp.

take. 1. To rob an addict or peddler known to be carrying a quantity of drugs. Knockout drops are sometimes used. The form most frequently encountered is the past participle. "I hear Sam was taken for ten O.Z. last night." 2. The proceeds of a racket.

take a sweep or **take a sweep with both barrels.** To inhale cocaine or heroin. Rare. Obsolescent. "Pass the quill, I want to take a sweep." The *quill* refers to the older custom of inhaling drugs, especially cocaine, from a soda straw, paper tube or hollow quill toothpick. The smoke from heroin is also sometimes inhaled by putting the dry powder in a tinfoil trough, heating it was a cigarette lighter and passing the smoking drug underneath the nostrils.

Take a trip. Using LSD, which is frequently taken in groups where experienced users like to observe the reactions of novices who have never had the drug before.

take a tumble. To be arrested. See *fall.*

take it in the line. To inject narcotics intravenously. See *bang 4, shoot.*

take it main. To inject drugs intravenously. See *shoot.* "Take it main, that's the way to put the test to it."

take off. 1. To smoke, as opium. "He took off about eight pills. . . ." 2. To take a shot of narcotics. "I just took off about an hour ago. . . ." 3. To rob a place, especially of narcotics. "I'm going to take off that croaker's office tonight."

take off artist. A type of strong arm man who preys on addicts and robs connections, peddlers, etc.

take the rope. To commit suicide by hanging. See *Gillete route*.

talcum powder. Inferior or fake narcotics. See *flea powder*.

tar. Smoking opium. Obsolescent. "Any tar around the Big Apple these days?"

taste. A small ration of narcotics. Also *bird's eye*. "Save me a lightweight taste for a get up."

tchi or **shy**. To roll a pill of opium preparatory to smoking. "This hop is like li yuen, it tchis (or shies) to a golden brown."

tea or **Texas tea**. Marihuana. See *muggles*. "Get some tea for Johnny's gal."

tea man. A marihuana user. Obsolescent. See *reefer man*.

tell it to the chaplain. To inform. See *rat*.

ten cent pistol. A *hot shot* or a heavy overdose sold to an informer with other capsules or *papers* and undistinguishable from the standard purchase.

that's all she wrote. There is nothing more; that is the end. Apparently originated in the Lexington Hospital around 1935-38.

thin dirties. Diarrhea accompanying withdrawal.

thin hips. An old-time opium smoker, the folk belief being that lying on one side to smoke makes the hips small. While it has been observed that most old-time opium smokers tend to be slender, especially about the middle, this condition probably stems from the tendency to neglect food. When these men go *off drugs* for a time, they tend to gain weight, losing it again when they go back on opium. "Old Charlie there is the original thin hips. . . ."

thing. See *emergency gun*.

three-day habit. 1. See *chippy habit*. 2. A *habit* which has not been satisfied for three days, by which time withdrawal distress is acute. Also *hung up, beat, hurting*. "Been beat for three days. And that three-day habit is getting tough."

throw a meter. See *Brody*. Rare, obsolescent. "He would throw a meter just to keep in practice."

tie up. 1. To distend a vein with a tourniquet preparatory to taking a *vein shot*. "Tie me up, will you?" 2. To block something or interfere with someone. "Don't do anything to tie up the connection."

tight. Intimate.

till tipping or **tapping**. Stealing from a cash register. Also *creeping*. See *heel*, which is a specialty among a certain class of thieves called *heels*, or *bank heels* if they operate through a cashier's window.

tin. 1. A tobacco can of marihuana. 2. Sealed or canned smoking opium.

tip. 1. A gang. 2. A crowd. 3. To inform. 4. To expose oneself, or someone or something. "Joe tipped his mitt by talking too much." "I looked at the spindle and tipped the gaff."

tired. Disgusted, quiet, ready to stop the action.

toby. Any good luck charm carried, especially by Negroes—a copper disc, piece of wire, rabbit's foot, etc. Also *mojo*.

tom cat. 1. A sewing machine, especially one in prison. 2. The needle from a power sewing machine, often used in making a *pen shot, q.v.* "All those guys from the West Coast rather use a tom cat." Also *point, q.v.*

too much. A superlative used to denote the utmost. Giving way to terms like *righteous* on the West Coast and *the end* in the East.

tools. Instruments for adminstering narcotics hypodermically. Obsolescent. See *artillery*.

top sarge. A very aggressive female homosexual. Also *sergeant, jasper,* etc.

tops. A male homosexual who practices fellatio.

tops and bottoms. A male homosexual who will practice his perversion orally and anally.

torpedo. 1. A drink (usually whiskey) containing chloral hydrate. See *Mickey Finn, knockout drops.* 2. To beg money by getting sympathy. 3. A gunman used by a *mob* to execute informers or other undesirables.

torture chamber. A jail or prison where an addict cannot secure drugs. "Most stirs in Canada are real torture chambers."

toss out. 1. A pretended fit or illness. See *Brody.* "He always pulls a toss out too fast." 2. A means used by *boot and shoe* addicts to beg money on the street by getting sympathy. "He is a toss out artist, gets him twenty bucks a day."

tough time. See *hard time.*

toy. 1. A small box of opium, or for containing opium. Small tin salve boxes are sometimes used; also half-shells from English walnuts are referred to as *toys* when filled with opium. *Toys* are put up usually to contain 5, 6 or 12 *fun* of smoking opium. In some areas like California, a toy contains 25 *fun*, in others 20 *fun*. Smaller quantities are put up in *papers, q.v.*

tracks. Supravenous scars. See *service stripes.*

train arrived. Narcotics successfully smuggled into prison. Also *drive* 4, *sail, boat sailed,* etc.

trained nurse. Narcotics (*white stuff* usually), especially drugs smuggled to an addict to "take care of him" while in prison or jail.

> *Funny as it may seem,*
> *See the prints upon my arm,*
> *They were put there by fingers, deft,*
> *Of my trained nurse, Miss Morphine.*

trap. Prison.

tray. 1. A quantity of narcotics on the retail level. 2. Or **trey.** Three of anything, as a three-year sentence.

tremble. 1. To ogle the female patients in the hospital. 2. To commit an adverse act, which may be discovered.

trick. 1. A person who is willing or looking for sexual gratification. 2. A victim of one of the rackets. 3. The sexual act performed to obtain money for drugs. Usually occurs as "*turn a trick.*" 4. Any foolish person. 5. Any customer serviced by a prostitute. A girl refers to him as "*my trick*," and from this usage comes such phrases as *trick hype*, meaning a "square" addict, or one only partly or very recently addicted.

trick bag. 1. The mythical place for victims, as, "He is in the trick bag." 2. Someone pretending to be too stupid to follow orders.

trick hype. See *Hoosier fiend, trick* 5.

trip. The experience of taking LSD.

tripper. A user of LSD.

tripping. Experiencing euphoria following the use of drugs. Now specializing to LSD users. See *high.*

trolley. 1. The secret channels through which narcotics and other articles are distributed inside prisons; sometimes an actual string or wire passing from cell to cell. "In a Canadian stir, the trolley was a string of plaited shoelaces and reached from No. 1 cell on the No. 3 gallery to the 33 cell on No. 1 gallery and it was called the telegraph, French pronunciation. . . ." 2. A low-type female *hustler.*

turkey. A *bindle* of bad narcotics, or a capsule containing only sugar or chalk. "Got a second turkey before we scored, but it was sure bonaroo stuff." See *blank.*

turn. To consent to sell drugs to an addict, applied to peddlers mostly, but also used of physicians. "That outfit won't turn to me; I'm on the cuff (credit) for two bills ($200.00) now. . . ." "He'll turn if you know somebody."

turn around. 1. To reform or go off drugs. 2. To confess. 3. To put somebody in jeopardy. 4. To upset someone. 5. To *flip over* or go homosexual.

turn a trick. 1. To prostitute. "My frame will have to turn a trick before we can score." 2. To cheat.

turn in or **turn up.** 1. To point out an addict or peddler to the law, with the implication that an arrest takes place. "The same broad turned him in before. . . ." 2. The arrest resulting from the act of a stool pigeon. "He had a turn up this month a year ago."

turn on. 1. To inject drugs by needle. 2. To introduce someone to drug use. "Nobody ever turned me on. I turned myself on, just from being in the life."

turn over. 1. To abstain from using or selling drugs. See *off drugs*.

TV action. Euphoria from drugs. See *high*.

twist. 1. A marihuana cigarette. 2. A girl, from Australian rhyming argot: *twist and twirl*. "I had a twist who hustled her Kelseys with every trick. She was a nympho."

twisted. Under the influence of narcotics.

twister. 1. A feigned illness or "fit" for the purpose of getting drugs. See *Brody*. "I threw a twister, but it cut me a duster." 2. An addict expert at this trick. "See Joe, he's the twister for the outfit." 3. A fit of violent retching or the vomiting of blood and mucus during withdrawal. Also *heaves*. "His habit was one twister after another. . . ." 4. A marihuana user.

uffi or **uhffi.** Morphine. Rare (New York City and Detroit areas). See *M*.

Uncle. 1. A Federal narcotic agent, or any Federal officer. "Blow, bub, Uncle is everywhere tonight. . . ." 2. The Federal Government. "No use spending big dough for a mouthpiece when Uncle has you. . . ." See *Sam* 1.

under the gun. 1. To be under observation by the police. See *on ice* 2. 2. To be taking a long chance, as having a pusher who sells for his *connection* just to support his own habit.

unkie. Morphine (New York City and Detroit areas). See *M*.

unwind. To relax by taking drugs; especially used by jazz musicians.

up and down the lines. Having ruined the veins by repeated puncturing. The phrase reflects the *vein shooter's* constant hunt for veins he can use. See *burned out*.

up tight. 1. Out of money. 2. To be in an uncomfortable position, as out of drugs, *sick* or in fear of being picked up by the police.

uptown connection. A big-time peddler. See *connection*.

user. See *gow head*.

vein shooter. An addict who uses drugs intravenously (*white stuff*), barbiturates and, on occasion, opium).

vein shot. An intravenous injection of narcotics. "I remember his first vein shot knocked him kicking."

verification shot. 1. An injection during or before which a little blood is drawn up into the needle to make sure it is in the vein. See *back up, register, boot shot, booting*. 2. A *shot* of narcotics taken to test its strength or quality. "After a couple of O.Z. are bought by a mob, the first round of shots before the stuff is chopped up are called verification shots."

vet. A prison or jail physician. See *croaker*.

vipe. To smoke marihuana. See *muggles, send*.

viper. A marihuana smoker. See *reefer man*.

viper's weed. Marihuana. See *muggles*.

V.S. A vein shot, the opposite of S.S. for *skin shot*.

wake up or **get up.** The first shot of the day, taken the first thing in the morning; a must for a *strung-out* user. "If I didn't save a *wake up*, I'd be up tight." Also *morning shot*.

washed up or **cleaned up.** 1. Temporarily off drugs, as when an addict is out on bond. See *away from the habit*. 2. To be forced to go off drugs for a long time, as when in prison, etc.

waste. To kill a person. "Some day we'll have to waste that fink."

wasted. 1. Under the influence of narcotics, especially when unconscious. See *gowed*. 2. Arrested as a *peddler*.

way out. 1. Incomprehensible. 2. The best.

Weasel. An undercover agent formerly in Atlanta Penitentiary. Widely known for his ability to sense that a man was using or getting narcotics. "Never knew the Weasel, but his name was Head and of his exploits I've heard plenty. . . ." "Mr. Head or The Weasel would stand in the chow line and dog eye each con. Knees and Elbows Jr. at the Annex (Leavenworth) got his start the same way."

wedge. To manipulate people by playing the opinion of one person in authority against the opinion of another (largely institutional usage).

weed. Marihuana. See *muggles*. "I don't like weed, the taste, the effect or the weed heads that use it."

weed head. A marihuana smoker.

weekend habit. A small, irregular habit which may be indulged over weekends. A kind of *chippy habit, q.v.* "An ex-addict can't have a weekend habit but two weekends. . . ."

what did you knock over? What brought you here? (refers to a prison, jail or hospital). Other common phrases: "What's your rap?" "What's your beef?" "What did you fall for?"

wheels. A car.

whips and jingles or **jangles.** The symptoms of withdrawal, especially in the early stages.

whiskers. 1. A Federal narcotic agent. "Second guy from the left at the bar is whiskers." 2. Any Federal officer. 3. The Federal Government. "Whiskers just returned a true bill against George and his old lady. . . ."

white angel. 1. A nurse or other attendant in an institution who can be bribed or persuaded to obtain narcotics for an addict. Obsolescent. 2. Morphine. "A white angel is one tablet or cube of morphine scored for in jail. . . ."

white scene. A state of advanced intoxication from ingesting amphetamines; a *benny jag*.

white nurse. A general term loosely used to cover cocaine, morphine or heroin, more often morphine.

white stuff. 1. Morphine, heroin, cocaine, Dilaudid. 2. Any drug which can be injected by an addict. 3. A cotton field or, by extension, penal labor or chain gang labor. There is a saying among underworld addicts: "You mustn't fall in Dixie, for white stuff will flip a junker" (meaning that an addict shouldn't get arrested in the South, for he can't stand penal labor). "Since I did that bit in Arkansas I can see a blade of white stuff for half a mile." "A *blade* of white stuff? A boll. . . ."

whites. Benzedrine tablets. See *benny*.

whiz bang. A mixed *shot*, usually morphine or heroin with cocaine. See *speed ball*. Rare, in this idiom, but the mixed *shot* is very common. "My favorite whiz bang is tincture of opium and C."

whizzes. See *jab*.

winder. A voluntary patient. Probably

originated at Lexington, and not widely used elsewhere. Also *crank handle* and many other terms. See *Mr. Fish.*

wing ding. A feigned attack or "fit." See *Brody.* "Then he threw a wing ding in the bath house to cover up the get."

wired on whites. See *benny jag.*

wired up. Under the influence of narcotics.

wolf. An aggressor in a homosexual affair.

wolf ticket. Harassment, as being *sold a wolf ticket,* is to be picked on. Here *wolf* does not necessarily have homosexual connotations.

works. 1. Instruments for administering narcotics hypodermically. See *artillery.* 2. A government agent or undercover man. 3. A sexual pervert.

write scrip. For a physician to supply an addict regularly with drugs. An old term among addicts. See *right croaker.* "He started to write scrip in '29, and now he has a gold pen and a Packard, and he's still writing scrip. . . ."

write up. To write an adverse behavior report on a prisoner. Also to *shoot (someone) down, put in a shot against (someone).* See *A.B.C.*

writing. 1. Porous paper, saturated with a drug in solution, on which a letter is written to a prisoner. See *satch.* "Big Nose Tommy got some writing today; you're invited." 2. Said of a doctor who is writing prescriptions for addicts.

wrong. 1. Untrustworthy. Usually means just the opposite of *right* from the speaker's point of view. Thus a *right* town has the *fix* for certain *rackets* while a *wrong* town does not; a *wrong* copper cannot be *fixed,* while a *right* one can.

Yale. A needle, from one brand of standard commercial hypodermic needle. See *spike, Luer.*

year. A dollar bill. Also *ace.*

yellow jacket. A capsule of Nembutal. Also *nimbie.*

yen. 1. A desire for narcotics, even though an addict may not be using drugs at the time. 2. The need for narcotics which recurs regularly with an addict using drugs. 3. By extension, a desire for anything. Originally used by pipe smokers, but now generalized.

yen hok. 1. The steel needle-like instrument on which an opium pill is made or shaped. Also *hook.* 2. A tall, slender person, usually an addict.

yen pok. 1. The pill of opium after it is cooked. 2. A pill which is taken away by the smoker to swallow in place of a smoke. "An opium pill is always an opium pill until it is removed (from the *joint*) to be taken by mouth, then it is referred to as a yen pok." "Fix me a couple of high hats for yen poks." "I used to wrap yen poks in cigarette papers to take to work. . . ." "Usually made of yen shee or sam lo. . . ."

yen shee. The residue of opium which forms inside the bowl of the pipe; it is removed with the *yen shee gow* and used to mix with more gum to prepare more smoking opium. It is very concentrated. In solution, it is known as *medicine* or *yen shee suey,* and is carried on the road when smoking is difficult or impossible. Some addicts eat *yen shee;* others mix it with alcohol as a drink. Mostly mixed with cod liver oil, peanut oil or cottonseed oil. Rarely used today.

yen shee baby. The difficult bowel movements from severe constipation which accompanies addiction. "Wrap it up in a towel and it'll live—it's a yen shee baby."

yen shee boy. Possibly a variant of *yen shee quoi.* An opium addict, especially one who eats *yen shee, q.v.* "In the old days there were many addicts, male and female, who used strictly yen shee. Most pipe smokers would give it away when hop was plentiful."

yen shee gow. The scraper (sometimes made from a brass door key) which is used to cut the yen shee out of the inside of the hollow pipe bowl. These scrapers are widely variant in form, but generally resemble the letter Z with an extra angle for a handle. "We often made a yen shee gow out of a shoe hook . . . for button shoes, that is." Rare except among old-time opium smokers.

yen shee kwoi. Also recorded as "quoi," "quoy" or "quay." An opium smoker. "Me yen shee quoi, you got pen yen?" "My little colored gal would holler upstairs, 'Elnay, you know yen shee quay?' She was being secretive, or so she thought."

yen shee suey. See *yen shee.* "Ng King had the best yen shee suey in San Francisco. Also the best string of smoking bottles."

yesca. Marihuana. See *muggles.*

yet low, yet lo. The second or third ashes of opium; *yen shee* which has been reworked several times, like *san lo* or *sam lo.* See *yen shee.*

zonked. Under the influence of narcotics. See *high, in high.*

INDEX

A

Abscesses, 47, 89, 90
Abstinence symptoms, 94-98, 213
   table of, 211, 213
ACTH, 217, 224
Adams, Professor Roger, 122
Adanon, see Methadone
Addiction-prone personality, 31, 81-84, 91, 93, 114, 131, 137-138, 141, 156, 157, 289, 315
Addicts
   and community, 220
   argot of, 318-398
   commitment of, 206
   juvenile, 302-316
   number of, 7, 8, 9, 21, 220, 229, 299, 302, 306
   personality of, 91
   sick person, 30, 39
   subculture, 265
   treatment of, 192-235
   women, 306
Addiction, 8
   and crime, 262-300
   and youth, 8, 9, 302-316
   argot of, 318
   brain surgery in treatment of, 217
   compulsion in, 31-37
   compulsory treatment, 205
   government clinics for, 7, 8, 198
   increase in, 7-9, 121, 262
   liability, 80
   marihuana used before, 20
   metabolic rate in, 85
   motives for seeking treatment, 207
   nature of, 28-33
   need of proof of, 159
   non-opiate sedatives considered in, 102-128
   physical dependence in, 33-36, 44, 60
   prevention of, 194
   prognosis or results of treatment, 225
   sexual secretions in, 85
   significant signs of, 164
   social aspects of, 192
   treatment of, 192
   use of hypodermic needle in, 42-47
   violations, 255
   where should be treated, 200
Addicts Anonymous, 208, 227
Adrenalin (epinephrine), 135
Afghanistan, 62
Africa, 14, 105, 251, 278, 279, 285
Alameda Rehabilitation Center, 169
Alcohol, 14, 16, 18, 37, 40, 41, 283, 298
   prohibited by Moslems, 14
   used with barbiturates, chloral hydrate, paraldehyde, 111
Aldrich, C. K., 126
Alkaloids, Mayer's test for, 176
Allentuck, Samuel, 280
Allybarbituric acid (also known as Sandoptal), 40, 104
Alpert, Richard, 144
Alurate sodium (also known as aprobarbital sodium), 40, 104
American Medical Association, 258
Amidone, see Methadone
Ammonium bromide, 113, 114
Amobarbital (Amytal), 40, 104
Amphetamine (Amphetamine Sulphate), 21, 156
   acute poisoning, 234
   discussion of, 135
   in acute barbiturate poisoning, 156
   urine test, 172
Amytal, sodium, 40, 103, 104
   in acute cocaine poisoning, 234
Andrade, Oswald Moraes, 280
Anhalonium lewinii, see Peyote, 144
Anileridine, 78

400   Narcotics and Narcotic Addiction

Anslinger, Harry J., 270, 304
Apaches
   use of peyote, 145
Aphrodisiac
   marihuana as, 125, 284
Apomorphine (Apomorphine Hydrochloride), 30, 39, 69
   discussion of, 71
   laboratory test for, 177
Aprobarbital sodium (also known as alurate sodium), 40, 104
Arabs
   knowledge of opium, 5
Argentina, 62
Argot of narcotic addicts, 318-398
   argots and the narcotic addict, 325-335
   changing character of, 332
   glossary of terms used by addicts, 335-398
   in literature, 321, 322
   of Benzedrine addict, 331, 332
   of cocaine addict, 331
   of heroin addict, 331
   of marihuana addict, 330, 334
   of Negro, 335
   origin of, 321, 322, 330
   social aspects of argot formation, 318-325
"Army Disease," 6
Artificial respiration
   in acute drug poisoning, 219, 230
   mouth-to-mouth, 233
Aspirin, 73, 103
Atropine, 89, 103, 176
   in combination with morphine, 68

B

Bakewell, W. S., Jr., 128
Barbital (also known as veronal, barbitone), 40, 104
Barbitone (also known as barbital, veronal), 40, 104
Barbiturates, 21, 40, 42, 44, 47, 102-110, 122
   acute barbiturate poisoning, 231-232
   alcohol used with, 92, 107
   amphetamine in acute barbiturate poisoning, 156
   blood pressure in addiction, 123
   discussion of, 102-111
   effect of ACTH on, 224
   effect of cortisone on, 224
   intoxication from overdose of, 107, 123, 231
   laboratory tests for, 182
   Metrazol in treatment of barbiturate depression, 232
   phenobarbital in withdrawal, 223
   picrotoxin in the treatment of barbiturate depression, 232
   post-withdrawal treatment, 225
   table of, 104
   taken with Benzedrine, 108
   taken with cocaine, 107
   used in opiate withdrawal, 217
   withdrawal from, 124, 223
Beam Test, 186
Belladonna, 88, 103
Bemidone, see Meperidine series, 76, 78
Bender Gestalt Test, 123
Benzedrex, 41, 138
Benzedrine (amphetamine sulfate), 21, 22, 41, 43, 47
   addicts, argot, 331, 332
   blood pressure using, 140
   discussion of, 135-138
   poisoning, 234
   taken with barbiturates, 108
   tests for body fluids, tissues, and complex solutions, 172
   tests for powder and simple solutions, 188
   Thin Film Test, 172
Bhang, 117
Blood pressure, 123, 231, 233
   in barbiturate addiction, 123
   in opiate addiction, 123
   in opiate and barbiturate poisoning, 231-233
   in withdrawal distress, 95
   using Benzedrine, 43, 47
Blue velvet, 47
Bolivia, 4, 133, 134
Bouquet, J., 125, 278, 279, 283, 284, 285
Bowman, Karl M., 180, 280
Brain surgery (in the treatment of addiction), 217

Index 401

Brazil, 131, 280
British System, 260
Bromides, 22, 40, 43, 47
  in blood, 115
  discussion of, 113-116
  inorganic tests for, 184
  organic tests for, 185
  quantitative tests for in blood, 185
Bromidia, 40, 113
Bromine water, 180
Bromobarb, 40, 114
Bromoseltzer, 40, 114
Bulgaria, 62
Bureau of Narcotics, see Federal Bureau of Narcotics
Burma, 62
Buss-Burke Test, 123
Butabarbital sodium (also known as Butisol sodium), 40, 104
Butallylona (also known as Pernoston), 40, 104
Butethal (also known as Neonal), 40, 104
Butisol sodium (also known as Butabarbital sodium), 40, 104

C

Caffeine sodium
  acute opiate poisoning, 230
Calcium bromide, 114
California, 9, 10, 24, 26, 30, 92, 139, 149, 205, 209, 210, 217, 251, 302, 316
  Alameda Rehabilitation Center, 169
  California Civil Addict Rehabilitation Program, 220
  California Rehabilitation Center, 220-226, 250, 304
  Department of Corrections, 24, 171, 222
  Department of Education, 316
  Narcotic Addict Evaluation Authority, 220
Camphorated tincture of opium, see Paregoric
Canada, 295
Cannabinol, 43, 117, 281
Cannibis indica, 116, 235
Cannabis intoxication, 235
Cannabis sativa, 116

Chapman, Kenneth, 32, 37, 79
Charas, 117, 235, 281
Cheyne-Stokes, respiration
  in cocaine poisoning, 234
  in opiate poisoning, 229
Chicago, 9, 251, 309
China, 5, 14, 62, 198, 244, 277
Chiras, 281
Chloral hydrate, 21, 40, 43, 111
  alcohol used with, 111-112
  discussion of, 111
  in body fluids, 184
  qualitative test for, 184
  quantitative assay, 184
Chloretone, 112
Chlorobutanol, 112
Civil War, 6
Clinics, 7, 8, 198
Coca leaves, 3, 4, 14, 131-133, 241
Coca-Cola, 133
Cocaine (Cocaine Hydrochloride), 3, 21, 36, 39, 42, 47, 131, 155, 234
  argot of cocaine addict, 331
  amytal sodium in acute cocaine poisoning, 234
  antidote for alcohol and opiate poisoning, 155
  Cheyne-Stokes, respiration in poisoning, 234
  discussion of, 131
  poisoning, 234
  relationship to violent crime, 276
  taken with barbiturates, 107
  taken with heroin, 156
  taken with morphine, 156
  tests for body fluids, 161
  tests for powders and simple solutions, 187
  urine test, 172
  use of nikethamide in cocaine poisoning, 234
  use of phenobarbital in cocaine poisoning, 234
  withdrawal treatment, 222
Codeine (Codeine Methylmorphine), 5, 39, 43, 86, 211
  discussion of, 72
  derivatives of, 73-74
  laboratory test for, 177
  urine test, 172

402   Narcotics and Narcotic Addiction

Cohen, Sidney, 149, 150, 155
Coleman, A. H., 171
Collector of Internal Revenue, 243, 260
Colorado Psychiatric Hospital, 114
Columbia, 131
Comanches
   use of peyote, 145
Commissioner of Narcotics, 34, 40, 243-244
Community services, 312
Compulsion, in addiction, 33-37
Compulsory treatment, 205, 226
Commitment of addicts, 206
Connecticut, 221
Copavin, 73
Cortisone
   effect on the barbiturate abstinence syndrome, 224
   in managing opiate withdrawal, 217
Cosa Nostra, see Maffia, 294-295
Courts
   juvenile, 264, 307, 313
Crime and addiction, 262-300
Criminal personality, drugs and, 267
Curare, 4
"Cut Downs," see Gangs, 27
Cyclobarbital (also known as Phanodorn), 40, 104

D

"Dangerous Drugs," 21
   see Amphetamines, Barbiturates, Tranquilizers
Drug Abuse Control Amendment, 304
Daprisol, 136
Death penalty, 307
Defoe
   argot in literature, 322
   Robinson Crusoe, 66
Dekker, Thomas
   argot in literature, 322
Delvinal sodium (also known as vinobarbital sodium), 40, 104
Demerol (Meperidine Hydrochloride), 39, 43, 47, 75-78, 169, 195, 211, 230-231
   discussion of, 76
   identification of, 179

Nalline treatment of, 230
   urine test, 172
de Monardes, Francisco, 11
de Quevedo, Francisco
   argot in literature, 322
DeQuincey, 65
Desbutal, 135
Desoxyn, see Methedrine, 22, 41, 136
Desyphed, 41, 135
Detroit, 9, 308
Dewey, L. H., 117
Dexamyl, 135
Dexedrine, 41, 135
Di-acetyl-morphine, see Heroin
Dial (also known as diallylbarbituric acid), 40, 104
Diallylbarbituric acid (also known as Dial), 40, 104
Diamba, 116
Dicodide (Dihydrohydroxycodeinone-Bitartrate)
   color of in various tests, 177
   discussion of, 74
   laboratory test for, 177
Dihydromorphinone, see Dilaudid
Dilaudid (Dihydromorphinone Hydrochloride), 36, 43, 47, 313
   discussion of, 70-71
   laboratory test for, 177
   urine test, 172
Dimethyltryptamine—(DMT), 143
   discussion of, 155
Dionin (Ethylmorphine Hydrochloride), 70
   laboratory test for, 177
DL-3-hydroxy-N-methylmorphinan, see Dromoran
DMT—Dimethyltryptamine, 143
   discussion of, 155
Dolantin, see Demerol
Dolophine, see Methadone
Dolantol, see Demerol, 76
Doriden, 128
Dover, Dr. Thomas, 66
Dover's powder, see Opium, Powder of Opium and Ipecac, 66
   laboratory test for, 177
"Draw a Man" test, 123
Drell, Hyman, 137, 140

Drinalfa, 22, 41, 137
  see Methedrine
Dromoran (Dl 3-hydroxy-N-methylmorphinan), 39
  discussion of, 77
  laboratory test for, 177
Drug Abuse Control Act, 242, 249
Drug dependence, 38, 110, 134
  World Health definition, 142
Drugs
  and criminal personality, 267
  and non-violent crime, 285
  and violent crime, 272
Drug poisoning
  amphetamine, 234
  barbiturate, 231
  cocaine, 234
  LSD, 235
  opiate, 229
  tranquilizers, 235
  treatment of acute, 228-235
Durall, 226

E

East India Company, 5
Ecuador, 133
Eddy, Nathan B., 32, 71, 78
Education in juvenile addiction, 307, 312-316
Egyptians
  knowledge of opium, 5
El Hodka, A. A., 296
Ellis, Havelock, 145
Ellingwood, E. H., Jr., 268, 270
Emotional dependence
  psychic, 60
Ephedrine, 135
Epinephrine (Adrenalin), 135
Equinal, 128
Ethylmorphine hydrochloride, see Dionin
Essig, C. F., 128, 235
Eucaine, 133
Eukodal (Dihydrohydroxycycodeinone Hydrochloride)
  discussion of, 73
  laboratory test for, 177
Evipal (also known as hexobarbital sodium), 40, 105

Executive Order, 243
Expert Committee on Drugs Liable to Produce Addiction, 33

F

Federal Bureau of Narcotics, 8, 9, 26, 70, 109, 121, 186, 187, 195, 244, 250, 262, 270, 279, 295, 297, 299, 304, 307
Federal Dangerous Drug Law, 155
Federal Food, Drug and Cosmetic Act, 242, 248, 260
Federal Narcotic Laws, 69, 198, 223, 239, 242, see Legal Control of Addiction
Federal Veterans' Hospitals, 206
Felix, Robert H., 32, 91
Fichelis, Robert P., 109
Fielding
  argot in literature, 322
Food and Drug Administration, 139, 148, 154, 242
Food, Drug and Cosmetic Act, 109, 242
  see Federal Food, Drug and Cosmetic Act
Fort Worth U. S. Public Health Service Hospital, 26, 77, 203, 204, 206, 306
Froehde's test, 177-178

G

Gaedkin
  first prepared cocaine, 131
Gangs, see
  "Varrio Nuevo," 27
  "Little Dukes," 27
  "Midgets," 27
  "Pee Wee Winos," 27
Ganja, 117
Gaulden, 85
Gautier, Theophile, 284
Germany, 71, 296
  Methadone, 77
  Morphine isolated, 5
Glue sniffing, 47, 310
  physical damage, 310
  physical dependence, 312
  solvents in, 310
Government clinics, see Clinics

404   *Narcotics and Narcotic Addiction*

Gordan, 144
Granulated opium, 65
Greece, 62
Greeks
  knowledge of opium, 5

H

Habituation, 33, 34, 37
  habit forming, 34
Hallucinatory drugs, 31, 41, 142
  discussion of, 142-157
  see (DMT), 155; Dimethyltryptamine, 143; LSD, 147; mescaline, 144; peyote, 144; psilacybin, 147
Harrison Narcotic Act, 7, 9, 73, 262, 264, 316
  discussion of, 243, 245
Hashish, 3, 4, 43, 47, 117, 143, 225, 281
Hawaii, 250
Hemp, 117, 119, 235, 281
  see Marihuana
Hepatitis, Jaundice, 90
Hernandez, Fransisco, 144
Heroin, 7, 10, 20, 39, 42, 47, 88, 313
  argot of heroin addict, 331
  "cure" for morphine, 69
  discovery of, 6
  discussion of, 69-70
  in crimes of violence, 272
  laboratory test for, 177
  taken in combination with cocaine, 70
  urine test, 172
  withdrawal, 215
Hexathal sodium (also known as Ortal sodium), 40, 104
Hexobarbital sodium (also known as Evipal sodium), 40, 105
Himmelsbach, C. K., 32, 71, 73, 76, 94, 140, 212, 213
Hoch, Paul R., 145, 146, 147
Hoffman, Albert, 143
Homatropine, see Eukodal
Hong Kong, 261
House of Representatives Appropriations Committee, 241
Hungary, 61, 62

Hycodan, see Dicodide, 74
  (Hycodan syrup, tablets, Hycomine compound)
Hypodermic needle, 6, 18, 42, 44
  abscesses from using, 47, 89, 90
  as used by addicts, 42-47
  first use of, 5, 6
14-Hydrooxydihydromorphine, see Phenazocine

I

Identification of drugs, 159-181
Immunity to addiction, 286
India, 5, 14, 61, 62, 117, 198, 278
Indo-China, 62
Inhalation of drugs, 47
Insulin, 216
Interdepartmental Committee on Narcotics to the President, January 1961, 315
Internal Revenue, 7
International Control, 249
International Criminal Police Commission, 241
Intoxication
  barbiturates, 108
  cannabis, 283
Ipral (probarbital), 40, 104
Iran, 61, 296
Isbell, Harris, 32, 37, 78, 79, 87, 94, 109, 123, 146, 232, 234
Iso-methadone, see Methadone
Isonipecaine, see Demerol

J

James, William, 145
Japan, 15, 62, 277
Juvenile addiction, 9, 243, 302, 316
  a fad, 309
  education in, 312
  factors in, 309
  increase in, 305
  treatment of, 314
Juvenile Protective Association, 315

K

Kansas, 250
Kashmir, 62

Kefauver-O'Conner Committee, 293
Kentucky, 117-119, 250
  University Medical Center, 128
Ketobemidone, see Meperidine series
  see Demerol, 76-79
King, M. R., 71
Kiowas
  use of peyote, 145
Kohs Block Test, 123
Kolb, Lawrence, 82, 94, 197, 266, 267, 270, 272, 273, 274, 276
Krueger, Hugo, 32

L

Laboratory tests
  for amphetamines, 188
  for barbiturates, 182
  for bromides, 184
  for chloral hydrate, 184
  for cocaine, 187
  for marihuana, 186
  for mescaline, 188
  for morphine, 177
  for opium and derivatives, 175
  for paraldehyde, 184
  for peyote, 188
La Guardia report, 280
Laudanum (Tincture of Opium), 39, 43, 88
  laboratory test for, 177
Laugier, Henri, 62
Law enforcement, 316
"Laws for Youth," 316
League of Nations, 239
Leary, 144
Legal Control of Addiction, 239
  Drug Abuse Control Act, 249
  Drug Abuse Control Amendment, 244, 304
  Federal Food, Drug and Cosmetic Act, 248
  Harrison Narcotic Law, 243
  international controls, 239
  local laws, 251
  Marihuana Tax Act, 245
  Narcotic Drug Import and Export Act, 245
  Narcotic Hospital Law, 246
  Narcotic Information Act, 245
  Narcotic Transportation Act, 245
  Opium Poppy Control Act, 246
  state narcotic laws, 250
  Uniform State Barbiturate Act, 109
Leritine, 39, 78
Levallorphane, 75
Levi, Mario, 123
Levine, Joe, 144
Levo-methadone, 79
Levophan, see Dromoran
Lexington U. S. Public Health Service Hospital, 7, 26, 75, 77, 92, 94, 109, 139, 146, 168, 183, 189, 196, 197, 203, 205, 206, 211, 213, 218, 223, 226, 232, 250, 260, 306
Librium, 128
Lipinski, Dr., 154
Lithium bromide, 114
"Little Dukes," see Gangs, 27
"Living Death," 315
Lobotomy
  in treatment, 217-219
Local laws, 251
Lomotil, 217
Lophophera williamsii, see Peyote, 144
Los Angeles, 149, 150, 260, 293, 309, 310, 313
LSD (lysurgic acid diethylamide), 31, 143, 313
  discussion of, 147-155
  poisoning, 235
  tests for, 189
  thorazine in, 235
Luciano, Lucky, 294
Luminal (also known as phenobarbital)
Lysurgic acid diethylamide (LSD), see LSD

M

Macedonia, 62
Macht, David I., 6
Maffia, 294, 295
Malaria, 90
Mallinkrodt Company, 88
Marihuana, 10, 20-22, 39, 42, 43, 48, 102
  argot of addict, 331, 334

as an aphrodisiac, 125, 284
chemical tests for, 186
discussion of, 116-122, 127
extent of, 126
in crimes of violence, 126, 283, 297
microscopic examination of, 187
physical and psychological effects of, 122, 125
poisoning, 235
suggestibility, 283
use before narcotic addiction, 298, 304, 326
withdrawal treatment, 222
Marihuana Control Act, see Marihuana Tax Act
Marihuana Tax Act, 117, 119, 257, 298
discussion of, 243
Marquis test, 177
Massachusetts, 250
Maurer, David W., 264, 320, 333
Mayer's test for alkaloids, 176
Mebaral (also known as mephobarbital), 40, 103-105
Mental Health, National Institute of see National Institute of Health
Meperidine, see Demerol (Meperidine series: bemidone, ketobemidone, Nu-1197, Nu-1779, Nu-1932)
Mephobarbital (also known as Mebaral), 40, 103-105
Merck, 88
Merrill, Frederick T., 187
Mescal buttons, 144
Mescaline, 31, 41, 143, 144, 313
intoxication, barbiturate treatment, 146
tests for body fluids, 189
test for powder and simple solutions, 188
Metabolic rate
in opiate addiction, 85
in withdrawal distress, 95
Methadon, see Methadone
Methadone (Methadone Hydrochloride), also known as Methadon, Amidone, Adanon, Dolophine, 39, 43, 78, 79, 88, 195
discussion of, 76
identification of, 179
in withdrawal, 211

Methedrine (Methamphetamine Hydrochloride), 21, 22, 24, 41, 47, 156
discussion of, 135
Methods of taking drugs
hypodermically, 42-47
inhalating, 47
inhaling
oral, 42-48
smoking, 5, 16-19, 43
Metopon (Metopon Hydrochloride), 39, 43
discussion of, 71, 72
laboratory test for, 177
urine test, 172
Metrazol
in the treatment of barbiturate depression, 232
Mexico, 62, 70, 117, 144, 294, 295, 316, 330
"Midgets," see Gangs
Miltown, 128
Mitchell, S. Weir, 145
Mongolia, 62
Monobromic camphor, 40, 114
Monroe, Russel R., 137, 140
Morning Glory seeds, 41, 143
Morphine, 5, 6, 19-20, 36, 39, 42, 47, 86, 313
atropine sulfate in combination with, 89
discovery of, 5
discussion of, 67-69
in crimes of violence, 272
test for, 176
urine test, 172
withdrawal, 212
Motives for seeking treatment, 207
Moslems, 11, 14, 279
Mushrooms, 143, 147
My Six Convicts, 198

N

N-Allylnormorphine Hydrobromide
discussion of, 75
in opiate poisoning, 75, 231
Nalline, 30, 39, 75, 169, 171-175, 230-231
Nalline Test, 168, 169
urine test, 172

Nalorphine, 75
Narcosan treatment, 215
Narcotic addiction and crime, 262-300
Narcotic Control Act, 243
Narcotic Drug Import and Export Act, 242, 245
"Narcotic Farms," see U.S.P.H.S.
Narcotic Hospital Law, 242, 246
Narcotic Information Act, 242, 245
Narcotics Anonymous, 208
Narcotics, Commissioner of, see Commissioner of Narcotics
Narcotic Transportation Act, 242, 245
Narcotine, 69
Narphen, 78
National Institute of Mental Health, 78, 314
National Quinine Company, 88
Nature of addiction, 28-33
Negro, 309
  argot, 335
Nembutal (also known as pentobarbital sodium), 40, 104
Neonal (also known as butethal), 40, 104
Neo-synephrin, 232
Nervine, 40, 114
Neurosine, 40, 114
New Hampshire, 250
New Jersey, 30, 222, 250
New York City, 205, 227, 309
New York Department of Education, 315
New York Department of Health, 260
New York (State), 8-10, 22, 24, 26, 30, 92, 149, 200, 205, 207, 250, 313
New York *Times*, 9
Nikethamide
  in cocaine poisoning, 234
  in opiate poisoning, 230
Noludar, 128
Non-opiate addicts, withdrawal of, 222
  treatment of, 222
Non-opiate sedatives considered addicting, 102-128
  physiological and psychological aspects of addiction to, 122
Non-violent crime, drugs and, 285
North Korea, 62

Nostal, 40
Novocaine, 42, 133
Nutmeg, 128
Nu-1197, Nu-1779, Nu-1932, 76, 78
  see also Methadone
Numorphan, 39, 78

O

Omahas
  use of peyote, 145
Opiates and their synthetic equivalents, 60-98
  allergy to, 84
  identification of, 179
  physiological and psychological effects of, 81-98
  tests for in body fluids, 179
  treatment of, 196
Opiate poisoning, acute, 229-231
  artificial respiration in, 230
  blood pressure in, 230
  Cheyne-Stokes in, 229
  metabolic rate in, 85
  N-allylnormorphine in, 230
  nikethamide in, 230
  symptoms, 229
  treatment of, 230
Opium, 3, 6, 15, 39, 42, 47
  American colonies, 5
  Arabs, knowledge of, 5
  as it appears in urine after administration, 172
  blood pressure in opiate addiction, 123
  camphorated tincture of, 66
  China, 5
  discussion of, 61
  eating, 5, 198
  Egyptians, knowledge of, 5
  granulated, 65
  Greeks, knowledge of, 5
  gum, 63
  India, 5
  laboratory tests for, 176
  Pantopon, 66
  Persians, knowledge of, 5
  powdered, 65
  powdered opium and ipecac, 66
  preparations and derivatives, 64-67

prepared, 64
smoking, 5, 16-19, 43, 58, 62, 198, 264
tincture of, 65
urine test, 172
War, 5, 62
Opium Poppy Control Act, 245
Opium Problem, The, 7, 32
Oral taking of drugs, 42, 43, 47, 48, 65, 88, 212
argot of addicts, 332
Ortal sodium (also known as hexethal sodium), 40, 104
Ortiz, Martin, 313
Osler, Sir William, 29
Ossenfort, W. F., 91

P

Pakistan, 62
Pantocaine, 133
Pantopon, 39, 43
laboratory test for, 177
Papaver Somniferum, 61
Papaverine (Papaverine hydrochloride), 74-75
laboratory test for, 177
Paraldehyde, 40
alcohol used with, 113
discussion of, 112
test for, 184
Paregoric, 39, 43, 47, 66, 88
laboratory test for, 177
Parker, Kenneth D., 180
Parole
California program, 220, 289
"Pee Wee Winos," 27
Pellens, M., 7, 32
Pentazocine, 39, 79
Pentobarbital, 40; (Nembutal), 104
in withdrawal from barbiturates, 223
Pentobarbital sodium (also known as Nembutal), 40, 104
Pentothal sodium (also known as thiopental sodium), 40, 104
Percobarb, 74
Percodan, 73
urine test, 172
Pernoston (also known as Butallylona), 40, 104

Persians
knowledge of opium, 5
Personality, addiction
see Addiction prone
Peru, 131-134
Pescor, Michael, 270
Pethidine (also known as Demerol), 76
Petronius
argot in literature, 321
Peyote (Lophophora williamsii), 31, 39, 41, 48, 143, 156-157
discussion of, 144
test for body fluids, 189
test for powder and simple solutions, 188
used by Apaches, 145
used by Comanches, 145
used by Kiowas, 145
used by Omahas, 145
Peyotyl, 144
Phanodorn (also known as cyclobarbital), 40, 104
Phenacaine (Holocaine), 133
Phenacetin, 73
Phenazocine, 78
Phenobarbital (also known as luminal), 40, 104, 105, 106
in cocaine poisoning, 234
Physical dependence
its role in addiction, 33, 36, 37, 60, 84, 112
tranquilizers, 128
Physiological and psychological aspects of addiction to non-opiate drugs, 122
Physiological and psychological effects of opiate drugs, 122
Physiological and psychological effects of stimulant drugs, 155
Picrotoxin
in the treatment of barbiturate depression, 232
Placidyl, 128
Poisoning
treatment of acute drug, 228-235
Potassium bromide, 40, 113-116
Potassium Bromobromide Reagent, 180
Prevention of addiction, 194
Prinadol, 39, 78

Index

Prohibition Amendment, 16
Probarbital (also known as ipral), 40, 104
Procaine, 133
Prognosis, in addiction, 225
Proof of addiction, 159-173
Psychedelic, see Hallucinatory
Psilacybin, teonanacatl
    discussion of, 147
Psychopath, 268, 269
Psychotomimetic drugs, 142
P.T.A., 312
Pupillometer, 169
Pure Food and Drug Law, see Federal Food, Drug and Cosmetic Act
Pyrahexyl compound, 121
Pyribenzamine, 47

R

Recidivist type addicts, 207, 227
Reichard, J. D., 18, 32, 273, 280
Remington's *Practice of Pharmacy*, 66, 79, 102
Rinkel, Max and Shultes, R. E., 147
Robie, Theodore R., 105
Robinson, J. L., 310
Rorschach Test, 123
Rossium treatment, 215

S

Sadusk, J. F., Jr., 139
Sanders, B. S., 71
Sandoptal (also known as allybarbituric acid), 40, 104
San Francisco, 149, 150, 153, 313
"Satyricon," see Petronius, 321
Schultes, R. E. and Rinkel, Max, 147
Scouts
    boy and girl, 312
Secobarbital sodium (also known as Seconal), 40, 104
Seconal (also known as secobarbital sodium), 40, 104, 123
Sedative drugs, 60-
    (opiate): See opium, 61; (prepared, 64; granulated, 65; powdered, 65); laudanum, 65; paregoric, 66; Dover's powder, 66; morphine, 67; pantapon, 66; heroin, 69; dionin, 70; Dilaudid, 70; apomorphine, 71; Metopon, 71; codeine, 72; eucodal, 73; eukodal, 73; Percodan, 73; Dicodide, 74; Hycodan, 74; papaverine, 74; levallorphan, 75; nalorphine, 75; demerol, 76; Dolantin, 76; isonipecaine, 76; Methadone, 76; pethidine, 76; Adanon, 77; Amidone, 77; Dolophine, 77; dromoran, 77; the meperidine series: bemidone, ketobemidone, Nu-1197, Nu-1779, Nu-1932, 78; anileridine, 78; narphen, 78; Numorphan, 78; lerithine, 78; levomethadone, 78; prinadol, 78; Winthrocine, 78
    (non-opiate), 102-105; see Amytal, 102; Nembutal, 102; barbital, 103; Evipal, 103-105; pentothal, 103; veronal, 104; barbitone, 104; tuminal, 104; phenobarbital, 104; amobarbital, 104; butabarbital sodium, 104; Delvinal, 104; Ipral, 104; pentobarbital sodium, 104; Neonal, 104; Ortal, 104; Mebaral, 104; Phanodorn, 104; cyclobarbital, 104; Alurate, 104; Alurate sodium, 104; Dial, 104; sandoptal, 104; Pernoston, 104; Seconal, 104; Evipal soluble, 104; aprobarbital sodium, 104
    See also chloral hydrate, 111; chloretone, 112; chlorobutanol, 112; paraldehyde, 112; bromides, 113; sodium bromide, 113; bromidia, 113; bromobarb 113; triple bromides, 113; Nervine, 114; Neurosine, 114; Bromo-seltzer, 114; ammonium bromide, 116; Cannabis sativa, 116; Cannabis indica, 116; marihuana, 116
Selective service, 307
Selkirk, Alexander, 66
Sexual secretions in addiction, 85
Shakespeare
    argot in literature, 322

Shen Nung, Emperor, 116
Small, L. F., 32, 270
Smollet
　argot in literature, 322
Smith, W. G., 268
Smuggling, 295-296
Sniffing, 41, 47
Social aspects of argot formation, 318
Sodium bromide, 40, 113-116
Sokol, J., 310
Solvents volatile, 47
　in glue sniffing, 310
South America, 113, 240
Spain
　argot in literature, 322
Spot test table, 177
State narcotic laws, 250
Sterne
　argot in literature, 322
Stimulant drugs, see amphetamine, 21, 135; cocaine, 131; Benzedrine, 135; Desyphed, 135; Dexamyl, 135; Desbutal, 135; Dexedrine, 135; Drinalfa, 137; Tuamine, 137; Vonedrine, 137; Benzedrex, 138; mescaline, 144; peyote, 144
　discussion of, 135
　physiological and psychological effects of, 155
Stone Age, 3, 318
Stovaine, 133
Strontium bromide, 114
Strychnine, 176
Suggestibility, increased with marihuana, 283
Sumerians, 61
Sumwalt, Margaret, 32
Superintendent of Schools in New York, 302
Synanon Houses, 221, 222
Syphilis, 90

T

Tat test, 123
Taylor, Norman, 116, 132, 144
10-8-20, see Methadone, 76
Teonanacatl—Psilocybe mexicana, 147
Terpin hydrate, 66

Terry, C. E., 7, 32
Terry, Dr. James, 169
Tests for body fluids, 189
Tetracaine, 133
Thailand, 62
Thebaine, 69
Thin Film Chromatography Urine Test, 172, 180, 183, 188
Thiopental sodium (also known as Pentothal sodium), 40, 105
Thompson, Dr. R. Campbell, 5
Thorazine
　in LSD poisoning, 235
Tobacco, 11-14, 37, 38
Tolerance, 33, 37, 43, 60
Tranquilizers, 28 (see Equinal, Miltown, Librium, Placidyl, Valmid, Valium, Doriden, Nolvdar)
　physical dependence on, 128
　acute poisoning, 235
Treatment, 192-235
　opiate addicts, 196, 212, 230
　ACTH in, 217
　brain surgery in, 217
　compulsory, 205, 226
　government clinics, 7, 8, 198
　insulin in, 216
　juvenile addiction, 312
　motives for, 207
　progress, 225-228
　where treated, 200
Triple bromides, 40, 113, 114
Tuamine, 41, 137
Tuinal (Amytal sodium and Secobarbital sodium), 40, 105
Turkey, 61, 296
Turner, Ralph F., 187

U

Uniform state barbiturate act, 109
U.S.S.R., 62, 116
United Arab Republic, 296
United Nations
　Commission on Narcotic Drugs, 62, 194, 195, 239, 241
　Economic and Social Council of, 133
　international control of narcotics, 249
　study of coca leaves, 4, 133-134

Index 411

United States
 colonial times, 330
U. S. *Department of Agriculture Year Book*, 117
U.S.P.H.S., 10, 40, 196, 204, 270, 314
 see Lexington, Fort Worth
U. S. Treasury Department, 241
Uniform state narcotic law act, 250
Urine, 173
 barbiturates in, 182-183
Vaillant, G. E., 226, 268, 270, 305
Valium, 128
Valmid, 128
"Varrio Neuvo," 27, 313
 see Gangs
Veronal (also known as barbital, barbitone), 40, 104
Vin Coca Mariani, 133
Vinobarbital sodium (also known as Delvinal sodium), 40, 104
Violent crime, drugs and, 272-297
 heroin in, 274
 marihuana in, 126, 297
 morphine in, 235
Violations in addiction, 255
Vogel, Victor H., 32, 37, 79, 270
Voluntary patients, 206
Vonedrine, 41, 137

W

Walton, Robert P., 116, 187, 280
Washington, 250
Watson, 28, 180
Welfare Planning Council, 313
Wieder, Herbert, 76, 216
Wikler, Dr. Abraham, 15, 128
Williams, John, 32
Wilson, Donald Powell, 198
Winthrocine, 78

Withdrawal, 94, 202-205, 209-219
 ACTH in opiate withdrawal, 217
 barbiturates used in opiate withdrawal, 217
 blood pressure in, 123
 cortisone used in, 217
 discussion of, 94
 distress, 94
 effect of Methadone on, 211-212
 management of opiate, 196
 metabolic rate in, 95
 new drugs used in, 224
 of barbiturate addicts, 124, 223
 of cocaine addicts, 222
 of heroin addicts, 215
 of marihuana addicts, 222
 of Methadone addicts, 211
 of morphine addicts, 212, 230
 of opiate addicts, 196
 post withdrawal treatment for non-opiate addicts, 225
 post withdrawal therapy, 219-225
 time required for opiate drugs, 209
 use of pentobarbital in barbiturate withdrawal, 223
Wolff, Dr. P. O., 32, 119, 126, 194, 197, 279
Women addicts, 306
Wood, Mrs. Alexander, 6
Woods, L. A., 189
World Health Organization, 33, 34, 36, 38, 69, 110, 127, 134, 141, 194, 241
World War I, 262
World War II, 62, 295
Wren, Sir Christopher, 6

Y

Yugoslavia, 61, 296